PROMISCUOUS POWER

PROMISCUOUS POWER

An Unorthodox History of New Spain

MARTIN AUSTIN NESVIG

UNIVERSITY OF TEXAS PRESS *Austin*

Requests for permission to reproduce material from this work should be sent to:
Permissions
University of Texas Press
P.O. Box 7819
Austin, TX 78713-7819
utpress.utexas.edu/rp-form

♾ The paper used in this book meets the minimum requirements of
ANSI/NISO Z39.48-1992 (R1997) (Permanence of Paper).

LIBRARY OF CONGRESS CATALOGING-IN-PUBLICATION DATA

Names: Nesvig, Martin Austin, 1968– author.
Title: Promiscuous power : an unorthodox history of New Spain / Martin Austin Nesvig.
Description: First edition. | Austin : University of Texas Press, 2018. |
Includes bibliographical references and index.
Identifiers: LCCN 2017048395 | ISBN 978-1-4773-1582-8 (cloth : alk. paper) |
ISBN 978-1-4773-1583-5 (pbk. : alk. paper) | ISBN 978-1-4773-1584-2 (library e-book) |
ISBN 978-1-4773-1585-9 (nonlibrary e-book)
Subjects: LCSH: Mexico—History—Conquest, 1519–1540. | Mexico—History—Spanish
colony, 1540–1810. | New Spain—History. | Michoacán de Ocampo (Mexico)—History. |
Inquisition—New Spain. | New Spain—Church history.
Classification: LCC F1229 .N47 2018 | DDC 972/.02—dc23
LC record available at https://lccn.loc.gov/2017048395

doi:10.7560/315828

FOR PATY, PARTNER IN CRIME,
FOR TITO, MICHOACANO, WHO TAUGHT ME
SO MUCH ABOUT MEXICO,
IN MEMORIAM PAUL VANDERWOOD

EL VOLCÁN DE PARANGARICUTIRIMÍCUARO SE
QUIERE DESPARANGARICUTIRIGUARIZAR, Y ÉL QUE
LO DESPARANGARICUTIRICUARIZARE SERÁ UN BUEN
DESPARANGARICUTIRIMIZADOR. (REFRÁN POPULAR)

CONTENTS

ACKNOWLEDGMENTS

Acknowledgments in academic books are fascinating reading, but the form is a little strange. For reasons I have never understood, authors inevitably tack on a last line about their spouses, partners, boyfriends, girlfriends, and their moral support, how nice it was they let the author ignore them for the past five to fifteen years, but thanks for the memories. What if people thanked their partners and families first?

First, thank you, Paty, for too many reasons: for putting up with me; for teaching me so much about language and life; for trying to teach me how to be a better person and husband; for your wickedly hilarious sense of humor. And I have not only benefited from your wisdom personally, but you've ever been my in-house linguistic adviser, Mexican history expert, and paleography companion. I could never have done this without you.

Likewise, I thank Tito and Chiquis not only for being great in-laws but for teaching me so much about Mexico. My parents also were ever supportive of the project even though, fortunately for them, they did not have to be subjected to the details.

I have been incredibly fortunate to have benefited from wide-ranging and thoughtful feedback on this project. I will attempt to enumerate those to whom I owe my gratitude. Several excellent historians read the entire manuscript in various stages of its development. Such a chore is a true labor of love. Tatiana Seijas read the complete manuscript *twice* and offered excellent and often desperately needed stylistic and methodological advice. Susan Deeds graciously offered her characteristic generosity, sharp eye, and good humor. Raphael Folsom gave the manuscript a remarkably detailed reading, and while I did not incorporate all his suggestions, the ones I did incorporate improved the resulting book. Jessica Stites-Mor read a good deal of the manuscript and likewise offered excellent commentary from the perspective of a non-Mexicanist and modernist. Finally, I received three extremely helpful reader reports from the press. Two of the readers—Sonya Lipsett-Rivera and Matt O'Hara—signed their reviews. Their evaluations were incredibly thorough, helpful, and conscientious. Both went well beyond the call of duty, offering insightful observations and methodological suggestions, and they even spotted several unfortunate errors. A third, anonymous reader provided incisive critiques that helped me think about asking better questions and about framing arguments. In all these cases, I offer my deepest gratitude.

At the University of Texas Press, Kerry Webb and Robert Devens believed in a project that others thought too crazy to publish. I will be ever thankful for their support. Katherine Streckfus polished up the manuscript in a superb job of editing.

In addition, I have benefited from innumerable suggestions and comments over several years of presenting bits and pieces of this material at conferences. It is fair to say that the Rocky Mountain Council for Latin American Studies (RMCLAS) has been a perennial academic home. I have not only made many excellent friends there but also benefited from an embarrassment of intellectual riches. I would like to extend generalized, across-the-board thanks to everyone from RMCLAS. If you don't find your name in the acknowledgments below, drinks are on me next time around.

I have been fortunate to have presented parts of this project in other forums, including too many conferences to name and from which I benefited from extensive and thoughtful feedback. I am also thankful for the opportunity and graciousness of hosts of invited events where I presented parts of the book: at the University of Oklahoma (Terry Rugeley and Raphael Folsom), the John Carter Brown Library (Edward Widmer), Universidad Nacional Autónoma de México (Gabriel Torres Puga), Universidad Michoacana de San Nicolás de Hidalgo (Ricardo León Alanís), the San Francisco Theological Seminary (Christopher Ocker), the University of California, Berkeley (Thomas Brady—fortunately *not* the quarterback of the same name), and the University of Miami's Atlantic Studies group (Ashli White and Tim Watson).

I also thank so many people who either offered feedback on the book, blew my mind with some observation, shared stories and ideas, provided welcome company and conviviality or generalized moral or intellectual support during the process, or inspired by example: William Beezley, Chad Black, Rafa Castañeda, Justin Castro, Mark Christensen, Chuchiak (who is larger than life and requires only one name), Richard Conway, Laurent Corbeil, Linda Curcio-Nagy, Hao Diwen, Carlos Eire, Bill French, Íñigo García-Bryce, Lori Gonzales, Amy Grant-Borja, Donna Guy, José Ángel Hernández, Steven Hyland, Lyman Johnson, Susan Kellogg, Kris Lane, Asunción Lavrin, Mark Lentz, Rosalva Loreto López, Cheryl Martin, Gabriel Martínez, Ev Meade, Ken Mills, Jim Muldoon, Fr. Stafford Poole, Francis Ramos, Monica Rankin, Matthew Restall, David Rex-Galindo, Colby Ristow, John F. Schwaller, Robert Schwaller, Jeffrey Shumway, Susan Socolow, Amara Solari, Michelle Stephens, Linda Tapachula, David Tavárez, Barbara Tennenbaum, Kevin Terraciano, Zeb Tortorici, Fr. Salvador Treviño, S.J., Sam Truett, Jonathan Truitt, Ann Twinam, Robert Tzintzinpundáquari, Eric Van Young, Dana Velasco, Javier Villa-Flores, Andrew Villalon, Ben Vinson, Nicole Von Germeten, Clark Whitehorn (my official biographer), Angela Willis, Eddie Wright-Rios, and Yanna Yannakakis.

In addition to having received welcome intellectual feedback and conviviality,

I have been blessed with the opportunity to work in some of the most fascinating archival and library environments a historian could imagine. I had the incredible experience of working in the Archivo General de la Nación (AGN) in Lecumberri. I conducted more than half of the research for this book back when they still let us thumb through the physical Inquisition volumes, but, as if it were a bad habit, I just could never quit the AGN—I made lasting friendships there and it is where I met my wife, Paty, and spent countless hours not only amid its magnificent collections but sharpening my ability to defend myself linguistically against some of the world's greatest *albureros*. Roberto Beristáin was still working in Galería 4 when I started the project, and, like so many historians of colonial Mexico before me, I enjoyed his knowledge of the archive, his sardonic humor, and his willingness to mock the arrogance of academics. I make a special mention of Linda Arnold, who has been incredibly generous and helpful over the years, eager to share her encyclopedic command of the archive and her personal catalog files.

I have had the good fortune to have been welcomed in other repositories as well. I spent a few lovely months in Morelia several years ago. Ricardo León Alanís was an ever-generous friend and colleague. Luise Enkherlin was equally both friend and guide. In Seville, I spent a sweltering few weeks enjoying the vast collections of the Archivo General de Indias. In recent years, I have, like many others, benefited from the Spanish government's project at pares.mcu.es, which has digitalized hundreds of archival files. The site allowed me to read several important case files. In Colima, José Miguel Romero de Solís was a true gentleman-scholar in the best sense of the term. He was gracious in providing open access to the Archivo Histórico del Municipio de Colima, with its unparalleled holdings, and he happily invited me to his office for regular chats over *botanas* and beers, as well as to his magnificent home overlooking the river, where we shared a terrific dinner with his wife and friends.

In 2009, I enjoyed one of the finest experiences someone in my field can have: a fellowship at the John Carter Brown Library, in my case for six months. The materials there are amazing, and everyone who spends time there has an opportunity to showcase these invaluable holdings. Ken Ward, Maury A. Bromsen Curator of Latin American Books, was his usual bibliophilic self.

And then there is the financial and institutional support, which is crucial to the successful completion of such a project. The National Endowment for the Humanities and the American Council of Learned Societies, through a Charles A. Ryskamp Fellowship, provided generous support that released me from teaching and gave me time to research and write. Likewise, the University of Miami has offered extensive support for this and other projects. I benefited from several Provost Research awards, which funded summer research trips to Mexico. Likewise, the University of Miami's College of Arts and Sciences, and its dean, Leonidas

Bachas, provided sabbatical leave as well as post-tenure associate professor re-search leave. Both proved exceptionally helpful in allowing me to complete the book. My own department—in particular, its successive chairs, Guido Ruggiero and Mary Lindemann—has been flexible, supportive, and encouraging, by back-ing such releases and research leaves.

I would like to thank my students collectively. I was lucky to be able to teach a lot of energetic, demanding, engaged students at the University of Miami as I re-searched and wrote this book. They keep me honest, and helped me think about how to tell a story—how to gain the interest of someone not necessarily into his-tory. Their constant, just demands that history be compelling, engaging, and well told have helped me think about this book and how to script it.

Finally, I would like to recount my good fortune in knowing Paul Vanderwood as a friend and mentor for nearly twenty years. I would never have written this kind of book had it not been for Paul. He was a generous, funny, and wonderfully irreverent friend. The last conversation I had with him, I had called from the pay-phone at the Vips next to the AGN. Only a day before he died, he told me to keep doing things the way I wanted to, to keep writing books that people might find interesting. I broke down and wept. It was exactly the kind of thing Paul would do—even on his deathbed he was thinking about others, about writing books, and about remaining original. I never heard his voice again. I hope he would have been happy with this result.

CAST OF CHARACTERS

Elvira de Arévalo, encomendera and grieving widow
Alonso de Ávila, parish priest
Licenciado Cristóbal de Badillo, law professor, priest, card shark
Licenciado Fernando de Caballero, court judge
Captain Juan Pablos Carrión, admiral and bigamist
Friar Maturino Gilberti, gouty humanist
Nuño de Guzmán, conquistador
Don Antonio Huitziméngari, indigenous governor
Juan Infante, encomendero
Doña Beatriz López, plantation owner and kidnapper
Friar Martín de Jesús, missionary
Diego de Medina, encomendero
Friar Juan de Medina Rincón, bishop
Cristóbal Muñoz, parish priest
Friar Diego Muñoz, hermit
Pedro Muñoz, field marshal, rancher
Alonso de Montúfar, imposter
Antonio Negrete, royal judge
Cristóbal de Olid, conquistador
Don Diego de Orduña, caudillo, priest, rancher, brawler
Don Diego Pérez Gordillo y Negrón, priest, arsonist
Cristóbal Preciado, plantation owner and drunk
Francisco Preciado, magistrate and land thief
Don Vasco de Quiroga, former lawyer, bishop
River crocodile
Jerónimo Rodríguez, diocesan judge
Doña Isabel Ruiz de Monjaraz, encomendera and grieving widow
Francisco de Sarriá, magistrate
Juan de Solís, assassin for hire
Tzintzincha Tangaxoan, the caltzontzin, king of Michoacán
Sebastián de Valderrama, priest
Friar Alonso de la Veracruz, professor
Francisco de Villegas, encomendero
Don Pedro de Yepes, cathedral treasurer and inquisitor
Rodrigo de Yepes, imposter
Juan Zurnero, cathedral canon

PROMISCUOUS POWER

INTRODUCTION

Michoacán was "enclosed like Eden," according to Alonso de la Rea, a Franciscan chronicler of the seventeenth century. He added, "The waters which irrigate this terrestrial paradise and fertilize its cup are the most abundant which this kingdom [of New Spain] enjoys; they are as sweet and drinkable as one could hope for."[1] A region of breathtaking physical beauty, it is home to lush green hills and mountains, lakes and rivers, cascading waterfalls, abundant fish, pine forests, and rolling valleys buffeted by volcanic peaks in mountainous highlands (the Tarascan Plateau).[2] In De la Rea's time, the subtropical zones were rich in avocadoes, papayas, and zapotes as well as river crocodiles, scorpions, and hallucinogenic mushrooms. Spaniards thought Michoacán was a kind of American paradise, a place where one could grow crops year-round, populated by tranquil and pious indigenous peoples.

Encompassing the modern-day states of Michoacán and Colima, as well as parts of Jalisco and Guanajuato, the viceregal province of Michoacán was topographically and ethnically complex. Prior to Spanish arrival, it remained independent from the Aztec (Mexica) Empire of central Mexico. Composed of a hereditary kingdom or federation, the Tarascans (Purépecha), and overseen by a hereditary king known as the *caltzontzin*, the province had satellite states of influence in Colimotl and the Motines mountain regions and was bounded to the north by the vaguely defined "Chichimec" groups. After contact with Spaniards and putative political conquest, the Spanish Crown divided the region into *encomiendas*. In exchange for spiritual oversight of their indigenous charges, the *encomenderos* received rights to labor drafts of these charges. In all practical terms, encomiendas developed into land grants, even if, technically speaking, the encomenderos held no formal title to land.[3] The region remained ethnically mixed, composed of Purépecha, Otomí, Colima-Nahua, Xilotlanzinca, and Piñol groups, followed by Spaniards and, later, mestizo and mulato peoples. Missionaries saw Michoacán as a region ripe for a kind of New World utopian communal Church overseen by simple friars. With its dense population, seemingly endless subtropical warmth, long growing seasons, and near-limitless freedom, Spaniards believed it could become a sort of cultural utopia. A dramatic showdown had already taken place between the Mexica Empire and Spanish conquistadors allied with Tlaxcalan auxiliaries. After the fall of the Mexica capital, Tenochtitlan, in 1521, Spaniards set their sights on the large kingdom of Michoacán to the west in the interest of imperial expansion.

In the century after Spanish-indigenous contact, in 1521, Michoacán hosted a series of antics so outlandish in all their macabre glory that it seems like some sarcastic deity has narrated the stories. The hereditary king, the caltzontzin, flayed Spaniards and made costumes of their skins, dancing inside them. The first Spanish missionaries demolished indigenous religious materials with glee. The region had no resident priest or magistrate for the first two decades of Spanish rule. Spanish landowners and settlers lived in an un-Christianized, stateless zone, free to drink, smoke, steal, gamble, screw, and do as they pleased. After Christianity arrived decades later, priests loyal to the bishop burned down a monastery in a factional dispute—while the friars were asleep inside. Parish priests hired their own personal militias and stabbed agents of the very Church they served when reminded of their legal duties. Friars gossiped that certain cardinals in Rome offered jobs for their male lovers. Ranchers laughed at inquisitional agents and called them punks, rogues, and thieves. The first inquisitional agent of the region was an inveterate gambler who loved a good dance party and silk suits. Priests punched each other out in the cathedral. Missionaries said the bishop was a lazy egotist. A gouty friar rode in a litter to preach to the indigenous for miles around, because local priests did not speak the local language, Purépecha. Royal magistrates ran drunkenly through the streets of small towns in their underwear, only to be reappointed for lack of royal representation on the ground. Other magistrates were murdered by their rivals. One had his ear chopped off in revenge. Mammoth coconut plantations supplied most of the illegal wine of the region. River crocodiles ate travelers but magically bore missionaries across river rapids. And the proverbial last man standing, a priest and inquisitional agent, stole so much land that the royal court was obliged to steal the land back. When it attempted to do so, the priest set his personal militia on the judge in attempted murder. A century after the conquest, an inquisitional agent was dispatched to Michoacán's countryside to deliver the good news that he was from the government and there to help the residents. They wondered, "What is this Inquisition you speak of, good sir?" And these are just a few of the true stories which littered the juridical and political landscape and which this book retells in an effort at rescuing largely forgotten histories of everyday forms of making (or undoing) empire.[4]

The case of western Mexico, the province of Michoacán, offers a detailed case study of the endemic difficulties of a transoceanic imperial authority, Spain, imposing a colonial order on a province of New Spain. This book provides a detailed portrait of Spanish agents of a global order relentlessly pursuing their own interests. Michoacán developed into a kind of outpost of empire, where the ordinary rules of law, jurisprudence, and royal oversight collapsed in the entropy of decentralization. In due course, Michoacán became a kind of region of refuge—refuge from imperial oversight, from juridical control, and from formal Catholicism.[5]

In the following pages, I examine the everyday exercise of authority by colonial agents of the Spanish Crown in Michoacán in the first century of Spanish presence. The Spanish Crown in the sixteenth century exercised far-flung global influence. Yet the Spanish Empire was diffuse, represented by a conquistador class that was largely a private enterprise in service of a state; an administrative class allied to local political interests; and a Christianization enterprise fractured into competing corporate groups. The Spanish Empire in the sixteenth century was less a cohesive empire than a "confederation of principalities held together in the person of a single king."[6] Nowhere was this loose archipelago of power more obvious than in sixteenth-century Michoacán.

This book examines the ground-level application of an imperial project in a viceregal province, avoiding interpretations of empire as all-powerful or empty. As one modern historian has put it, agents of empire lived in a sixteenth-century world where "power relationships . . . were intermittent, incomplete, and complicated by many conflicting obligations and loyalties . . . [without] a single, unified, coherent ruling class."[7] In the quotidian activity of making, or, rather, unmaking, empire, one sees the remarkable ability of local political actors to flout royal will even when tasked with defending royal justice, global Catholicism, or a universalizing Inquisition. Analysis of Spanish actors who presumably represented the imperial project—landowners, magistrates, missionaries, priests, bishops, inquisitional agents, and notaries, for example—reveals divided mini-empires. Indigenous aristocrats, *pipiltin*, also acted as agents of empire, as the Spanish Crown delegated to them rights and privileges in exchange for acting as intermediaries between indigenous commoners, or *macehuales*, and the Crown. In this frontier, a few men wielded what amounted to promiscuous power, drawing strength and authority from overlapping institutions (such as royal court, municipal government, parish church, mendicant order, cathedral chapter, and Inquisition).

Resident Spaniards, acting as the little hands of empire, worked toward their own goals, usually to the detriment of royal justice. The book's focus on Spaniards inverts the usual ethnographic practice of studying indigenous responses to colonial authority. The sustained analysis of Spanish perceptions and practices articulates the instability of empire. The focus on local, quotidian politics distinguishes this study from the many excellent global treatments of Spanish Empire and the transatlantic world.[8] We know a good deal about the obverse side of this book's analysis. Studies about indigenous polities (*altepeque*) and their collective responses to Spanish imperial or colonial rule abound.[9] But given the stark silence about the ordinary enforcers of Spanish rule, I set out to write a book about the banality of local imperial rule.

Activities of the everyday and local representatives of colonial rule reveal the domestic quality of the enterprise of making empire. This study focuses on ranchers and encomenderos as representatives of Spanish control of land; on magistrates and judges as functionaries of royal law; on missionaries as ideological agents of Catholic evangelization; on parish priests and bishops as representatives of the Spanish royal control of the Church; and on inquisitional deputies as agents of social discipline. Conquistadors, land speculators, ranchers, and encomenderos presumably served to expand the Spanish orbit literally at the ground level by usurping indigenous land claims. In practice, they were concerned with personal enrichment. Royal legal agents—magistrates—were supposed to enforce the royal law. Yet their distance from centralized jurisprudential oversight (in Mexico City and Madrid) lent them an impunity to enforce civil law in capricious ways. Religious officials sought to Christianize Michoacán for diverse reasons. Friar-missionaries—Augustinians and Franciscans—hoped to convert the indigenous population to Christianity. But these friars were relatively uninterested in making the indigenous peoples into Spanish citizens or members of a secular empire. The bishops and parish priests who followed in the wake of the missionaries more clearly identified with a project of Hispanicization. Secular priests—that is, priests who were not monastics—viewed friar-missionaries as too independent—financially and administratively—for the broader good of global Spanish Catholicism. And the Inquisition viewed Michoacán as culturally out of control. Scholarship and popular imagination presumed the Inquisition to be the highest expression of a global Spanish Catholicism in a negative, punitive way. Yet Spanish citizens in the region mocked the Inquisition. Overall, one sees a deeply quotidian enforcement of imperial theory.

MICHOACÁN'S FIRST SPANISH CENTURY, SERIALIZED

Individual narrative dramas organize this book. Each chapter offers a snapshot of the everyday processes of colonialism of a particular region during a delimited period of time. These narrative chapters portray the extent to which local interests pursued their own powers with few overarching political-legal theories of empire or colonialism. Microhistorical biography fleshes out colonial actors as individuals caught up in the intrigues, violence, and drama of imperial showdown just as residents of indigenous towns resisted Spanish control.[10]

While methodologically microhistorical, this book takes epistemological and stylistic cues from Russian theorist Mikhail Bakhtin. In his study of Dostoyevsky, Bakhtin made a critical point that has influenced my thinking about human biographies.[11] In telling their stories, a novelist may utilize life-stories to represent concepts (piety, redemption, sensualism, cynicism) — as Dostoyevsky did so famously, for example, in *Brothers Karamazov*. Michoacán's imperial agents represent conceptual explorations — a friar might represent idealism; a bishop, regalism; an encomendero, colonial territorial expansion; a cathedral canon, *caudillismo* — rule by a strongman; a drunken womanizer, anarchism; a rancher, sedition. But these symbolic biographies are implicit rather than explicit, hiding behind the mask of the ordinary.

Stylistically, I have long found inspiration in Bakhtin's assessment of Rabelais (to say nothing of Rabelais himself). In Bakhtin's telling, Rabelais, an erudite, elegant, and witty theologian and writer, combined the language of the market, of the street, of the "lower-bodily stratum," with the language of the monastery, the classroom, and the court.[12] Rabelaisian style was thus a perfect synthesis of the crass and the elegant, of the grotesque and the sublime, of the ordinary and the exceptional, of the scatological and the angelic. The stories of everyday Spaniards in Michoacán reveal in their ribald detail the kind of symphonic range that might have pleased Bakhtin's sensibilities.

Slippage between official and popular comes out in the language and mentality of those who were accused of doctrinal offenses. In 1577, a Franciscan friar preached a sermon in Celaya in which he claimed that the Virgin Mary gave birth to Jesus like any other woman.[13] The naval captain Andrés López claimed (in 1566) that "Saint Catherine was an adulterous whore, and Saint Magdalene, a dyke."[14] Friar Joan Díaz, the guardian of the Franciscan monastery of Pátzcuaro in 1605, thought that "the guardian of Naples and definidor (regional superior) of the Roman province was Cardinal Matteo's lover and the cardinal was his bitch and that the Cardinal had given him the position as guardian because he was so handsome."[15] Others had more mundane ideas. The ecclesiastical court accused Alonso Gómez of blasphemy in 1563 in Pátzcuaro. His crime was that he had traveled from Michoacán to Mexico City, where he said he "rode a horse in Mexico without a bit and that he had gotten the horse to stop like a seraphim, to which the witness asked, 'How do seraphims stop?'" Alonso Gómez replied that "it was simply a manner of speaking."[16] In 1561 in Ensamala, in the *tierra caliente*, the diocesan court accused a rancher named Hernando de Coca for blasphemy. While eating a spicy stew he had casually remarked that it "had a chile sauce as red as the blood of Christ."[17] He had only thought to compare the sacred with the ordinary. In 1569, a Spanish rancher named Pedro de Ávila of Tangancícuaro found his servants' request to attend an Ash Wednesday mass to be ridiculous. He told them "to go down to the river which passed by his ranch and bring back a lot of willows and burn them and from them they could make ash which he would apply to their fore-heads."[18] Such a naturalistic approach seemed easy enough, but inquisitors were not satisfied, since it rejected the liturgical tradition of burning the palm fronds blessed on the previous year's Palm Sunday to make the ashes. Such everyday asso-ciations of the lurid and natural with the sacred were ubiquitous in Michoacán and serve, stylistically, to reiterate the prosaic nature of global Catholicism.

I begin my tale in 1521 with the first contact between Spaniards and Purépecha. Chapter 1 examines the sketchy military-spiritual conquest and colonization of Michoacán from 1521 to 1538. The main goal of the Spaniards was, theoretically, to claim the region for the Crown. More plainly, their goal was to get rich. The early period of conquest and colonialization set the tone for decades to come. The Crown quickly divided much of Michoacán's best lands into encomiendas.[19] The encomenderos came to wield outsized political and economic power in the re-gion.[20] In 1529, a high court (*Audiencia*) with known antipathy to Hernán Cor-tés ruled New Spain.[21] The court's president, Nuño de Guzmán, led a notoriously violent campaign of conquest of New Galicia (modern-day Jalisco); en route, he blazed a fiery trail through Michoacán, executing Tzintzincha Tangaxoan, the last independent caltzontzin of Michoacán, in 1530.[22] The initial contact period in Mi-choacán set the stage for the political culture of the region. Between 1521 and the early 1530s, the region was home to only the occasional priest and itinerant friar. In May 1522, Pope Adrian VI issued a series of bulls, known as the Omnimoda, that empowered Franciscans with privileges ordinarily restricted to the parish clergy— the construction of churches and celebration of the mass, marriage, and confes-sion. The mendicant missionaries, in turn, claimed that the American mission needed a special, zealous kind of priest—a friar.[23] In due course, Franciscans, in 1525, and Augustinians, in 1537, established the first residential Catholic presence in Michoacán, forming a bulwark against attempts at diocesan centralization.[24]

Chapter 2 examines the spiritual conquest of Michoacán, which was fitful and corporatist.[25] Rather than a centralized religious program, or even a unified mis-sionary expansion, the earliest stages of Christianization in Michoacán engendered bitter factional feuds. Analyzing the topic through the lens of the disputes between friars and diocesan powers, the chapter covers the years 1538 to 1565. A lawyer and former court judge, Vasco de Quiroga, became bishop of Michoacán at the beginning of this period, and a vicious struggle for political supremacy erupted. Quiroga sought to rein in the corporate powers of the friars while simultaneously taking aim at the social and economic power of the encomenderos. It did not end well, and Michoacán became ground zero of the battle for the soul of Mexican Catholicism. Ideologically, the friar-mendicants promoted an idealized mission project focused on Christianizing the indigenous population without oversight of bishops or any parish priests. Quiroga was having none of this, and the mendicants dug in their heels. Franciscans and Augustinians enjoyed economic support from the region's encomenderos and the indigenous elite. The bishop was the agent of the Crown, sent to centralize the region under a firm imperial grasp. The bishop's supporters became, in turn, armed partisans. In 1561, under the tutelage of Don Diego Pérez Gordillo, a priest and cathedral canon, the bishop's partisans torched the Augustinian monastery of Tlazazalca as punishment for refusing to obey Quiroga's reform.[26] The rivalry between bishop and friar smoldered for decades.

These two initial chapters set the stage for a region perennially unfriendly to centralized rule. Chapter 3 tells the story of an Inquisition that did not frighten anyone. Much recent scholarship has shown that the Inquisition was much less effective in its repression than the old stereotype presumed.[27] Yet the popular imagination and even some modern scholarship continue to see the Inquisition as an institution of omnipotent power, or capable of harnessing sociological paranoia and cultural hatreds for religious and cultural minorities.[28] How did Spanish residents—the judicial subjects of the inquisitional court—react to this supposedly omnipotent apparatus? Yes, the inquisitional court had the power to arrest, imprison, punish, and even torture suspects. But in that respect, the Inquisition functioned like other criminal courts of the early modern Hispanic world.

Chapter 3 thus examines the widespread resentment and mockery of inquisitional attempts to impose social control. For example, diocesan officials threatened the wealthy encomendero Pedro Muñoz with legal action in 1569 for refusing to pay the tithe. When told he would be excommunicated if he did not pay up, he told the church officials that he would "shit on the excommunication order."[29] The local inquisitor was not amused, but the rancher suffered no long-term consequences for this response. If Spanish residents mocked the Inquisition, how did inquisitional agents understand their role as defenders of orthodoxy? Their goals appear to be largely financial. Don Pedro de Yepes, a cathedral treasurer, was the diocesan inquisitor from 1569 to 1571. He made a fortune on land speculation and real estate.[30]

Chapter 4 describes a judicial theater of the absurd in which the Mexican Inquisition could not even seat its own agent in the province. A centralized Inquisition took office in Mexico City in November 1571, voiding the claims of inquisitional power by the bishop of Michoacán. The new inquisitor general dispatched a deputy, the law professor Cristóbal de Badillo, to Michoacán to establish order. It was a farce. The cathedral canons opposed his installment, assaulting the new inquisitional deputy both physically and legally. These expressions of masculine public power functioned as variations on the semiotics of power.[31] Thus expressions of violence in the public sphere were often about the most ordinary slights. A lawyer refuses to don his bonnet; a priest deliberately sits in the presence of a presumed social superior. While much of the rivalry between friars and diocesan priests in Chapter 2 centers on questions of ecclesiological power, the politics of everyday masculine violence detailed in Chapter 4 was often an expression of this most quotidian semiotics of power.

Chapter 5 offers a case study of a quintessential region of refuge from the norms of royal oversight. Colima, located in the far west and southwest of Michoacán, was a province within a province. It also was a good place to escape the law, murder one's rivals, or start a secret cult. Geographically and topographically remote, with its principal city 120 miles south of the government of New Galicia in Guadalajara, Colima was nonetheless subject to Mexico City, which was 500 miles away. It was therefore an excellent place to escape governmental authority. Simultaneously, however, Colima's residents found themselves cut off from practical attempts to appeal abuse of local power: since the court of appeal was in Mexico City, any journey to make such an appeal would be arduous and costly. Thugs and criminals ruled Colima at the local level. How could a region nominally under the rule of royal law become a sort of outpost of criminal governance? The region was home to a vast plantation economy (in cacao and later coconut) as well as some of New Spain's most coveted encomiendas.[32] The outsized wealth from the plantation system combined with isolation to produce a culture of impunity. A long, illustrious series of criminals and scammers held the office of *alcalde*, or town magistrate, in the region; they were famed as drunken womanizers through the end of the sixteenth century.

Chapter 6 recounts another part of the saga: the tale of the caudillo-priest Diego de Orduña. In 1583, Badillo's career in Michoacán ended when the bishop exiled him for assaulting another priest, and Badillo fled to Spain to seek legal redress. Orduña stepped into the jurisdictional vacuum and applied to become the inquisitional deputy of Michoacán's capital city. In 1592, he succeeded in becoming the inquisitional deputy.[33] Then, in 1598, Mexico's Audiencia condemned Orduña for an elaborate theft of indigenous lands and dispatched a royal inspector to seize his ranch and livestock. When the royal judge arrived, Orduña attempted to have him murdered, mocking him and calling him a *calabaza*, or "squash," an insult implying arrogance.[34] The Mexican Inquisition voided the judgment against Orduña, and he remained in office for nearly two more decades, until his probable death in 1616.

How could a man who was both an ordained priest and a felon with multiple offenses establish himself in Michoacán as the province's most influential and powerful churchman? Chapter 6 examines the concept of caudillo-priests. A *caudillo* today is usually associated with Latin American strongmen, such as the nineteenth-century Argentine dictator Juan Manuel de Rosas.[35] Yet even as early as 1602, court cases in Mexico show, the term was used to refer to a man who commanded a private militia and who looked to the maintenance of his clients in the patron-client relationship.[36] Local factotums, priests even, mocked the royal monopoly on military force.

The book's conclusion reflects on the state of Michoacán's church in the 1620s. The Franciscan monastery of Valladolid, built as an affront to Quiroga's Pátzcuaro project, was falling down, and the Franciscans had to plead for a massive loan to restore it.[37] The new inquisitional agent made a tour of the region only to discover that most places not only had no resident priest but had never seen an agent of the Inquisition.[38] Armed bandits who worked for caudillo-ranchers assaulted the inquisitional mailmen in order to destroy evidence.[39] Spanish citizens were eating hallucinogenic mushrooms and peyote in open defiance of the law.[40]

(UN)MAKING EMPIRE

The story of decentralized power in Michoacán offers a finely grained case study of the complexities of making church and empire at the ground level. Even though Philip II had a "grand strategy" (which, ahem, did not turn out very well), or if a grand vision of empire existed in royal courts, personal gain, not love of king, motivated prosaic agents of colonialism, who were emboldened by the lack of oversight, and deeply committed to their own corporate memberships.[41] The king dispensed justice and ruled as the defender of Christendom while defending rights of the citizenry. By the time Cortés arrived in Mexico in 1519, the Spanish Crown was united under Charles V, a Hapsburg, and the old Castilian kingdom had become a truly global empire.[42] The Crown presumably owned a monopoly on justice—meaning the resolution of legal disputes—but it drew its power as a representative of the collective interests of the citizenry.[43] When the Crown flouted the will of the citizenry, armed revolt occurred, as in the *comunero* revolt of 1520, effectively demonstrating the limits of royal authority.[44] The establishment of a viceregal system in Mexico in 1535 after fourteen years of political chaos following Cortés's spectacular defeat of Tenochtitlan was subject to such exigencies.[45]

What were the aspirations and goals of the Spaniards involved in the various themes analyzed in this book? What motivated them to travel to or live in Michoacán? Did *letrados*—the legally trained royal functionaries assigned to the region to enforce royal law—and other magistrates have a fully articulated understanding of empire? How interested in colonial hegemony were the encomenderos? Did friar-missionaries support Spanish globalism? Did bishops and parish priests want to centralize colonial power? And did the Inquisition succeed in imposing its version of cultural-ideological order? Such are perennial questions of political theory. There is a state, a king, or an empire. For most people the concept of a state that oversees their lives is vague. In western Mexico in the sixteenth century, no one ever saw the king, and rarely, if ever, the viceroy. Why do people go along with the system when they have such a tenuous connection to the state itself? People agree, usually unconsciously, to support the state apparatus in the most banal and ordinary ways. Answering questions about the motives of colonial representatives and royal subjects means examining their public lives and personal attitudes.

How did letrados effect the royal legal system in local, rural settings?[46] Magistrates (alcaldes and *corregidores*) were the direct representatives of the royal legal system and acted as judges of first instance.[47] Appeals thus could be sent to a royal court (Audiencia)—in the case of Michoacán, the one in Mexico City. Magistrates were supposed to enforce imperial rule, but, in practice, to be adapted to local circumstances, the application of law required flexibility.[48]

What were the goals of encomenderos? In a word—wealth. Empire was an instrument for enrichment through channels of conquest and the spoils of war. The Spanish Crown dispensed grants of labor drafts to encomenderos after the political-military conquest of Mexico and Michoacán. This practice continued the centuries-long tradition of the Reconquest in which private armies fought wars of conquest for Iberian kings. Victory ensured social promotion, titles, and lands. Theoretically, the encomenderos were to oversee the doctrinal conversion of indigenous peoples and act as Catholic models of behavior.[49] Yet the encomenderos of Michoacán had a complicated relationship to Catholicism. They were often irreverent but often supported missionary-building projects in Michoacán as a method of political diversification.

How did the Christianization program proceed? Why was Catholicism in Michoacán so variegated? Answering these questions means examining the fractured loyalties that derived from two conflicting versions of Catholicism: one based on friar-missionary complexes and a second overseen by a strong bishop and loyal parish priest class. Michoacán's Catholicism was born out of a primal struggle between these two visions of the Church.[50] The mendicant church answered to Rome and its corporate overseers in Spain. The diocesan church answered to the Spanish Crown, which controlled the institutional Catholic Church in Mexico through its system of royal patronage (*real patronato*). This system prohibited direct communication between the Mexican Church and the hierarchy in Rome; it also allowed the Crown to appoint bishops and archbishops with perfunctory approval from Rome.[51] The Church in the Americas answered only indirectly to the pope; the Crown placed the Council of the Indies as the direct intermediary between Spanish America and Rome.[52] This created a religious sociology of layered and overlapping jurisdictions and claims to authority.

What did inquisitional agents hope to achieve in Michoacán? Theoretically, their charge was to police the Spanish population's beliefs and religious behavior, but inquisitional agents found that a lot of Catholics did not like being told what to do. The Inquisition acted as the enforcer of orthodoxy and social ortho-praxis throughout the Spanish Empire. And here, too, the Inquisition was a pawn of the royal state. In the 1470s, the Catholic Monarchs extracted privileges from the papacy that allowed the Spanish Crown to appoint and oversee its Inquisition and inquisitors; only in theory did the pope have any say in the operation of the institution.[53] By extension, the Spanish Crown oversaw the appointment of bishops in New Spain, who from the 1520s through the 1560s oversaw a series of diocesan Inquisitions. In 1569, the Spanish Crown revised this system and created a central Mexican Inquisition under the direct purview of the Crown.[54]

How did ordinary Spanish residents react to this system of cultural and ideological control? This study analyzes the inquisitional prosecutions and investigations of Spanish residents of Michoacán in the period, stories that unfold in all their insolent glory. The idyllic and utopian visions of Michoacán as a pristine and unspoiled paradise ripe for easy Christianization provide a clear contrast with the "elemental, instinctive materialism" of rural peoples, both encomendero and rancher.[55] By analyzing the mentalities of those targeted by the Inquisition in Michoacán one can appreciate the nuances of early modern Catholicism in a rural area—and the inability of the Inquisition to impose social discipline. So, too, do the political lives of inquisitional agents elaborate the human element of a presumably repressive institution.[56] These "agents of orthodoxy" adapted to and profited from local politics even when their orthodoxy was questionable.[57]

The biographies of the varied and often bizarre individuals who made up the Spanish order in Michoacán elucidate the humanity of empire. To that end, this book does not presume to explain the theories of empire imposed from above—from pope, Crown, inquisitor general, or viceroy. Instead, the focus here is on the practical, the lived, the experiential, and banal.[58] Yes, royal law existed in large tomes, such as the *Leyes de Toro*, *Fuero Real*, *Siete Partidas*, and *Digest*. The *Decretum* and the *Decretales* explain Catholic, ecclesial law. Inquisitional manuals, including the *Directorium Inquisitorum*, instructed inquisitional agents on how to pursue cases. But one cannot find extensive discussion of these codes in Colima, Pamatácuaro, or Apatzingán, because few people in Michoacán owned these books. In fact, sixteenth-century New Spain in general encountered a chronic shortage of such books, and local officials rarely possessed even a single printed law code.[59] The argument in the ensuing pages relies on a reading of more than one hundred inquisitional trials and hundreds of testimonies in civil lawsuits and land disputes, as well as voluminous official and officious correspondence. In only a small handful of cases, as in Quiroga's lawsuits against the Augustinians, did citation of law even occur. By following how individual actors interpreted empire in customary, practical ways, this book elucidates how ordinary Spaniards effected ground-level rule.

OUTPOSTS OF EMPIRE

Some of the still highly readable and influential scholars from a much earlier generation have shown that logistical complications characterized Spanish imperial projects at local levels.[60] Recent scholarship on colonialism and empire has emphasized themes such as negotiated empires, the limited influence of empire on frontier regions, the ethno-political variegation of new conquest history, and the persistence of indigenous culture.[61] With these traditions in mind, this book looks to the "ambivalent conquests," political and religious, of western Mexico even as they were begun by the agents who had been sent to undertake them.[62] Thus it offers a cultural interpretation of political and religious violence.[63]

The stakes in Michoacán were high for a variety of reasons. It was the first large-scale attempt by the Spanish Crown to expand imperial power out of the core region of central Mexico. Michoacán had incredible wealth—a large, dense population for labor exploitation; extensive mining deposits (copper, silver, and gold); and a fertile landscape for agricultural and livestock development. The region was strategically important: if the Spanish could dominate the region, they could settle it and employ it as a locus of power from which to expand ever northward into the Chichimec frontier.[64]

Given the high economic and political stakes in securing Michoacán, the effort at colonial hegemony was remarkably haphazard. For example, in 1570, some 200 Spanish families lived in Valladolid and Pátzcuaro, in a region which still counted in the central Tarascan Plateau (or *meseta tarasca*) close to 100,000 indigenous residents.[65] These colonial agents and families represented a simulated hegemony. Colonial representatives were all too human; theoretically, they represented an imperial project, but in practice they sought advantage where they found it. Scholars have written reams on the men in the high ranks of empire—king, viceroy, conquistador, inquisitor—but little about these provincial agents.[66] Likewise, there is a full historiography regarding indigenous contestations of imperial authority.[67] This study builds on such work by reconstructing the history of Spaniards who were charged with implementing royal justice in a largely rural, frontier, and provincial region.

These local imperial agents were all subaltern to the upper echelons of power—king, viceroy, royal judge, archbishop, inquisitor general. Yet in their local setting, for all practical purposes they *were* the Crown, Church and Inquisition.[68] The argument of this book calls attention to the political, cultural, personal, and ideological diversity of royal representatives. New scholarship on the Americas has reoriented our understanding of a presumably top-down Spanish sociopolitical conquest,[69] showing that in reality, the Spanish conquest was semi-privatized, incomplete, multidirectional, and composed of multiethnic alliances.[70] Indigenous peoples of Mexico operated less as oppressed and conquered victims and more as shrewd and self-interested operatives involved in a complex process of mitigation.[71] By contrast, we know little about the more prosaic Spaniards who benefited from representing imperial rule; in the account that follows I aim to rectify that situation.[72]

In this book I also engage five themes about conquest, colonialism, and imperial aspirations. First, I consider the theoretical construction of regions of refuge. Gonzalo Aguirre Beltrán conceived regions with topography hostile to the intrusions of state power as zones of refuge, where indigenous peoples and escaped slaves fled the authoritarian or colonial pretentious of empire.[73] I invert the model to interrogate the extent to which agents of the empire tasked with imposing state power fled the royal oversight of their local power.

Second, I examine the efforts to impose Catholic social orthodoxy in Michoacán. Landowners, settlers, traders, priests, and bureaucrats were freewheeling in their behavior and attitudes toward orthodox Catholicism. Inquisitional investigations reveal the extent of Spanish hostility to the Inquisition's conservatism and the venality of its own agents. While some see in the Inquisition a precursor to modern totalitarianism, this book analyzes the limited nature of inquisitional power in Michoacán.[74]

A third consideration of everyday empire is the extent to which the Spanish Crown struggled to maintain a monopoly on coercive power. Michoacán's royal agents asserted particularist authority. Even the earliest colonial efforts in Michoacán were expressions of a type of caudillo rule, or rule by individual strongmen. Michoacán's most notorious conquistador, Nuño de Guzmán, clearly sought out the conquest of Michoacán for pure and simple spoils. But what were the goals of later colonial agents? To what extent did the Crown succeed in maintaining that monopoly on force? And how did the corporations—mendicant orders, the cathedral chapter, plantation owners—respond to assertions of might in the region? My analysis focuses on local representatives of royal interests and how they operated as local power brokers within the theoretical orbit of the Crown.

Fourth, Michoacán historiography has tended to describe the region as a kind of terrestrial paradise. In this interpretation Quiroga was a beloved father figure who oversaw a utopian ordering of indigenous communities.[75] I examine instead how Quiroga undertook his Edenic mission and sociopolitical utopian system. Rather than offer hagiography, I scrutinize the granular, local struggles between Quiroga's regalist view of the Church and the mendicant ideal.

Fifth, I engage the history of colonial political authority by generally rejecting the Black Legend, or the depiction of the Spanish Empire as an especially egregious form of imperialism. Although a generation of historians has now demonstrated the limits of colonial rule in Latin America, few have challenged the assumption that the royal state and the institutional Church colluded to produce a powerful Catholicism that crushed heterodoxy, punished cultural difference, and ruined indigenous worlds. I thus ask whether the Crown-Church alliance produced effective regulation of everyday life in Michoacán.[76]

The following chapters lay out in stark relief the everyday negotiation of empire. There was spectacular personalism in this project, a collective middle finger for officialdom. In place of sobriety one finds mockery of order, insult to the dignity of law, and uproariously sarcastic contempt for decorum. I tell the story of the lives of ranchers, priests, lawyers, missionaries, land speculators, judges, murderers, rapists, drunks, scammers, thieves, saints, sinners, and everyone in between. Stylistically, I evoke the mood of the region, adding layer upon layer of improbability. Their stories remain all too human; their home was Michoacán, a mordant simulacrum of empire.

CHAPTER 1

THE CONQUEST OF MICHOACÁN,
PARADISE'S LOST AND FOUND

Setting: Tancítaro, Taximaroa, Tzintzuntzan
Years: 1521–1538

On 14 February 1530, Nuño de Guzmán, president of Mexico's First Audiencia, ordered the execution of Michoacán's hereditary king, Tzintzincha Tangaxoan, the caltzontzin. The charges were treason, human sacrifice, idolatry, and sodomy. The real reason Guzmán had him killed was that he stood in the way of westward colonial expansion and led stubborn indigenous resistance to Spanish land and labor claims in Michoacán. A villain of Mexican history, Guzmán personified the earliest royal officials of the region—personalist and drastic.

Guzmán has been one of the single most reviled conquistadors in the popular imaginary. Juan O'Gorman's 1941 mural depicting the conquest of Michoacán, painted in Pátzcuaro's public library, succinctly expresses the revulsion for Guzmán felt by later generations.[1] Scholars also depict Guzmán as particularly vicious, starting with his days as a slaver in Pánuco in the 1520s.[2] The venerable historian Leslie Byrd Simpson described the conquistador as "one of those rare characters whose exclusive function seems to have been that of destroyer . . . [and whose] capacity for hatred was only equaled by an apparent delight in sadistical orgies of burning, torture and destruction."[3] Against this image of barbarity, historians and muralists found a convenient foil in Michoacán's first bishop, Vasco de Quiroga, whom they depicted as a benevolent humanist—faithful to study of the classics but also dedicated to the idealized betterment of indigenous communities.[4]

The trial and execution of the caltzontzin represented a crucial turning point in Michoacán's political culture. Although Spanish expeditions had made tentative contact with the Purépecha kingdom as early as 1521, Spanish efforts at military conquest and spiritual conversion in Michoacán had been itinerant in the 1520s. In 1533, the Crown formally recognized the central part of Michoacán, in and around Pátzcuaro and Valladolid, as part of New Spain.[5] In 1538, the region was organized

FIGURE 1.1. Juan O'Gorman, mural in Pátzcuaro public library, 1941. Photo by Ernesto Perales Soto (2006), Creative Commons license, https://commons.wikimedia.org/wiki /File:242292072_ab49824e72_b.jpg.

as a diocese of the Catholic Church. By this time any hope among the Purépecha that Michoacán could remain an independent indigenous federation had vanished. Accordingly, Guzmán's actions set the tone for the development of political and religious culture in Spanish Michoacán as particular and corporatist. The first practical Spanish rulers were not judges, magistrates, bishops, priests, or inquisitors. They were planters, ranchers, and friar-missionaries.

Guzmán and his allies—dozens of Spanish horsemen and thousands of indigenous forces—swept through Michoacán with furious, terrible violence. The terror he inflicted on Michoacán through an especially cruel form of warfare, in which

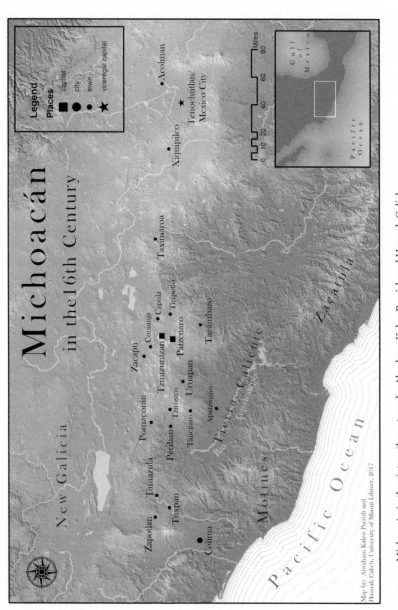

MAP 1.1. Michoacán in the sixteenth century, by Abraham Kaleo Parrish and Hannah Calich.

Michoacán's elites often sacrificed their own subjects for fear that Guzmán would enslave them, is well known. It presaged his invasion of New Galicia and the spectacularly vicious Mixtón War, where even Guzmán's indigenous forces engaged in human sacrifice and cannibalism.[6]

Guzmán's invasion of Michoacán and concomitant execution of the caltzontzin illustrate the early stages of conquest and imperial rule on multiple levels. First, these events traumatized Purépecha society. Although the indigenous residents were accustomed to warfare, the scale of Guzmán's brutality must have been shocking. Furthermore, Guzmán departed without establishing any lasting form of governance, leaving the region in literal and sociopolitical ruins. After the trauma of 1530, Spanish incursions in the region let up, and a semblance of governing order emerged. Taking office in 1535, New Spain's first viceroy, Antonio de Mendoza, was eager to assert a peaceable transition of authority to a royal system of governance, but it proved difficult given that the region had experienced wars, territorial divisions, and encomendero predation for fourteen years without royal or viceregal oversight.[7]

Guzmán's entrada and assassination of the caltzontzin opened the door to a corporatist and privatized form of governance. No residential magistrate was vested in these early years; a magistrate (corregidor) was assigned to Tzintzuntzan in 1529, though there is no evidence that a regularly installed residential magistrate oversaw the city of Michoacán before the 1540s.[8] Guzmán's bloody actions also set the stage for a coercive form of evangelization, even if it was undertaken by corporations presumably opposed to conversion by the sword—Franciscan and then later Augustinian friars. Ultimately, these first seventeen years established Spanish Michoacán as a region where private interests dictated imperial efforts in the wake of political violence, and where corporatist rivalries and alliances of cynical convenience dominated the political landscape.

DECENTRALIZED CENTRAL RULE, NO HOME OFFICE

From 1521 to 1538, Spanish colonization of Michoacán developed against the backdrop of a sparse Christianization project, expansive encomendero wealth, and a small number of residential royal officials. An itinerant string of royal inspectors traveled to Michoacán, and many of them arrested their predecessors on charges of abuse of authority. The province's capital (first Tzintzuntzan and then Pátzcuaro) had its first residential magistrate in October 1536.[9] Evidence of judicial activity by a resident magistrate did not occur until 1542.[10]

Encomenderos formed the most politically powerful group of Spanish residents in the 1520s in Michoacán. They developed a well-deserved reputation for flouting the normal rules of Catholic decorum. But by the 1530s, they also began to forge a calculated political relationship with the Franciscans and Augustinians in efforts to solidify their cultural and economic power against royal and diocesan oversight. In 1525, the Franciscans became the first Catholic religious to reside in Michoacán. They had been dispatched from Mexico City, where they had already established a missionary presence. In Michoacán they claimed special status as the Crown's favored agents of evangelization. In May 1522, Pope Adrian VI issued the bull *Exponi nobis fecisti*, known also as the Omnimoda, which gave the Franciscans (and, later, the Augustinians) the right to engage in activities normally under the purview of a bishop—to build friary-churches, to hear confession, to celebrate the mass, and to perform weddings.[11] The friars relied on the bull as legal precedent and customary proof that they had free reign to act without oversight of diocesan power.

Michoacán became a region of refuge from global imperial oversight. Neither of the twin pillars of Spanish global expansion—the Crown or the Catholic Church—was represented in the first seventeen years of Spanish presence there. Instead, state and church were only present in corporate entities—in the form of encomenderos and mendicants, respectively. The only royal officials in Michoacán in the 1520s and 1530s were a series of royal inspectors (*visitadores*). Encomiendas formed the socioeconomic backbone of the Spanish project. In religious terms, the province was home to no parish priests, and only to a couple of Franciscan friars prior to 1537, when Augustinians arrived. It was not until the summer of 1538 that a bishop arrived to oversee the Church. The foundations of Michoacán's missionary project were moored entirely in the Franciscan and Augustinian orders.

A detailed portrait of how the colonial project played out in its earliest years enumerates the decentralized politics of the region. On the eve of Spanish contact, the ethno-geographic world of Michoacán was variegated. Encomendero wealth fostered distrust of external authority, setting up a constitutional disregard for imperial monopolies of force and for religious programs of social discipline. The earliest forms of spiritual conquest were punitive: militias strove not to Christianize the indigenous population, but to extirpate the pre-Hispanic religious culture. The region ceased to be (if it ever was) idyllic once these extirpation campaigns arrived.

Michoacán was strategically important for the early colonial project in Mexico. Cortés's hold on power in central Mexico was tenuous after the fall of Tenochtitlan. The Spanish Crown viewed westward and northward expansion as useful for its broader imperial designs on Mesoamerica. Yet the privatized and caudillo style of conquest of Michoacán meant that the Crown never had a firm control over the conquistadors, encomenderos, or missionaries of the region. These early speculators successfully established a pattern of political, economic, and martial power only theoretically overseen by the Crown.

THE TARASCAN FEDERATION

Most of what became the province of Michoacán of New Spain belonged to a loose federation of ethnic groups, often called the Tarascan Federation, that, ethno-linguistically, were predominantly Purépecha. The region had a hereditary monarch, which in Nahuatl was called a caltzontzin and in Purépecha an *irecha*. It was centered in the mountainous plateau west and northwest of today's Morelia, the meseta tarasca, with Tzintzuntzan as its capital.[12] Subject regions in Motines, Colima, and Tuxpan fell within the orbit of Purépecha rule, paying tribute in cotton, copper, maize, turkeys, and pottery. The Mexica had never subjugated the region, and as such the Purépecha enjoyed relative political autonomy from Nahua states.[13] The region is topographically diverse and at contact presented a bewildering array of ethnic groups and linguistic clusters. To the east nearing the border of Mexico one found a mixture of Purépechas, Otomíes, Matlatzincas, and Nahuas.[14] To the north, in today's Guanajuato and the northern part of Michoacán state, were a mixture of various Chichimec groups. The southwestern section of the province of Michoacán, in Zapotlan and Tuxpan, was ethnographically elusive. Colima and Tuxpan-Zapotlan appear to have been outposts of Nahuatl-speaking groups.[15] This western region had never been subjected to Purépecha rule prior to Spanish-indigenous contact, so Purépecha was not used.[16] Nahuatl was probably introduced as a lingua franca after the conquest.[17]

This ethno-geographic complexity provided the backdrop to a region that proved difficult to govern. Regional micro-cultures—often separated by mountains or rivers—jurisdictional overlap, and ethno-linguistic confusion characterized the province. One finds deserts dry enough to produce mummies in Guanajuato, whereas in Colima, the lush tropical heat produces growth on top of growth, and summer thunderstorms rip through with terrifying ferocity. Rivers come raging down the mountains so intense and full of caimans that they become impassable even by canoe. Much of the tierra caliente lies below 1,000 feet above sea level, but with steep rises to the mountainous plateaus. The meseta tarasca lies high in an area of pine forest that is impossibly green. Alonso de la Rea compared Michoacán to legendary Trinacria (Sicily) of the *Odyssey*, ancient Italy's most abundant region.[18] The Augustinian chronicler Matías de Escobar called Michoacán the American Thebaida, the birthplace of Augustine, and as fertile as Italy for its array of produce—avocados, membrillos, zapotes, European-introduced limes and lemons, and apricots and peaches.[19]

While the Spanish laity saw the region as topographically ideal, missionaries viewed the religious cosmology as essentially satanic. The Purépecha practiced a polytheistic religion that included ritual human sacrifice, which was common

FIGURE 1.2. View of Lake Pátzcuaro from the ruins of the Purépecha ritual complex in Tzintzuntzan. Photo by Thelmadatter (2009), Creative Commons license, https:// commons.wikimedia.org/wiki/Tzintzuntzan,_Michoac%C3%A1n#/media /File:VwPalB2.JPG.

throughout Mesoamerica. The principal deity was Curicaueri, who was represented as a massive stone figure in the ritual complex of Zacapu. The high priest overseeing the cult was called the *curicaneri*. So powerful and central to the Purépecha cosmology was the priest caste that even the caltzontzin prostrated himself before the curicaneri when he led a major annual pilgrimage from Tzintzuntzan to Zacapu to pay respects to the god—and make a human sacrifice.[20]

Franciscan and Augustinian missionaries viewed the ritual practices and polytheism with both horror and respect. Although De la Rea saw the idolatry in negative terms, he also considered the Purépecha to be naturally inclined to respect for authority and social hierarchy. Escobar praised the complex social value of ritual observance as the reason why the Purépecha were later among the best Catholics of the New World: "I say, in fact, that the Tarascans are ceremonious and as a result careful in their reverence; . . . thus today they are very reverent and serious in the [Christian] law which they profess; their churches are the best served and decorated in the Western Hemisphere."[21] The Purépecha occupied the collective missionary conscience as peaceable and controllable, ideal Christians, even when these memories came centuries later.[22]

THE CONQUEST AND NON-CHRISTIANIZATION
OF MICHOACÁN, 1522–1529

Spiritual and military conquests were slow to come to Michoacán. These two strands of conquest were closely linked, with evangelization wed to military violence. Priests accompanied early expeditions, and later, in 1525, Franciscan friars began to establish a tenuous presence. Because Michoacán was never a tributary of the Mexica Federation, the Purépecha leaders saw a chance to curry favor with Cortés and the Spanish Crown. Indigenous military resistance to the Spanish was fitful at best. Spanish contact with Michoacán began in 1521. Conquistador and Cortés ally Antón Caicedo led the first expedition, arriving in Tzintzuntzan in the fall of 1521. Later, a Spanish expeditionary force, sometime in 1522, made brief contacts with Otomí border guards along the Tarascan-Mexica frontier.[23]

Early depictions of the initial contacts are not definitive. The *Relación de Michoacán*, composed between 1539 and 1541 on the orders of Viceroy Antonio de Mendoza, tells of two Spaniards arriving in Taximaroa on the festival of Purecoraqua, 23 February (presumably in 1521).[24] The *Relación de Michoacán*, the oldest illustrated manuscript chronicling pre-contact Michoacán, is a compilation of indigenous descriptions and witness statements of the history of the Purépecha world before contact and of the subsequent political fallout from Spanish conquest and the execution of the caltzontzin. Franciscan Jerónimo de Alcalá managed the project, but as with all such manuscripts, the collaboration of indigenous scribes, authors, and witnesses was central to its production.[25]

The first ideological exchange of Spanish Empire with Michoacán occurred with an expedition led by Cristóbal de Olid, who had once been a loyal lieutenant of Cortés in the conquest of Tenochtitlan. Olid later led an expedition to Honduras, where he declared his independence from Cortés, prompting Cortés's disastrous Honduran expedition. Olid died during Cortés's counterinvasion to rein in his former protégé.[26]

Olid traveled to Michoacán with Tlaxcalan auxiliaries, and the caltzontzin, Tzintzincha Tangaxoan, dispatched a relative, Don Pedro Cuinerángari, to act as his emissary and meet with him in Taximaroa. Olid's combined forces, which massively outnumbered Don Pedro's, arrived in Taximaroa for the meeting on the Purépecha festival of Cahera-cósquaro, 17 July 1522.[27] The Spaniards then questioned Don Pedro through an interpreter. It remains uncertain if Olid had Don Pedro bound or confined or if he provided testimony willingly. It is also unclear which language they used, but Olid's interpreter, Xanaqua, was a Purépecha; he had been captured by the Mexica and later given to either Olid or Cortés in Tenochtitlan as a war captive. The *Relación de Michoacán* describes Xanaqua as a *nahuatlato* (a ge-

FIGURE 1.3. Spaniards arriving in Michoacán. Illustration in Fray Jerónimo de Alcalá, *Relación de Michoacán* (ca. 1540), Creative Commons license, https://commons.wikimedia .org/wiki/File:Relaci%C3%B3n_de_Michoac%C3%A1n_L%C3%A1mina_18.JPG.

neric term for an indigenous language interpreter) and mentions that he spoke the languages of Michoacán (Purépecha) and Mexico (Nahuatl).[28] It is unclear, however, whether he spoke Spanish. Don Pedro later recounted the event for the *Relación de Michoacán*. According to his testimony, Olid's forces included about two hundred Spaniards.[29] Although the number of indigenous auxiliaries in Olid's forces is unknown, seventeenth-century chronicler Fernando de Alva Ixtlilxochitl estimated it at thousands. In any case, the encounter between Olid and Don Pedro quickly turned violent, developing into an extirpation campaign against the Purépecha religious system.[30]

Don Pedro's testimony in the *Relación de Michoacán* describes the encounter as one full of mysterious rituals and swift retribution against the Purépecha gods. Olid demanded a series of tribute payments as a peace extortion, and the Spaniards celebrated a Catholic mass. Francisco Martín or Pedro Castellano, both horsemen in Olid's entourage who may have been secular priests, probably celebrated this first mass in Michoacán.[31] Don Pedro, observing the priests with their chalice, speaking ritual words, concluded that they "must be medical men like ours, since they look into the water to see what will happen."[32] Surely the confusion about the intent of Spanish visitors changed when the Purépecha began to observe the close connection between military expedition and religious evangelization.

Olid's expedition was typical in its punitive nature. Soon after the Spaniards celebrated the first mass of Michoacán in Taximaroa, Olid sent Don Pedro back with the presumed mission of negotiating a truce between the caltzontzin and the Spanish forces. With his combined Spanish-indigenous armed forces, he then traveled to Tzintzuntzan. Olid's men rooted out Purépecha stone deities, demolishing, in particular, a stone representation of Curita-caheri, a messenger of the gods, or possibly referring to Curicaueri, the principal Purépecha god. Olid ordered Purépecha religious ornaments, feathers, and masks to be gathered up and burned.[33]

Olid's entrada was a bad sign for the Purépecha ruler. There are conflicting reports about whether or not the caltzontzin fled because he heard that Olid had at least temporarily captured and then released Don Pedro, or as a preventative defensive measure before Olid and his forces arrived. Don Pedro's statement, as recorded in the *Relación de Michoacán*, suggests that the caltzontzin fled the capital.[34] Later statements, however, such as the account of service to the Spanish Crown offered by the caltzontzin's son, Don Antonio Huitziméngari, dispute the claim.[35] The Purépecha leaders worried about the Spanish presence, however. In the summer of 1522, Purépecha rulers massacred eight hundred of their own slaves, fearing that in the event of a military-political defeat by Olid's forces, the Spaniards would take the slaves as war captives.[36] Shortly after Olid's entrada it became clear to both sides of the conflict that the Purépecha could not defeat the combined forces of the Spanish and their Texcocan and Tlaxcaltecan allies. The

Spaniards quickly turned their attention to rumors of a vast fortune of gold and silver owned by the caltzontzin.

The caltzontzin and other Purépecha elites watched with dismay as the balance of power shifted. Conversion to Catholicism in Michoacán among the Purépecha elite was a strategy of political survival. Shortly after the skirmishes of 1522, Cortés ordered Don Pedro brought to Mexico City to answer to charges that he was an active idolater. He dissimulated, claiming Catholic conversion. He had seen an opportunity to remove the caltzontzin from power, and to thereby promote his own position within the Purépecha world, he told the Spaniards. If this was true, Don Pedro's gambit failed. The caltzontzin remained the indigenous ruler of Michoacán. But it was clear that the political-military balance was shifting in favor of the Spanish. Don Pedro returned to Michoacán and lived in an uneasy truce with the caltzontzin.

MISSIONARY ARRIVAL

Following Spanish forays into Michoacán, initial Christianization efforts in the region were limited in scope through the 1520s. These first efforts came, ironically enough, through the Purépecha elites' embrace of Franciscans. The caltzontzin and Don Pedro traveled to Mexico City in the summer of 1524 to meet with the Spanish rulers, and the Purépecha elites deposited several of their sons in the newly founded Franciscan friary in Mexico City to receive doctrinal instruction.[37] In what was possibly a traditional Mesoamerican show of respect for the gods of a conquering army, the caltzontzin received baptism as a Catholic and was renamed Francisco (in deference to the Franciscans) in 1525. Franciscan chronicler Juan de Torquemada claimed that the caltzontzin then asked the friar Martín de Valencia if one of the Franciscan missionaries would accompany him on his return to Michoacán.[38]

The caltzontzin's conversion was probably a political stratagem intended to appease Spanish authorities in Mexico City and retain Michoacán as a Purépecha kingdom. But the Purépecha leader was a shadow king in 1524. It was unclear if and when Michoacán would follow the path of Tenochtitlan and pass to Spanish rule. Spanish royal authorities arrested and imprisoned the caltzontzin at least twice in 1524 and 1525, doubting the sincerity of his political pacifism and Christian conversion. The royal factor Gonzalo Salazar, the encomendero of Taximaroa, imprisoned the caltzontzin in the winter of 1525 on charges of idolatry in a ploy to remove him from power.[39] For reasons that remain unclear, however, the caltzontzin was then released from prison and permitted to return to Michoacán.

At this point, the Purépecha elites allied themselves with the Franciscans. It is unclear whether the caltzontzin had personally requested Franciscan missionar-

FIGURE 1.4. Ex-Convento de Santa Ana, Tzintzuntzan. Photo by eurimaco (2013), Creative Commons license, https://commons.wikimedia.org/wiki/Category:Tzintzuntzan#/media /File:Ex_Convento_de_Santa_Ana,_Tzintzuntzan_-_panoramio.jpg.

ies, but he did return to Michoacán in 1525 with the Franciscan Martín de Jesús (de Coruña) and one or two other Franciscan friars.[40] Friar Martín was one of the "apostolic twelve" Franciscans who came to Mexico in 1524 under the leadership of Martín de Valencia. When the small group of Franciscans arrived in Tzintzuntzan, there were no resident priests—no parish priest resided in the Tarascan highlands during the 1520s.

It is also unclear whether any other Franciscan friars had ever been to Tzintzun-tzan by the time Martín de Jesús arrived in 1525.[41] The first Franciscan missionary efforts focused on the destruction of indigenous religious iconography.[42] Francis-can chronicler De la Rea described Martín de Jesús as a Moses delivering the popu-lace from blind idolatry. Rumors claimed that the friar walked Michoacán's entire length and breadth, more than 400 miles by 150 miles.[43] Friar Martín also engaged the assistance of Purépecha elites when, convinced to do so by the caltzontzin, he had the friars and Purépecha commoners erect a small thatch church in Tzintzun-tzan dedicated to Saint Anne.

Indigenous depictions of the early Franciscan mission diverge considerably from those of the Spanish chroniclers. The *Relación de Michoacán* is the earliest

source. There is considerable debate about the relative knowledge of the Purépecha about the Spanish, the authorship of the *Relación*, and the question of indigenous participation in its production.[44] But details slip out from the *Relación* indicating that the Purépecha were suspicious of the friars. The Purépecha who offered
information to Jerónimo de Alcalá for the *Relación* said they initially viewed the
friars as sorcerers, but when they saw that the friars had no wives, and were not
interested in silver, they started to believe that they might be true emissaries of
a god. Out of political circumspection, the witnesses for Alcalá portrayed themselves as good, converted Catholics, but their suspicions of the Spaniards were
clear. The Purépecha witnesses said that in the earliest days of evangelization their
people had been cautious because the friars wore strange robes. Some Purépecha
viewed the robes as shrouds that they shed at night; they thought the friars might
actually be skeletons who traveled to hell at night to visit their wives.[45]

Surely Michoacán's first Franciscan mass, which was not a particularly mel-
low affair, did not endear the Purépecha to the friars. Nor, presumably, did anyone understand anything on either side. The friars had not yet studied Purépecha,
and the mass would have been celebrated in Latin, possibly with some Spanish or
Nahuatl explanations. After Friar Martín de Jesús (de Coruña) celebrated the mass
before the assembled Purépecha and the caltzontzin and his family, he systematically demolished their religious symbols:

> On finishing preaching the word of the Gospel and explaining the true adoration
> the population saw before it, he had to reprove their false sect, demolishing and
> destroying all the temples in Tzintzuntzan. And all their idols of gold and silver
> were gathered up and smashed into pieces and Coruña gathered them up into
> a great heap and tossed them into the lake with the disdain they deserved . . . so
> that everyone would see their gods entombed in the lake. Others he gathered up
> in the plaza and burned them so that the ashes snatched up by the wind would get
> in their eyes so that they would be removed from their blindness and realize the
> trickery of the past and see the truth of the present.[46]

Such early evangelization efforts placed a premium on the annihilation of religious
idolatry to pave the way for active Christianization. In many ways, the approach
mirrored Guzmán's political strategy, which involved removal of indigenous rule
even if no permanent Spanish governance was ready to take its place.

The Franciscan presence may have been minimal, but it eagerly sought to ex-
terminate Purépecha iconography. This harsh but diffuse approach proved indicative of Christianization efforts for decades in the region. No more than six Franciscans ever resided in Michoacán from 1525 to 1529, and there were never more than
three resident friars at any given moment. The friars had mastered Purépecha to

the point of being able to act as interpreters, but six missionaries for a vast region is simply not enough to convert a population.[47] Even after the Franciscans established their primitive friary in Tzintzuntzan, they abandoned the mission "two or three times" in those early years.[48]

The activities of one other friar in Michoacán, Antonio de Ortiz, presaged the temporary end of Franciscan efforts in the region. The Crown, weary of the political disorganization of conquistador and treasury official rule in Mexico City, created Mexico's First Audiencia by decree in December 1527. The Audiencia took power in 1528 with Nuño de Guzmán as its president.[49] The new bishop of Mexico, however, the Franciscan Juan de Zumárraga, joined Ortiz as an outspoken critic of Guzmán and the Audiencia.[50] By 1529, Ortiz had returned from a short stay in Michoacán. On Easter Sunday 1529, Ortiz delivered a sermon in Mexico City lambasting the Audiencia and its predations. The sermon precipitated a brawl, during which an Audiencia judge, with the support of Guzmán, clamored for Ortiz's removal. A bailiff for the court hauled Ortiz down from the pulpit, and excommunications and lawsuits ensued.[51] Faced with lawsuits over their actions, the Franciscans fought back. In an appeal before the Council of the Indies, Zumárraga stated that as the Audiencia judge "is not content with constantly defaming the bishops and priests of Mexico before the royal court, . . . I beg you to punish him as a calumniating slanderer. His vices, his exorbitance, and his poor treatment of the natives awoke my zeal to rebuke him."[52] In response to the sermon kerfuffle, as presumed political punishment, the Audiencia forbade friars from going to Michoacán.[53]

Three salient details emerge from the primitive evangelization efforts of the 1520s in Michoacán. First, the church of Michoacán was from its very beginning one of friar-missionaries unmoored from diocesan rule. Second, by 1530, nearly a decade after the presumed conquest of Mexico, Michoacán was virtually devoid of Catholic presence. Catholicism could only count a thatch church to Saint Anne in Tzintzuntzan and presumably some roughly designed adobe chapels in places somewhere in Colima or Motines, but no one really knows. Third, the Purépecha religion continued to be robust. A royal inspection of the region in 1528 uncovered numerous idols and god-stones, which the inspector ordered demolished.[54] If one reads the missionary accounts, one might conclude that extirpation had been effective. Yet the conversion of Purépecha elites to Catholicism was a political, not a spiritual, strategy, and Purépecha religion existed parallel to the fitful introduction of Christianity in the region by the missionaries.

ENCOMIENDA DISTRIBUTION

Like efforts at spiritual control, land and labor oversight was delegated to private interests, in this case, in the form of encomiendas. Michoacán's encomenderos solidified their political power in the region, laying the foundation for another important corporate interest group. The cumulative effect of encomienda holdings proved telling for Michoacán's religious and political history. Unlike in Mexico City, which had an extensive royal bureaucracy, a large urban center, and professional variegation, in Michoacán encomienda and plantation holdings—particularly in cacao, coconuts, cotton, and chiles—characterized the Spanish presence. The concentration of rural estates also meant that Spanish residents in Michoacán lived in a region where oversight by magistrates, priests, or inquisitors arrived after they had already developed a modus vivendi outside the regulations of imperial rule.

From its inception, the encomienda system in Michoacán was an exercise in blatant land grabs and naked assertions of clan power, especially by Cortés. Cortés dispatched Antonio de Carvajal in the summer of 1523, for example, to conduct a judicial inspection of the region (*visita*), but, as one historian put it, the visita became a "carnage of destruction and extirpation."[55] The inspection was the first Spanish accounting of the demography and cultural geography of Michoacán.[56] The report, which described the region's dense population, its vast agricultural potential, and its silver and gold mines (which it overestimated), instantly made Michoacán a valuable target of further conquest and spoils in encomienda grants.

The Crown divided Michoacán's lands and peoples into encomiendas soon after Carvajal delivered his report in 1524. Many of the encomiendas were to be counted among the most lucrative of New Spain. The core regions of the meseta tarasca boasted a dense population, useful for labor and tribute. Regions to the north and east proved ideal for livestock. The power to award encomiendas remained in legal limbo; in theory, only the Crown could award them. Cortés nevertheless claimed vast regions of Michoacán as part of his personal estate of the Valle de Oaxaca. Zapotlan and Colima, for example, were rich in mines and had extensive populations, and Cortés personally reserved several massive encomienda estates in the region, including most of Tuxpan and Zapotlan. The estates remained personal encomiendas of Cortés's estate at least until 1528, when the Audiencia began to challenge Cortés's massive holdings.[57] By 1535, Tuxpan, Zapotlan, and Tamazula had become royal possessions: to provide a sense of their outsized worth, the *Suma de visitas* (1548–1550) listed the province of Zapotlan as bringing in more than 100,000 pesos annually. So lucrative were the mines of the region that Cortés forbade Spaniards from entering the province under pain of one hundred lashes, for fear that someone might attempt to usurp the estates.[58]

Although the population of Michoacán as a whole at contact is unknown, it was surely well above 200,000, and possibly as high as 1 million. The *Suma de visitas* indicates that mortality rates from the 1545–1548 epidemic cycle may have been as high as 15 to 20 percent in Michoacán, a rate owing in part to enslavement, mining, and excessive tribute demands. Pátzcuaro and Tzintzuntzan surely had more than 15,000 residents combined as late as 1551; Tiripetío was rumored to be home to as many as 12,000 men (not to mention women and children) in 1551.[59] Even pueblos such as Tuxpan and Tamazula counted 4,000 residents each in 1550.[60] Smaller, more rural towns, including Capula, Zacapu, and Taximaroa, had nearly 2,000 residents each in 1550.[61] These figures, along with the mortality rates, suggest that the Pátzcuaro basin may have had a population as high as 30,000 to 40,000 at contact. In short, the province of Michoacán was surely home to well over 100,000 residents in 1520, though the claim by one member of the first Spanish expedition of 1522 that the Purépecha had an army of 200,000 men (which would imply a population of over 1 million) is probably an exaggeration.[62]

Despite the large, dense population of Michoacán, mystery surrounded much of the process of assignment, transfer, and litigation of encomiendas in Michoacán before 1528. In addition to Tamazula, Tuxpan, and Zapotlan, Cortés assigned himself the Pátzcuaro basin centered in Tzintzuntzan. The Crown vacated many of these grants. The First Audiencia also litigated these estates, endeavoring to despoil the original encomiendas held by Cortés and his partisans in Michoacán.[63] Although the history of these holdings is beyond the scope of this study, encomienda possessions proved politically crucial to the earliest development of Michoacán under shifting Purépecha-Spanish rule.

In 1528, the Crown dispatched another royal inspector, Juan de Ortega, whose report listed the status of the encomiendas and encomenderos at the time: there were no fewer than forty-seven individual encomenderos, who together possessed sixty-three distinct encomiendas.[64] The Spanish encomenderos in Michoacán were, depending on one's point of view, either typical or abusive. The use of indigenous slaves, captured in "just wars" of conquest, was common in silver mining regions. Alonso de Mata was an especially sadistic encomendero whom Ortega judicially sanctioned. But most were like Francisco de Villegas, who received Uruapan, and Diego de Medina, who received Tancítaro. They relied on tribute payments in kind, in cotton textiles, chiles, beans, and corn, for example. Indicative of the essential nature of encomiendas to Michoacán, it remained a primarily rural region throughout the colonial period, with only Pátzcuaro, and later Valladolid, as provincial cities.

The imbalance between the extensive encomienda holdings and the scarcity of Catholic priests is striking. Ortega's inspection noted the presence of only one priest in the entire province, the Franciscan Antonio Ortiz.[65] It is likely that one or two, or possibly three, other Franciscans were resident off and on in 1528—possibly Martín de Jesús and Diego de Santa María, Ángel de Salcedo, or Miguel de Bolonia.[66] Between 1522 and 1537, there is evidence of only one parish priest in the vast province: a secular priest named Francisco Martínez was in Colima as early as

1524, and became resident priest of Zacatula sometime between 1525 and 1529,[67] perhaps most likely in 1528.[68] In any case, Martínez did not stay long, and it appears that the entire Motines lacked for a parish priest until around 1546, when the priest Juan Venegas was installed.[69]

The nearly comical imbalance between land interests and Christianization is clear. In the same province that assigned forty-seven encomenderos to manage the massive, usurped landholdings, there were only one or two priests to minister to them and to Christianize the tens of thousands of indigenous residents. In 1528, Tuxpan supplied 100 men to transport provisions to mines.[70] Twenty years later, Tuxpan was a Crown possession but still had some 4,000 residents, though the mortality rate in the interim was probably as high as 15 percent.[71] Tancítaro was obliged in 1528 to provide five *cargas* (about 50 pounds each) of corn and beans and one carga of chiles daily.[72] These astronomical figures were impossible to deliver but nevertheless demonstrate the vast agricultural resources delivered to encomenderos. By 1548, half of Tancítaro was still held by Medina, though the population figures are uncertain—it had somewhere between 800 and 4,000 inhabitants, yet it was still required to provide 120 pesos every seventy days as tribute to Medina along with 10 men weekly as labor drafts.[73] In 1551, Pátzcuaro still had some 15,000 men subject to labor drafts, according to claims made by the viceroy.[74]

Although most of Michoacán's encomiendas were established by 1528, a few more continued to be assigned. The most notorious of the Spaniards to receive encomiendas between 1528 and the 1530s was Juan Infante, who, unlike many earlier encomenderos, was not a conquistador, but a sort of professional con man. On the death of the encomendero Juan de Solís in 1528, Infante asserted rights to Pomacorán, Comanja, Naranja, and several towns subject to Tzintzuntzan, and a series of lawsuits questioned the authenticity of his grants. Villegas, for example, sued Infante for infringing on his encomienda of Uruapan. No one was ever able to discern how Infante had done it, but in several lawsuits he produced copies of royal decrees of an encomienda grant for Comanja. Although most of the authorities doubted the authenticity of the documents, he was able to assert these rights for decades.[75] Infante continued to make enemies in the new world of the Spanish encomendero. Gonzalo Gómez, whom the Inquisition of Zumárraga tried for blasphemy, even hired a man to assassinate Infante as revenge, though the hit was unsuccessful.[76]

By 1530, large Spanish-held estates dominated Michoacán's landscape. The Purépecha remained culturally dominant, with the indigenous elite retaining titles of governor. But the assignment of vast tracts of land to encomenderos forever transformed the region. The outsized political-economic power vested in Spanish landowners meant that political culture responded to the interests of the encomiendas, at least through the 1540s when the encomienda system dominated the landscape.

THE KING IS DEAD; LONG LIVE THE KING

The fate of the caltzontzin is well known. On 14 February 1530, a Spanish tribunal operating under Guzmán's authority tortured and then executed him. Putatively for treason and human sacrifice, the trial was an assertion of particularist power. The impetus for the trial came from encomenderos who were vying with the Purépecha elites for economic control of the region. As encomenderos expanded their control of Michoacán's land in 1528 and 1529, disputes over land control were rampant, and Don Pedro and the caltzontzin became rivals for the title of indigenous governor. The Spanish policy throughout the Americas was to delegate local power over indigenous towns to pre-Hispanic aristocrats (or *pipiltin*), whose titles were known variously as caciques, or governors. These indigenous elites were afforded their own labor drafts from indigenous commoners, the *macehuales*.[77] Encomenderos accused both Don Pedro and the caltzontzin of deliberately hiding the provenance of their macehual labor forces.

The Purépecha—both elite and commoner—did not simply lay down their arms and give up. The defeat of the caltzontzin and the Purépecha polity was the result of being simply outnumbered—the Purépecha offered resistance, but it was not enough. The result was disastrous, since any heir to the caltzontzin inherited only vague recognition as a kind of indigenous cacique in the service of the Spanish Crown. However, the caltzontzin's actions did reveal the continued vibrancy of the Purépecha religion. While Franciscans, aided by royal officials, engaged in the destruction of Purépecha religious iconography, the trial against the caltzontzin made it clear that indigenous peoples continued to worship their deities and engage in ritual sacrifice.

Guzmán's 1530 invasion marked a turning point in Michoacán's political history, as it spelled the official end of a Purépecha kingdom and marked the beginning of a more official kind of colonialism. The expedition also set a precedent for high levels of political violence. Guzmán virtually press-ganged Nahuas and Huejotzincas to serve in his expeditionary force to pacify New Galicia and extend Spanish power out of central Mexico. In December 1529, Guzmán set out from Mexico City with a large force, including some 400 Spanish foot-soldiers and anywhere from 600 to 12,000 indigenous allies.[78] His first stop was Michoacán, where he imprisoned the caltzontzin, Don Pedro, and Don Antonio (the caltzontzin's son) in January 1530 in Tzintzuntzan. Guzmán demanded from the caciques some 8,000 subject Purépecha to serve in his expedition to New Galicia. After having tortured the caltzontzin, Guzmán reportedly told him that if he could not muster the requisite number of men, he would be sure to pay for it.[79] Before his execution, the caltzontzin said that he would raise the 8,000 men for Guzmán. When the Spaniards later arrived in Cuinao, where the presumed soldiers awaited them,

they found that the entire population had been massacred—presumably by Purépecha warriors by command from the caltzontzin and his advisers—in advance
of Guzmán's arrival.[80]

The trial against the caltzontzin laid out in stark terms the extent to which
Spanish landowners could manipulate a global system of imperial rule to their advantage. In fact, the principal fulminators for prosecution of the caltzontzin were
encomenderos. Witnesses against the caltzontzin, such as the encomendero Fernando Villegas and the Purépecha Cuaraque, listed a series of incredible charges
concerning human sacrifice, sodomy, and peculation of labor drafts.[81] Guzmán's
court interrogated and tortured not only the caltzontzin but also Don Pedro and
Don Alonso and two indigenous interpreters in a trial of summary justice between
the 5th and 13th of February.[82]

The trial showcased lurid accusations. "Show me the skins of the Christians
which you have here; if you do not bring them to me, we will have to kill you": so
demanded Guzmán of Don Pedro on 11 February, referring to the most sensational
charge against the caltzontzin—that he had flayed Spaniards and used their skins
as ritual costumes.[83] On being threatened with the death penalty if he did not comply, Don Pedro reported that he would bring the skins the next day.[84] In a morbid
twist, Don Pedro produced as exhibits human skins that the caltzontzin had used.
One can only imagine the repulsion the Spaniards felt on seeing the human pelts.

On 14 February 1530, Guzmán pronounced the caltzontzin guilty of idolatry,
treason, and human sacrifice.[85] The caltzontzin received a defense attorney, De la
Peña, who appealed the verdict, but Guzmán ignored him. De la Peña was a known
partisan of the anti-Cortés faction and could be counted on to defend Guzmán,
who was Cortés's most important political enemy. The court condemned the caltzontzin to be burned alive, though he reportedly repented and was executed in a
different way before his immolation at the stake—by the garrote, a cord wrapped
and tightened around the neck.[86]

Guzmán's expedition represented the culmination of a series of judicial-
military inspections of Michoacán. Pedro Sánchez Farfán had conducted a royal
inspection in Motines in 1527, with Ortega conducting the wider inspection in 1528.
These inspections were designed to regulate the newly emergent encomiendas to
the advantage of the Spanish and the detriment of indigenous caciques. Addition-
ally, the visitas were doctrinally instructive. Led by civil authorities, these quasi-
evangelization campaigns offered compelling negative reasons to convert, since
obdurate idolatry could lead to a death penalty. The royal officials on these expeditions engaged in widespread desecration of religious symbols. Under Ortega and
Carvajal, the inspection teams demolished stone and wood deities. Sánchez Farfán
executed some indigenous men for sodomy, though we will never know if they had
engaged in sex between men or if these were trumped-up charges.[87] The caltzon-

tzin's presumed taste for anal sex with men was also scandalous, though certainly sex between men among Spaniards occurred with regularity, despite the fact that it was a capital offense in Spanish law.[88]

The royal inspections facilitated the ability of encomenderos to exploit the royal system of visita in order to exact terrible political revenge on their Purépecha cacique rivals. Two encomenderos, who became involved in the religious politics of Michoacán for decades, stood out for their collaboration with Guzmán. The first is Pedro Muñoz, the *maese*, or field-captain, of Roa.[89] Muñoz arrived in New Spain in 1525 and quickly acquired Acolman and Capula in encomienda, though both were removed from his ownership and reassigned as Crown possessions in 1528.[90] We do not know exactly when he acquired it, but Muñoz also held Xiquipilco as an encomienda from at least 1537, though possibly from as early as 1529.[91] When Guzmán's court called Muñoz as a witness in the caltzontzin's trial, the encomendero said that he recalled an earlier visita by Juan Xuárez in which the royal authorities had tracked down and destroyed many idols and sacrificial items.[92] Muñoz also provided important logistical support for Guzmán's expedition. After assembling his forces and departing from Mexico City in late December 1529, for example, Guzmán traveled to one of the encomiendas belonging to Muñoz, probably Xiquipilco.[93]

Other encomenderos piled on in order to secure their hold over their indigenous charges. Villegas brought the original judicial complaint before Guzmán as judge, claiming that the caltzontzin had hidden wealth from the Crown and engaged in sodomy. Villegas's complaint included testimony from nine Spaniards as witnesses, including Pedro Muñoz. Although it mentioned sodomy, most of the ire stemmed from the caltzontzin's refusal to fulfill his tribute demands in the form of macehual labor. Other Spanish witnesses, as summarized in Villegas's complaint, said that the caltzontzin had been actively involved in killing dozens of Spaniards. Don Pedro, long the caltzontzin's political rival, added the damning testimony that the caltzontzin had ordered the execution of Spaniards.[94]

These early royal inspections and military incursions folded Christianization into their activities. They set out to quash the still active if underground Purépecha religious ritual complex. Nine years after Spanish entrance into the region, the indigenous religion of Michoacán was still going strong: people were murdering and ritually sacrificing Spaniards and peeling their skin off and dancing around in them. It had to stop—it was too scandalous and scary. Thus the Guzmán expedition was a sort of militarized spiritual conquest in the truest sense—not persuasion by catechesis (a method Guzmán found decidedly effete), but old-fashioned military subjugation.

The caltzontzin's trial also exemplified the implementation of local power and the attempt by one faction (pro-Guzmán) to exercise absolute power, even when royal oversight intended to put a check on that power. The Guzmán invasion and the trial were thus symbolic of the kind of imperial-religious politics to come: factional (Guzmán represented an unstable government that both Cortés and the Franciscans impugned) and undertaken by a caudillo (Guzmán's legal authority for the trial has long been questioned; his status as a caudillo is legendary—he had been a notorious slave-trader in Pánuco prior to his arrival in Michoacán).

The Guzmán moment in Michoacán led to no lasting political infrastructure. Instead the incursion left much of the previous system in place—a nascent Church, a wealthy encomendero class, and an extensive indigenous population. One big thing did change—any claim by the hereditary line of the caltzontzin to kingship was stopped cold. The execution was a cruel reckoning for the Purépecha elite and demonstrated the possibilities of political violence. By March 1530, Guzmán and his force had departed for New Galicia, leaving the region to rule by encomenderos. Guzmán's heavy-handed treatment of the caltzontzin and Don Pedro led to criticism from at least three friars. Martín de Jesús admonished the caltzontzin's Spanish jailers for their treatment of him. While we cannot be certain, Friar Martín may also have played a role in convincing Guzmán to garrote the caltzontzin immediately before his scheduled immolation.[95] Guzmán kept Don Pedro a captive, though he was presumably badly injured from his torture—the *Relación de Michoacán* noted that a decade later his arms were permanently marked from the cords that had dug into his flesh.[96] But after the failure to raise Purépecha troops, Guzmán continued to Jalisco with Don Pedro as his prisoner. Franciscans Jacobo de Testera and Francisco de Bolonia reportedly intervened on Don Pedro's behalf, asking Guzmán to allow him to return to Michoacán, which, presumably, he was able to do, as he remained indigenous governor until the 1540s.[97]

SEEDS OF DISSENT AGAINST CATHOLIC SOCIAL CONTROL

Michoacán's earliest Christianization program was absurdly diffuse. Simultaneously, encomienda expansion was meteoric. It is difficult to know exactly what encomenderos thought of their newfound wealth, their indigenous charges, or the oversight of a putative Catholicism. But we can surmise that encomenderos were, by and large, motivated by economic interests and a sense that as conquistadors and first *pobladores* (or settlers, a term that implied civic privileges and status), their service to the Crown entitled them to fantastic wealth.

However, it is unclear how many of Michoacán's earliest encomenderos made Michoacán their permanent home. For example, Diego de Medina, an employee of Cortés in Mexico City in 1524, received Tancítaro in encomienda along with Pedro de la Isla, another Cortés employee. Medina probably lived in Pátzcuaro and maintained his personal household there.[98] It is unclear how much time De la

Isla spent in Pátzcuaro or Tancítaro, but Michoacán's mild climate, dense indigenous populations, and attendant fabulous tribute contributions, combined with
the virtual complete absence of religious oversight, created a powerful enticement
for men interested in economic wealth unencumbered by social control.

Rodrigo Rangel, a captain in Cortés's conquering army of Tenochtitlan, was
dying of syphilis in 1529 and was in a spectacularly terrible mood. For starters, the
syphilis was giving him terrible migraines, which no amount of booze relieved.
The evenings, when horrifying chills swept over his skeletal structure, were the
worst. Fevers plagued him, and he awoke at night in a lagoon of his own sweat.
Sores covered his scalp and legs. A gruesome sight, Rangel, like others who died
of syphilis in the sixteenth century, served as a convenient example for the Dominican friars who targeted conquistador morality.

Rangel, a notorious blasphemer and enemy of the Dominican friars—and also a
good friend of Diego de Medina and Pedro de la Isla—ruminated on the perceived
easy life of Medina as he lay dying of syphilis: "Fucking friars. We had things good
in Tenochtitlan and then that self-righteous bastard came along with his robe and
rosary. I should have taken the advice of Medina and De la Isla, who told me that
Michoacán didn't have any priests and only a couple friars who ignored them anyway. They sat in the warm evenings drinking pulque and doing as they pleased."[99]
He hated friars, especially Domingo de Betanzos, who prosecuted and sentenced
Rangel for blasphemy. Among Rangel's lewder comments was his reference to the
Virgin Mary as a "whore." He was a big fan of interjecting his language with many
"*goddammits*." Given his scandalous critiques of friars and Catholicism, we can
also imagine his mental world. He loved booze, gambling, and hookers, and he
had learned from Medina of the expansive wealth, mild climate, and superabun-
dance of Michoacán. During his trial for blasphemy, witnesses claimed that he
had encouraged his encomienda subjects to attack friars with bows and arrows as
sport. He had a mordant sense of humor. He may have annulled the wedding of
one of his encomienda subjects in order to make the woman his concubine.[100] Perhaps he gave her syphilis.

Rangel and Medina were typical of an early generation of encomenderos who
saw Mexico as a large expanse with land and indigenous labor ripe for exploitation. Rangel received Cholula as an encomienda, among other endowments. His
fame also derived from holding political office in Mexico-Tenochtitlan (*regidor*)
and for being an early inquisitional target.[101] The Dominican Betanzos, who exercised inquisitional authority in Mexico between May 1527 and September 1528,
deliberately targeted Cortés's friends and partisans for blasphemy.[102] Indeed, Betanzos made of Rangel a political example of conquistador hubris, encouraging
Franciscan Toribio Motolinía to pass a spectacularly harsh sentence against him.[103]
Rangel's punishment for the guilty verdict included a five-month imprisonment in

a monastery; the public humiliation of holding a lit candle during a mass, marking him as a convicted blasphemer; a fine of five hundred pesos, an unheard-of sum for such a trial and, in 1520s currency, a fortune. He was also ordered to use his encomienda subjects to build a hermitage in Tacuba.[104] In short, Betanzos put the political screws to one of Cortés's closest political friends.[105] And then Rangel died in 1529 of syphilis.[106]

We will never know whether Medina shared Rangel's hatred for friars, though they clearly shared an ethos of labor exploitation for personal wealth. But Rangel's story and his close friendship with the encomenderos of Tancítaro call attention to Michoacán's unique social circumstances, where Spanish colonists wielded egregious power over their indigenous encomienda subjects and openly flaunted the authority of ecclesiastical officials. By 1530, Spanish landowners in Michoacán had adapted to life unregulated by imperial oversight. The absence of resident priests and permanent royal judicial officers meant that for most Spanish residents, life was a kind of free-for-all. Spanish settlers viewed Michoacán as nothing short of paradise — spoils, physical pleasure, easy sex, and endless liquor. There was no priest — just the occasional Franciscan friar in Tzintzuntzan — and they came and went and were not interested in Spaniards in any case. In places like Tancítaro, there were only Purépecha residents, in addition to the Spanish men and an occasional Spanish woman. In fact, Tancítaro remained an encomienda as late as 1630.[107]

We know even less about Spanish women in Michoacán in the 1520s. It was common for Spanish men to have indigenous mistresses, or, in some cases, wives, so it is a safe assumption that some Spanish encomenderos in the region became involved, consensually or not, with Purépecha women. The extent to which Purépecha women exerted a kind of domesticating force on these men remains a mystery. But we do know that in the 1530s, after the execution of the caltzontzin, Michoacán had some Spanish women who held power as encomenderas, and usually they had inherited the encomiendas as widows.

ENCOMENDERAS — MICHOACÁN'S FIRST SPANISH WOMEN?

The narrative thus far has been exclusively male. There is no evidence that many Spanish women lived in Michoacán in the 1520s, though we know that wives accompanied encomenderos throughout New Spain; with the exception of Purépecha (and other indigenous) women, few women show up in the chronicles. The relative paucity of source material restricts our ability to understand the role Spanish women played in the earliest imperial efforts in the region. That women by convention were excluded from the roles of priest, magistrate, or bishop only exacerbates the analytical gaps. Perhaps some study in the future will examine the cultural influence of Purépecha women on Spanish men.

Several Spanish women did exert power and influence as encomenderas in Michoacán in the 1530s, precisely at the time the region was opening up to further Spanish ideological incursions. Although Spanish law allowed for women to hold their wealth and property as their own, the paterfamilial social system provided that husbands and fathers administered that wealth in the name of their female family members. Nonetheless, Michoacán was home to some very wealthy encomenderas beginning in the 1530s.

Among the earliest (if not the earliest) encomenderas of Michoacán was Leonor de la Peña, who had been married to Álvaro Gallego, a former encomendero of Santo Domingo and a member of Cortés's entrada to Mexico in 1519. For his role in the conquest of Tenochtitlan, Gallego had received Chocándiro in the mid-1520s.[108] The encomienda covered at least nine *estancias* (ranches), and we can safely assume that the tribute value was substantial. When Gallego died around 1530, De la Peña had inherited the rights to Chocándiro, and though she held these encomiendas with her second and third husbands, the rights remained hers. We do not know if De la Peña took up residence in the rural region, far from any Spanish settlement, or lived in Mexico City. If the latter, she could have appointed a *mayordomo* (superintendent or steward) to oversee the tribute collection. In any case, unlike male encomenderos, Spanish women who oversaw such estates did not seem to share the enthusiasm for blasphemy or sexual acrobatics that characterized men like Rangel.

Coming later to Michoacán, Doña Marina Montesdoca was perhaps Michoacán's wealthiest Spanish woman of the period. She was married to Antón Caicedo, a man of vast encomienda wealth counting 18,000 indigenous tributaries in 1535 from encomiendas including Periban, Tingüindín, Tarecuato, and Texcaltitlan (southwest of Toluca). When he died around 1535, Doña Marina inherited at the least Periban and Texcaltitlan and possibly Tarecuato.[109] Portions of Tingüindín which remained in her estate included well over 1,000 tributaries.[110] She held these encomiendas through the 1560s, though Texcaltitlan became embroiled in a lawsuit between Doña Marina and her daughter-in-law's widower in 1564.[111] While we do not know the precise extent of her wealth, it is safe to assume she did not want for economic stability.

Women like Doña Marina Montesdoca and Leonor de la Peña were exceptions in the rustic, male-dominated world of Spanish colonials in Michoacán in the 1520s and 1530s. The relative absence of Spanish women is sociologically important, however, for explaining the peculiar political culture of Michoacán. The region developed a culture based almost entirely on male perceptions of status, honor, and public power. Even in cultures like Spain or North Africa in the early modern period, which placed a heavy premium on public honor and shame, male honor was always contrasted to assumed ideals of feminine passivity and purity, and women were seen as being responsible for the domestic softening of male brutishness.[112] That so few Spanish women were present in the earliest stages of Michoacán's imperial settlement simply added one more layer of public violence.

AN EMERGENT BUT FRAGILE STRUCTURE

When Mendoza assumed office as viceroy in 1535, he attempted to impose political order on both central Mexico and Michoacán—regions that had seen rather little of it. Neither Tzintzuntzan nor Pátzcuaro had a resident corregidor, to say nothing of an alcalde, in this period. Then, in 1536, Mendoza began to assign a handful of corregidores to towns in Michoacán. In many cases, the newly installed corregidores were also encomenderos, and it is not clear how much time these new functionaries spent in Michoacán.

It appears that for his first magisterial appointments Mendoza privileged areas perceived to be peripheral, of strategic importance, or located in densely populated encomienda regions. In the tierra caliente basin, Asuchitlan (or Ajuchitlán) probably had a corregidor as early as 1533. Though the region included valuable encomiendas, for the most part royal magistrates ignored them in the 1530s.[113] In a sign of the perceived importance of the region, Mendoza assigned a lawyer, the *licenciado* (or licentiate, recipient of a university degree conferring a license to practice law, medicine, or theology and the right to teach the subject in a university) Juan Altamirano, Cortés's mayordomo and estate governor, as the corregidor of Asuchitlan in September 1536, renewing the appointment in 1537. Altamirano received an outlandishly high annual salary of 300 pesos for his position—much higher than other corregidores in the same decade. Indeed, when the viceroy assigned Francisco Moreno to be Asuchitlan's corregidor in December 1537, the salary was reduced to 120 pesos.[114] In a harbinger of royal governance to come in Michoacán, Altamirano was also a wealthy encomendero, holding Metepec, Tepemaxalco, and Calimaya.[115]

Mendoza assigned several encomenderos as corregidores in Michoacán. Luis de Ávila became corregidor of Yuriria (Yuriripúndaro, Urirapúndaro) in September 1536. Ávila, who served as a page in Cortés's siege of Tenochtitlan, was one of Michoacán's earliest Spanish citizens; he had received Xuxupango in encomienda but the grant was never confirmed.[116] Given the town's location at the northern reaches of the province of Michoacán, Yuriria was important to Mendoza. In November 1537, the viceroy assigned not only a corregidor, Juan de Sandoval, but also a *teniente* (substitute or lieutenant), Antonio de Castro, to Yuriria. Both men had their terms renewed in December 1538.[117]

Other *corregimientos* (areas overseen by corregidores) may have paid less but were of strategic importance. The pueblos of Tamazula, Tuxpan, and Zapotlan, subjects of bitter dispute between Cortés and the First Audiencia, appear to have had numerous corregidores who received lavish salaries. Subject to Colima's alcalde, the corregidor Andrés Ortiz was assigned in March 1536 at an annual salary of 320 pesos. Manuel Guzmán was appointed corregidor in 1537 and again in 1539 at the same salary. Presumably, the charge was to bring some form of royal stability to a region of dense indigenous population, a task entailing perennial violent attempts to control tribute labor. Neighboring Amula also had a teniente, Diego Allo, who was assigned in December 1536 at the much-reduced salary of 120 pesos annually.[118]

We cannot know how much time these earliest magistrates spent in their assigned regions. In some cases, the corregidor may have lived relatively close—Luis de Ávila, for example, became a citizen of the city of Michoacán, although whether in Pátzcuaro or Valladolid it is not clear. Other magistrates may have simply conducted judicial inspections of their assigned regions only to return to Mexico City. In the aftermath of the Guzmán invasion and the caltzontzin's assassination, the new viceroy hoped to stabilize the region. But the apparatus of royal law was far too thinly spread to be effective on a large scale, and the encomenderos by then had amassed too much control of everyday land tenure politics to provide much entrée to this handful of magistrates.

A MISSION SETTLEMENT

The uniquely male culture of Spanish imperial aspiration in Michoacán continued in its evangelization efforts. For example, the early missionary efforts by Augustinians, in particular, were construed in cultural terms associated with crusading and chivalrous knights. Martín de Valencia, the founder of the Franciscan mission in Mexico, was promoted as possessing singularly virile moral qualities.[119] Diego de Basalenque and other chroniclers emphasized the martial courage of early Augustinian missionaries to the tierra caliente.[120] Despite the establishment of friaries in Michoacán by the Augustinians and Franciscans, no nunneries were founded there during the sixteenth century, unlike in Mexico City and Puebla.

In the aftermath of the Guzmán expedition, a new phase of missionary activity began that reflected this ethos of chivalry and conquest. Christianization solidified the interests of two corporations: the Franciscan and Augustinian orders. The execution of the caltzontzin paved the way for the entrance of more Spaniards. During the next eight years, from 1530 to 1537, there was a rise—though far from meteoric—of a more organized Christianization project in Michoacán. But this Christianization continued along its corporatist lines, far from metropolitan oversight (whether by Mexico City or Madrid). Even the friar-missionaries were conflicted about the early results. De la Rea tells us that it was not until the arrival of the Franciscan Jacobo Daciano, probably in 1545, that indigenous peoples first received the Eucharist.[121] Friar Juan de San Miguel traveled to Uruapan, probably sometime between 1533 and 1535, to form a monastery there, though the dates are uncertain.[122]

The Franciscan mission emphasized a kind of primitivism—baptism accompanied by destruction of idolatry. Curicaueri, the principal Purépecha deity, was represented as a kind of massive obsidian stone idol. Purépecha elites and priests led elaborate pilgrimages to the site of the deity in Zacapu. Franciscan missionaries viewed the Purépecha religion as clearly pagan and vaguely satanic with its worship of a stone god, which they found horrifying. The friars eagerly sought out the religious iconography of the Purépecha in order to destroy it.

Yet Franciscans viewed the social and clerical hierarchy of the Purépecha as signs of political sophistication.[123] De la Rea, for example, associated Zacapu with Rome in his description of Purépecha veneration of Curicaueri. On the one hand, De la Rea noted that the Purépecha sacrificed people to their deity, extracting a beating heart from each sacrificial victim. On the other, in describing the social order of the annual pilgrimage from the Purépecha capital in Tzintzuntzan to the site of Curicaueri in Zacapu, he called the capital the "metropolis of Michoacán and womb of its greatness, as Rome in all the world."[124] An elaborate procession accompanied the caltzontzin in this annual rite, in which the caltzontzin kissed the hand of the high priest and offered obeisance to the Purépecha god.

Franciscans praised the cultural circumspection and subtlety of the Purépecha. According to De la Rea, one of the most admirable and notable things about the Purépecha was their "liveliness of spirit." Moreover,

> In everything one admires their readiness of wit and . . . their egalitarianism. . . . [T]hus as much in their politics as well as their ancient religion they were so circumspect that they lacked nothing in comparison with how Saturn, Lysanias, Radamanthus, or the lawmaker Lycurgus established laws, that as much in rectitude as in observance that they are judged to be the most severe in the compliance of laws concerning government, republics and temples, which today is repeated in the west [in Michoacán].[125]
>
> Circumspection is so native to the Tarascans that one sees it daily in the vividness of their words and in the subtlety of their actions and business. They are preeminent in all trades, especially in sculpture in which they are considered to be the most famous in New Spain.[126]

Here the creation of an idyllic imagination expanded far beyond mere topography and encompassed what missionary chroniclers imagined as the sociocultural purity of Michoacán.

If the Franciscans emphasized the religious naïveté of the Purépecha, the first friars engaged in extirpation campaigns. Franciscan Pedro de las Garrovillas may have been the first friar to promote Purépecha conversion.[127] From Extremadura, he was considered the first Franciscan of the tierra caliente, though he probably had spent time in Tzintzuntzan to learn Purépecha—the sixteenth-century Franciscan chronicler Diego Muñoz tells us that Garrovillas was among the first Franciscans to learn the language.[128] Muñoz described Garrovillas as a pious and devout man who had no patience for trivial conversation. These earliest linguistic-catechetical activities remain vaguely understood, and the dates of Garrovillas's activity in Michoacán are unclear.[129] He traveled to Motines de Zacatula, where, Muñoz reported, idolatry was rife. Garrovillas was a kind of crusading warrior. According to Muñoz, the indigenous people "used horrendous and abominable sacrifices. . . . [I]t was a land of extreme heat and incredible harshness. . . . [I]n every town [Garrovillas] destroyed idolatry, often putting himself in mortal danger, planting the holy catholic faith in which the residents remain today, liberated from diabolic subjection. He burned more than 1,000 idols together and made those who adored them help him in burning them."[130] It is unclear which language he employed in the tierra caliente, though Nahuatl and Coacoman were dominant there.[131] Because there were so few priests with any skill in Purépecha, Garrovillas returned to Tzintzuntzan to instruct baptized Purépecha in the Catholic doctrine. We do not know when Garrovillas was active in Zacatula. Nor do we know when he returned to Tzintzuntzan, though the seventeenth-century chronicler Agustín de Vetancurt claims that the friar died there on 19 July 1530.[132]

Linguistic study was emblematic of Franciscan efforts in Mexico, but the extent of their early studies in Michoacán was limited. Although Garrovillas may very well have been part of the early nucleus of Franciscans in Tzintzuntzan in 1525–1530, others took up more expansive Purépecha study as part of a broader Christianization effort. Jerónimo de Alcalá, who was notable among the earliest Franciscan friars to study Purépecha, composed a Purépecha language doctrine around 1537. Zumárraga approved the doctrine in his capacity as bishop and it was published, but no copies are extant.[133] Alcalá's involvement in the production of the Relación de Michoacán established him as a key missionary Spanish-Purépecha cultural mediator.[134] It fell to later missionaries in Michoacán, such as Maturino Gilberti, to produce a fuller corpus of Purépecha-language pastoral material. It is symptomatic of the diffuse efforts in Michoacán that the first comprehensive works on doctrinal instruction and sacramental education for priests came not in the sixteenth but at the very end of the seventeenth century.[135]

The Franciscans' founding of Uruapan exemplifies their goal of restructuring indigenous society in the image of idealized communities through forced resettlement and spatial organization into grid-style towns. Originally Uruapan and Tzirostro were included in a single encomienda granted to Francisco Villegas, a mine operator and a proponent of the introduction of pigs into Uruapan as livestock to be raised for food, as his workforce needed to be fed.[136] The region was home to the earliest social experiments in radical socio-spacial and ecological reconstruction, since the pigs were an invasive species. Some animals, especially sheep, wrought environmental havoc in New Spain, although some studies suggest that the introduction of European livestock impacted Mexico's environment less than previously assumed.[137]

Friar Juan de San Miguel viewed Uruapan as having the perfect climate but believed it was inhabited by savages in dire need of sociopolitical reeducation. Franciscan chroniclers idealized Friar Juan as a brave and fearless David in the face of a Goliath; in these accounts, he seems to be unfazed by danger or adversity, exemplifying the chivalric ideal of the spiritual conquistador:

He went through mountains and canyons looking for souls to convert, and the barbarians, showing him claws as if to tear him apart, did not frighten him, but rather the virtue of his words turned them docile, and when he would return to his convent they would seek him out, bleating, following his footprints, to return as if to be reborn in his tender arms. There was no summit, grotto, or mountain in the entire province that he did not cross by foot, barefoot, fasting almost the entire time, without missing once the hours of the divine office, even though he was among lions and tigers whose rudeness would have challenged more ordinary disciples.[138]

The deconstruction of idolatry emphasized both the agility of friar-missionaries and the religious savagery of indigenous peoples, especially those outside the Purépecha core.

Friar Juan traveled extensively up and down the steep escarpments of the Uruapan region as early as 1532, becoming guardian of the *doctrina* (proto-parish for indigenous peoples) by 1536.[139] He told Quiroga during the Audiencia judge's 1533 inspection that the residents in and around Uruapan were little better than savage beasts: "They go about naked and flee priests in order to hide their idolatry and in their drunkenness serve the devil."[140] Having decided to apply a forcible resettlement (*congregación*) of the residents in order to establish good government, he used his authority as an agent of royal will—though he was only a friar—to order at least seven pueblos in the region to be reestablished in the new town of Uruapan.[141]

A crusading, masculine ethos thus formed a central part of missionary memory. In De la Rea's estimation, Friar Juan was the lawgiver that David requested in the Old Testament—to support the belief that it was up to the Spaniards to make the indigenous peoples civilized, he invoked Psalm 20: "Appoint, O Lord, a lawgiver over them that the Gentiles will know themselves to be but men." This, he believed, was the best way to establish *policía* (good government). De la Rea argued that

> to deprive someone of their normal and natural tastes can only be done by force. And thus we see the impossibilities that this servant of God would face in trying to tear these Indians away from their natural place, from the delights that they had enjoyed with the ease of barbarism, without tightening their liberty, toward the law that impedes the power of appetite, and to make submit forcefully to the will of a head or ruler those who had never had one before. This is because for Chichimecs' nature this is the most repugnant thing in the world, because their life, being, and nature is to go about like vagabonds in the mountains, hunting beasts and clothing themselves in their skins.[142]

De la Rea echoed common beliefs among the Spanish about the incivility of the Chichimec peoples, contrasting them with the Purépecha, whom he viewed as having more pacific and devout qualities.

Friar Juan relocated thousands of indigenous people into towns with plazas surrounded by straight-line streets, comparing the locations to the Flemish countryside and the towns to the orderly cities of the ancient Romans.[143] The Purépecha and vaguely defined Chichimecs who were resettled probably did not view this process through the same rosy lens. The ideological seeds of the later, more widespread congregación project of 1598–1605 were already planted in the "fecund soil" of Uruapan.[144]

When the Augustinians arrived in Michoacán, they viewed the Franciscan project as woefully inadequate and set out on an ambitious project of wide-scale Christianization. Having arrived in Mexico in May 1533, they quickly established their earliest house in Mexico City and resolved to send missionaries "to go to Michoacán to set out nets and fish, since many of the nets set by the Franciscans were breached, and there were many more fish to be caught."[145] Whereas the Franciscans had sent only two or three friars to Michoacán in the years after 1525, the Augustinians determined to establish a college, in Tiripetío. It became a center of indigenous education and an important educational and catechetical center for western Mexico.[146] The Franciscans' rudimentary evangelization project in Michoacán focused on didactic, but not necessarily doctrinal or theological, instruction. The Augustinians, in contrast, while engaged in moral didacticism, dedicated themselves to educating the Purépecha nobles along with Augustinian friars. Alonso de la Veracruz and other friars adopted indigenous elites, such as Don Antonio Huitziméngari, as their tutors in Purépecha language.[147]

During the earliest years of the college in Tiripetío, then, Purépecha nobles and Spanish novice friars sat in the same classrooms for training in scripture, logic, and theology. The experience of Augustinians in the mountains southeast of Mexico steeled them for their ambitious project in Michoacán. The Augustinians fretted over the perceived idolatry of the Purépecha. But unlike the Franciscans, the Augustinian chronicler Matías de Escobar explained, the Augustinians arrived in Tiripetío with the experience of a previous encounter with un-Christianized Nahuas in central Mexico behind them.[148] In Escobar's version, when the friars Juan de San Román and Agustín de la Coruña had gone to Chilapa (southeast of Mexico, near the border of Puebla), unfriendly pagans surrounded them. Escobar even evoked a kind of knightly tradition of the type one could find in popular medieval novels, such as the *Amadís of Gaul*.[149] Thus the friars "encountered Circes and Medeas, even visible demons in the form of dragons," at every step of their journey. They were trapped in the mountains of Ocuituco (east of Cuernavaca) and, huddled on humble *petates* (woven mats), defending the souls of the soon-to-be-converted, blessed their first indigenous Catholic congregation.[150]

The Augustinians recalled their mission in apostolic terms. At the beginning in Tiripetío, there were only two friars—Juan de San Ramón and Diego de Chávez. The devil was no match for San Ramón, however, who had already faced down the devils of Ocuitulco. Upon their arrival, the two Augustinians had spent an extraordinary amount of time instructing the local residents in Catholic doctrine, though the content and extent of this instruction are unclear. It is also unknown whether San Ramón and Chávez studied Purépecha in Mexico City prior to their arrival in Michoacán. If not, perhaps they administered their doctrinal instruction in Nahuatl.

Despite the potential confusion that the language barrier may have caused, Escobar was effusive in explaining the success of the first Augustinians in Tiripetío in 1537. The friars presumably convinced the Purépecha to form monogamous marriages and abandon their veneration of Curicaueri. During Easter week of 1538, Escobar claimed, when some 30,000 indigenous residents confessed en masse before the two friars, they were so numerous as to appear like a swarm of "rational locusts."[151]

The most impressive aspect of the Augustinian missionary triumph was their presumed victory over idolatry. According to Escobar, San Román and Chávez were so persistent and patient in their doctrinal instruction that the Purépecha happily tossed their deities onto bonfires of extirpation. When the Augustinians expanded to Tacámbaro in 1538, again led by San Ramón and Chávez, they encountered more veneration of idols (Xarantaga and Curicaueri). So beloved was the peaceful yet firm evangelization of these friars that Escobar invoked a martial victory in telling the story: "Entire pueblos came dancing in their ancient tradition, filling the countryside with boughs and flowers in triumph, . . . whose happy jubilation made the death of idolatry apparent to all."[152] Once again, religious images went into the bonfire through the happy acquiescence of the Purépecha catechumens.

The founding of the Augustinian project in Michoacán was not all abstruse intellect; it also foreshadowed the abiding ties the missionaries developed with encomenderos. Diego de Chávez was the nephew of encomendero Don Juan de Alvarado. The very first Augustinian mission—linked by family wealth and encomendero land—could scarcely have been more corporatist. The Franciscans also eventually developed ties with encomenderos, though their connections were less explicitly familial. In either case, the Franciscans and Augustinians shared a common belief in the need for Christianization as well as a corporatist interpretation of Catholicism. Both orders claimed special privileges for the evangelization of Michoacán as derived from the Omnimoda. They viewed parish priests as unnecessary—the Christianization of the indigenous populations of Michoacán, and, indeed, of New Spain, was, in their view, best left to the friars.

REFLECTIONS

Paradise is relative, and the paradise for Spanish settlers in Michoacán came at the rather obvious hell of indigenous peoples. Several tendencies in the earliest colonial order in Michoacán are clear, some of which became more pronounced throughout the sixteenth century. The religious trend reflected coercion and corporatization. Christianization efforts were largely punitive, as seen most symbolically in the trial and execution of the caltzontzin Tzintzincha Tangaxoan. The extirpation and demolition of the physical artifacts of Purépecha religion were central to the missionary program. Yet extirpation campaigns were less prominent after the 1530s, when conversion efforts tended to become more parochial and patronizing, both in the sense of patron-client relationships and in terms of the friar-missionaries' treatment of indigenous peoples. There were no resident parish priests—it is possible that some encomenderos attempted to fulfill their Christianization duties by appointing curates to oversee their indigenous charges, but no evidence exists for this as a regular practice.[153] Only two or three itinerant Franciscan friars had been working in the region prior to 1537 when the Augustinian friars arrived. The friars of both orders hoped to turn the idyllic region into a Catholic paradise.

In the public political realm, power in New Spain was untethered from royal reach. The conquest of Michoacán from 1521 to 1538 took place without the oversight of a viceroy. In fact, most of this earliest conquest-period was removed from all oversight. By extension, the conquest itself (undertaken by Guzmán) was remarkably privatized. Guzmán himself engineered a largely private armed force composed of Spanish shareholders in the endeavor and indigenous allies. Moreover, land and political authority at the local level were vested in private corporate interests in the form of encomiendas. In many cases, the local corregidor was also an encomendero, setting up a corporatized state. The sheer economic wealth of the encomenderos resulted in centralization of political power in personal, clan, and corporatist groups.

Finally, Spanish political culture in Michoacán in the 1520s and 1530s was exceptionally male-oriented. The inscribed record tells us of military and spiritual conquest in the manner of crusade and masculine virtue. It falls to a different study—a new kind of psycho history—to examine the so-called hidden transcripts of male-female interactions in Michoacán during the period.[154] Surely unspoken power dynamics characterized such encounters. Michoacán had its share of micropolitics, much of it concerning everyday gender relations.[155] Indigenous women, as we know, sometimes voluntarily entered relationships or marriages with Spanish men, while others were coerced; the Spanish women who accompanied Spanish male landowners also engaged in subtle forms of interactive power. But those moments remain largely hidden from historical recall.

This political culture of masculinity set the tone for a region of Spanish men performing public power by appealing solely to other men. In a Hispanic culture of honor and shame, such concentration of masculine public order laid the foundation for future interactions.[156] The overwhelmingly male presence among early Spanish colonials in Michoacán influenced the type of political culture it developed—in this case a culture of violence and demonstrative public power, which became ever more complex in the second half of the sixteenth century.

These early years set the stage for the ways in which Spanish residents of Michoacán expressed power for generations. Thus, in 1538, when agents of the Crown and Church began to try to assert oversight over the region, the result was rebellion, political violence, mockery, and satire.

CHAPTER 2

BURNING DOWN THE HOUSE, IN WHICH
THE SPIRITUAL CONQUISTADORS GO TO
WAR WITH EACH OTHER

Setting: Pátzcuaro, Tiripetío, Tlazazalca, Uruapan
Years: 1538–1565

One fine day in 1560 in Tlazazalca, in the northwestern reaches of Michoa-cán province, a priest grabbed an indigenous nobleman (known as a *principal*) and punched him in the face, breaking his jaw. When the man's wife screamed in protest, the priest had her arrested, stripped naked in the makeshift jail, and flogged until her blood flowed as copiously as the bailiff's sweat. The priest in question was Don Diego Pérez Gordillo y Negrón, a cathedral dignitary, a parish priest, and the appointed strongman of Bishop Vasco de Quiroga. The indigenous residents testified before Audiencia officials that the bishop's loyalists had beaten and threatened them on numerous occasions.

Why would an ordained priest knock out this prominent man and sadistically order the flogging of his wife? The actions reflected a desire for power and control, for they were meant to show rival Church factions that parish priests had to be re-spected and feared as agents of God and of the Crown, and also, most importantly, as representatives of the local bishop. The indigenous man had unwisely decided to hear a mass celebrated by an Augustinian friar in a town that was in the legal domain of the diocesan church. Bishop Quiroga had specifically mandated that only priests—and not friars—had the right to celebrate mass outside of mission-ary towns. As such, the indigenous nobleman's decision to attend the mendicant mass was an affront to the diocesan order.

Attending the friar's mass in this context demanded a personal rebuke to the indigenous nobleman for his symbolic support of the Augustinians. Gordillo was only too happy to deliver the assault as a warning to anyone else who dared chal-lenge his priestly authority and the supremacy of the diocesan power.

Apart from blows and whips, Gordillo was also fond of arson. The violence he brandished in a two-year period, 1560 and 1561, illustrates his temper. He im-

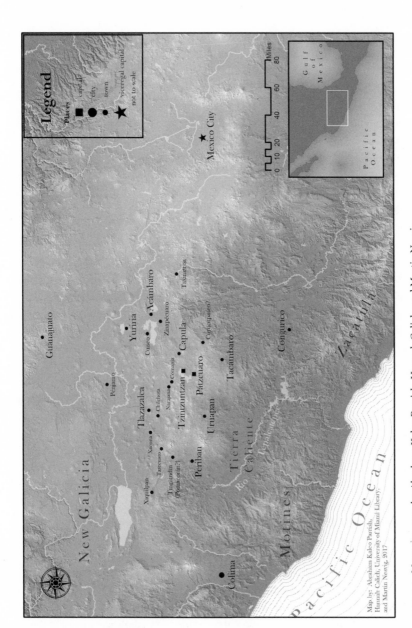

MAP 2.1. *Meseta tarasca*, by Abraham Kaleo Parrish, Hannah Calich, and Martin Nesvig.

prisoned dozens of indigenous men and women for refusing to attend a mass he conducted in the parish church of Tlazazalca. He burned down the Augustinian monastery of Tlazazalca while the friars were inside sleeping. He demolished the baptismal font of the Franciscan church in nearby Pátzcuaro. He disinterred dozens of corpses from the cemetery of the Augustinian monastery in Tlazazalca. He snatched a baby from his parents' arms while the family was awaiting the child's baptism with such force that the infant died.[1]

What made Gordillo act with such fury? Was this kind of violence common among priests, or just one of his own little idiosyncrasies? Contextual analysis of the religious politics of Michoacán in the 1540s and 1550s reveals that the region evolved into a fractured ecclesial polity and that mendicants formed alliances with indigenous elites and encomenderos to create a corporate interest. Gordillo's actions were part of a judicial war between Bishop Quiroga and his partisans against the mendicants that often culminated in ground-level violence. Thus, as Quiroga's loyal servant, Gordillo became, in effect, the enforcer of a vision of centralized Spanish Catholicism that was obedient to a strong bishop. This vision promoted the interests of the Crown as patron of the Church in a very real worldly sense. Accordingly, Gordillo set out to contain the ambitions of the friar-missionaries, who saw themselves as answerable only to the pope. Gordillo's actions make sense if placed within the context of this factionalism. Many chose to turn a blind eye to his violence for the sake of achieving the larger goals of control of the religious polity. Although it was a politically cynical choice, the stakes were certainly high enough. Assaulting indigenous residents was illegal and could lead to criminal convictions, fines, exile, or the stripping of office.[2]

From 1538, when Quiroga assumed the see, the conflict and violence grew in a steady crescendo of bitter animosity between Quiroga and his partisans, the encomenderos, and the mendicants. Quiroga ran into immediate intransigence upon assuming the see. Colonists were not simply one-dimensional sadists; nor were churchmen grotesque caricatures of piety. But the Spaniards and indigenous residents of Michoacán in the 1540s and 1550s both sought to maximize their self-interest. Churchmen—such as Bishop Quiroga, the Augustinian friar Alonso de la Veracruz, and the Franciscan friar Maturino Gilberti—all had a genuine interest in converting the Purépecha and elaborating their vision of a Hispanic civic order and a Catholic religious order. But the process of implementing that order had to be effected. The quotidian application of each vision of Catholicism distorted their idealism, producing a legal and personal free-for-all. Moreover, the indigenous elites, many of them associated with the Huitziméngari clan, descendants of the caltzontzin Tzintzincha Tangaxoan, sought alliances of political convenience with the friars in order to protect their privileges as *pipiltin* (indigenous aristocrats).

Among the greatest ironies was that the encomenderos threw their social and economic support behind the same friars who were allied with the Purépecha elite—for many of the same reasons, especially to invest in a stable system blocking the global aspirations of the Crown through its agent, Bishop Quiroga.

The Franciscans and Augustinians thus crawled into a financial bed with the encomenderos of Michoacán. Far from offering any sustained critique of the encomienda system, the friar-missionaries drew extensive support from the encomenderos. No central or united spiritual Catholicism claimed a presence. The need to arm ground-level operatives in this showdown, legally and physically, engendered a political fracas. The riotous and freewheeling politics of Michoacán were about as far from Eden as one could imagine.

SPIRITUAL CONQUISTADORS OR MAGISTRATES OF THE SACRED?

Consider the spiritual conquistadors of Michoacán—a contentious lot.[3] The idea that Spanish friars, missionaries, and bishops operated essentially as spiritual arms of the political-military assault on Mesoamerica has held remarkable staying power. Lest we sweep the spiritual conquistadors entirely into the historiographic waste-bin, it is worth recalling that the inventor of the term "spiritual conquistador," Robert Ricard, in 1933, had little sympathy for actual military conquistadors. While Ricard referred specifically to friars, his concept has been adapted to refer to priests and missionaries in general in early Latin America. He described the prototypical conquistador, Hernán Cortés, as "greedy, debauched, a politician without scruples [who] . . . despite his weaknesses . . . had deep Christian convictions."[4] His depiction of Cortés reflects a broader characterization of Spanish colonial authorities and missionaries as zealous but prone to violence.

Spanish landowners and encomenderos functioned as lay spiritual conquistadors through their patronage of mission projects. Rather than paint spiritual conquistadors—clerical and lay—as inherently susceptible to violence, we might understand them as individuals with a range of motives, from pious to cynical, who struggled with the reality of Michoacán, a region with little legal oversight. We know a fair amount about the high-profile leaders of major mission programs, such as Bernardino de Sahagún.[5] We also know a good deal about indigenous society in mission settlements.[6] But we know less about the sort of everyday builders who undertook the plans of this spiritual conquest. The sociopolitical nexus of the friar-missionaries, parish priests, and landowners who built the first Catholic church of Michoacán was complex and far-reaching. These spiritual conquistadors were drawn ever closer into the promiscuity of everyday struggles for prominence, struggles that grew out of a bewildering number of overlapping claims to authority in local towns and the baroque social and economic alliances that accompanied them.

As a formal Church presence expanded in Michoacán, so, too, did the conflict over power. Theoretically, according to the historian William Taylor, "parish priests were located at sensitive intersections between Indian subjects and higher authorities, and the state religion was an important source of public discipline and restraint.... [N]o sharp lines ... divided secular and religious life."[7] In this telling, priests were magistrates of the sacred, to borrow Taylor's term. Yet, in Michoacán, parish priests were often magistrates first and only secondarily interested in the sacred. The blurred lines between secular and religious polities in the sixteenth-century world also meant that the civil (in the form of encomenderos and indigenous elites) and the sacred (in the form of friars and secular priests) often battled for preeminence.

Two powerful mythologies persist in evaluations of the Christianization process in Mexico. First, the historiography generally continues to assume that "the Church" was relatively centralized, organized, powerful, and orthodox. Recent scholarship on conversion, missionaries, and Christianization programs in the Hispanic world has focused on the mediation of the message, but has taken for granted that the message itself was fairly uniform.[8] Early modern populations— Mesoamerican, rural Castilian, or French—often reacted to presumably "foreign" urban Catholic conversion mechanisms with distrust.[9] We know how Catholicism adapted to its Mexican context, and how indigenous populations resisted certain elements of Spanish Catholicism.[10] We also know a good deal about how, in some cases, missionaries, such as the Jesuits in Naples, viewed local populations as a kind of devilish urban horde of pagan quasi-Christians.[11] Thus we understand the Church as it interacted with the targets of Christianization, but we lack detailed portraits of the quotidian architects of that Christianization.[12]

The second strand of idealized memory offers a benevolent appraisal of both friar-missionaries in general and of Michoacán's first bishop, Vasco de Quiroga, in particular. Much scholarship and popular lore have depicted Quiroga as a pacifist, lionizing him as a sort of sixteenth-century hippie and proponent of utopian Catholicism. This depiction largely ignores the internal discord that took place and the extent of power of the Catholic orders present in the provincial region in which he operated.[13]

THE "TATA" VASCO LEGEND, RECONSIDERED

Don Vasco de Quiroga, licenciado, was an idealist; his degree was in law. Born in 1478 in Castile, after studying canon law he had acted as a royal administrator in

Oran in North Africa. Quiroga was a prototypical letrado, and his loyalties to royal justice ran deep. In 1531, his powerful connections in the royal court secured him appointment to the Second Audiencia of Mexico, which had supplanted the First Audiencia, which the Crown viewed as out of control, in 1530. In 1533, Quiroga became the royal inspector (*visitador*) of Michoacán, and his inspections inspired him to develop a vision of Michoacán as a place of self-sustaining towns based on Thomas More's *Utopia*.[14] His idea was that its Spanish overseers, in the form of a bishop and loyal parish priesthood, would relocate the indigenous population into fabricated towns, based on a grid layout, that would be agriculturally self-reliant. It was a brilliant idea, except for three inconvenient facts: Spain had never had such towns, the project relied on labor extortion and cultural dislocation, and it gave rise to social resentment among the indigenous peoples, who would lose their original lands.

Quiroga believed that only a strong bishop with the obedient force of local parish priests could implement his utopian village system on the scale he desired. There are hints of this joint project in his 1535 "Información en derecho," a document in which Quiroga criticizes a recent decision of the Spanish Crown to reverse restrictions on indigenous slavery. He viewed the indigenous population as ethnically inferior but still human and thus deserving of certain rights, including freedom from enslavement. But Quiroga's critique was also a precursor to his assault on encomendero power, since enslavement of indigenous peoples cut into the monopoly on social organization that he wanted as bishop.[15]

Quiroga joined his idealism with his belief in the supremacy of a legal-minded Church. When he was legally appointed as Michoacán's first bishop in 1536, he was still a layman, and he had to be ordained as a priest before he could take possession of the diocese. By the time he became bishop in August 1538, rudimentary structures were already in place: the Franciscan enterprise was centered in Tzintzuntzan, the Augustinian one in Tiripetío. Quiroga saw Michoacán as ripe for reform. His political goal was to centralize clerical authority and to bring both groups of friars under his purview, a task that proved to be as complex as it was contentious. A small retinue of secular clerics accompanied Quiroga to Michoacán to aid him in this project. Quiroga also founded a new seminary, the Colegio de San Nicolás, in 1540, to train a diocesan clergy.[16] His long-term plan was to surround himself with loyal clerics who were specifically trained to bring his project to fruition— indigenous relocation, a royalist Church, and an obedient mendicant mission.

The new bishop moved quickly to achieve his goals. He moved the cathedral see from Tzintzuntzan to Pátzcuaro on the day of his arrival, 6 August 1538. As there was no actual cathedral church in Pátzcuaro, the move was symbolic; though the relocation was official, it was also a bit absurd. A bishop oversees a diocese from its administrative home, which is called a "cathedral," or, in Spanish, the *catedral*—a term ultimately derived from the Latin *cathedra* (chair or seat); a cathedral is thus the place where the bishop sits and holds his court. Perhaps Quiroga sat in an inn or private residence. Royal instructions had directed him to establish the nascent cathedral chapter and diocesan seat in Tzintzuntzan and to use the Franciscan church of Saint Anne as the cathedral church. Quiroga viewed that location as unfavorable, however — too wet and too cold.

Quiroga made the decision to move the see unilaterally, and the Franciscans felt threatened immediately, as it seemed that Quiroga had abandoned them. When the viceroy, Mendoza, became aware of the decision to relocate the see, he was peeved, and his relationship with Quiroga became somewhat frosty. Mendoza traveled to Michoacán in December 1539 after receiving numerous pleas for royal justice from encomenderos, who disliked the idea of the capital's relocation to Pátzcuaro, because, they said, the road was poor and the location too cold.[17] They were, in a word, miffed: What was the problem with this Quiroga guy, anyway? Mendoza sympathized with the encomenderos: he didn't like Quiroga either.

Quiroga made enemies quickly. For example, he sued Juan Infante over the tributes from the vast encomiendas in the Pátzcuaro basin to which Infante laid claim.[18] Quiroga asserted that the indigenous residents were direct subjects of the Crown and not of an individual encomendero, reasoning that, as such, they had no responsibility to pay tribute to Infante. Viceroy Mendoza sided with Infante, and Quiroga lost the lawsuit. Another political clash was brewing between the bishop and Spanish settlers. Spanish encomenderos — in particular, Cristóbal de Oñate, Diego de Medina, and Juan de Alvarado — militated for moving the capital of Michoacán east to the Guayangareo Valley in what became known as Valladolid (today Morelia). Mendoza assented, and in May 1541 a small group of anti-Quiroga and anti-Pátzcuaro Spanish settlers formally occupied the valley, declaring it the "city of Michoacán."[19] When Luis de León was made corregidor of the province of Michoacán, he made his residence not in Pátzcuaro, but in Guayangareo, which he immediately began to call the city of Michoacán.[20] Other pro-Guayangareo encomenderos followed suit, and the political feud deepened.

There were clear and open tensions as jurisdictional confusion reigned. For the next two years, Mendoza continued to reaffirm the legal primacy of Guayangareo over Pátzcuaro.[21] No physical church had been established in Guayangareo, however, even as Quiroga was intent on building a cathedral church in Pátzcuaro.

Encomienda subjects rebelled amid the jurisdictional confusion. In 1540, Francisco Vásquez de Coronado was on the Michoacán-Chichimec frontier getting ready for his notorious northern expedition; provisioning and preparation for the invasion to the northwest provoked mayhem.[22] In June 1542, at the height of the Mixtón War in New Galicia, hundreds of Juan Infante's encomienda subjects fled Comanja. They claimed that Infante had press-ganged them into unpaid mining work. In turn, Infante filed a countersuit before Viceroy Mendoza, demanding that his indigenous charges be forced to return. Mendoza reconfirmed Guayangareo's superiority over Pátzcuaro by sending the order to investigate the matter to the corregidor Luis de León in Guayangareo.[23]

No one knew who was really in charge. In June 1542, Pope Paul III formally convoked the Council of Trent, and the Spanish Crown summoned Quiroga as a delegate. Quiroga traveled to Veracruz but did not arrive in Spain, as summer storms in the Gulf of Mexico delayed his journey. The see remained a kind of administrative no-man's-land in the bishop's absence. Quiroga returned to the province in 1543.[24]

The defiant move to Guayangareo upended the labor and tribute system. By May 1543, Spanish residents had complained to Mendoza that indigenous peoples were refusing to travel to the new city of Michoacán to sell food or supplies. Mendoza was compelled to order the Purépecha to be more interested in setting up a marketplace, but he noted that they could not be compelled.[25] On 28 May, Mendoza reaffirmed the judicial supremacy of Guayangareo, vacating all claims to royal justice that Guayangareo did not recognize.[26]

The willful abandonment of Pátzcuaro by the Spanish founders of Guayangareo underscored the deteriorating relationship between Quiroga and the Spanish landowners. Their action was galling to Quiroga for several reasons. First and foremost, Viceroy Mendoza's decision to grant approval to Guayangareo as the "city of Michoacán" was a backhanded response to Quiroga's decision to move the cathedral see to Pátzcuaro without consulting the viceroy. Second, the open defiance of the anti-Pátzcuaro Spaniards spelled trouble for the bishop. In June 1543, the citizens of Guayangareo protested to the viceroy that Quiroga had refused to place a parish priest in the new town. Quiroga replied that this was because the uppity settlers had defied his decision to relocate the cathedral see. The Spaniards of Guayangareo offered a riposte, noting that although the Franciscans had established a primitive church in the new town, they still were ill served by the absence of an actual priest, as the friars only administered to the indigenous. This was a political move, not a genuine spiritual one, and it paid off. In May 1545, Viceroy Mendoza wrote a blistering letter to Quiroga, suggesting that as he (Mendoza) was the direct representative of the Crown, the bishop answered to him, not vice versa, and that he would do well to install a parish priest.[27] For Quiroga, the viceroy's support of the pro-Guayangareo faction was surely the cause of personal humiliation.

ENCOMENDEROS, THE FRIARS' NEW POLITICAL FRIENDS

Although many encomenderos viewed friars as morally self-righteous, in Michoacán they formed alliances of political necessity with them. Friars, notably Bartolomé de las Casas, had frequently criticized the encomienda system, and yet the friars of Michoacán formed deep social and economic ties with the encomenderos.[28] In the abstract, the friars defended indigenous rights—especially, in the case of the Augustinians, the right to education—but these ideals foundered on the shoals of the financial necessities of their monastery building programs and everyday practical necessities. The friars happily accepted the largesse of encomenderos, and expedience expressed itself in the furtherance of corporate structures—plantations and mission complexes.

The predations of encomenderos in New Spain in general, and Michoacán in particular, are well-known. The consensus view is that encomenderos abused their authority, extracted labor and tribute demands well beyond what was permitted, engaged in illegal slaving, and were generally immoral. The actions of Infante, the encomendero of Pomacorán, Comanja, and Naranja, have been held up as especially egregious.[29] When, in 1541, the Spanish Crown commissioned friar Alonso de la Veracruz to conduct an inspection of the Michoacán province, his findings led to charges against Infante for abuse and enslavement of indigenous subjects. In 1542, Viceroy Mendoza ordered the corregidor Luis de León to determine whether Michoacán's indigenous peoples were working in Infante's mines willingly. The viceroy's order stipulated that if Veracruz's inspection uncovered evidence that Infante had forced indigenous peoples into unpaid mining work, he must cease and desist such practices.[30] Mendoza ordered other investigations in 1542 and 1543 into Infante's abuse of indigenous land rights in Guaniqueo.[31] Infante filed a countersuit to force many of his indigenous charges to return to his encomiendas.[32]

Despite their reputation for abuse, the encomenderos became a linchpin in the developing factional rivalry between Quiroga and the mendicants. The Franciscans happily accepted Infante's financial support, transforming him into the central financial backer in the construction project for the Franciscan monastery of Guayangareo. His support of the Franciscans was orchestrated to snub Quiroga. Franciscans had founded a rudimentary church and an adobe convent building in Guayangareo in 1543. By the early 1550s, Infante was providing the funding for the new Franciscan monastery in the form of cash infusions and indigenous labor drafts from his subjects in Pátzcuaro.[33] Infante saw his cash donations to the Franciscans as a wise investment in a corporation that might shield him from the bishop's attempts at reforming encomienda holdings.

The Augustinian project also benefited from the encomienda system. When they established their first monasteries in Tiripetío and Tacámbaro in the late 1530s, the Augustinians were the direct and immediate beneficiaries of the Alvarado encomienda. Don Juan de Alvarado, brother of Pedro de Alvarado, held Tiripetío in encomienda in 1537, when the Augustinians were considering the initiation of their evangelization project in the tierra caliente of Michoacán, and he gave the friars a warm welcome. So moved was Alvarado by the Augustinian project that he donated "nearly all of the lands" of his encomienda, including the "opulent mines" of Curucupaseo (near Tacámbaro), for the new monastery.[34] He even donated the encomienda house to be made into a hospital for the indigenous residents.[35] These donations presumably occurred immediately, and were not bequeathed on his death but rather as he was alive, though the chronicle accounts may have been exaggerated for effect. No contemporaneous documents exist to corroborate the bequest account. In 1538, the Augustinians established their second monastery, in Tacámbaro, and in similar fashion, the encomendero Cristóbal de Oñate prostrated himself before the friars in an elaborate show of welcoming them and praising them for bringing Christianity—or at least social order—to his territory.[36] Oñate's lands included a mine and a mill, and the proceeds of these assets found their way into Augustinian coffers.[37] The Augustinians quickly formed close bonds with other encomenderos as well, receiving important financial backing from them, and, in some cases, even acting as the collectors of tribute in lieu of a local tax authority.[38]

The Augustinians also received conscripted tribute from indigenous pueblos for construction of monasteries and churches. In 1541, the Crown established a series of *repartimientos*, or forced labor arrangements, for the construction of the new city of Guayangareo and for drainage projects within it.[39] Like the Franciscans, the Augustinians supported the transfer of the capital from Pátzcuaro to Guayangareo, and they had established a primitive church-monastery in the new town. As early as 1552 the Augustinians were receiving cash payments from the royal tributes of the province of Michoacán for the construction of their monastery in Guayangareo. The Augustinians became, in turn, a lending agency for the early Spanish settlers of the new town.[40]

Encomenderas were as active as male encomenderos in pushing their economic interests, but because their vested interests often fell within the broader economic portfolios of their husbands, their actions are more difficult to trace. It is clear, however, that women encomienda holders expanded their social and financial networks at this time, both as patrons of building projects and as lucrative landowners in and of themselves.

In this regard the story of the Alvarado clan is more intricate and nuanced than its obvious support of the Augustinians would suggest. Doña Leonor de Alvarado, a niece of the conquistador Pedro de Alvarado, married Gil González de Benavides. Before her husband's death in 1543 she bore him a son, Alonso de Ávila Alvarado—who became notorious for his presumed role in the so-called Martín Cortés conspiracy of 1566, for which he was beheaded.[41] Doña Leonor never formally held the title to Cuauhtitlan; when Gil González died, the encomienda passed to their son Alonso. Two lawsuits against Doña Leonor suggest that in practice, how-

ever, indigenous residents viewed her, and not her son, as the rightful encomendera. In 1543, the Otomíes of Cuauhtitlan filed a lawsuit against her for abuse of
land rights, demanding that the court force her to remove her livestock.[42] As the
case is not extant, we do not know its outcome; nevertheless, the fact that the local
Otomí population sued Doña Leonor for redress instead of her son is telling.

Doña Leonor diversified her landholdings over the next two decades, and in so
doing, established herself as an important player in Spanish expansion beyond the
Chichimec frontier. In 1544 she married Luis de Moscoso, a conquistador of Peru
and Guatemala and field marshal of Hernando de Soto's Florida expedition.[43] In
response to the Otomí demands against her and her estate, Doña Leonor appealed
to the encomendero of Acámbaro, Hernán Pérez de Bocanegra, who suggested
that the valley of Chamacuero, just north of Celaya, was an excellent place to settle
her livestock. She succeeded, despite indigenous protests, in establishing herself
as the principal landowner of the region until her death in 1551.[44] Doña Leonor's
expansion was part of a broader expansion of Spanish claims to land beyond the
Chichimec frontier and into the northern parts of the province of Michoacán. As
her family was a loyal supporter of the Augustinians, this expansion also had the
effect of pushing Yuriria farther within the Michoacán province, since her actions
effectively moved the frontier line farther north.

Amid this bewildering array of patronage connections, parish priests were
largely absent. As William Taylor has observed, "for much of the colonial period
the local priests were regarded by the royal government as counterweights to the
corregidores and their lieutenants."[45] The irony in Michoacán was rich, since few
parish priests were settled before the 1560s to act as such counterweights. The new
viceregal government helped to cement encomendero and corregidor power—in
some cases in the same person, much to the detriment of Quiroga's plan to establish religious authority in the province's towns. Pedro Méndez de Sotomayor, for
example, was, through marriage, the encomendero of Maravatío in 1540. Viceroy
Mendoza made Méndez the corregidor of Ucareo, which oversaw the region of
Maravatío during the years in which Méndez acted as magistrate (1542–1544).[46]

In other cases, encomenderos oversaw stateless regions where no parish priest
was seated. Maravatío, for example, had no parish priest until the 1570s.[47] Enter
Hernán Pérez de Bocanegra, a friend of Doña Leonor. Pérez de Bocanegra had
received the lucrative encomienda of Acámbaro from Mendoza in 1538—and, lo
and behold, Pérez de Bocanegra had recently acted as Mendoza's representative in
purchasing vast ranching lands in Maravatío.[48] In a possible quid pro quo, the viceroy granted Pérez de Bocanegra's request to establish an inn (venta) in the same
region, in Zinapécuaro, in 1542.[49] In short, a byzantine web of favors, patronage,
friendship, and encomienda relationships coalesced to put Quiroga on the defensive. Mendoza, a clear antagonist of Quiroga, must have understood the utility of

empowering encomenderos in Michoacán when it suited his broader goals: political pacification, and irritating the bishop.

PIPILTIN PATRONAGE

The nexus of economic and political arrangements between mendicants and the laity was not limited to Spaniards. Michoacán's pipiltin—indigenous aristocrats—sought to capitalize on the emerging political rivalries by aligning themselves with mission settlements. By the end of the sixteenth century, indigenous elites throughout New Spain began to see that their appeals to the Spanish Crown as loyal subjects and trust-inspiring Christians had limited effect.[50] The pipiltin of Michoacán were similar to other indigenous elites, but in the case of Michoacán, they invested in what they saw as their best potential social and financial partners in an ironic choice—monastery complexes and friar-missionaries.[51]

The Purépecha elite developed important alliances with both Franciscans and Augustinians. The legitimate son of the caltzontzin, Don Francisco Turiácuri, supported the Franciscan project, though certainly this arrangement was designed to be mutually beneficial. Turiácuri appealed to Viceroy Mendoza in 1542 for a license to marry a Spanish woman and to wear Spanish clothing. The viceroy consented, noting the long period of time Turiácuri had spent as a resident of the Franciscan convent in Michoacán.[52] Yet in their efforts to conscript indigenous workers, the Franciscans had to appeal to the royal justice in the same year. The viceroy replied that the friars were forbidden from conscripting Purépecha in their efforts to construct a church in Zinapécuaro.[53] Given the shortage of paid Spanish labor, the Franciscan friars sought encomienda subjects to build their mission complexes. They obtained this labor both from encomenderos, who held indigenous subjects as tributaries, and from indigenous governors, who possessed similar conscription privileges for macehual labor.

Don Antonio Huitziméngari, one of the Augustinians' main financial backers, became the indigenous governor of Michoacán, inheriting tribute payments, exemptions, and certain rights and privileges, as was common for indigenous nobles throughout New Spain. He and his brother, Tariácueri, likely received baptism from Franciscans in Tzintzuntzan. In 1535, the two Purépecha nobles went to Mexico City, where they served as pages in Viceroy Mendoza's court and received an education typical of Spanish letrados in grammar, logic, and law.[54] On returning to Michoacán sometime around 1540, Don Antonio Huitziméngari became Alonso de la Veracruz's star pupil in Tiripetío. He studied Latin, Greek, Hebrew, and theology and even became Veracruz's professor of the Purépecha language. The bond of patronage was important, as the Augustinians received bequests from the Huitziméngari estate through repartimiento labor and cash donations.[55]

As the founder of the Augustinian colleges in Tiripetío and Tacámbaro, Veracruz had a close relationship with Huitziméngari. Viceroy Mendoza had believed that the relationship was too close, and he had reprimanded Veracruz in 1542 for establishing too many houses of doctrinal instruction. Mendoza had also forbidden the Purépecha nobles from being attended by their macehual servants in the Augustinian colleges, as he viewed this as an unnecessary extravagance.[56]

THE CATHEDRAL THAT REFUSED TO BE

Rivalry was brewing. While the Augustinians and Franciscans were expanding their mission complex and patronage networks, Quiroga embarked on his own program of diocesan expansion and church construction. Yet he was hard pressed to dislodge the entrenched interests of the mendicants. Quiroga's first and most famous project was the establishment of the Santa Fe hospital in 1533, which he funded with his own money. This hospital formed the basis for his famed hospital-pueblos—idealized villages inspired by Sir Thomas More's *Utopia*.[57] The villages were, in effect, a forced resettlement program. But the hospital-pueblos could not compete with encomienda wealth or with the majestic monasteries built in places like Yuriria or Cuitzeo, where the Augustinian churches remain to this day impressive monuments to mendicant wealth.

The bishop forged on with his project for Pátzcuaro, proposing two massive projects: a college-seminary and a cathedral church. Neither went far in the first years, in large part on account of the local economy. Guayangareo was siphoning off indigenous labor drafts and repartimientos, a program that Viceroy Mendoza actively supported. The concentration of indigenous labor in encomiendas belonging to Infante, Villegas, Oñate, and Alvarado hamstrung Quiroga's plans. Even Huitziméngari offered macehual subjects to projects in Guayangareo. Encomenderos and pipiltin were committed supporters of mendicant building projects. Quiroga's building projects and college seminary, lacking the requisite labor sources, had to wait.[58]

Between 1543 and 1547, although Quiroga had to fight a virtually never-ending uphill political battle with the Guayangareo settlers and the anti-Pátzcuaro landowners, he was able to lay some of the groundwork for his diocesan structure. As part of his strategy of creating a residential priesthood loyal to the diocese, for example, he began to ordain non-friar clergy (secular priests) in Michoacán. The political situation was absurd: although Quiroga had established a cathedral chapter in 1540, it had no place to conduct business, and its first meeting did not take place until 1544 or 1545.[59] A cathedral chapter, in theory, formed the basic government of a diocese, with a head, or dean (*deán*), *maestrescuela* (schoolmaster), *chantre* (choirmaster), treasurer, archdeacon, and shareholder-dignitaries (canons

FIGURE 2.1. Ex-Convento de Santa María Magdalena, Cuitzeo, Augustinian monastery, sixteenth century. Photo by Armando Pineda Ortiz (2011), Creative Commons license, https://commons.wikimedia.org/wiki/File:Santa_Mar%C3%ADa_Magdalena,_Cuitzeo .jpg.

and *racioneros*, clerics who performed certain duties). But these structures were ad hoc at best. In fact, in the 1540s Quiroga's cathedral had no permanent structure, no dean, and no maestrescuela. Juan Rebollo had become the diocesan *vicario* (the bishop's principal substitute agent; the title was often attached to that of provisor, or chief ecclesiastical judge of the diocese) around 1545.[60] Similarly, the amount of income the cathedral received from tithes is unclear, as records are not extant from the earliest period. Judging from Quiroga's decision to travel to Spain to plead his case for the cathedral-building project, one must assume that the tithe income was meager.[61]

In any case, Quiroga became cranky, and by 1547 he viewed the situation as so unstable that he felt compelled to travel to Spain to plead his case before the Crown. It is unclear whom he appointed to act as the governor of the diocese in his absence.[62] Few formal dignitaries of the cathedral corporation had even been vested. Alonso Álvarez became the archdeacon in 1546, shortly before Quiroga's departure, but no cathedral dean was seated.[63] Quiroga was absent for seven years, and in that interim the absence of a bishop and the escalation of rivalries indicated a divided Church in Michoacán.

During his stay in Spain, Quiroga, a skilled lawyer, lobbied the Council of Indies relentlessly. His legal writs are complex, and they make fascinating jurisprudential reading. But above all else, he was a man convinced that legality could rule Michoacán. While in Spain, from 1547 to 1554, Quiroga scored important victories before the Council of the Indies, but they proved hollow. For example, he received formal approval of the move of the see from Tzintzuntzan to Pátzcuaro, but he could not formalize the decision from afar.

Back in Michoacán, the Augustinians and Franciscans waltzed into the power vacuum created by his absence. The patronage network of the friars was deep, whereas Quiroga's cathedral was only a legal concept lacking an actual home. Quiroga loyalist Juan Zurnero became the provisor sometime in 1548, though the precise date is not clear.[64] In technical terms, Zurnero ruled in Quiroga's absence, though the power he wielded in practice proved tenuous; his tenure in fact revealed the deep factional ties among Quiroga's parish clergy. Zurnero counted on the support of Quiroga's allies among the secular clergy, especially Gordillo. But the mendicants continued to assert the independence that the Omnimoda assured them.

Jurisdictional competition erupted into violence in 1548 when Quiroga loyalists demolished a small church in Congurico. The See of New Galicia (Guadalajara) and Michoacán had begun a long-term dispute over boundaries in the north in the Chichimec frontier as well as to the southwest. The dispute was fiercest in what is now the state of Guanajuato. The recently elected bishop of New Galicia had sent an expedition east from Guadalajara. The expedition removed the physical boundary markers and the crosses demarcating Michoacán and New Galicia in Congurico, twenty miles due south of Pénjamo, and then farther east and north, to Acámbaro.[65] In doing so the bishop was signaling his intent to claim these lands, along with their rich livestock tithes, for New Galicia. Doña Leonor de Alvarado's ranch in Chamacuero was only just north of the region and must have offered comfort for the Michoacán partisans. When later, in 1568, her estate became the subject of a second lawsuit, she appealed not to New Galicia, but to the Audiencia of Mexico, indicating that Michoacán had effectively claimed the region for itself.[66]

The skirmish soon expanded into a legal battle. Acting on Quiroga's behalf, Zurnero dispatched diocesan agents to Guanajuato to file a lawsuit on behalf of Michoacán before the alcalde of the Chichimec territory, a vast and vaguely defined region to the north. Gordillo, the parish priest of Pátzcuaro, traveled to Congurico with a cohort of Michoacán's Spanish citizens. There, the group razed and demolished the small church that had been erected by New Galicia. The diocese of New Galicia rebuilt the church, and in June 1548, Zurnero, along with several of Michoacán's diocesan clergy, went back to Congurico and again demolished the church. They arrested the parish priest, who had been placed there by New Galicia, and embargoed his property.[67] This skirmish offered a preview of events to come.

AUGUSTINIAN FORTIFICATIONS, 1547–1553

While Quiroga waged a courtroom battle in Spain against the friars, the Augustinians' political network became ever more baroque, and the mundane politics of land litigation began to suck the Augustinians into juridical and literal mire. Their connection to the Huitziméngari estate proved politically embarrassing. Macehuals resented the extortion of labor, not only by encomenderos but by indigenous governors as well, and they often sued the indigenous go-betweens before royal courts.

Huitziméngari acted in the same sort of duplicitous political self-interest as the encomenderos. But the Purépecha governor was also embroiled in a long series of lawsuits with his macehual subjects. In 1550, for example, he found himself in the ironic position of being ordered by the new viceroy, Luis de Velasco, to widen and improve the road from Valladolid to Curucupaseo, a town that sat above the mining region below.[68] The Crown ordered Huitziméngari to pay for the improvements to a road that would speed up the demographic decline of the Purépecha macehuals, on account of their brutal work in the mines.

Lawsuits against the Purépecha governor piled up. In 1550, Huitziméngari filed a countersuit against his indigenous subjects in Tzintzuntzan for their failure to pay the tribute they owed him as the governor.[69] In 1553, he filed an "información y méritos" brief—a recapitulation of his service to the Crown intended to draw favor, privileges, and rights.[70] The macehuals of Tzintzuntzan, in turn, disputed their tribute requirements, suing Huitziméngari.[71] The governor also filed a case against Capula, Tarímbaro, and Chocándiro, claiming that their communities were encroaching on his personal lands.[72] But Huitziméngari continued to face lawsuits claiming burdensome tribute demands for decades. The indigenous commoners of Chilchota sued him in 1559, and the Crown appears to have sided against him.[73]

It was not merely guilt by association with an indigenous governor's economic peccadillos that dragged the Augustinians into the metaphoric and literal muck of Michoacán's land. Indigenous communities sued the Augustinians directly on several occasions, claiming that their friaries had usurped lands, despoiled crops, or illegally diverted water supplies. The indigenous pueblo of Capula, for example, appealed to royal justice when the residents detailed a series of land abuses by the Augustinian convent. These included encroachment, setting livestock to roam freely on the crops of the indigenous people, and diverting river water, condemning them, according to the lawsuit, to starvation.[74] Far from the idealism of the classrooms of Tiripetío and Tacámbaro, which were filled with discussions of ancient Greek and the translation of Scripture, these disputes were all too grubby and real. But they were the outcome of the intimate patronage network that the Augustinians had forged with encomenderos and the Purépecha pipiltin.

Despite the alliances between the Augustinians and the encomenderos as well as the Huitziméngari clan, there was relatively little ideological Christianization going on in these regions. The Augustinians had an idealized catechesis that depended on the classical education of indigenous elites. But the conversion of the macehuals lagged. In November 1555, the viceroy, Luis de Velasco, was forced to order the corregidor of Taximaroa (still an encomienda of the Salazar family) to compel at least sixteen indigenous cantors to remain in the town to serve in the newly established Franciscan church, for fear that no one would staff the nascent Christian project in the town. Velasco went so far as to place the entire indigenous population under geographic hold, forbidding them from moving out of the town so that the region's Christianity would be preserved.[75]

The friars were idealists, but their worldly and financial needs brought them back to earth. No matter how ideal their vision of spiritual purity, they still had to lay the groundwork for actual churches, friaries, colleges, and chapels. This work was often squalid, both physically and politically. By the 1550s, the friars and the encomenderos were firmly allied in their social and economic interests, which proved useful to both in resisting the imposition of diocesan rule and imperial hegemony.

THE COMING CONFLAGRATION

Tensions mounted. News of the mission expansion rattled Quiroga, even though he was an ocean away. The bishop began to view the friars as enemies rather than allies in the Christianization of Michoacán. In 1552, Quiroga litigated mendicant privileges before the Council of the Indies. The Franciscans, for example, had ignored previous orders that they obtain a license from the bishop before building a new monastery. They appealed, as did the Augustinians, to their exemptions expressed in the Omnimoda. The Franciscans signaled their intent to build a monastery in Erongarícuaro on the west coast of Lake Pátzcuaro. Quiroga obtained a royal decree blocking the erection of the friary as superfluous, given its proximity to Tzintzuntzan and Pátzcuaro.[76]

Quiroga was playing a dangerous game. The bishop was astute in court politics, but New Spain's viceroys found him pompous and irritating. Viceroy Mendoza had been openly hostile to Quiroga, but in 1549, the Crown named Mendoza the viceroy of Peru. Quiroga probably hoped for a replacement who would be more receptive to his plans to solidify control of the Michoacán church. Unfortunately for Quiroga, Mendoza's replacement, Luis de Velasco, proved to be just as supportive of the friar-missionaries as his predecessor. Velasco, named to the post in 1550, was a thorn in Quiroga's side for a decade. Upon his arrival in New Spain, while Quiroga was still abroad in Spain, the new viceroy expanded the licensure of monastery building. Quiroga complained to the Council of the Indies, and on 17 March 1553, the council ordered the viceroy not to issue new licenses to build friaries without the consent and express license of the bishop, particularly in the diocese of Michoacán.[77]

Quiroga rebuked mendicant claims to the independent administration of sacraments and clerical activity. He rejected the friars' argument that by the privileges provided by the Omnimoda the friars could administer sacraments without diocesan license, and their claim that mendicants could act as ecclesiastical judges in marital disputes (as deriving from their sacramental charge of the indigenous). On 18 December 1552, the Crown issued a decree stating that friars could not act as judges in marital disputes but were compelled to refer any such cases to a competent diocesan judge ordinary. Moreover, Quiroga obtained two other writs from the Crown that compelled the mendicants to "treat secular clergy well" and not to disturb their activities.[78]

The diocese became increasingly unstable. Quiroga, however, having secured several victories from the Council of the Indies, viewed his time in Spain as well spent. The president of the court, Luis Hurtado de Mendoza, the Marquis of Mondéjar, may very well have been the key to his success. Quiroga had befriended Hurtado's confessor, the former inquisitional censor and Dominican friar Alonso de Montúfar. In 1551, the Crown had appointed Montúfar as the new archbishop of Mexico; by 1554, Quiroga felt that he had achieved as much as he needed and planned to return to Michoacán. Quiroga returned to Mexico in the same fleet as the new archbishop, armed with royal decrees and fortified by his new friendship. The archbishop was just as determined as Quiroga was to rein in the Augustinians and Franciscans.

Although Quiroga returned to Michoacán a transformed bishop, when he saw the state of his diocese, he was furious. It had taken fifteen years for him to obtain royal approval of the new location for the see in Pátzcuaro.[79] The parallel capital in Guayangareo created a practical inertia. The Franciscans and Augustinians had by then established close to thirty monasteries within the diocese of Michoacán, many of them licensed by Viceroy Velasco. The massive Augustinian and Franciscan building projects rose in ostentatious defiance of Quiroga's presumed legal right to control building permit grants. The grandeur of monasteries like Yuriria only humiliated the bishop further as he cogitated on the absence of his own monument—a cathedral church. Quiroga embarked once again on his own ambitious plan to build a cathedral church in Pátzcuaro, reportedly spending as much as 18,500 pesos from the *real hacienda* ("royal estate," or colonial treasury) on the massive building project, which would be staffed largely by repartimiento Purépechas between 1554 and 1563.[80]

At long last, a jurisdictional war erupted. Quiroga came to view Alonso de la Veracruz as a dangerous rival and the leader of a dissident faction, and he believed he was attempting to found a new church, unanswerable to Quiroga or Montúfar.[81] Indeed, Veracruz argued that the American Christianization effort only required friars; that the Indies did not need bishops; and that friars should administer the sacraments of baptism and marriage.[82]

Quiroga found not only intransigence but a politically well-equipped faction in the mendicants. Viceroy Velasco continued to act as a powerful ally of the friars. He provided financial backing for missionary projects, exacerbating tensions between Quiroga and the friars. In June 1555, Velasco granted the Augustinians 200 pesos for their continued work on their monastery of Tacámbaro.[83] Cristóbal de Oñate, the longtime patron of the Augustinians, who had been a close ally of Nuño de Guzmán and previously had been the governor of New Galicia, also received a 200-peso contribution from the viceroy to be administered in building the monastery. He was no friend of Quiroga's.

The Yuriria monastery placed tensions in high relief, with the Alvarado clan once again offering critical support for the Augustinians. The Yuriria monastery project began in 1550 under the direction of friar Diego de Chávez, the nephew of Don Pedro de Alvarado. The viceroy, Luis de Velasco, granted the Augustinians 200 pesos for construction of the monastery, and an encomendera, Doña Luisa de Acuña, who held Paguatlan in Veracruz province (today in the state of Puebla), also received 150 pesos to contribute to the project.[84] Apparently not satisfied with these cash grants, the Augustinians appealed to the viceroy for a labor draft as well. Their efforts were rewarded, and in December 1555, Velasco granted the Augustinians a repartimiento of fifty indigenous workers to build the church and monastery—twenty from Tiripetío, twenty from Cuitzeo, and ten from Matalcingo.[85]

The fact that the Augustinians depended on support from indigenous elites for funding while at the same time using semi-enslaved macehual labor was ironic: it meant that pipiltin, such as Huitziméngari, were supporting a project that exploited their own ethnic group, though surely the pipiltin saw such labor uses as traditional perquisites of their class. Completed by 1559, the Yuriria monastery was a soaring architectural achievement. But it was also a monument to corporate interests and defiance of diocesan control—a fitting statement of the ambivalence of the Augustinians toward the indigenous labor which made the building possible.

Like Mendoza, Velasco favored the mendicants. He funded the construction of a Franciscan monastery in Guayangareo, again inflaming Quiroga, who continued to insist that Pátzcuaro was the true capital. The viceroy disagreed, mocking Quiroga by referring to Guayangareo as the "city of Michoacán." The viceroy granted the Franciscans a repartimiento of subjects from neighboring Capula, which, at the time, the Franciscans held as a doctrina.[86] The Franciscans also benefited from encomendero wealth and sugar production. They were tied to the royal factor, Hernando de Salazar, the son of the factor Gonzalo de Salazar, who bequeathed Taximaroa as an encomienda to his son Juan in 1553.[87]

While the political rivalry grew on the ground in Michoacán, in Mexico City Archbishop Montúfar convened the First Council of the Mexican Church in 1555. Designed to set several issues into law, the council was characterized by remarkably anti-indigenous attitudes, setting the stage for the abolition of the Franciscan college for indigenous elites at Santa Cruz de Tlatelolco.[88] Montúfar opposed the cultivation of indigenous education and distrusted the Franciscans and Augustinians in general. Politically, the council strove to limit the privileges of the mendicants by reaffirming the primacy of diocesan control of marriage, baptism, and the regulation of the building of churches.[89] Quiroga attended the council and was among Montúfar's closest allies in promoting the diocesan line.

Veracruz took up the opposition mantle, defending mendicant privileges and articulating an assault on the claims of Montúfar's council. The Augustinian argued that the pope had conferred dominion to the Crown and the Spanish Church to convert the indigenous peoples. Because the Crown had chosen the mendicants as his special agents in that Christianization process, the friars were operating as vicars of the pope.[90] Montúfar and Quiroga were not pleased. In 1558, Montúfar sent off a series of letters to the Crown to complain that the mendicants were vain and disobedient, that they had far too many monasteries already, and that these, especially the Franciscan and Augustinian monasteries, were monuments to ostentation. He complained bitterly that in Mexico, such was the "power, favor, and control" of the friars that a "mere lay brother [Pedro de Gante] was esteemed more than an archbishop."⁹¹ Montúfar's ideology of centralized church power may have fueled his legal assault on the mendicants, but he was also clearly motivated by his own pride and animosity—to Veracruz in particular, and to the Franciscans and Augustinians in general. It was ironic—or maybe simply hypocritical—but Montúfar never aimed his anti-mendicant ire at his own order, the Dominicans.

Ideologically speaking, nothing enraged Quiroga and Montúfar more about Alonso de la Veracruz than the Augustinian's insistence that the indigenous people should not have to pay the tithe and that the Mexican Church needed no actual priests. Veracruz had argued that the indigenous were too impoverished to pay the tithe in his treatise *De decimis*. Furthermore, in Veracruz's assessment, if the tithe was required, it would only go to the diocesan clergy, whom he viewed as superfluous. In 1558, Montúfar went so far as to denounce Veracruz before the Inquisition in Spain, although no formal charges were ever leveled against him.⁹²

THE BISHOP'S HUMANIST ANTAGONIST

Into this controversy over diocesan control of Michoacán stepped Maturino Gilberti, who was born in Poitiers to an Italian family around 1507. He joined the Franciscan order as a teen in 1524 and was ordained a priest around 1531. In the autumn of 1542, when he arrived in Mexico, he may have gone directly to Michoacán, though we have no direct evidence of his presence there until 1556, when he was living in Tzintzuntzan.⁹³ He returned to Mexico City in 1557 though for the rest of his life he lived in and around Uruapan and Pátzcuaro.

Gilberti became a well-known scholar of the Purépecha language. He authored several works, and although some of them have been lost, and others were censured and destroyed by ecclesiastical authorities, the ones still extant remain the principal sources of Purépecha religious scholarship, which was humanist in approach. Gilberti was the best Spanish student of the Purépecha language (though Juan Baptista de Lagunas produced an important Purépecha grammar and dictionary in 1574).⁹⁴ One parish priest, Francisco de Monjarrás Godínez, claimed that Gilberti learned Purépecha in a few days, though this was certainly an exaggeration.⁹⁵ De la Rea called him a Cicero or Jerome of Purépecha—such was his rhetorical elegance.⁹⁶ Gilberti produced more than a dozen works in Purépecha. His best-known books were humanist in the manner and ideas of Erasmus—emphasizing simple prayer and devotion over external exhibitions of piety—and in style, especially the *Diálogo*. In addition, he produced the first comprehensive Purépecha *Vocabulario*, and he translated several popular spiritual works into Purépecha, including the *Flossantorum* (lives of the saints) and the Dominican Felipe de Meneses's *Luz del alma cristiana en lengua tarasca* (*Light of the Christian Soul in the Tarascan Tongue*).[97]

Gilberti was also riddled with gout.[98] Rumors suggested that the Purépecha carried him from Uruapan in a litter for miles so that he could preach sermons, as no resident priests spoke their language. De la Rea claimed that "there were so many Indians to hear him that like the children of Abraham they were like grains of sand in the earth or stars in the sky."[99] Some Spaniards even considered Gilberti a living saint.[100] But the gouty friar had advised the Purépecha not to listen to masses celebrated by bishop-appointed clerics—they were not to be trusted.[101] He said they were instruments of the Prince of Lies—lazy, corrupt men interested only in collecting money for their own enrichment.[102] Gilberti publicly criticized the bishop as an egotist who had killed many Purépecha from overwork on the construction of a cathedral church without access to clean drinking water, adequate food, or legal payment.[103] Gordillo saw in Gilberti everything he and Quiroga's supporters hated—an adherent of Erasmian humanism who rejected the authority of the diocesan structure. Gilberti repaid the hatred in kind, viewing priests like Gordillo as intellectually corrupt—coddled holders of sinecures.

Gilberti's Purépecha-language works drew immediate scrutiny from Quiroga's loyalists—Gordillo, principally. The ideological assault on Gilberti's material put both his orthodoxy and his obedience into question. For example, Gilberti had translated the calendar's liturgical cycle of scriptural passages into Purépecha sometime around 1559, though it was never published.[104] The Purépecha manuscript circulated for decades despite the legal suspicion surrounding his works.[105] The translation was among the most controversial of his projects: the Spanish Inquisition had explicitly forbidden vernacular translations of the Bible in 1554.[106]

Other legal issues bedeviled Gilberti as well. Tradition held that one had to receive approval from the local bishop to publish doctrinal works. In June 1558, Gilberti looked to publish two works, both in Purépecha, one called *Arte* and the other *Grammar*. He sought prepublication approval not from Quiroga as bishop, however, but from a friar, Jacobo Diacono, the Franciscan provincial, as well as from the viceroy, Velasco, for *Arte*. Shortly thereafter, in August 1558, Velasco approved the publication of *Arte* (Gilberti had not explicitly solicited that approval for his grammar).[107] Whether this was a deliberate snub of Quiroga or not, the bishop repaid him in spades.

Quiroga embarked on a legal battle to quash Gilberti's Purépecha-language works, arguing that the Franciscan had broken the law for having printed them without his license.[108] More effectively from a political standpoint, however, Quiroga impugned Gilberti's works as heretical. Quiroga insisted that the works be subjected to inquisitional review by Montúfar, the archbishop and inquisitor of Mexico. Quiroga entrusted the theological review of Gilberti's works to his partisans Diego Pérez Gordillo y Negrón and Francisco de la Cerda, a cathedral canon. Both Gordillo and De la Cerda were presumed to be Purépecha-language experts, but the rather obvious reason for their selection as censors was their known antipathy to the mendicants. The censors suggested that Gilberti had argued in his books that the Purépecha should be discouraged from worshiping images of Christ and the saints, and, in January 1560, recommended banning the works. Montúfar agreed, and in April 1560, he ordered that the works be recalled from circulation.[109]

While on the surface, the censorship of Gilberti's works was ideological, in reality it was primarily political and personal. Gilberti's refusal to seek the approval of the bishop was likely more galling to the bishop than the content of the works or any suspected iconoclasm. This ideological strife was a precursor to more serious jurisdictional battles to come. At last, the conflict that had long simmered in legal and philosophical paper battles was about to boil over into full-fledged armed violence.

THE BISHOP'S ARSONIST

The flames were roaring. It was early on the morning on 24 June 1560, and the Augustinian monastery in Tlazazalca was on fire. Waking up in the middle of the night to the smell of smoke and the terrifying rush of the fire, Alonso de la Veracruz shouted, "We are being burned down!" And, indeed, they were. The church was on fire. The friars rushed to save what they could and enlisted the help of indigenous residents to bring water from a nearby irrigation ditch. The church was not burned entirely to the ground, but by the time the fire was extinguished, much of it lay in ashes. Several statues of saints were destroyed. And then the rumors began to spread.[110]

The tensions released in the Tlazazalca monastery fire had been building for years. Veracruz had obtained a 1553 license from Viceroy Velasco for the Augustinians to build five new monasteries in the towns of Jacona, Tlazazalca, Ixtlan, Jiquilpan, and Chilchota along the Chichimec frontier.[111] The Augustinians had long argued that the Chichimec frontier was poorly staffed and in dire need of Christianization. They had already established monasteries in Yuriria, Cuitzeo, and Guango in 1550.[112] The Chichimec frontier of the northern reaches of the diocese had been largely without priests until the 1550s. In towns like Pénjamo, Tlazazalca, Jacona, and Guanajuato, the indigenous people and a small number of Spanish settlers had to travel dozens of miles to find the nearest resident priest to administer sacraments. Anyone interested in attending regular mass was out of luck.

The Augustinians wanted to establish posts farther beyond the Chichimec frontier. They viewed this as fertile territory for conversion, and so, on 3 January 1553, Velasco granted them license to build the Tlazazalca, Xiquilpa, and Chilchota monasteries. Quiroga was having none of it. Still acting in Quiroga's stead, Zurnero viewed this action as a threat to the diocesan claims on the northern flank of the province. In November 1553, Zurnero installed a parish priest in Tlazazalca as a counterweight to Augustinian influence.[113]

Further provocation came in September 1556, when Quiroga named Cristóbal Cola as the parish priest of Tlazazalca. The Augustinians viewed the appointment as a deliberate juridical assault even though, with license in hand, they had not yet occupied the town. Cola did not speak any indigenous language; consequently, during Lent of 1558, he heard no confessions from the indigenous residents of Tlazazalca. The Augustinians saw an opening, arguing before the viceroy that Tlazazalca was in effect sacramentally abandoned. Velasco agreed and ordered that work get underway on the Augustinian monastery. In April 1558, the friar Sebastián Trassierra occupied Tlazazalca as the Augustinian prior, asserting a sanctioned presence as the de facto parish priest.[114]

The diocesan counterattack followed immediately. Cola spent the next several months harassing Trassierra. Rumors spread that Cola had even assaulted the Augustinian friar and interrupted mass on occasion. Francisco de la Cerda replaced Cola as the parish priest in 1559, and by the summer of 1559 De la Cerda was spending his time watching the progress of the Augustinian building project in Tlazazalca. He filed a lawsuit before the diocesan court against the friars for celebrating mass without diocesan license. De la Cerda was especially incensed that the Augustinians had allowed the indigenous parishioners to celebrate the Feast of the Assumption on 15 August. Quiroga made repeated appeals to the Augustinian comisario general, Diego Chávez, to remove the friars from Tlazazalca. Fat chance—Chávez was the same friar who had initiated the Yuriria monastery project. The Augustinians did not budge.

The conflict over Tlazazalca quickly became a judicial war. In February 1560, Quiroga filed a lawsuit before the Audiencia of Mexico against the Augustinians for their presence in Tlazazalca. Quiroga's argument was simple: the Augustinians had no legal right to occupy Tlazazalca because they could do so only with diocesan license. This was an appeal to the older, traditional rights of bishops as expressed in canon law.[115] A legal title (a specific section of the canon law) known as the *Auctoritate* stipulated that no one could build chapels or churches without explicit license from the relevant bishop. Quiroga argued that this principle trumped any later claims to licenses issued by a royal authority, such as the viceroy. Moreover, he cited various royal decrees he had secured in Spain, which had instructed the viceroy to cease issuing licenses for monastery construction. The Augustinians and Veracruz replied that Tlazazalca and the Chichimec frontier in general lacked sufficient Catholic presence, so that the construction of a monastery in Tlazazalca was good, just, and appropriate. Moreover, the Augustinians continued to insist that the papal privileges granted them in the Omnimoda exempted them from the ordinary law expressed in *Auctoritate*.

The showdown demonstrated the legal confusion that could result from trying to apply Spanish or canon law to a remote region. Yes, there were theoretically binding decisions on both sides of the debate, but in practice, on the ground, those legal writs were scraps of paper. As the lawsuit wound its way through the machinery of the Audiencia, the practical situation in Tlazazalca proceeded according to the principles of human revenge. Gordillo emerged as the leader of the diocesan faction. On 25 May 1560, he entered the Augustinian church and demanded that the friars remove the baptismal font within one hour. The Augustinians refused. Aided by several armed men, Gordillo proceeded to personally demolish the baptismal font. A week later, on 2 June, the Feast of the Pentecost, a friar named Pedro de Medina was about to baptize an indigenous child, and Gordillo entered the church and declared before all that the Augustinian friar was acting illegally. Gordillo threatened to subject both the friar and the indigenous worshipers to a beating. Witnesses claimed that as Gordillo made these threats, he wrested the young child from his parents' arms with such force that he killed the infant.

More violence followed. Gordillo and the acting diocesan representative in the town demolished the small jar that the Augustinians began to use in place of the now demolished baptismal font. On the next Sunday, 9 June, the Feast of the Trinity, Gordillo, along with his deacon and an indigenous *fiscal* (an indigenous steward of a physical church), Uapo, burst into the church during mass.[116] Gordillo grabbed the cantor of the church by the chest, a melee broke out, and the deacon started stabbing anyone who attempted to interfere. The cantor was dragged out of the church in the midst of shouts and taken to the curate, where Gordillo ordered him flogged and then jailed for five days. The cantor, sufficiently cowed, agreed never to sing for the friars again.

And then things really deteriorated. The Feast of Corpus Christi was approaching—a festival of particular importance. The Augustinians had prepared for the feast day, and the indigenous residents had designed several *retablos* (devotional paintings or statues in the form of altarpieces) for the occasion. Gordillo threatened both the Augustinians and the indigenous residents, saying that they would pay dearly if they insisted on celebrating the feast at the Augustinian monastery and not at the diocesan church. Gordillo arrived at the monastery on 13 June and demanded that the residents remove the retablos and deliver them to the diocesan parish. At first, they refused. But then Gordillo punched the indigenous alcalde in the face. Gordillo rounded up several residents and had them tossed into jail and flogged.

The bloody fiasco called for measured intercession. The Augustinians dispatched Veracruz to Tlazazalca to reinforce the monastery with his moral presence. On 23 June, the eve of the feast day of the nativity of St. John the Baptist, the small Augustinian atrium and hut that served as a church were decorated with boughs for the procession to be held on the following day. Gordillo and his retinue arrived and informed Veracruz that he was prohibited from leading any such procession. Veracruz refused to relent and insisted on the Augustinian right to lead religious ceremonies in Tlazazalca. The secular priests reportedly told Veracruz that he would regret any scandalous fracas if he followed through with the Augustinian-led procession. An hour later, Gordillo and company returned, armed with staffs, and threw all the decorative boughs to the ground. They left the scene, and the friars retired for the evening, apparently assuming that tempers had cooled. By morning, the monastery was largely a smoldering heap of ash.

Although the monastery was not completely destroyed, the assault on a sacred space and the destruction of holy images were outrageous acts of sacrilege. The Augustinians blamed the most obvious suspect: Gordillo. Others claimed that a lightning strike had lit the fire, as there had been a strong thunderstorm the evening before the fire. But even if Gordillo did not organize the arson, he was blamed for it. The lines were now irrevocably set. So shocking was the event—the destruction of a monastery immediately following weeks of open hostilities from the diocesan partisans—that Quiroga's lawsuit was stopped cold in its tracks. The Audiencia demanded a full investigation of the case.

In normal circumstances, church officials viewed the destruction of a church by arson and the burning of images of saints as the worst kind of sacrilege. Indeed, the Calvinist and Reform "war on the idols" was fresh on the Catholic and Spanish mind.[117] Martin Luther may have assaulted the privilege of the clergy, but in many ways the Calvinist impulse to iconoclasm seemed more viscerally terrible to Catholics. And yet Quiroga did not invoke an Inquisition; nor did anyone insist that the destruction of the Tlazazalca church was a doctrinal crime of sacrilege, though a decade later, in November 1571, Gilberti, in making his critique of Gordillo, listed the Tlazazalca arson and the disinterring of corpses as worthy of inquisitional attention.[118] The reason for Quiroga's inaction was all too obvious: he had called in the hit.

The hostilities grew ever more grotesque. Immediately following the torching of the Augustinian church, Gordillo and his partisans had dozens of indigenous residents jailed in an attempt to prevent them from testifying in court. The Audiencia dispatched a special judge to Michoacán to investigate. In the end, at least fifty-eight witnesses testified in the case. No one was able to identify Gordillo as the person who actually set the fire, but this was the only area of disagreement among the witnesses. There was remarkable similarity in the witnesses' accounts, and all of them agreed that Gordillo was a dangerous, violent man. He had demolished the baptismal font of the Tlazazalca friary; punched an indigenous alcalde in the face; rounded up dozens of indigenous residents and had them flogged for worshiping in the Augustinian church; and murdered an infant awaiting baptism.

In the aftermath of the Tlazazalca fire, Quiroga and the Augustinians engaged in a lengthy, vicious lawsuit. Each side impugned the other as vain and peremptory. Eventually, Mexico's Audiencia weighed the evidence and ruled in the case, issuing a sentence on 11 March 1561 and making a public announcement on 18 April. The conclusion pleased neither the Augustinians nor Quiroga: The court affirmed Tlazazalca as a diocesan parish and the right of the bishop to install his own parish priest. The town was to remain definitively under the bishop's control. But the court also ruled that the Augustinians who remained, and the buildings still standing, must stay.

Quiroga and Gordillo were livid. Quiroga issued an order to Gordillo empowering his faithful servant to proceed to Tlazazalca as the diocesan judge. He was to notify the Augustinians that they were forbidden to celebrate mass, bury the dead, or officiate over any other religious service. Quiroga told Gordillo to dismantle the church, take down its bells, and remove the altar and its crucifix. In effect, Quiroga dared the Audiencia to enforce its own ruling while signaling his intent to appeal the entire case to Rome, bypassing the ordinary appeal to *real patronato* (royal patronage) and the Council of the Indies. The events that then followed went beyond what anyone could have imagined.

The feud took a gruesome turn. On 18 June, Gordillo ordered the indigenous noble of Tlazazalca to dig up graves. With a heavily armed retinue of clerics and Purépecha men, who had been excused for the time being from the drudgery of building the monument to Quiroga's ego in Pátzcuaro, Gordillo then watched as several indigenous men unearthed corpses from the atrium of the Augustinian monastery.

Gordillo had chosen a palpable display to reiterate the right of bishops to control the physical landscape of Catholicism: the disinterring of corpses. The Augustinians had buried the dead in their monastery as sacred ground. Gordillo showed the entire town that this was not to be the case. The corpses were in various states of decay. We cannot know with certainty the ages of the corpses, but the Augustinians had not been in Tlazazalca for more than five years. The corpses were then loaded onto carts and moved across town to the graveyard of the nonmonastic church. The stench made many swoon; others retched. Gordillo offered a perverse grin of triumph, daring anyone to protest. No one did.

The following day, 19 June, Gordillo and his armed guard systematically sacked the monastery, taking with them very little of value, as the place had been partly abandoned. In an added bit of malice, Gordillo had Friar Trassierra arrested and placed in chains. He was taken to Pátzcuaro and deposited in the episcopal jail. The friar refused to acknowledge Quiroga as his judge and was excommunicated forthwith. Upon his return to Pátzcuaro, and now empowered as the choirmaster (*chantre*) of the cathedral chapter, Gordillo then proceeded to demolish the baptismal font of the Franciscan monastery in Pátzcuaro. In the middle of the night, Purépecha residents bribed the jailers and smuggled friar Trassierra out of jail, humiliating Gordillo.[119]

The scandal was so great that Gordillo, along with several of his allies, were summoned to Mexico to appear before the Audiencia. The saga of animosity continued for more than ten years. The Crown summoned Gordillo to Spain to answer for the assaults, and Quiroga gave him a sealed copy of the depositions to take with him, along with witness statements from the Tlazazalca case and the Trassierra prosecution. And, so it seemed, ended one of the more scandalous cases of religious politics in Church history—the year of rage in Michoacán.

THE SMOLDERING EMBERS OF RIVALRY

Anyone who has worked in an academic or political institution knows that rivalries refuse to die. Gilberti returned to Michoacán at some point in 1560, and he preached a sermon in Taximaroa on 17 November. Gordillo appeared before Montúfar in Mexico City along with several Purépecha from Pátzcuaro only five days after the event; Gilberti later claimed that the Purépecha were planted as spies. In their testimony before the archbishop-inquisitor, some of Pátzcuaro's Purépecha residents claimed that Gilberti had preached that only mendicants were true to the Christian faith and that secular priests would fail the Catholic Church in a coming calamity to befall Mexico.[120] Later, Gilberti submitted a complaint to Quiroga, saying that Gordillo was engineering a campaign of libel against him—hardly a novel claim, given Gordillo's earlier violence against the mendicants.[121]

Gilberti shared the millennial thinking of many of his contemporaries. Many Franciscans, influenced by Joachim of Fiore, conceived of the history of the world in stages: in the end stage, only the friars would remain as the faithful members of the true church. This eschatology had a profound impact on the Franciscans in Mexico, who had imbibed this vision under the direction of Martín de Valencia and Francisco de los Ángeles, leaders of the Franciscan province of San Gabriel of Extremadura and intellectual leaders of the early mission to Mexico. Valencia had spearheaded the first mission to Mexico. When the archbishop-inquisitor Montúfar investigated Gilberti, this vision came under scrutiny as well.[122]

Gilberti's suspicious eschatology emboldened Quiroga and Montúfar. In May 1561, Quiroga continued his assault on Gilberti's works, asking Montúfar to ban them once and for all.[123] The next year, Montúfar succeeded in forcing Veracruz to travel to Spain to answer the charges of heresy that Montúfar had leveled against him. Veracruz appeared, presumably before the inquisitor general and Philip II, and was absolved of heresy. He also was instrumental in having Pope Pius V, in 1567, issue a reaffirmation of mendicant privilege in Mexico, despite Pius IV's previous revocation of such privileges not specifically covered by the conclusion of the Council of Trent in 1563.[124]

The assault on indigenous nobles, the flogging of indigenous women, the disinterring of corpses, and even arson and attempted murder were not enough. There was more. By the time Gilberti returned to Tzintzuntzan in the spring of 1561, Gordillo had been elevated to a dignitary post in the cathedral chapter. Although the Crown ordered Gordillo to return to Spain to answer for the events in Tlazazalca before the Council of the Indies, he seems to have continued his campaign against Gilberti in Spain. On 15 March 1563, the Crown issued an order to the Audiencia and viceroy that they recall all copies of Gilberti's works from circulation, after having been persuaded by Gordillo of their doctrinal dangers.[125]

Gilberti decided to push back. On 4 February 1563, he penned a denunciation of Quiroga, to be delivered to Spain by a fellow Franciscan. He originally had hoped that it would be presented before the Crown. This "Memoria," however, never reached Spain. It is unclear where it went, but after Quiroga's death, it came into the possession of the new bishop, Antonio Ruiz de Morales y Molina, who forwarded it to the Inquisition in Mexico, and it was entered into evidence in the growing criminal file against Gilberti being engineered by his enemies.[126]

Gilberti's appraisal of Quiroga offers glimpses into the contempt with which he held the bishop. He claimed that Quiroga was a fanatic who was obsessed with his own fame; that he placed onerous tribute burdens on the Purépecha, to the extent that many had died in building the cathedral church in Pátzcuaro in forced servitude. Gilberti also claimed that Quiroga exacted summary justice against indigenous peoples who refused press-gang service, imprisoning them without food or clothing, and that the bishop had obliged many to travel several miles, without food, to fulfill their duty to work on the cathedral construction. Gilberti also implicitly criticized Quiroga for not even having learned the Purépecha language. Quiroga, he said, had once instructed the indigenous residents of Tiripetío, when he stopped there on a trip to Mexico City, to ignore the Augustinians, who, the bishop claimed, had no right to teach the doctrine. But the bishop had informed the residents of this through an interpreter. Clearly, Quiroga had minimal fluency in Purépecha more than a decade after becoming bishop.[127]

Gilberti also critiqued Quiroga's seminary. He said it had little value; the diocesan clergy trained there and supported by Quiroga were "idiots born here and raised on the breasts of Indian women."[128] They administered the sacraments not out of any concern for spiritual well-being but for a desire to extract money from indigenous parishioners. Likewise, Gilberti argued, Quiroga refused to respect the privileges the papacy had conferred on the mendicants. Quiroga established parish priests in locations entirely too close to the mendicants and with no respect for the needs of Christianization or the administration of sacraments. Gilberti's critique enraged the diocesan authorities, especially Gordillo and Quiroga's successor.[129] Presumably, Gilberti's criticism was publicly known. When the new bishop Morales y Molina, wrote to the new inquisitor in November 1571, he said it was well known throughout Michoacán that Gilberti and Quiroga had been enemies.[130]

Amid all of the controversy, Juan Infante, long the Franciscans' patron in Pomacorán and Uruapan, continued to provide cover for priests who used his encomienda as a kind of free tap. Although the Franciscans had churches in Uruapan and Tancítaro in the 1560s, much of the mountainous region belonging to Infante seemed untouched by genuine evangelization. In May 1563, the indigenous subjects of Pomacorán and Sebina filed a lawsuit against a priest named Juan Díaz along with an unnamed priest of Naranja and Comanja, in the mountainous and remote region north of Uruapan. Infante was only implicated in the case by association. Nevertheless, the lawsuit claimed that as encomienda subjects, they were not only required to provide tribute, in kind and in labor, to Infante, but that Infante had allowed the two priests to exact domestic service (three men and one woman weekly), along with three hens, three *cargas* (loads) of "yerba" (probably hay), two of firewood, fruit, and one *fanega* (close to two bushels) of corn weekly. That the residents felt the need to appeal to the viceroy in Mexico City suggests that Infante was allowing the clerics to treat them as a source of free goods and services.[131]

The Infante-Pomacorán case is telling, especially when compared with a similar case between the indigenous subjects of the neighboring encomienda of Periban (northwest of Uruapan) between 1557 and 1564. Sometime in 1557, the encomendero of Periban, Francisco de Chávez, demanded payment of tribute from his subjects, and the Audiencia of Mexico granted his wish. Pleading poverty, the indigenous subjects filed an appeal before the Audiencia.[132] The region had originally been given to Antón Caicedo, the conquistador and leader of the first Spanish contingent to reach Tzintzuntzan and meet with the caltzontzin. He received Periban, Tarecuato, Tingüindín, and Tecascaro before 1528. After Caicedo's death in 1535 or 1536, his widow, Doña Marina Montesdoca, received the encomienda. When she remarried, the grant remained in her possession through her husband Francisco Chávez, who was named in the 1557 Audiencia case as the encomendero of record. He died in 1561.[133] By 1564, the Periban portion of the encomienda had been assigned to Antonio de Luna, who had married one of Caicedo's daughters, presumably receiving Periban as part of a marital agreement between the Luna and Montesdoca families.[134]

In September 1564, Periban's indigenous residents filed a suit against Luna, claiming that Luna had extracted unfair tribute demands, especially in cotton.[135] The judge assigned to the case, Juan Baeza, had formerly been *alguacil* (bailiff) of the city of Michoacán.[136] Among the witnesses called was none other than Gilberti. In his testimony, he sided with the Periban residents, apparently having served at the time as the resident priest (though it is not clear if the Franciscans had a friary in the town).[137]

Most revealing is that Gilberti only too happily reported to the royal judge that the encomendero, Luna, did indeed extract far too many demands of the indigenous residents.[138] It strains the imagination that Gilberti, who was open in his criticism of Gordillo and offered sworn testimony concerning Periban's encomendero, had simply never heard of the Infante lawsuit. One may very well suspect that the implicit pact between Infante and the Franciscans, who had several monasteries in and around the Infante encomienda, continued well into the 1560s, three decades after the original congregación of the 1530s effected by the Franciscans in Uruapan.

Gilberti's critiques of encomenderos continued. In 1564, he became the resident priest of Periban and launched a critique of an encomendero who, in his view, was putting unusually onerous demands on his subjects.[139] Gilberti also accused the parish priest of Periban, Joaquín Gutiérrez, of placing ridiculous and unfair labor demands on the indigenous residents.[140] Between 1564 and 1570, Gilberti seems to have lived quietly in and near Uruapan. Through the 1560s, his works were under the interdict, and he was only tenuously absolved, it seems, of inquisitional investigations. He made his home in Uruapan, where he was guardian of the Franciscan monastery, yet he openly flouted the inquisitional ban on his works.

DEATH OF A BISHOP

By early 1565, Quiroga was quite ill—and not just from politics. He was mortally ill, and he died in March. At the time of his death, Michoacán was a kind of scorched earth of political rivalry. The indigenous population was in drastic decline. The friars hated the bishop. Strongmen like Gordillo were sullen with rage, even if they had largely succeeded in scaling back the friar-missionary project. Monasteries lay in ashes. There were still few parish priests, and even fewer who spoke Purépecha. Quiroga set the example by not mastering the language himself.

The multiple instances of real-world actions belie a presumably ideological battle for Michoacán's church. These events elucidate an ethnography of communication. Skirmishes and showdowns—the deliberate snubbing of Quiroga by the pro-Guayangareo settlers; the investment by encomenderos in monasteries; the assault on the Augustinian monastery of Tlazazalca; the ecclesiastical censure of Gilberti's Purépecha works—all had underlying philosophical politics. The violence was based on ideological disputes, but effected in very tangible action. Anthropologist Steven Caton suggests that we understand local or tribal disputes through their public displays; in order to "analyze ideology, then, one must examine its mediation through signs in concrete social acts."[141] In Michoacán, the ideological dispute may have been about the role of friars in Catholic governance, but the concrete public acts that burst forth in the ethnography of communication were often violent, brutish expressions of political control.

One thing was clear—residents viewed the Church as the most worldly of mechanisms. The rivalries were voluminous enough to be hilarious. Disputation of the Christianization process was endemic, not exceptional. The spiritual conquest in Michoacán in the 1540s and 1550s looked more like an internecine war. Tata Vasco's utopian dream came up against practical squabbling over local power. And those squabbles, though theoretically tied to imperial goals, brought everyone down to a level they could understand: land, bricks, mortar, baptismal fonts, altars, monasteries, ranches, roads.

Internal dissent, political rivalry, and violent opposition to the centralized power of a bishop all characterized the corporations of Christianization in the province. As the friar-encomendero-pipiltin faction dug in its heels against diocesan power, Michoacán's Spanish residents mocked attempts at imposing Catholic orthodoxy and social piety. The chapter that follows looks at the earliest efforts to impose inquisitional authority in Michoacán. They were not well received.

CHAPTER 3

"I SHIT ON YOU, SIR"; OR, A RATHER
UNORTHODOX LOT OF CATHOLICS WHO
DIDN'T FEAR THE INQUISITION

Setting: Michoacán countryside
Years: 1556–1571

Pedro Muñoz was having a bad day. It was 8 December 1569, and representatives of Michoacán's newly convoked Inquisition arrived at his ranch in Irapuato. As a wealthy rancher, Muñoz normally spent his days making money by selling livestock and produce, bossing around indigenous workers, screwing indigenous girls, drinking wine, and smoking cigars. There were no sensitivity trainings or anger-management classes. But there was an Inquisition, and the organized church was not pleased—not pleased at all—when people with money refused to pay the tithe. On the day in question, Muñoz was apparently truant in his tithe payments for 1558, 1563, and 1567. The bishop's agents were determined to collect them. The official dispatched for the job, Pero Gómez de Ávila, went to Irapuato with a writ of excommunication in hand should the encomendero refuse to pay up. When Muñoz told the official that he had no intention of doing so, Gómez served him with the excommunication order. Then Muñoz threatened to shit on it.[1]

The tithe represented a key component of religious politics, and the attempt to excommunicate Muñoz did not exactly work out. The Church had a tenuous ability to command social and economic obedience. Threatening to shit on a legal order does not, after all, show deference. All Catholics were expected to provide the tithe, and rural peoples especially loathed this responsibility. The threat of excommunication was not enough to bring Spanish residents to heel; even the Inquisition had limited success in punishing errant Catholics for mocking the power of the Church. Surely Muñoz, like many other Spanish landowners, often did pay the tithe, but such positive actions went unrecorded in legal documentation. A bad crop, a drought, or an epidemic had the potential to destroy rural economies. The recurrence of these natural disasters in Michoacán made tithing among the most hated aspects of official Catholicism.[2] Spaniards begrudged the Church's power

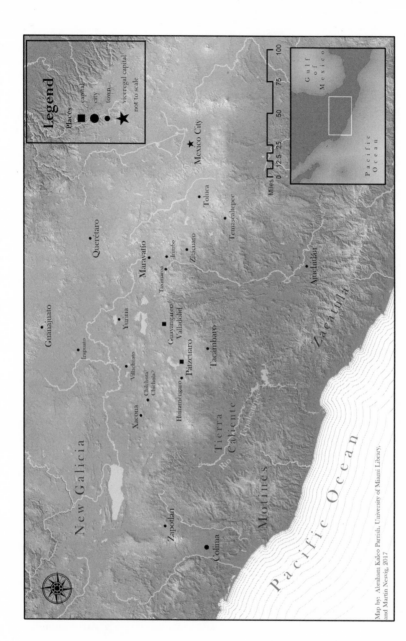

MAP 3.1. Broader Michoacán Province, by Abraham Kaleo Parrish and Martin Nesvig.

to make personal demands on their property and livelihood, but they viewed this demand as even worse when the institution threatened their souls to collect it. Blasphemy was never particularly ideological, but rather practical and economic, employed as a political device to express the contempt that many ranchers, encomenderos, and Spanish settlers reserved for the Church as an institution.[3]

Individuals such as Muñoz acted out their antipathies toward the tithe or the Inquisition in the broader context of a weak organ of religious control. Refusal to obey the Church and the Inquisition—understood as arms of the royal state—and the concomitant lack of effective punishment for such disobedience show that the state-church alliance was weak in Michoacán. Spanish landowners viewed attempts by Catholic priests to regulate their behavior with cool suspicion or blatant hostility. Similarly, the spectacularly vicious political feuds between friars and the diocesan Church consumed the Christianization program. Little energy remained for ideological repression.

The motor of Catholic social discipline, the Inquisition, sputtered from the beginning in Michoacán. Catholic law allowed for a variety of local courts. A bishop oversaw a general ecclesiastical court, which claimed jurisdiction over issues concerning marriage, the tithe, clerical behavior, and doctrine. Traditional Catholic law stipulated that, in the absence of a delegated inquisitor, bishops held the right to appoint an inquisitor or act himself as the inquisitor.[4] Vasco de Quiroga never exercised this legal prerogative. Perhaps he was too busy arranging monastery arson and suing the Augustinians. He was absent from the diocese for nearly a decade, and upon his return the cathedral project and political bickering consumed his energy. Nevertheless, a bishop had the right to invoke an Inquisition to prosecute doctrinal crimes such as heresy, blasphemy, sorcery, and sacrilege.

The Inquisition was supposed to be an ideological arm of the Spanish imperial order. Yet, as it played out on the ground in Michoacán, the court inspired little dread. The Inquisition was institutionally weak and culturally ridiculed. The lack of implementation of a formal inquisitional office in Michoacán before 1568 surely set the tone for religious repression of any sort in the region. It was not until 1568 that a diocesan judge in Michoacán adopted the title of inquisitor.[5] Whereas other provinces of New Spain, such as Oaxaca, had vigorous Inquisitions overseen by bishops, Michoacán's constant factional battles occupied center stage of ecclesiastical politics for decades. Indeed, the first inquisitional cases in Michoacán, in 1536, 1537, and 1544, came from external courts—the diocese of Mexico and a royal inspection. The first doctrinal cases ordered by Michoacán's diocese did not begin until 1556. From 1562 to 1568, diocesan prosecutors oversaw eighteen cases.[6] Between 1569 and 1571, they prosecuted another seventeen.[7] The diocesan Inquisition of Oaxaca, by comparison, was fully functional by 1538 and especially active in the 1550s and 1560s, prosecuting forty-eight cases between 1555 and 1564.[8] The contrast highlights the organizational pitfalls of Michoacán's inquisitional power.

Despite the loose organization of the diocesan Inquisition in Michoacán, the risks one took in openly mocking it were clear. Inquisitors were legally empowered to impose a wide range of punishments for a variety of sin-crimes. The most serious offense was heresy, which was the open rejection of an established article of Catholic doctrine, such as the validity of the sacraments, the existence of the Trinity, or the truth of the virgin birth of Christ. Mockery of religious symbols or saints was blasphemy and could mean criminal conviction. Denigration of sacred sites and images (sacrilege), bigamy, and soliciting sexual favors in the confessional also could be punished. Theoretically, the inquisitors could prosecute sorcery, but in Michoacán they rarely did. The most severe penalties ranged from the death sentence (rarely imposed in Mexico) to forced servitude in the royal galleys. The most common sentences were cash fines, public humiliation, whipping, fasting, and temporary civic death through exile.[9] The possibility of receiving any of these sentences for a conviction was quite real. Yet mockery of inquisitional authority was still common in Michoacán.

Spanish settlers in Michoacán had become accustomed to the juridical and geographic isolation of the region. The outsized social and economic power of Spanish landowners also lent them a sense of impunity. Landowners viewed the clergy with disdain even if they possessed abstract respect for pope and king or the mass. But expressions of contempt for the rule of Catholic law were not limited to the laity; the clergy, too, thumbed its nose at oversight. Some parish priests, when faced with discipline, called on armed guards to assault court officials. Even as the laity demonstrated its propensity to debauchery in a region with sparse forms of social control, the decentralized nature of power in the region seduced agents of that social control—the clergy.

In Michoacán, inquisitional prosecution was uniformly directed at Spaniards and some mestizos. In 1569, indigenous peoples were excluded from inquisitional oversight throughout the Americas, but even before that time, although it is not clear why, diocesan inquisitors refrained from prosecuting indigenous peoples in Michoacán.[10] This lack of inquisitional oversight over indigenous peoples may suggest that the disciplining courts were inner-looking and banal, petty and factional. It may also reflect a general contempt on the part of the polity for indigenous ritual; apparently, rather than making it a priority, the diocese relegated its suppression to the missionaries as particular to their activities.

The fact that rebukes of inquisitional power were so common reveals disdain for the Inquisition rather than fear among the local Spanish population; the court was incapable of imposing widespread penalties for disobedience. Far from imposing theological or cultural uniformity, the diocese spent its time battling the obstreperous local population. Try, try as they might, diocesan inquisitional agents simply could not control Michoacán's Spanish laity, as the laity kept threatening to shit on them.

AN INQUISITION THAT NEEDED ITS OWN INQUISITORS

Inquisitional attempts at social discipline in Michoacán were laughable, often in a quite literal sense—local residents actually did laugh at inquisitional deputies. And indeed, there is evidence of only four inquisitional cases being tried in Michoacán between 1522 and 1555. The nature of the heterodoxy involved in these cases and the impetus to control it are telling. Mexico's bishop from 1530 to 1548, Juan de Zumárraga, acted as apostolic inquisitor between 1536 and 1541, prosecuting cases largely from central Mexico. The diocese of Mexico encompassed Michoacán in 1536, Zumárraga's first year as inquisitor.[11] In that year, Zumárraga prosecuted an indigenous man in Michoacán who claimed that he was a god and had come from heaven—though the trial of this case is not extant, and we only have the cover sheet.[12] The case is in line with other high-profile prosecutions of indigenous caciques by Zumárraga, such as the prosecution of Andrés Mixcoatl, in 1537, and Don Carlos de Texcoco, in 1539. Zumárraga's overly zealous prosecution of caciques led the Crown to strip him of inquisitional authority in 1541.[13] But in Michoacán such cases—which, when they did occur, typically involved extirpation and anti-idolatry efforts—were only loosely organized, and not by the bishop but by friar-missionaries.

In this early period Bishop Zumárraga also pursued at least two cases against Spanish settlers in Michoacán, but no organized, systematic campaign ever materialized. One of these cases, in 1537, concerned Gonzalo Gómez, the first Spanish resident of Guayangareo.[14] His political enemies had compiled a wide range of probably falsified claims against him, seeking to displace him and seize his land assets.[15] Gómez and encomendero Juan Infante were such bitter rivals that Gómez admitted to having hired an assassin to try to kill Infante.[16] The assassination attempt failed. But his case caught the attention of Zumárraga, who accused Gómez of crimes ranging from blasphemy to being a crypto-Jew. The inquisitor-bishop found it especially scandalous that the settler hung a crucifix on his patio, where he dried his chiles. In Zumárraga's mind the physical proximity of a crucifix to domestic items, in this case indigenous Mesoamerican food stuffs, demonstrated lack of respect for the figure of the crucified Christ. Gómez nevertheless received only a scolding from the bishop.[17] In the other inquisitional case from those years, in 1538, Zumárraga commissioned a judge, Juan Ruiz de Olvera, to prosecute a Spanish woman named Beatriz González for bigamy in remote Zacatula.[18] The court summoned her to Mexico City for the trial, convicted her, and sentenced her to make a pilgrimage to Nuestra Señora de los Remedios.

Inquisitional repression in Michoacán in its first two decades under Spanish rule was therefore hardly a coordinated assault. For example, in 1544, the Crown sent a royal inspector, Tello de Sandoval, to New Spain. He had inquisitional authority, but he undertook only a limited caseload in that capacity—although he did prosecute the guardian of Zapotlan's Franciscan church, the friar Arnaldo de Basancio, in 1544 for preaching against the most recent Bull of the Holy Crusade, which Basancio had said was pointless.[19]

The prosecution of Basancio foreshadowed things to come on many levels. Basancio had referred to the Bull of the Crusade as a mockery of the Holy Crusade itself.[20] Bulls of the Crusade, issued by the pope, acted as fundraisers: they authorized the sale of indulgences to support what was deemed a "just war"—at this time, a war focusing on the Moors, or North African Muslims. In exchange for making a donation, to fund the wars in North Africa, the donor received plenary indulgence and remission from purgatory according to the amount donated. The indulgences that Johann Tetzel had peddled in German lands had received similar criticism, especially by Martin Luther. So any criticism of the Bulls of the Holy Crusade was tinged by association with Lutheranism.

The royal treasurer, Rodrigo de Albornoz, oversaw this particular Bull of the Holy Crusade in Mexico in late 1543 or 1544. As part of this effort, he sent two men, Alonso Carrillo and Jorge Castillo, to Colima to sell indulgences. They, in turn, employed a parish priest, Francisco Sandoval, to preach a sermon in Colima supporting the bull and announcing the indulgences. The three men then traveled up to Zapotlan, an almost exclusively indigenous pueblo, to call on the Franciscan guardian, Basancio, to announce the bull and the indulgence opportunity in town. Basancio refused to preach a sermon promoting the bull; instead, he openly mocked the bull and encouraged his indigenous charges to boycott the sale. In fact, if Sandoval's testimony is accurate, Basancio was essentially an unreconstructed Lutheran who succeeded in preventing the sale of the indulgences in Zapotlan.[21] The case does not appear to have been adjudicated.

A TENTATIVE INQUISITION

Michoacán's diocesan court remained largely inactive in terms of doctrinal prosecution throughout the 1550s, consumed as it was in legal battles with the friars.[22] Quiroga never appointed an inquisitor. While the bishop was in Spain, provisor Juan Zurnero completed three extant cases of ecclesiastical justice between 1556 and 1559.[23] All three of Zurnero's targets were Spanish men, and they were prosecuted for broadly defined "social" crimes, such as bigamy; in fact, the scarcity of doctrinal regulation in the period is remarkable.[24] A 1555 investigation against a Spanish resident of Colima, Juan Ruiz, for vaguely polytheistic beliefs, for example, required more than a year to be heard. The Church could not even bring such cases to trial unless the diocesan prosecutor traveled the lengthy journey to the southwest to prosecute it, and in Ruiz's case, that was not until January 1557.[25]

During the spectacular showdown between Quiroga and the Augustinians between 1554 and 1561, the diocesan court ground to a near standstill in regulating Catholic doctrine. In 1561, a cathedral canon, Jerónimo Rodríguez, became the provisor and vicar general of the diocese. He exercised this office for several years, yet only nine cases of ecclesiastical justice between 1561 and 1565 on his watch are extant.[26] His investigations targeted Spanish men who expressed suspicious disregard for conservative ideas, but he uncovered little actual Lutheranism or other heresies. For example, in September 1563, the judge condemned a student of the San Nicolás seminary for vaguely Lutheran-sounding statements asserting that faith was more important than good works. The student, Atanasio de Solís, repented and received a mild sentence of seven Fridays of fasting.[27]

THE LAND OF NO PRIESTS

After Quiroga's death in March 1565, the diocese remained without a bishop for nearly three years. During this period it became evident that the Church had little everyday control over the celebration of the mass in remote towns, as most of them lacked a parish priest. Catholic clergy possessed a monopoly on sacraments, including the celebration of the mass, hearing confession, and sanctifying marriage. The Lutheran assault on confession and other Catholic sacraments challenged this monopoly, and inquisitors and bishops throughout the Spanish world saw Lutheranism as among the worst menaces of the sixteenth century.[28]

In the spring of that year, following Quiroga's death, a traveling huckster in eastern Michoacán impersonated a priest in several towns. When witnesses came before the diocesan court, they suggested they did not know or care whether the man was a priest. Worse, in the view of the court, was the collusion of Spanish residents in indigenous towns in the fraud that had been committed. Diocesan officials were incensed. Other inquisitional cases against such impersonation had taken place in New Spain, and the precedent for severe punishment was set. In Oaxaca in 1555, for example, the local inquisitor convicted two men for impersonating priests and celebrating the mass, sentencing them to public whippings in the towns where they had perpetrated their crimes as well as to perpetual exile from Oaxaca.[29]

That same spring, Provisor Rodríguez investigated charges that a mestizo named Alonso de Montúfar (not to be confused with the archbishop of the same name) had celebrated mass, heard confessions, and administered the sacrament of marriage in numerous indigenous towns from Pátzcuaro to the eastern end of the province near Maravatío. Montúfar was the servant of the priest Juan de Balderas.[30] According to his confession, he was a mestizo who had been raised in the Temascaltepec mines in the southwestern part of the diocese of Mexico. In this predominantly Nahua region, Montúfar probably grew up speaking Spanish as well as the dominant Nahuatl, but may have understood Matlatzinca.[31] Montúfar said he was a baptized Catholic, but he held no particular office.

The case revealed the absence of priests in the region. The provisor had Montúfar arrested on 17 July 1565, after he learned that Montúfar had celebrated a false mass in Huiramángaro (just west of Pátzcuaro) the preceding Sunday.[32] He asked Montúfar if he had ever dressed himself as a priest, and if so, how many times. The defendant admitted that he had done so two weeks earlier—he later confessed to numerous other such instances—when he had come from Mexico City on his way to Pátzcuaro on the main road, which went through the Maravatío-Taximaroa area. Eastern Michoacán is a mountainous region of mixed ethnicities, including Nahuas, Matlatzincas, and Otomíes. Of varying altitudes, it had several large sugar mills (*ingenios*) in its warmer regions, such as Taximaroa and Zitácuaro. These mills in fact rivaled those of Tacámbaro and Tingambato, in the regions heading toward the tierra caliente.[33] The communities where Montúfar held masses were populous enough that he had found large and willing audiences. The presence of the Church in this region was tenuous at best. The Franciscans had established a church in Taximaroa in 1555, but there is no indication of any missionary activity. Maravatío had no missionaries and functioned as a diocesan *doctrina* (protoparish) in the 1560s.[34]

Montúfar's confession reads like an improbable tale of a wandering man in a region abandoned by Catholicism. When he went to Irimbo, an Otomí pueblo subject to Taximaroa, for example, he met a priest named Pedro Yáñez who gave him wine and wafers for the mass. He had told Yáñez that he would deliver the Eucharistic items to Don Diego Pérez Gordillo y Negrón, the arsonist who was still the cathedral choirmaster. Montúfar claimed that Gordillo was on his way to meet Yáñez. But instead of delivering the elements of Communion to Gordillo, Montúfar traveled north and performed a mass in the church of Maravatío before dozens of indigenous residents. At the conclusion of the mass he told the indigenous residents that if they so desired, he would hear their confessions. As many as twenty individuals received absolution from Montúfar.[35]

How did Montúfar understand their confessions and how did he communicate with them? The region was ethno-linguistically complex. For example, people in Taximaroa spoke both Purépecha and Otomí. Nearby Maravatío was probably monolingual, using Purépucha. To the south, in Zitácuaro and Tuzantla, people spoke Nahuatl and Purépucha. Matlatzinca speakers were also common through-out the region.[36] Nahuatl, however, was beginning to replace Purépucha in eastern Michoacán. Montúfar may have spoken Nahuatl, which he probably learned as a child. Or he may have used Purépucha, which was traditional to Maravatío. The testimonies do not say.

It is also unclear how Montúfar knew how to celebrate the mass. He had been the servant of a priest, so perhaps he had learned by observation. Even if he had memorized the liturgical order of the mass, however, this does not explain how he could have known the Latin well enough. Perhaps he celebrated the masses in Nahuatl or Purépecha instead, and just mumbled and fumbled his way through the entire exercise. In regions with extremely low priest-to-resident ratios, such as colonial Guatemala, indigenous peoples viewed priests not as people to admin-ister ordinary, daily pastoral functions, but as privileged experts who could cele-brate specific ritual acts.[37] Rural Michoacán may have been similar, and indigenous residents may have imbibed Catholicism without caring for the theological dis-tinction between ordained priest and laity.

Montúfar admitted that he had performed these rites in other towns as well. On Friday, 13 July, for example, Montúfar went to Curunéndaro, and on Satur-day the 14th he celebrated a requiem mass with the necessary vestments. He also heard the confessions of some fifty indigenous residents. On those two days, he administered the Eucharist to more than one hundred residents and married two indigenous couples.

Montúfar's activity in Huiramángaro on 15 July relied on the collusion of Span-ish residents—and of the indigenous governor (*indio principal*) of the town. Ac-cording to the sworn statement of the governor as well as of the town's fiscal (or church steward), Pedro Tzinzun, Montúfar had arrived early that morning and sent some residents to fetch some wine for the Eucharist from Pátzcuaro, twelve miles to the east. Montúfar then celebrated mass, confessed more than 140 in-digenous residents, and married three couples. Other confessions confirm these activities. Spaniards Juan Martínez and Juan de Solís (perhaps related to the en-comendero of the same name) had traveled to Huiramángaro on that date, and the provisor later deposed them before the court. Both men testified that they had found Montúfar in the sacristy, confessing an indigenous woman. The Spaniards and Montúfar must have understood Purépecha, as the town was monolingually Purépecha. Both the Spaniards told the inquisitor that they knew Montúfar per-sonally. On the day they found him in the sacristy, they had told Montúfar that the provisor was looking to arrest him, and that he would do well to flee the town be-fore the diocesan agents caught him.[38]

Martínez lent Montúfar his horse so that he could make an escape, and Montú-far departed. Tzinzun had seen them talking, and on seeing Montúfar leave in such haste, asked the two men what they had been doing "with that priest." Martínez responded with a racialized insult, telling him that the so-called priest was no priest at all but a mere mestizo. Provisor Rodríguez nevertheless jailed Martínez for aiding Montúfar and, when receiving his confession, reprimanded him for not apprehending Montúfar as an enemy of the Church. Martínez hemmed and hawed, saying that it was not his job to arrest him, since he was not a "competent authority" (*juez competente*) for the case. He was clearly dissembling—he and Solís both knew when they saw Montúfar in the sacristy that he was breaking ecclesiastical laws, and they had nevertheless even aided his escape. The provisor later condemned Martínez for aiding in sacrilege and fined him: he had to purchase eight pounds of wax for a local church. Despite all of this, there was still a clear network of support for Montúfar: as Montúfar and Martínez awaited sentencing, a priest named Diego López Fuenllana smuggled knives into the jail to help them escape.

Montúfar's motives are unclear. He probably charged residents for the sacrament of marriage, and he may have taken up a collection during the offering portion of the mass. But the testimonies do not mention this. Resident curates, in theory, received salaries, which the diocese paid, but they also collected fees for endowed masses, baptisms, and marriages. Montúfar may have played on these traditional functions in order to charge indigenous communities for his services.

The Montúfar case shows that clerical presence in Michoacán remained tenuous, and often nonexistent, in many towns—even four decades after contact. Indigenous residents may have seen Montúfar's activities as a bargain, since they never saw an ordained priest. Parish priests were reluctant to travel to remote indigenous parishes, whether for lack of linguistic skill or out of mere sloth. This general failure to attend to remote indigenous towns was one of the failures of the Michoacán church. A reforming bishop, Ramírez de Prado, remarked in his 1641 inspection that—more than a century after the presumed spiritual conquest—parish priests rarely spoke indigenous languages and seldom resided in their appointed beneficed towns.[39] Montúfar may have fulfilled a social purpose by offering mass, legitimizing marriages, and hearing confessions. It is clear from the testimonies that he received considerable local support for his actions.

Montúfar's imprisonment was brief, but his sentence was severe. Diocesan court cases tended to move swiftly once an accused was apprehended. In Montúfar's case, the judge had already amassed several witness statements by the time the case was heard; Montúfar confessed immediately, and on the same day, 19 July, received a guilty verdict and his sentence. In contrast to the people living in the local communities, Rodríguez considered Montúfar's activities gravely offensive. It must have also been humiliating for diocesan officials to discover how the complete absence of clergy in the region was playing out. The provisor ordered that on the first feast day following the trial, the civil officials of Michoacán were to remove

Montúfar from the ecclesiastical prison in Pátzcuaro and place him on a horse, "stripped from the waist up, with a rope around his neck with his hands tied and a peaked crown on his head," adding, "They are to give him two hundred lashes in public. A public crier is to announce his crime to the populace and after he is whipped he is to be placed at the entrance to the church where he is to remain until the mass concludes."[40] The provisor also sentenced Montúfar to have the same sentence, with one hundred or two hundred lashes, carried out in each town where he had committed the same crimes. Finally, the provisor sentenced Montúfar to four years as a slave in the royal galleys. Presumably, if he survived this misery, he was then to spend ten years as a kitchen servant in a monastery.[41] The punishment was designed to remind the laity of the seriousness of Catholic order and the control of the sacraments by the clergy. Yet the activities show that local residents were indifferent to rules about the ordination of priests. And the province, at the local level, continued to lack actual priests.

VIOLENCE AND FACTIONALISM

The see remained without a bishop for three years, and the inertia of political foot-dragging went on. Ecclesiastical justice halted, its court in effect suspended. It was another reprieve for the laity from oversight. The arrival of the newly consecrated bishop, Antonio Ruiz de Morales y Molina, in February 1568 signaled a shift in the efforts of the diocesan loyalists to exert inquisitional control. These activities were directed against their rivals. The main issues were blasphemy and generalized disobedience. Although a massive increase in inquisitional investigation was never forthcoming, the new bishop did appear to make a conscious decision to assert a diocesan office of Inquisition.

One of the first such cases came in March 1568, when Provisor Rodríguez began investigating claims that many Spaniards had walked out of the Franciscan church in Pátzcuaro one Sunday in the middle of mass, publicly snubbing the officiating priest, the friar Pedro de Aciénaga. According to witness statements, on 28 March, when the friar ascended the pulpit to preach the sermon, the Spaniards had left; then they went to hear mass at the indigenous church (*capilla de indios*).[42] Their motives remain unclear—perhaps they simply did not like the friar or the message of his sermon. There is little information about Aciénaga himself.

The provisor had attended the same mass, and he viewed the incident as a public scandal. He finished listening to the sermon and marched across town to the indigenous church to reprimand the Spaniards. He ordered the chapel's curate, Joachim Rodríguez, to tell the Spaniards not to leave the church in such a way again. If it happened again, there would be legal hell to pay: he would charge them with sacrilege as an inquisitional crime. The curate obeyed the provisor and informed a number of Spanish citizens and civil authorities of the provisor's threat, especially the men who had walked out of church, who apparently included Roque de León (the city's bailiff, or *alguacil mayor*), Hernando Ortega, Diego Madaleno, Francisco Madaleno, Francisco Roque the younger (*el moço*), Juan Bautista, Josepe Carrión, and Doña Ysabel de Arébalo. The curate also warned Luis de Montesinos, a fiscal (presumably the indigenous steward of the church), about the importance of obeying the inquisitional agent's instructions. The curate explained that the Spaniards had disparaged the word of God and held the faith in contempt.

The Spaniards explained that they had only held the word of a priest in contempt. The provisor was not amused. He had them hauled before him in court within days. Perhaps the threat of criminal condemnation or jail time would bring them to heel. The provisor's gambit failed. According to the judge, the Spaniards mocked him. For example, the city bailiff, Roque de León, said that he was a Christian, just like the provisor, but that the provisor could not make him hear a sermon by force. León said that the Spaniards who had left the church "were not a bunch of Indians he can order around."[43] Hernando Ortega said something similar, telling the judge that they were not "a bunch of mining coolies" to order around.[44] Francisco Madaleno said that nobody could force him to listen to a sermon, and that he would come and go as he pleased, thank you very much.[45]

The verbal insults were a prelude. When Provisor Rodríguez served them with subpoenas, they assaulted him physically, beating him with their staffs. This action could not stand in decent Catholic society, so the judge prosecuted several Spaniards for sacrilege. Yet the court failed to extract any lasting penalty. The provisor convicted the accused of crimes against the faith, but the sentences amounted to a slap on the wrist. Several of the Spaniards received simple fines, equivalent to two or three weeks of wages: for Ortega, it was twelve pesos; for Diego Madalena, Francisco Madalena, and Francisco Roque, eight pesos each, and for Juan Bautista, four pesos.[46] It is unclear whether Arébalo or the indigenous fiscal was convicted or sentenced. The fines were unwelcome, irritating but unsubstantial. There was no exile, no public lashing, no galley servitude, even though they had openly insulted and assaulted the diocese's prosecutor.

Priests defied the diocesan court as well. In fact, priests were even more violent than the bailiff and his friends. Late in 1568, Provisor Rodríguez ordered the arrest of Alonso de Ávila, the curate and vicar of Chichola, a small town on the north-central Tarascan plateau. The original charges against Ávila were not specified in the ensuing trial.[47] A year passed before any arrest warrant was issued, and when the court did order Ávila's arrest, things did not go well for the church officials. On 11 November 1569, the diocesan prosecutor, Francisco Hidalgo de la Fuente, recounted the fracas in a letter to Rodríguez. When De la Fuente went to arrest Ávila, the priest refused to accept the legality of the warrant and physically resisted the arrest—with armed assistance. Ávila's armed retinue included another priest, Cristóbal Muñoz; a layman, Lázaro de Ávila; a black man named Gaspar; and a black slave of Muñoz's named Juan.[48]

None of the witnesses agreed about the order of events, but one thing was clear: the priest's private guard tried to murder the court representative. When De la Fuente arrested Ávila, the armed men hooted at the official, calling him a "knavish traitor" and demanding that they release him.[49] When it became apparent that the official had no intention of releasing Ávila, Lázaro de Ávila (presumably a relative of the priest) assaulted the official. De la Fuente explained, "They launched a thrust of the lance and wounded me in the face on the left side. It cut me through the skin and the flesh and I lost a lot of blood. They charged at me with their lances and staffs and pulled me down from my horse. They threw me to the ground. . . . Had it not been for the grace of God they would have killed me."[50] Witnesses claimed that Alonso de Ávila actually struck the prosecutor in the face, drawing blood.[51] At some point, one of De la Fuente's men assaulted Muñoz, and in defending Muñoz, Gaspar gouged the judge with a lance.[52]

Insult accompanied literal injury. De la Fuente was on the ground, blows and lance cuts raining down. Lázaro de Ávila said to Gaspar, "Kill this thieving, knavish traitor, highway bandit, punk-ass bitch."[53] Muñoz testified in court that they considered De la Fuente a thief and a bandit because he had stolen their haciendas. At last the real reason for their animosity was in the open: the tithe and the onerous demands of the Church were at the heart of the dispute. Alonso de Ávila and his friends, including ranchers and landowners, were willing to assault, to the point of near murder, anyone who attempted to extract money or legal obedience from them.

The diocesan court found several individuals in the case guilty.[54] The penalty was rather severe. The court sentenced Muñoz to a two-month suspension of his office and benefices, which was in itself not especially harsh, though economically painful. But the court also sentenced him to a ten-year exile from the diocese of Michoacán, which would have effectively ended his career in the church in Michoacán. In addition, he was fined twenty pesos. It is unclear what became of Muñoz, but his disappearance from archival records suggests that he withered away in anonymous poverty or left Mexico.

TITHE POLITICS

Local residents demonstrated their contempt for diocesan authority in particular concerning the tithe. In 1568, Provisor Rodríguez prosecuted a Spanish rancher named Pablos de Vargas for "certain heresies" regarding his tithe payments. Vargas held several ranches with livestock in Villachuato along the Chichimec frontier, and Bishop Morales had ordered him to pay tithes that were past due. The diocesan court served him with the order while he was in Querétaro, but, before several witnesses, Vargas refused to hear it read. The bishop's messenger read the order to him anyway; Vargas replied that he did not owe even two *maravedíes* (a paltry sum) for the order.[55] His defiance growing, he then said he owed the bishop nothing. He would not pay up even if the bishop threatened excommunication, or if they brought a letter from the archbishop of Mexico. But now he had gone too far: the diocesan officials prosecuted him for disobedience, securing a conviction, and sentenced him to pay sixty pesos. It was a sizable amount, roughly equivalent to the annual salary of a ranch hand.[56]

The case of Pedro Muñoz (he who would shit on a writ of excommunication) is exemplary for its assault on the dignity of diocesan authority. Also known by the title *maese de campo* (field marshal), Muñoz had arrived in New Spain in 1525 and quickly made his fortune, starting with the accumulation of several encomiendas.[57] He was happy to give Nuño de Guzmán and his forces land on his encomiendas as a staging area for the invasion of Michoacán, and Muñoz was one of the principal fulminators against the caltzontzin in 1530.[58] He then diversified his capital and became a merchant in Mexico City. In 1543, the Crown awarded him two estancias (ranches) in the Toluca region.[59] Muñoz was also among the first estancia owners of Guanajuato in 1561, and he appears to have installed himself in Irapuato around 1568, some thirty-five miles south of the mines of Guanajuato.[60] For all we know Muñoz was a typical Spanish Catholic who attended mass sporadically, baptized his children, and usually paid the tithe. He does not appear to have been especially heterodox, but when money was involved, his religion became distinctly secular, given his encomienda and ranch holdings.

By 1568, Michoacán's diocesan officials, primarily cathedral canons like Rodríguez, were running the inquisitional office and adopting the title of inquisitor. The prosecution of anyone who refused to pay the tithe was obviously an expression of self-interest, since cathedral chapter shareholders derived their income from collections of the tithe. Thus Muñoz's apparent refusal to pay the tithe in 1558, 1563, and 1567 brought him to the attention of diocesan officials. Muñoz's behavior had clear political and economic underpinnings. Diocesan inquisitional officials threatened to excommunicate him if he refused to acknowledge the jurisdiction of Michoacán to exact tithes.[61] The diocesan representative announced the threat, and, on hearing the judicial writ, Muñoz replied with this pithy gem: "I shit on the excommunication and he who informs me of it."[62] Once informed of the rancher's insolence, the cathedral treasurer and inquisitor, Don Pedro de Yepes, opened a case of inquisitional justice against him for blasphemy and disobedience. The case file is incomplete, and we are left to speculate on the outcome.[63] It is likely that the diocese had already threatened to sue Muñoz over the tithe. Thus the court followed through with a threat of excommunication and inquisitional prosecution.

The Muñoz case was symptomatic of a contempt for Catholic social order. Muñoz was no outlier; he expressed the visceral hatred that Michoacán's Spanish laity reserved for the two things they detested the most about formal Catholicism: the tithe and the Inquisition. Nor was Muñoz a self-professed Lutheran; he was the most mainstream kind of Spaniard of western Mexico. It was a population that consisted of ranchers, encomenderos, and farmers. And among the members of this group, little was sacred, not even the saints: "I offer little balls of shit for the saints" was a favorite phrase of one rancher in Colima, Pedro de Trejo.[64] He reportedly told his wife that she had "damn well better" call on the saints while he beat her, because he had Satan on his side. Both Muñoz and Trejo expressed a shocking level of disregard for the official Church, even as they were avowed Catholics.

These scatological insults seem extreme, but they were common in blasphemous assaults on unpopular institutions. In rural society, feces are everywhere. Encomenderos and ranchers used corporeal and scatological terms to express their hatred of the stultifying cultural control symbolized by the tithe, forced attendance at mass, the annual confession, and the Inquisition. Such comments constituted a socially taboo way of speaking that was used for maximum effect to express disdain for ecclesiastical officials.[65]

The historical record of these interactions and insults, as recorded by notaries, reveals a vibrant linguistic past in the region. A historian writing on scatological language offered this charming dictum: "farts supplement shit as does living speech to the archive of writing."[66] It is unclear to what extent these Spaniards experienced more deep-seated doubts about priests and sacraments.[67] Perhaps they had been influenced by Martin Luther.[68] Brother Martin had, after all, once said, "I shit on the law of the pope."[69] Sixteenth-century Lutheran propaganda was notoriously scatological, and images of Germans farting on the pope were used to uproarious political effect.[70] In some cases, inquisitional notaries—not exactly known for demurring from controversial language—redacted "offensive" statements as just that. But on most occasions the notaries recorded the offensive words quite happily.

Refusal to pay the tithe, and contempt for threat of excommunication, were blatant assaults on the worldly expression of Catholic authority. It is surprising that Michoacán's diocesan courts could not punish such actions more severely, as such actions assaulted the power of the Church to extract rudimentary obedience. Even Michoacán's principal royal officials refused to pay the tithe. In 1570, when Pedro Díaz Carvajal, the regidor of the city of Michoacán, was excommunicated for refusing to pay the tithe, he told the diocesan prosecutor-inquisitor to go to hell. He also said, "I swear to God that I do not till land in order to pay the tithe."[71] Apparently these were not his only offenses to Catholic dignity. The Inquisition also accused him of having bedded not one but two indigenous women. It was a lurid case: the women in question were Cecilia and her daughter Ana—Carvajal had committed a form of incest. In 1570, two diocesan inquisitors prosecuted the magistrate for blasphemy (and for lechery). The court condemned him as guilty of offenses against the Church and sentenced him to a fine of twelve pesos and four months exile.[72] The sentence is moderate and suggests that attempts to impose harsher penalties could have resulted in violence.

SORCERY AND ACCUSATIONS AGAINST WOMEN

Although Michoacán had no inquisitional trials against indigenous "idolaters" or "dogmatizers," its inquisitional apparatus did pursue some Spaniards, mestizos, and mulatos for holding rites viewed as demonic. In 1562, for example, Provisor Rodríguez prosecuted Isabel de Vera, a woman of mixed but undetermined ethnicity.[73] In this case, Vera, a resident in Guayangareo, was a kind of sorceress who treated broken toes with a potion derived from a stew of sheep heads, onions, milk, and herbs. Witnesses considered her a witch who should be burned. The diocesan court viewed her as suspicious, but not as an actual witch. She received a relatively light sentence—a four-month exile of five leagues (or about twenty miles) from the vicinity of Guayangareo and a fine in an amount covering the costs of the trial.[74]

The prosecution of Isabel de Vera was one of only two inquisitional cases against women in Michoacán in the 1560s. The other case was lodged against a wealthy Spanish woman from the Canaries, Catalina de Peraza, a resident of Guanajuato in 1569. Convicted of sorcery, Peraza was exiled from the diocese for a year and disappeared from the historical record.[75] There are probably several reasons for the relative paucity of cases against women. First, there were very few nonindigenous women in the region, and Michoacán's diocesan court ignored indigenous residents. Women represented less than 20 percent of all Spanish immigrants to the Americas before 1560, and in the 1560s this figure rose to just below 30 percent. Michoacán in that decade probably had fewer than 1,000 Spaniards in total, so it is possible that the entire province had fewer than 300 Spanish women, even accounting for *criolla* (creole, or American-born Spaniards) girls.[76] Nevertheless, such demographic figures do not explain why the population of several hundred Spanish men received such proportionately greater attention from inquisitional judges.

Sporadic inquisitional prosecution of women focused on folk medicine and sorcery. Such a focus could indicate an assumption about the kinds of heterodox behaviors women engaged in, or it could suggest that women in the period were less likely to engage in the kinds of public-honor–related heterodoxies that men were accused of, such as blasphemy and sacrilege. After the installation of a formal tribunal in Mexico City in 1571, a slate of prosecutions of bigamy was common throughout New Spain, and women were often accused of the offense.[77] Curiously enough, in 1575, the Mexico City inquisitors brought a bigamy case against a woman named Ysabel de Vera. It is unclear whether this was the same woman accused of sorcery, though in the 1575 case the woman was identified as a mestiza — she claimed that her mother was a Nahua and her father, a conquistador. She was convicted and given a severe sentence: two hundred lashes in a public auto-de-fé and exile from New Spain for five years.[78] Maybe Spanish women in Michoacán were simply better behaved or more pious than the men, who set the bar low — or high, depending on one's perspective. But such tendencies also suggest that Spanish men in Michoacán used public displays of blasphemy as part of a strategy of asserting power and will, operating in the hypermasculine public culture that had developed in the region.

The court's emphasis on prosecuting cases like sacrilege, blasphemy, and other forms of disregard for clerical authority reflected the diocesan concern for imposing social order. But such prosecutions also reveal underlying contempt for diocesan oversight of people's personal lives. When a new bishop in 1568 intended to pursue an Inquisition, it was rather late in the proverbial game. Michoacán's residents had grown accustomed to having no real inquisitional presence.

THE LIBERTINE INQUISITOR

Although the Spanish laity demonstrated contempt for orthodoxy, agents of orthodoxy in Michoacán appeared to be more interested in personal power than in imposing orthodoxy. Installed as the diocesan judge sometime in 1569, Don Pedro de Yepes acted as inquisitor ordinary of Michoacán until November 1571. In fact, it was Yepes who prosecuted Muñoz, though no sentence in the case is extant. Nothing in his activity suggests theological purity.

Yepes, the man who charged Muñoz with a crime, had become the provisor in 1569; as such, he was the ranking ecclesiastical judge in the province. Born into a wealthy merchant family of Toledo around 1515, Yepes arrived in Mexico between 1535 and 1538, during which time he was ordained.[79] He was Quiroga's representative (*procurador*) in the 1539 lawsuit over Santa Fe, in which the diocese sued the encomendero Juan Infante.[80] Ordained in Michoacán, Yepes was among the first parish priests of Michoacán. His first position was in Jacona in 1544 with a salary of one hundred pesos. Witnesses who attested to Yepes's blood purity in a genealogy in 1555 in Toledo said that he had served as an interpreter of Purépecha and that he was well versed in the language, though we do not have any extant cases which demonstrate his role in that capacity.[81] The genealogy was probably commissioned in order for Yepes to apply for a dignitary position, as in 1555 he was parish priest of Tlazazalca and a canon. He became the cathedral chapter treasurer in 1557, and in 1568 he became the diocese's inquisitor ordinary.[82] He prosecuted at least eighteen cases in his three years as inquisitor.[83] In November 1571, the establishment of the Holy Office in Mexico City nullified his claims to inquisitional power, though he remained diocesan provisor for several years. He died in late 1579 or early 1580.[84]

As inquisitor, Yepes focused his activity on Spaniards for their unseemly statements about saints, religious decorum, or the veracity of purgatory or hell. He prosecuted Martín González, a resident of Guanajuato, in May 1570, for example, for believing that if a man confessed and completed his penance, he would go directly to heaven after death, thus rejecting the existence of purgatory. Yepes sentenced the man to a fine of twelve pesos.[85] In August 1571, Yepes prosecuted and convicted a Spanish settler of Colima, Juan Fernández Lázaro de Ocampo, for telling people that there was no hell. He was condemned to pay a fine of thirty pesos and exiled from Colima for one year.[86]

Yepes had a long career as a pro-Quiroga partisan and supporter of Pátzcuaro as the capital. He assumed the post of parish priest in three towns, Jacona (1544), Yuriria (1545–1548), and Tlazazalca (1553–1555), as part of Quiroga's project of expanding the diocesan clergy.[87] But his salary was hardly enough to justify the vast fortune he amassed. His parish priest salary of 100 pesos a year was a respectable if middling sum.[88] He became a regular canon of the cathedral chapter some time before 1554, a position that would have netted him somewhere between 100 and 150 pesos annually.[89] Thus Yepes had an explicit vested financial interest in the collection of tithes, as cathedral chapter members' salaries were derived from a share of tithe income.

Yepes's financial stake in Pátzcuaro increased in the 1560s. By 1562 he owned various stores in Pátzcuaro, and later he owned mills and rental real estate.[90] In 1565 he became the cathedral treasurer, which increased his financial interest in tithe collection and in the expropriation of lands for the diocese. He may very well have used that position to obtain low-interest loans or to make business deals below the radar. In the 1560s, the diocese averaged about 7,700 pesos annually in tithes, and presumably much of this was deposited as cash assets of the diocese after the division of salaries. Yepes's salary was unlikely to have been much higher than 200 pesos annually, though he surely made money from officiating at masses, burials, and weddings, if he was so inclined.[91] Later, in March 1568, he sold "some houses," eight stores, and three mills in Pátzcuaro for 1,044 pesos.[92] His interest in keeping the diocesan capital in Pátzcuaro grew ever larger.

Most of the members of the cathedral chapter seem to have viewed Michoacán as a kind of hellish provincial outpost. One canon left for Mexico City soon after his appointment to the region and never returned, but collected his salary for at least eight years. He was not alone: many canons for the region declined to live there. By all accounts only three cathedral chapter members were present to attend chapter meetings in the 1560s, including Yepes, who was the treasurer. The dean, Diego Rodríguez, was away for more than three years but continued to collect his salary. The choirmaster, Gordillo, was the curate of Asuchitlan. One canon, Antonio de Ayala, and the shareholder (*racionero*) Alonso Pasillas accompanied Bishop Morales on his general inspection (*visita*) of the diocese. The former provisor and maestrescuela, Juan Zurnero, collected his salary from Spain. The remaining canons, possibly four or five of them, were mysteriously absent as well.[93]

Yepes, by contrast, was a loyal citizen of Pátzcuaro, and he benefited from the absence of his colleagues. His will, drawn up in the late 1570s, portrays a wealthy man. It registered ownership of several mills—expensive investments that probably paid well. He endowed no fewer than nine hundred masses to be celebrated for his soul, and another three hundred for the souls in purgatory and his family members. Celebrating those masses, according to the going rates at the time, would have cost thousands of pesos. Yepes also donated 700 pesos outright toward the building fund for the cathedral church of Pátzcuaro, and he donated various mills to the Colegio de San Nicolás.[94] This was a will of a devoted partisan of the diocesan structure and the cathedral building project.

Yepes's will also included suggestive details about his personal life. In addition to his mills and considerable cash assets, Yepes noted ownership of three slaves. Two were adults: a black man, Juan, and a black woman, Juana. He noted the slaves as assets to be sold as his property after his death. But the will also noted a two-and-a-half-year-old mulata girl, Ursulila, the daughter of Juana. Yepes explained that Ursulila lived in his house and had been raised by him. By definition, Ursulila's father was a Spanish man. Yepes's will stipulated that Ursulila was to be manumitted on his death.

The subtext is all too clear: Ursulila was most likely his daughter. Such an arrangement was hardly unusual; priests often had amorous relationships with their domestic servants or slaves. If Ursulila was not Yepes's daughter, it would mean that Yepes had taken in the daughter of a different Spanish man who had impregnated Juana. In any case, we have the inquisitor of Michoacán bowing to sexual custom: the recognition of an illegitimate daughter (*hija natural*) as either his own daughter or a proxy daughter, to be freed on his death, presumably as a nod to his extended clan.

As a wealthy man, Yepes had every reason in the world to keep the capital of Michoacán in Pátzcuaro. He remained entrenched in the control of the cathedral chapter—a wealthy and influential corporation. But his status took a blow when the diocese lost control over the inquisitional office in November 1571. Between 1569 and 1571, the Crown had reformed its imperial system, and in so doing it had created two individual Inquisitions—one in Lima and one in Mexico City. On 4 November 1571, the newly installed inquisitor general of Mexico, Pedro Moya de Contreras, took office.[95] His arrival in Mexico City was well known (he had been officially nominated in 1569), and diocesan authorities throughout New Spain were compelled to turn their pending cases of inquisitional justice over to the new court's authority. The new inquisitor general also quickly began to appoint local inquisitional deputies in the viceregal provincial cities.

Yepes complied with the orders, but one of his very first letters to the new inquisitor general revealed a, shall we say, embarrassing situation. Prisoners were escaping from Michoacán's ecclesiastical jail—probably with armed support, as had been the case with the mestizo Montúfar. Yepes dispatched a letter and summary of the history of Michoacán's diocesan Inquisition. The report listed the cases it had taken up from 1563 to 1571. The inquisitor general received the letter and the report into evidence in Mexico City on 27 November 1571.[96] Yepes's letter admitted that his Inquisition had ordered the arrest of a notorious blasphemer, the rancher and poet Pedro de Trejo (he who would offer shit balls for the saints).[97] There was one small problem. Trejo had escaped from the local jail and was nowhere to be found. This is not exactly the kind of letter a new administrative overlord wants to receive. Yet it perfectly sums up the situation in Michoacán. Left to local interests, devoid of metropolitan oversight, Pátzcuaro and Guayangareo partisan players determined who would be imprisoned. For all we know, Trejo had help in evading justice. He was able to avoid arrest for several months, although someone—it is not clear how, as the case file is incomplete—eventually managed to apprehend the blasphemous rancher. By 11 March 1572, Trejo was in the inquisitional jail in Mexico City.[98]

The transfer of power from the diocese to the central Inquisition in Mexico City came in fits and starts. When Maturino Gilberti had accused Gordillo of heresy, for example, Yepes at first oversaw witness statements from various Purépecha men. This took place in September 1571 in Pátzcuaro. Informed of the imminent arrival of the new inquisitor general, Yepes sent the entire case to Mexico City a few weeks later, on 22 October.[99] He probably did so to remove himself from the Gordillo-Gilberti clash. Similarly, a case of ecclesiastical justice against two Spanish men in Guayangareo began in December 1571; Yepes received the depositions in Pátzcuaro, but forwarded the resulting paperwork to the inquisitor in Mexico City on 21 January 1572.[100]

PEDAGOGY OF SATIRE

In the winter of 1571–1572, inquisitional authority vanished in Michoacán in a technical sense. But it never had really exerted any practical power over the laity—or over the clergy, for that matter. In the 1550s and 1560s in Michoacán, smirking dissent and open defiance were the norm, supplanting any pedagogy of fear or hegemony of orthodoxy. Ranchers and Spanish residents openly mocked the social discipline associated with orthodox Catholicism. Local politics was endemically sarcastic and irreverent. Even the agents of Catholicism appear quite cynically libertine, as in the case of Yepes. Catholic political culture in Michoacán grew out of the fecund soil of decades of factional rivalries. The ashes of those rivalries provided the sociological nutrients for the mockery and disdain that characterized popular responses to religious law. By reading court transcripts one is likely to find criminal behavior—an obvious conclusion. But it was the lack of any real negative consequences for defiance of the law that made the Michoacán case fascinating.

We still find depictions of the Inquisition as a force of repression that successfully employed a "pedagogy of fear" in imposing its will.[101] This interpretive model assumes that a persecuting culture harnessed to Catholic social discipline assaulted weaker socioeconomic groups and peoples.[102] Theoretically, Hispanic Inquisitions were supposed to work by harnessing the terror the institution inspired through the use of public, instructive spectacles of repression—autos-de-fé, public humiliation, lashing, parading guilty individuals around town on a donkey, making penitents wear *sanbenitos* (a sackcloth garment) during an auto-de-fé and then hanging those sanbenitos in cathedral churches as permanent reminders of the guilty party's infamy. Spiritual violence was to be instructive, and the Inquisition was to employ the laity to further the broader interests of inquisitional repression. The model may have worked in some contexts, but in Michoacán it did not. There was little widespread fear of inquisitional power in the region. Instead, defiance and mockery of the Inquisition went to the highest levels of political culture—from encomenderos and wealthy ranchers to magistrates and parish priests. The Inquisition in Michoacán faced serious limits to its ability to impose social control. Scholarship has shown such limitations, especially in port cities, in Catalonia and in rural areas throughout the Iberian early modern world.[103] Yet for all the complexity of the social history of the Inquisition, an image of an efficient court of spiritual terror remains, even in some scholarly treatments.[104]

Inquisitors in Mexico had their hands all over the documentation of sixteenth-century Michoacán. I draw the stories told here from that extensive documentation. There is vast correspondence; the inquisitional court prosecuted dozens of cases in Michoacán and investigated hundreds more that never saw an actual judge. The omnipresence of inquisitional documentation telling the story of an institution that wielded little power may appear strange, even unlikely to be correct. But there was a wide gap between discussion and repression: surveillance and recording did not always result in effective repression.[105]

The Inquisition's repressive capability in Michoacán did not map onto the extensiveness of documentation. Instead, the Inquisition in Michoacán offers a paradox. As an institution, it did a remarkably good job of keeping track of people's private lives and spiritual peccadillos, but as an apparatus of repression it was farcical. Rather, the Mexican Inquisition seems to have succeeded primarily in making life easier for modern historians, because of all the documentation it provided, while making life for Spaniards in sixteenth-century Mexico moderately irritating. As the stories of inquisitional investigation in 1550s and 1560s Michoacán make clear, the Mexican Inquisition only intermittently extracted long-term negative consequences against those it deemed a menace to social order. No effective state-church alliance existed in Michoacán to form the bonds that could hold an Inquisition together. This tool of global Catholic hegemony stalled for decades. The next chapter tells the story of the Inquisition that was not there.

THE INQUISITION THAT WASN'T THERE, IN WHICH THE LOCALS REMOVED THE INQUISITION'S AGENT FROM OFFICE AND THE INQUISITION GAVE UP

Setting: the City of Michoacán (i.e., depending on whom you ask, Pátzcuaro or Guayangareo-Valladolid)
Years: 1572–1584

In Michoacán in the 1570s, the eyes of the Inquisition went blind. The Inquisition's first choice for the unenviable job of deputy in the rowdy province was Licenciado Cristóbal de Badillo, a law professor at the University of Mexico. Like Vasco de Quiroga, Badillo had traded his legal career for an ecclesial prebend. It did not turn out well. In the spring of 1573, Badillo arrived in Pátzcuaro in a full cassock with an ostentatious green silk sash and a lawyer's bonnet. The ranchers, plantation owners, and local officials must have thought, "This guy?" Priests were expected to dress modestly in a black cossack, and custom said that ostentation in dress, especially damask or silk, for a priest was immoral, while ecclesiastical law said it was illegal in public. Later, residents and officials assembled a litany of complaints about his lack of regard for decorum.[1]

A series of acts of the judicial absurd ensued. When Badillo arrived, he forced the cathedral chapter to read his commission as inquisitional agent aloud in the cathedral church.[2] It seemed pretentious, even if technically permissible. No one was amused. The cathedral chapter stonewalled him, preventing him from reading the Edict of Faith until October 1574. Reading this document, an enumeration of sins and heresies, was his opening gambit; once that was done, he would be able to start carrying out his inquisitional duties. The fact that the cathedral prevented him from doing so for more than a year was symbolic of the tension and the struggle for preeminence. After Badillo finally read the edict, he spent a year trying to track down a renegade bigamist in the mountains, to no avail.[3] Tensions mounted. Pedro de Yepes, the cathedral treasurer and diocesan provisor, attempted to install his nephew as some kind of inquisitional authority parallel to Badillo.[4] And then, one day in 1575, a convicted criminal showed up in Pátzcuaro

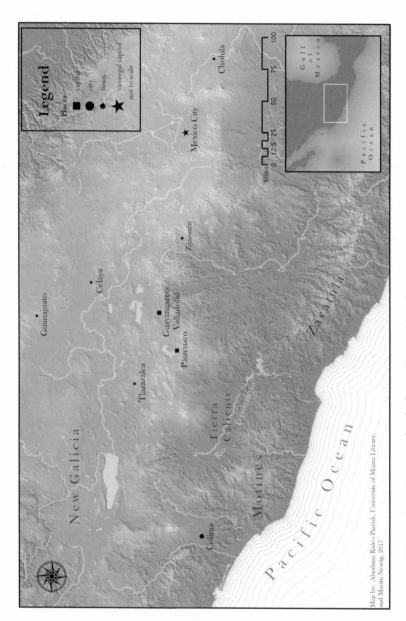

MAP 4.1. Cities in western New Spain, by Abraham Kaleo Parrish and Martin Nesvig.

claiming to be a member of the cathedral corporation. Though he looked like a rancher, he was anything but common. Badillo called him a shameless rogue.

The rancher, a priest named Don Diego de Orduña, slapped Badillo in the face, and then, in what became his signature move, smacked the lawyer's bonnet from his head.[5] Public orchestrations of assault on authority through such semiotics of power went much further than hidden, silent resistance to inquisitional authority. Indeed, denigration of authority scripted public events. The residents of Michoacán proceeded to have Badillo replaced by publicly opposing his authority. They accused him of abuse of power. Ultimately, the inquisitors summoned Badillo and stripped him of his commission as inquisitional deputy. He returned to Michoacán in 1578 to claim his lesser position, archdeacon, and the province returned to its state of perpetual judicial entropy.[6]

These events foreshadowed a much more profound schism in Michoacán and in the provinces of New Spain in general. On one level, the rivalry between Badillo and Orduña was intensely personal; they fought and quarreled and lodged complaints about each other in the inquisitional court. But the spectacular feud took on a deeply symbolic nature, because each man was a kind of synecdoche in the ever-complex saga of local versus global authority. To local interests, Badillo represented urbanism, cosmopolitanism, Mexico City, and the world of university-trained lawyers and clergy. In short, he symbolized external authority. Orduña represented localism, rural life, and the world of the everyman. Though many locals hated or feared Orduña, he symbolized local defiance of external power.

The attempt to install a satellite of the Inquisition in Michoacán failed spectacularly in the 1570s. The rejection of inquisitional oversight highlighted the conflict between urban, juridical conceptions of power and local, rural development of power among residents of Michoacán. Inquisitional law explains how it is supposed to work as a court. From the twelfth and thirteenth centuries, the canon law allowed bishops to regulate doctrine. The papacy began delegating inquisitors in the 1230s, and the Spanish Crown extracted privileges from the papacy to run its own national inquisition in the 1470s. A delegated inquisitor acted as a doctrinal judge.[7] But in Michoacán prior to 1572, no specifically delegated and centralized inquisition existed, and such authority fell to diocesan judges. As inquisitor ordinary from 1568 to 1571, Yepes acted as an arm of the local polity in the form of the diocese. After his claims were voided in November 1571, the Mexican Inquisition held the power to appoint a delegate, which it did in the form of Badillo.

But obviously, the Mexican Inquisition could not be in all places at all times. The Inquisition in Mexico seated a central office in Mexico City that was overseen by one, or sometimes two — and very rarely, three — inquisitors. These inquisitors, in turn, dispatched their deputies to the capital cities of provinces as far south as Honduras and as far north as Zacatecas. But beyond the capital cities, inquisitional agents were scarce in Mexico, and, for all practical purposes, almost nonexistent until the seventeenth century.

Inquisitional deputies were empowered to do most of the same things inquisitors could do. They could summon witnesses, compel appearances, and arrest and interrogate witnesses or prisoners. They could recommend prosecution, though at that point they had to consult with inquisitors. Inquisitors could ask the deputy to carry out some punishments in their stead, but generally, inquisitors in Mexico took one of three courses of action: ignore the investigation, ask for further investigation, or demand that the accused be arrested and delivered to them in Mexico City. On taking office, inquisitional deputies were required to deliver the Edict of Faith, normally in the cathedral church—or in a church or a public square—formally enumerating the crimes regulated by the Inquisition, including heresy, Lutheranism, and Judaism. Those with guilty consciences were told to come before the deputy to cleanse their souls, and then to denounce anyone they knew to be a heretic, a blasphemer, or a religious criminal.[8]

No one in Michoacán really quite knew how this new central Inquisition was supposed to work. Instead, rivalries over inquisitional power became proxy battles for control of the system of spoils, over the salaries of the cathedral chapter, and over preeminence in local society. Local custom subsumed those willing to adapt; others it crushed. In short, the Inquisition was no match for the concentration of everyday local power in Michoacán.

During the 1570s, the capital of Michoacán was in dispute; there was not even agreement as to where the actual "city of Michoacán" lay. Although Yepes and others loyal to Pátzcuaro insisted that their city was the province's capital, the Crown began an official move to Guayangareo, and by 1580, Guayangareo, renamed Valladolid, had been legally recognized as the capital city.[9]

In the space of seven years, 1573 to 1580, political struggles for the control of the capital city, the cathedral chapter, and the inquisitional office turned into a series of broken bones, blood, lawsuits, counter-lawsuits, exiles, and floggings. Although the violence suggests that Michoacán was always embroiled in conflict, this is not the case—there was still a good deal of Eden left in Michoacán. In many small towns and mountain hamlets, ensconced among the membrillos and avocadoes, and in the perpetual spring of Uruapan, many pious and devout Catholics dutifully obeyed the Church's dictates. But inquisitional inspections were not interested in those people. The broader implication is that the very men—magistrates, cathedral dignitaries, even the inquisitional deputy—charged with enforcing Catholic order flouted that social order. This defiance was spectacular for the role-inversion it represented—it was an inquisitional system that defied the Inquisition.

The seeds sown in decades of local hostility to external governance bore fruit.

Plantation interests, encomiendas, absentee cathedral canons, topographic isolation, and generalized distrust of Mexico City and Madrid transformed Michoacán into a region of refuge where localism triumphed. Local repudiation of the doctrinal message of the Inquisition was so thorough that, in 1578, the Inquisition gave up on the province.

MICHOACÁN'S FIRST INQUISITIONAL AGENT

Badillo had a promising start to his career. Born in Seville around 1540, he studied canon law at Spain's most prestigious institution, the University of Salamanca, where he received the basic letrado degree of *bachiller* (a kind of semi-degree— prior to a licenciatura—which indicates a rudimentary education without having completed the full course of study for the licenciate degree) in 1560 or 1561.[10] He was most likely from a middling socioeconomic background; documents only sporadically refer to him as "Don."[11] He probably moved to Mexico City in 1563.[12] He seemed drawn to the possibility of socioeconomic advancement, but by all appearances had no family in Mexico. He studied canon law at the University of Mexico, where members of Mexico's intellectual elite noticed him. Doctor Don Sancho Sánchez de Muñón, the archdiocesan maestrescuela, considered him one of the university's best students. So great were Badillo's academic prospects, in fact, that in 1565 the University of Mexico appointed him to the Chair of Decretum, the second-highest position in the canon law faculty, even though he did not yet have a licenciate degree. According to Diego López de Agurto, a cathedral shareholder of the archdiocese, although Badillo was a brilliant student of the law, he was too poor to pay the expenses for the ceremony awarding him the licenciatura in 1566, and that was enough to keep him from receiving his degree.[13]

In January 1566, Badillo petitioned the Crown, through the Mexico Audiencia, for a position as cathedral dignitary somewhere in New Spain. Anywhere would do, he explained. The court said it would grant the request once a position became available.[14] While awaiting an opening, Badillo became the provisor and vicar general of Yucatán. That was at some point in 1565, and he was reappointed in 1568. Between 1566 and 1570, Badillo also earned the title of presbyter and became the maestrescuela of the Yucatán diocese.[15] He was not an active ecclesiastical judge; there is only one extant case over which he officiated in 1568 in the Yucatán.[16] But there were dark rumors about Badillo's behavior down south. Years later (in 1577) in Michoacán, the notorious choirmaster Don Diego Pérez Gordillo y Negrón said that Badillo had lived in Campeche and had insulted a priest during his time as the provisor. The incident turned violent, and someone had stabbed Badillo twice.[17]

Badillo's career moved ever upward, but his long-term goals of becoming a Mexico City cathedral canon proved difficult to attain. In March 1570, he returned to Mexico City as a licenciado—presumably, he had raised the funds in the meantime to obtain the university degree. He then became a practicing attorney before the Audiencia. Because he was a priest, he sought and received exemptions from the ordinary rules prohibiting a priest from arguing cases in a civil court.[18] Once again he petitioned the Crown, this time specifically for a position as a canon in the archdiocesan cathedral, in the wake of the death of one of its members. Witnesses who vouched for his morals and professional qualifications included high-profile members of the metropolitan elite, and no one mentioned the events in Campeche. Doctor Pedro Farfán, an Audiencia judge and occasional rector of the University of Mexico, said he had seen Badillo's successful licenciatura exam, which he considered a model exposition on the canon law in the Decretals (papal decrees).[19] Badillo did not receive the position he sought; instead, he returned to the university, where he held the Chair of Civil Law of the Institutes in 1570 and 1571.[20] In 1572, he once again held the Chair of the Decretum.[21] The Yucatán cathedral chapter then nominated Badillo as its inquisitional deputy, and in 1572, Badillo appealed to both the inquisitors and the Crown to appoint him as a cathedral dignitary or an inquisitional official.[22] At last Badillo's request was granted. He was made the archdeacon of Michoacán's diocese in 1572.[23] Shortly thereafter, the Inquisition made him its deputy in the same province.[24]

Badillo was unprepared for provincial life. He had spent more than a decade, from 1560 to 1572, in the cloistered world of the university, and he had grown accustomed to academic debate and the philosophy of law. He was a creature of classroom lectures and of the intricate hierarchies and cultural niceties of academia, its ceremonial buffoonery and false collegiality. If testimonies against Badillo five years later can be trusted, he was also remarkably witty and had a distinctly urbane and dramatic sense of humor. He must have been accustomed to the more liberal form of Catholic culture that typified the early modern Hispanic urban world—one of bullfights, theater, poetry contests, street prostitution, taverns, card games, and elaborate dinner parties.[25] He was, in short, utterly ill-equipped for the rough edges and brute honesty of life in a provincial town. His high-minded legalism and worldliness met with the gritty personal interests of the cathedral chapter and lay landholders.

Habituated as he was to a hierarchical world of court and university ritual replete with false flattery and pompous pronouncements, Badillo immediately ran into obstacles as he confronted a more direct, rural population. He arrived in Pátzcuaro sometime in the spring of 1573 with the supercilious formality of a professor and ordered his commission as inquisitional deputy to be read aloud in the cathedral church of Pátzcuaro. The commission was read on 13 July 1573.[26] In August, he heard his first depositions as inquisitional agent. It was a bigamy case.[27] At first, the cathedral canons supported their new colleague. But sometime between July and

October, Badillo arrested an indigenous man as a witness in a case of ecclesiastical justice, setting off an imbroglio with the royal magistrate.[28]

Badillo's actions offended the sensibilities of the alcalde mayor, Licenciado Fernando Caballero, who had set his sights on centralizing his own power. There was surely a personal reason for the feud, as the magistrate had been one of Badillo's mentors. Caballero was alcalde mayor of Michoacán from February 1573 through March 1574.[29] Like Badillo, he had been a lawyer before the royal court in Mexico. In fact, the two had had a mentor-pupil relationship—Caballero had testified on Badillo's behalf in 1566 for the aspiring young law professor's first petition for a cathedral benefice.[30]

When Caballero had first taken office as the alcalde mayor of Michoacán, he had ordered all "vagabond" Purépecha to take up permanent residence, report to a census, and live under a master or someone whom they would serve.[31] In March 1573, he attempted to limit the authority of the alcaldes *ordinarios*, prohibiting them from overseeing lawsuits involving indigenous persons. Caballero's thinly veiled intent was to control the repartimiento labor drafts and tribute payments by pronouncing himself the sole civil judge over the indigenous. The alcalde ordinario Alonso Orejón attempted to block Caballero's ruling, but his challenge to the order did not appear to have any effect.[32]

The patron-client bond between Caballero and Badillo dissolved in the dusty streets of Pátzcuaro. In October 1573, Caballero objected to Badillo's decision to apprehend an indigenous person without explicitly asking for the cooperation of royal justice—in this case, the alcalde mayor. Perhaps Caballero felt personally betrayed—someone he had once protected was now challenging his legal authority. Caballero said Badillo's action was an outrage, and Badillo replied that it was, in fact, not an outrage. Several witnesses claimed that this response angered the alcalde so much that he ordered the provisor, Pedro de Yepes, to arrest this "shameless greedy man who looks like a sad old man."[33] The cathedral canons largely supported Badillo at this stage, noting that he had responded to the calumnious words of the alcalde "with modesty, asking, Is this how you treat the Holy Office's deputies?" However, support from the cathedral chapter proved short-lived.

The inquisitors soon received news of the scuffle. Sufficiently perturbed in their response of 5 November, they ordered Yepes, as provisor of the diocese, to open an investigation.[34] Yepes took witness statements from the cathedral dean, Diego Rodríguez, and from the canons Garci Rodríguez Pardo and Francisco Beteta. Yepes also deposed one other man—Don Diego Pérez Gordillo y Negrón, the architect of the Tlazazalca fire. Incredibly, despite his many criminal convictions, Gordillo was still the diocesan choirmaster.[35] Maybe he had a good voice.

The fact that the alcalde was not put on trial is suggestive of many issues. First, there was immediate resistance from civil authorities to the prerogatives of the Inquisition. Inquisitional officials were exempt from ordinary civil prosecution, and as such, they could not, under normal circumstances, be prosecuted by alcaldes, even for murder. Rather, the Inquisition prosecuted its officials in its own court for such nondoctrinal offenses. Second, royal magistrates viewed men like Badillo as undermining their privileges—even though Badillo was a trained lawyer, he did not care about the customary application of the law. As soon as a juridical breach opened in Michoacán between the alcalde (Caballero) and the Inquisition's man (Badillo), the inquisitors were compelled to issue a special commission, nominating Yepes as the judge in the case. Yepes sided with Caballero, perhaps out of dislike for Badillo.

Badillo then alienated the cathedral chapter, which attempted to unseat him as inquisitional deputy. There is no extant inquisitional documentation for Michoacán between November 1573 and April 1574, which, given the early-modern Hispanic world's prolixity of administrative documentation, implied that nobody was pursuing investigations. On 24 April 1574, the acting members of the cathedral chapter sent a report to the inquisitors in Mexico City. When Badillo had first installed himself as inquisitional deputy in July 1573, he had done so without asking permission from the cathedral chapter to publish his commission in public. It was most irritating. Moreover, they quibbled, the original commission had come from Moya de Contreras, who, a year before, in 1573, had been the sole inquisitor. Because, by 1574, Mexico had two inquisitors (Moya de Contreras and Alonso Fernández Bonilla, the former prosecutor), Michoacán's cathedral chapter demanded that the inquisitors send a new commission ratified by both inquisitors. Legally this was pure nonsense; it was intended to mire Badillo's commission in technicalities and bureaucratic inertia. The cathedral chapter members viewed Badillo's university penchant for declaration as an offense to the more practical world of local politics and a huge pain in the ass. They complained that he had ordered the bull of immunity of inquisitional officials from royal law to be affixed to the doors of all the churches in Michoacán, ostentatiously signing his name to it. The cathedral chapter complained of this excess, asking the inquisitors how to proceed.[36]

Political stonewalling against the implementation of inquisitional authority in Michoacán had begun. But Badillo was determined to move forward against the forces of political practicality. On 18 October 1574, he succeeded in forcing a reading of the Edict of Faith in the Pátzcuaro cathedral.[37] Ultimately, his decision to ignore the rebuke was politically toxic, though it took several years to become fatal. Michoacán's residents began to defy Badillo more openly. For years, for example, the Inquisition in Mexico attempted to apprehend a well-known naval captain, Juan Carrión, who had been living in bigamy somewhere in the mountains near Colima. Despite numerous arrest warrants, the residents said they had no idea who Carrión was. Their collective message was: nothing to see here, inquisitors, move along. Lacking their cooperation, a humiliated Badillo was forced to report to inquisitors, on 10 November 1574, that he had been unable to find any information about the man; alas, he could not locate him.[38] Presumably, Badillo had begun to see the extent to which local interests could resist outsiders who refused to adapt.

ANOTHER TENTATIVE INQUISITION

The Inquisition was off to a rocky start in Michoacán. Placement of its deputy proved a hollow victory. From December 1574 to April 1575, inquisitors heard nothing from the querulous province, however, and they were probably relieved. The lull was rudely broken when they learned that the nephew of Pedro de Yepes, whom they had installed as some kind of inquisitional official, had been arrested by the residential magistrate.

The confusion involved Rodrigo de Yepes. Born around 1550 in Toledo, Rodrigo, the nephew of Pedro de Yepes, made his way to Michoacán sometime in the 1570s. In March 1575, he applied before the inquisitors in Mexico City to become an inquisitional official in Michoacán. The application suggested that he would have accepted any appointment. The Mexican inquisitors appear to have granted him the office of inquisitional notary, though the original application was for a position as comisario (deputy). After he submitted a lengthy genealogy proving his old Christian bona fides and his connection to Pedro de Yepes, the inquisitors Alfonso Fernández de Bonilla and Alfonso Granero Ávalos ratified his appointment as notary of the Inquisition, on 23 March. But there was confusion in Mexico City, as later scribes, presumably archivists of the Inquisition, wrote across the cover sheet: "nominated as deputy [comisario] of the Holy Office."[39] Pedro de Yepes thus installed a loyal family member (his nephew) as an inquisitional agent in a horizontal expansion of his clan's political clout. Another member of the family, Gonzalo de Yepes, became a canon of the cathedral in 1577.[40]

But in Michoacán no one knew whether the inquisitors had commissioned Rodrigo de Yepes as a notary, a deputy, or maybe even a *familiar* (that is, a lay collaborator, a sort of official snitch who surveilled communities and sometimes effected arrests). Others doubted whether he had actually received a position from the inquisitors. The situation was most confusing. He could not produce a physical title, and everyone in Pátzcuaro seemed a little unclear about whether they had even actually issued a commission to him. Rodrigo alienated royal officials upon his arrival. Indeed, less than two months after receiving a commission as inquisitional notary, in May 1575, he began to make a series of demands on the alcalde, Francisco de Sarriá, that Sarriá resented. Yepes claimed that the city was obligated to purchase hay for his household.[41] The repartimiento labor drafts of indigenous subjects customarily provided hay and the city distributed it to its citizens. When Yepes demanded his share, the alcalde refused, claiming that Yepes was not a duly recognized citizen of Michoacán, and as such had no right to the customary hay. Yepes retorted that not only was he a citizen of Michoacán, but he was a much better one than the alcalde, as he was a notary of the Inquisition. Sarriá clapped Yepes in irons and jailed him for insulting his honor. Yepes demanded that the inquisitional deputy, Badillo, be summoned. Badillo succeeded in having Yepes released to house arrest in Badillo's residence, after which Badillo undertook an investigation. No sentence was handed down in the case, but the tense standoff set the tone for further conflict.[42]

THE ARRIVAL OF THE RANCHER-PRIEST

When the rancher-priest Don Diego de Orduña showed up in Pátzcuaro, some of the local residents knew the man. But no one had any idea what was about to happen, and nothing could have prepared the poor professor, Badillo, for the maelstrom that would consume his life. Orduña appeared in the Augustinian monastery church on 28 August 1575 in the middle of the mass for St. Augustine, as it was the saint's feast day. He proceeded to plop himself into a chair in the middle of the church in front of the cathedral dean and the other members of the cathedral chapter who were present. He then claimed to be a canon and demanded that the cathedral recognize him as such.[43] He had upended the acceptable semiotics of power, and his actions demanded a rebuke.[44]

Orduña's provocation was deliberate, and it set off a monumental feud, but it was a feud that Orduña was prepared to fight. When Badillo saw the roguish-looking rancher-priest appear in the church, demanding to be recognized as a member of the cathedral, he was dressed immaculately in an ostentatious silk suit, wearing his lawyer's bonnet. Badillo muttered, *sotto voce*, "What a shameless man." But when Orduña saw Badillo's mincing, smug look—a look that is universal to all men with an inflated sense of their own importance in the universe—he boiled over. He was determined to wipe that pedantic look off the licenciado's face. Rumors began to circulate that someone—perhaps Badillo, the inquisitional deputy—might prosecute Orduña for his assault on the dignity of the monastery, as Orduña was an uninvited guest.

Two days later, Orduña confronted Badillo in the town square. "Words were spoken." Alas, the case file does not tell us what those words were, but we can certainly imagine them, given the kinds of words Orduña used at other times. Perhaps he called Badillo a rogue or a bastard, or perhaps a thief. And then he slapped Badillo across the face with his gloves—a grave insult to his honor. Orduña then slapped Badillo's lawyer's bonnet right off his head, punched him in the face, and dragged him to the ground.[45] This was the first act in a long saga of alternating periods of friendship and bitter hatred between the two men.

Who was this man who had seemingly appeared out of nowhere and proceeded to start fistfights, claiming that he was a member of the diocesan government? Orduña was, in fact, an ordained priest, but he had spent the previous four years living in exile from the province of Michoacán. Though only a handful of people knew it, he had been a parish priest of Santa Ana de Guanajuato in 1568 and 1569, and then, in 1570, he had been convicted of assaulting a magistrate and condemned by Pedro de Yepes, acting as the inquisitor.[46] It was the first of at least five convictions Orduña received during his long and illustrious criminal career. And yet, here he was, in the capital of the province, claiming to be a canon of the cathedral and slapping down the inquisitional deputy. One has to admire his gall. Orduña spent four decades as Michoacán's most powerful clergyman-criminal. He was a dangerous man.

Orduña's background is a little shady, which is fitting. He was born in Zamora, Spain, around 1535, and sometime around 1565 in Mexico City, he commissioned a genealogy that upon execution proved to be vague.[47] The genealogy was drawn up in his home town in 1566. It appears that the purpose of getting a respectable genealogy drawn up was to give him a better chance of being appointed as a beneficed priest in New Spain—though we can only infer this, as there are no written documents attesting to the specific goal. For all we know, Orduña intended to use the genealogy for an application for a different position.[48] Witnesses, primarily citizens of Zamora, agreed that Orduña had been born there as the legitimate son of Pedro de Orduña and Catalina Paloma and that he was an ordained priest. Beyond this we know nothing of his life in Spain; nor do we know when he traveled to New Spain. He may have been related to the conquistador Francisco de Orduña, but there is no evidence for the connection. Likewise, he may have received his theological training as a *bachiller* in Pátzcuaro's Colegio de San Nicolás in the 1560s.[49] As we simply have no documentation of his early life, however, his past remains a mystery. Given the many times that he was involved in fraud, theft, and assault, it would not be surprising if he had been criminally condemned in Spain in the 1550s and had come to Mexico to reinvent himself.

Orduña made his political and economic fortune entirely in Michoacán. Although he claimed the honorific "Don," he lacked a university degree. No document ever refers to him as a licenciado; most of them explicitly call him a bachiller. His career was much like that of Pedro de Yepes—another parish priest who was not a licenciado who formed deep personalist and clientelist connections in Michoacán's rough world of politics.

Orduña probably began his clerical career as a parish priest in 1568 in Guanajuato, where he was the curate and vicar of Santa Ana, one of two parishes in the mining town.[50] This would have been a fairly routine first appointment for a young graduate of the seminary, especially considering that the diocese sought to establish Guanajuato as being within its territory, in order to bring in the mining wealth. His annual salary of three hundred pesos was high, but in keeping with the higher salaries for benefices in mining areas.[51] Then, in 1569, a series of scandals erupted in Guanajuato. The local lieutenant magistrate, Andrés de García, publicly accused his onetime paramour, a Canarian woman named Doña Catalina de Peraza, a daughter of the Count of Gomera, of being a prostitute and a witch. She was neither, and her lawyers sued García for libel. In the interim, García was pursuing a man accused of refusing to pay his debtors. The man sought sanctuary in a small church within Orduña's parish, and García and his bailiff had the man dragged out of the church kicking and screaming and clutching a crucifix. Yepes, unamused, initiated an inquisitional investigation against García for sacrilege, libel, and perjury.[52]

The scandal became a quagmire for Orduña. The existence of two parishes in Guanajuato—Santa Ana and Santa Fe—muddied the jurisdictional waters. García had dragged the man from the church within the parish of Santa Ana de Guanajuato. Rodrigo de Orejón was the cura of Santa Ana de Guanajuato from 1566 to 1568.[53] Presumably Orduña replaced Orejón, though the latter still was present in Guanajuato at the time of the assault. Both of the benefices lay within walking distance of each other, but legally the parishes were separate. By the summer of 1569, both Orduña and Orejón resided in Guanajuato, but it was unclear which of them exercised authority as vicar, or whether they both did so simultaneously. Though Orduña was the acting ecclesiastical judge, he did not order an immediate investigation against García for sacrilege after he and his bailiff violated the sanctuary of the church. Nevertheless, Yepes chose to charge García, but the case lay idle for a year. By summer 1570, the García case had mushroomed, becoming a public scandal. On 17 July 1570, Yepes dispatched a priest, Francisco de Hermosilla, to act as an investigator in the matter. Hermosilla attended a mass celebrated by Orduña in Santa Fe de Guanajuato. It is unclear if Orduña had been transferred to the other parish or if he was simply officiating at a mass. Hermosilla confronted García in front of the parish church, demanding that he recant his libelous statement against Peraza. García refused, and Hermosilla called on Orduña, as the acting ecclesiastical authority of the town, to excommunicate him.[54]

Witness statements offer conflicting versions of the events that followed. Many claimed that Orduña only made a perfunctory threat of excommunication to García, should he refuse to comply with Hermosilla's order. The witnesses all agreed that García openly refused to comply with any order from the ecclesiastical court, claiming that he had appealed the case both to the archbishop and the Audiencia of Mexico and did not view Yepes or Hermosilla as competent judges in his case. Responding to the threat of public excommunication, García said to Orduña, "You and the judge here are suspicious and both in league with the bishop and I will have you recused." Hermosilla defended the bishop's honor. Orduña told García, "That is roguish speech for a man like you to speak about the bishop."

And then the fight broke out. Witnesses did not agree who threw the first punch, but they all said that García and Orduña brawled, and that Orduña struck García with a judicial staff. The alcalde, Juan de Torres, punched Orduña in the face, breaking his nose.[55]

With blood streaming down his face, Orduña turned to the alcalde and said, "I am an important and well-known priest. You had better not seize me."[56] Torres's royal staff of office lay broken on the ground. Undeterred, he shouted for someone to place Orduña in chains. Into custody the priest went, hauled off to jail.[57] Hermosilla convened an investigation and charged Orduña with making an unprovoked assault; he also charged Torres with assaulting a member of the clergy and declared him excommunicated pending a trial.

On learning of the donnybrook, Yepes excommunicated Torres, and in September 1570, Torres presented himself before Yepes. In Torres's version of events, he had simply defended García from Orduña, who had struck García unprovoked; he was therefore simply carrying out his duty as an alcalde. There was some blood, yes, but this was only because Torres, in the scuffle, had ripped a scab from Orduña's face; it was not because he had struck him.[58]

Yepes also ordered Orduña to present himself in Pátzcuaro before the diocesan court. On arriving in Pátzcuaro in September, Orduña asked for, and received, a grant of house arrest during the investigation and trial, instead of being placed in the local jail. When Yepes interrogated him, Orduña claimed that he had acted in self-defense, and the provisor rejected the argument.[59] Yepes concluded by finding Orduña guilty of debasing the dignity of his office as parish priest by assaulting a royal official without provocation. His sentence was exorbitant: a fine of two hundred pesos and four years in exile from Guanajuato.[60] The exile theoretically stripped Orduña of his benefice, though we do not know if he received his salary in spite of the conviction.

Orduña's whereabouts between the September 1570 sentencing and the summer of 1575 are a mystery. It is unclear where he went during his four-year exile. He appears in no documentation for the period, though he did apparently steer clear of criminal accusations during that period. Perhaps he went to New Galicia or Mexico City; he was not technically exiled from Michoacán in general, so he could have invested in (or stolen) land in the region. He did eventually own several ranches north of Valladolid.[61] After receiving a punishment of exile or mandatory reclusion (as in a monastery or hospital), a convicted person often presented a sworn statement from the prior or guardian to attest to the completion of the sentence, in order to obtain legal relief and final absolution. So far, no such statement has been found for Orduña's first mandatory exile. He simply disappeared from the historical record for a while. Maybe he beat up a couple of licenciados or stole some land to while away the time.

RIVALRY BREWING

Rivalries are often born in a single moment. We will never know when the rivalry between Badillo and Orduña began. Like most academics, Badillo had an inflated opinion of himself. He was a professor, after all—a very important and serious job. People should nod reverently at his erudition—for he was a licenciado, after all, with a silk dignitary sash and a lawyer's bonnet. Perhaps in Mexico City, this would have been normal, but a man with an ostentatious green or pink silk sash, something usually reserved for high dignitaries—in addition to a lawyer's bonnet—strutting around a rural town on the shores of Lake Pátzcuaro, among the dogs and chickens, and the shit and bales of hay, and farmers and indigenous daylaborers—well, he looked a bit out of place.[62]

Though ambitious, Orduña was a regular guy. He had a clear grasp of street vernacular—something the hapless law professor lacked. Orduña had only a rudimentary formal education, but this was probably a social advantage in Michoacán's rural world. Ironically enough, once he made enough money, Orduña also began to wear ostentatious suits. But in the 1570s he was still very much a product of ranching society. True, he was a priest, but as he had no university education, he thought that licenciados were pompous assholes. Orduña learned his politics from the metaphor of livestock slaughter, where one is either killer or the killed. Orduña was also a fighter who knew how to throw a punch and wield a dagger. While he had been brawling in Guanajuato, Badillo had been delivering somber lectures on law in Mexico City. The contrast could not have been clearer.

Orduña's brash appearance in Pátzcuaro in the summer of 1575 set off yet another brawl, but this time, it was an extended legal battle. Orduña's slapping down of Badillo precipitated the legal battle. He was intent on reestablishing himself in the region. In August 1575, correspondence concerning his second criminal investigation noted that he was a cathedral canon of the Michoacán cathedral chapter.[63] Some local officials knew Orduña, but this turnaround was astonishing. He probably had been gambling on three factors: first, that enough people did not know about his criminal past to prevent him from rising politically; second, that no one really cared enough to prevent it; and third, that people were too terrified of him to hold him back. Obviously, Yepes knew him, though, and he did not like him one bit. It is unclear how Orduña obtained his commission as a member of the cathedral chapter—or if, in fact, he even ever received such a commission. For all we know, he may simply have arrived and demanded that he be recognized as a canon of the cathedral. The alcalde Francisco de Sarriá claimed that it was well known that Orduña had been prosecuted and sentenced for his assault on García. So there was some local knowledge that Orduña was a convicted criminal.

Orduña's return to Pátzcuaro enraged Yepes and Badillo. On 30 August, Badillo, as inquisitional deputy, and Yepes, as diocesan prosecutor, opened parallel investigations. Both asserted their authority to hear the case of Orduña's assault of Badillo, and each impugned the jurisdiction of the other. Badillo sent his report to the inquisitors in Mexico City, who were not amused to discover that Yepes had opened his own investigation. On 12 September, the inquisitors ordered Yepes to cease and desist, ominously threatening Yepes with excommunication for interfering in an inquisitional investigation. In another twist of baroque complexity, Rodrigo de Yepes acted as the notary to record the investigation.[64]

Caught in the crossfire, and with too many damning testimonies against him, Orduña had no choice but to answer to the inquisitors. Inquisitional bailiffs arrested him, perhaps as early as September 1575, and he traveled to Mexico City to appear before the inquisitors in their chambers. Orduña then offered what the inquisitional prosecutor called a "studied, contrived, artificial confession in which he added crime upon crime by committing perjury."[65] Orduña disputed the claims against him, arguing that at the time of the assault, he had not known that Badillo was the Inquisition's deputy, and therefore had not recognized his authority. For good measure, he claimed that Badillo had defamed him in public by calling him "shameless."

As was his right, Orduña demanded further investigation, impugning the prosecutor's case. Witnesses for the prosecution had sworn that Orduña had been fully aware that Badillo was the acting inquisitional deputy when he had assaulted him. But Orduña had powerful friends. The most telling witness for his defense was none other than Gordillo, who testified that Badillo was a well-known troublemaker. But witness after witness came forth to declare that Badillo had been involved in a series of public scandals. It came out that Badillo had clashed with his former mentor, Caballero, and that Caballero had publicly called Badillo "a Moor." This charge—that Badillo's mother was a Muslim, or a Moor—was repeated again in 1577, when Badillo was finally brought up on charges himself.[66]

Orduña's witnesses painted a grim picture of Badillo as loud, obnoxious, arrogant, and "Turkish." Nevertheless, Orduña was compelled to remain a guest of the inquisitors throughout October and November. He filed several briefs, complaining that his health was deteriorating, and that *forasteros* (outsiders who could not claim citizen status, or vagabonds) were invading his ranches back in Michoacán. He pleaded with the inquisitors to release him so that he could return to attend to his properties, lest he lose control of them. The inquisitors happily took their time in completing their investigation.

TRANSFERRING THE CAPITAL

Meanwhile, plans to transfer the capital of Michoacán from Pátzcuaro to Guayangareo-Valladolid marched forward. Despite the efforts of the Yepes clan and others to keep the capital in Pátzcuaro, the Crown and the papacy supported the move to Guayangareo. Beginning in October 1575, Badillo was obliged to begin taking an occasional deposition in the future capital.[67] The bishop of Michoacán, Antonio Ruiz de Morales y Molina, had formally proposed the move of the diocesan seat, and Pius V had confirmed the move in November 1571. But Bishop Morales became the bishop of Puebla in 1572 and died in 1576, before the move from Pátzcuaro could take place. An Augustinian friar, Juan de Medina Rincón, accepted the position of bishop of Michoacán in 1575 and encountered the final opposition from Pátzcuaro to the transfer of the see. On 25 December 1575, Viceroy Martín Enríquez ordered the cathedral chapter and municipal council to be moved to Guayangareo-Valladolid.[68] Medina Rincón submitted the plan to his cathedral chapter, and the chapter voted to approve construction of a cathedral church in Guayangareo. Philip II approved the move in 1576.[69]

The imminent transfer of the capital led to conflict between the Yepes family and the cathedral chapter, and on 2 November 1575, Rodrigo de Yepes was involved in a public shouting match about it. The debate erupted in the public square, right in front of the municipal administrative buildings, with Canon Francisco de Beteta stating that the move was legitimate, and Yepes rejecting that claim. The move, he said, was not a fait accompli.[70] Yepes claimed that the report filed on behalf of the Crown was a fraud—it had been deliberately falsified to favor those who had economic interests in Guayangareo. Diego Sánchez, an erstwhile magistrate of Michoacán, then called him a liar.

And then the fistfight broke out. It is unclear who threw the first punch, but when all was said and done, Sánchez's royal staff lay broken on the ground. The alcalde mayor, Juan del Hierro, clapped Yepes in chains and dragged him off to the city jail, where he was left, bound, to cool his heels.

Pedro de Yepes immediately called on the notary Juan de Benavides, who was his friend, to compose an affidavit condemning the arrest of his nephew. This he quickly dispatched to the inquisitors in Mexico City. He argued that royal involvement in the matter should be prohibited, and for good measure, he added that he stood to lose 1,000 pesos in rents if the capital were moved out of Pátzcuaro.[71] Badillo stepped into the shitstorm, claiming authority as the inquisitional deputy, and took depositions in the case. He, too, demanded the release of the younger Yepes from jail. Both Pedro de Yepes and Badillo argued in their correspondence with inquisitors that Hierro, as alcalde, was not a competent judge in the case. Rodrigo de Yepes was—maybe?—an inquisitional official, and therefore exempt from civil prosecution by a form of legal protection called *fuero*, which barred royal judges or magistrates from prosecuting inquisitional officials. Hierro responded by arguing that Rodrigo de Yepes was not a duly appointed inquisitional notary.[72]

The legal maneuvering in the case proceeded with alacrity. Badillo had taken depositions within twenty-four hours of the 2 November fight, and had demanded Hierro's recusal within hours of Yepes's arrest. Badillo sent the case for recusing Hierro and for asserting inquisitional fuero for Rodrigo de Yepes to inquisitors in Mexico City, who received it on 10 November. Initially, Pedro Farfán, an Audiencia judge and onetime mentor of Badillo, advised the inquisitors to forbid Hierro from prosecuting Yepes. But then, on 16 November, inquisitors made a decision, claiming, alas, "Our hands are tied." They proceeded to vacate Rodrigo de Yepes's rights as an inquisitional official, saying his judicial frivolity and poor behavior had given them little choice in the matter.[73] Although they also offered some mealy-mouthed statements about the complexities of such cases, the clear hand of the viceroy must be seen here—even though inquisitors often refused to obey viceroys' demands. The inquisitors had offered Rodrigo de Yepes as a sacrificial victim to the broader interests of the viceroy in seeing Michoacán pacified and the capital transferred out of Pátzcuaro. But the brawl and legal battle had also grown out of the resentment of Pátzcuaro's residents toward the Yepes family. They increasingly distrusted the concentration of power in the family; they had also wondered openly whether Rodrigo de Yepes was even a duly commissioned inquisitional official.

Legitimacy was a serious problem for the Inquisition in Michoacán. The cathedral canons may have impugned Badillo's commission, since it was only signed by one inquisitor. But outright impersonation was a grave offense. Once inquisitors learned of such impersonation, they tended to punish it severely, since such actions threatened their monopoly of coercion. Moreover, by hijacking the instruments of the "pedagogy of fear" that the Inquisition was supposed to control, such imposters seriously undermined the power of inquisitional repression.[74]

In short, the inquisitors refused to defend the right of fuero for Yepes and turned him over to the Audiencia for judgment. Mexico's Audiencia, in turn, dispatched the archdiocesan prosecutor Mateo Arévalo Sedeño to judge the case, presumably on appeal to the alcalde's authority. On 30 November, Badillo informed the Inquisition that he had received Sedeño's sentence in the case. In making the announcement, he explained to the inquisitors that he was simply carrying out orders, despite the clear animus he said Pedro de Yepes demonstrated toward him. Nevertheless, he still seemed to hold some animus toward Yepes as well, and there was a hint that he might want to take revenge against him in the future.

The conviction and sentencing of Rodrigo de Yepes suggested either that hatred of his family ran deep among Mexico City officials or that the Audiencia was determined to make an example of him for impugning the move of the capital from Pátzcuaro to Valladolid.[75] The royal judge prosecuted and convicted him — between 16 and 29 November — and moreover, Sedeño seemed intent on making an example of him. The penalty he handed down was mind-boggling: 200 lashes, a lifetime of galley slavery, and a fine of 3,000 pesos. The penalty mocked the law; no one received such sentences for anything less than treason. Indeed, one would be hard pressed to find a similar sentence even for heresy in the same period — this was even greater than the kinds of sentences meted out to English and French corsairs in the same year, who typically received sentences of ten to twelve years of galley service.[76] The sentence has all the hallmarks of vengeance.

On 29 November, the residents of Pátzcuaro gathered before the jail eagerly, itching to see the young man flogged and humiliated, fulsome in the collective societal sadism accompanying such events. At the last moment, on leaving the jail, however, Rodrigo de Yepes pled for the opportunity to appeal. It is impossible to know whether his reprieve was granted, because the Audiencia trial is not extant. He may very well have been publicly flogged and sent into exile as a galley slave.

In the aftermath of the scandal, the entire province was on the brink of a jurisdictional civil war. The definitive legal transferal of the see came in December 1575. Technically, but only sporadically, Badillo acted as inquisitional agent.[77] And inquisitors finally released Orduña, convicting him in December 1575 for public insult and assault on an inquisitional official. In a prescient detail, the prosecutor added that Orduña had behaved more like a soldier than a priest, by asserting his authority and public office with force. The accusation offered a remarkable bit of foreshadowing.[78] Mexico's inquisitors condemned Orduña to a one-year exile from the province of Michoacán and the archdiocese of Mexico, of which Orduña was to spend at least six months in reclusion in a monastery. For good measure, inquisitors fined him 200 ducats, more than a year's salary.[79] So it was that Orduña went into exile a second time, traveling to Cholula to spend his time in a monastery.

ORDUÑA'S RETURN

Badillo hoped that at long last order would come to Michoacán and that the population would have respect for the law. His hopes were premature. He heard some depositions shortly after what he hoped would be a prosperous new year on 3 January 1576.[80] The residents of Michoacán had probably learned that Orduña would soon be safely in exile, and many of them no doubt hoped he would never return. Orduña reported for his stay at the Franciscan friary of Cholula on 15 February 1576, and the guardian received him, reporting that the convicted priest was in poor health.[81]

Badillo's position was tenuous, as he surely understood after witnessing the fate of Rodrigo de Yepes. Although we do not know if the draconian sentence against Rodrigo de Yepes was exacted, he did disappear from the archival record, and for all we know, he spent the rest of his days on some hellish galley barge in the Philippines or the Caribbean. Even if he wasn't there to enjoy it, though, Rodrigo de Yepes—and, indirectly, Badillo—scored a hollow legal victory later that year. On 19 May 1576, the Supreme Council of the Inquisition in Madrid wrote to the inquisitors of Mexico. Presumably, this part of the case originated on appeal by Rodrigo de Yepes or his attorney. The inquisitors general affirmed the tradition of fuero for inquisitional officials. They reprimanded Mexico's inquisitors for denying it, reminding them that inquisitional law did bar royal judges or magistrates from prosecuting inquisitional officials. True, the inquisitors conceded, it was wise to consult with Audiencia judges, or even the viceroy, when doubts arose. But, on principle, they vacated Yepes's conviction.[82] We are left to speculate about Yepes's fate, and Badillo must have taken cold comfort in the decision.

Orduña took steps to return to Michoacán. On 9 June 1576, the newly arrived guardian of Cholula, Friar Antonio Salazar, reported that Orduña had spent his exile in the friary as obediently as any novice.[83] Forthwith, Orduña applied to the Inquisition to be reinstated as cathedral canon and beneficed priest.[84] On 23 June, inquisitors granted Orduña the request, issuing a formal license for his reinstatement and return. Orduña lamented that during his exile he had lost his salary as well as his hacienda, at an estimated loss of 3,500 pesos. It is unclear where he held his estate, though he owned a ranch in Apaceo by 1580, so the comment may refer to this area.[85] Even if he exaggerated his financial loss, forasteros probably did occupy his properties in his absence.

Orduña's arrival in Pátzcuaro in July 1576 could not have been more cleverly timed, though it may have been dumb luck. Badillo was in Colima, ostensibly to take witness statements as an inquisitional deputy.[86] Pedro de Yepes was furious; on 11 July 1576, he drew up a legal complaint against Orduña. According to Yepes, Orduña had returned to Pátzcuaro, entered the cathedral church, and celebrated mass without presenting evidence of having completed his inquisitional sentence. Yepes was intent on blocking Orduña's reinstallation as a cathedral canon, demanding that he present written evidence of his purged sentence. He ordered Orduña to travel north to Cupándaro to see the bishop, who had traveled there, in order to receive exoneration from excommunication.[87] Orduña then wrote to the inquisitors, on 12 July, asking for relief in the case.[88]

On 17 July, the inquisitors instructed Yepes that because Orduña had fulfilled his sentence, the diocese must recognize him as a fully vested cathedral canon.[89] Surely, one of the reasons Yepes tried to block Orduña's reinstallation on his return from Cholula was that he had become too powerful a rival. Orduña received a kind of final exoneration in the case on 2 September, when the prior of the Augustinian monastery in Cupándaro, Friar Luis Mingolla, wrote to the inquisitors to report that he had absolved him of excommunication.[90]

The absurdity of sending a twice-convicted criminal back to Michoacán, not only to live but to exercise authority in the cathedral, suggests that Orduña had powerful friends, that the Inquisition didn't care what happened in Michoacán, that the Church was desperate for someone—anyone—to rule the newly transferred capital of the diocese, or that the entire system was just too disorganized to function very effectively.

DEAR INQUISITORS: WE DEMAND A NEW GUY

Everything went terribly wrong for Badillo in 1577. A massive showdown, which had been brewing between Badillo and his growing list of enemies for years, finally erupted. By May 1577, Orduña had become the maestrescuela of the Michoacán cathedral chapter. No trace of the appointment can be found, but it became a fact. The irony was rich: a man with a rudimentary education and rather obvious contempt for the formal legal system became the highest-ranking doctrinal instructor for parish priests in the diocese.[91] And then things really deteriorated. Several of Michoacán's citizens began to demand that inquisitors replace Badillo. His enemies struck, and their revenge was swift and vicious. The simmering hostility toward Badillo and the Inquisition boiled over. One of his opponents, the acting deputy magistrate Juan de Santa Cruz, of Pátzcuaro, sent a letter to the inquisitors in Mexico City on 29 June 1577:

> Very reverend sir: The deputy Badillo deals with inquisitional matters openly and does not keep them secret, creating a lot of fuss and noise, threatening men and defaming them. He is a man who does not have the qualities required for the office. He appears fickle and light and unserious, especially for a priest, archdeacon, and agent of the Holy Inquisition. He goes to any wedding and nuptial, wherever it might be. He drinks and eats too much. He openly admires women. He is loose and goes about armed at night, threatening people. He pretends to be wealthy. He is boisterous and has bad taste. He dances with the bride at weddings

even though he is wearing his cassock, dignitary sash, and lawyer's bonnet. He makes jokes with his hands and acts like a woman and wears petticoats. He jokes that he wishes he could give birth and wishes people would call the midwife. He giggles like a girl saying, "Look, I am pregnant," and other things like this which are typical of low and plebeian men not of his station. People also publicly say that he is of suspicious Moorish blood, that he is Turkish. . . . He plays prohibited card games. For all of these reasons I beg your reverence that you be aware of the qualities of the man who serves you. . . . I regret that my handwriting is poor but I am greatly afflicted with gout and am an old man. . . . Your humble servant kisses the feet and hands of your excellence.[92]

The letter, which goes on at some length, is darkly hilarious. It was a gouty man complaining that the archdeacon drank and ate too much, a rural man serving the Crown as a deputy magistrate bitterly criticizing the sartorial ostentation of the university-trained jurist, an aging man lamenting that the cathedral dignitary (who, at the time, was probably less than forty years old) was getting too much attention from the ladies. More telling, the letter outlined the case that the bishop eventually brought against Badillo for gambling and public scandal. Santa Cruz's letter, however, is remarkable for the venomous personal quality of the claims, all hinting that Badillo was a kind of foppish, ostentatious, city-educated lawyer.

The letter was symptomatic of a broader and more serious tendency. Complaints to inquisitors show that it was unclear how exactly an inquisitional agent was supposed to behave or how far his authority reached. Local residents rejected Badillo's claims to power—Santa Cruz was not the only one to complain to inquisitors. The bishop, Friar Medina Rincón, wrote a similar letter, demanding that the inquisitors, in effect, send a different deputy. Juan Ruiz, the former diocesan prosecutor, penned a letter explaining that surely the inquisitors could find someone with the proper gravitas for the job. Ruiz even helpfully offered to appear before the inquisitors in their chambers to swear to this. He was probably ingratiating himself in a backhanded attempt to vie for inquisitional appointment.[93]

Local interests resented the imposition of an outsider as the inquisitional agent. Of course, the charges against Badillo had a backstory. Residents already hated his peremptory way of announcing his status. During the investigation into Orduña's assault on Badillo, for example, witnesses that Orduña produced expressed their hatred for Badillo. Their statements were only part of a chorus of accusations. Badillo made inquisitional investigations public. He was noisome and unethical. He was a Moor. He had a habit of insulting people in public and threatening them with inquisitional prosecution for the slightest provocation.[94] These claims were all offered simply to defend Orduña from charges that he had been unjustified in his altercation with Badillo.

The new accusations against Badillo tipped the balance against him. At some point in 1576, he traveled to Colima. Upon his return to Pátzcuaro in early 1577, he found that the cathedral chapter would refuse to reimburse his expenses. Oh, the privileges of petty tyranny. Badillo sued the corporation in February 1577, but the bishop reported that Badillo, who had been made the mayordomo of the cathedral in 1576, was puffed up with pride. The bishop refused to reappoint him. Lawyer that he was, Badillo pressed forward, summoning the cathedral's accountant, who concluded that the cathedral did in fact owe Badillo sixty-four pesos, one *tomín*, and eight *granos*, to be exact, thank you very much. Badillo sent the report to the inquisitors in May, and they wearily wrote back to the cathedral chapter that it must pay up.[95]

There was more to the story than reimbursement. According to the bishop, the cathedral chapter had made a terrible mistake in electing Badillo as mayordomo. He had refused to turn over account books and receipts valued at 80,000 pesos— although it is unclear whether the bishop meant to say that Badillo was personally sitting on a fortune of 80,000 pesos, or that he had refused to deliver the receipts functioning as sureties for the amount. In either case, the charge was serious. The diocese was simultaneously litigating the vast estates of Juan de Infante, encomendero par excellence, who had died in 1574. As fate would have it, Infante was the brother-in-law of the Audiencia judge Pedro Farfán, Badillo's onetime patron. The coincidence was too convenient.[96]

Payback, as they say, is a bitch. The accusations against Badillo flew. Santa Cruz's letters reached inquisitors on 9 July 1577. Diego Caballero Bazán, a cathedral canon of Michoacán, delivered the letters from Santa Cruz and confirmed the events they outlined. On 10 July 1577, Caballero Bazán testified before inquisitors, and he aimed for the jugular by corroborating all the most salacious details that Santa Cruz had provided. And then all hell broke loose. As Bishop Medina was attending to the litigation of the Infante estate, he was not in Pátzcuaro to supervise matters. The residing magistrate, Juan Hierro, had left on business, leaving Santa Cruz to act as his lieutenant. Santa Cruz arrested and fined Badillo's nephew, Pedro de Ortega, for illegal gambling and card playing. Badillo, in turn, publicly threatened Santa Cruz with inquisitional action in retaliation if he did not release his nephew and turn over the materials concerning the civil proceeding. Badillo denied the accusations of abuse of power and said the inquisitional investigation was unrelated to his nephew. He threatened to have Santa Cruz arrested and accused him of blocking the exercise of inquisitional authority. In due course, Badillo and Santa Cruz feuded publicly, trading insults in the city square. Santa Cruz later said that Badillo became so enraged that "he had fire coming out of his eyes," adding, "[He] put his fingers in my eyes, disrespecting me as a man with a royal staff."[97] Moreover, Badillo had forced Santa Cruz to appear before him in the municipal offices, where he refused to allow him to sit in the comisario's presence, which Santa Cruz correctly interpreted as a deliberate insult to his honor. The assault on the magistrate's honor was too much for him to stand—that it was an assault on royal justice only exacerbated the offense.

The inquisitors ordered Badillo to surrender and appear before them and instructed Medina to open an inquiry. Between 12 and 27 July 1577, Medina took depositions against Badillo. Several witnesses attested to the hubbub, and a lurid portrait emerged. Witnesses against Badillo included the choirmaster, Gordillo; canons of Michoacán's cathedral; the lieutenant magistrate, Santa Cruz; and Diego Caballero Bazán. One curious detail emerged: although Santa Cruz named him as a witness, Orduña does not appear to have made a sworn statement against Badillo in the summer of 1577. In fact, when the cathedral chapter convened on 22 July, five canons, along with the dean and choirmaster, attended, but Orduña was notably absent.[98]

The accusations against Badillo were broad, ranging from inappropriate legal activity to economic fraud, public scandals, vendettas, and gambling. The issues fall into the illegal and punishable category as well as the lurid and vaguely scandalous, but not especially illegal, category. By all appearances, the inquisitors did not view the accusations as sufficient to charge or condemn Badillo for a crime. The cover sheet for the investigation includes a notation saying the case was suspended.

But the accusations grew ever more bizarre. Several witnesses told stories of Badillo as a con man and partier. First there were several corroborated accusations of economically questionable activities. Badillo had bought and sold several cacao plantations—for example, he had gone to Colima in 1576 not in his capacity as an inquisitional agent, but on private business, to buy and sell cacao, hay, wine, cloth, and salt. He had sold these products at profit back in Pátzcuaro. Several witnesses considered this outrageous, considering that he was a priest. There were insinuations that Badillo was therefore a Jew, given the stereotypes about usury. Santa Cruz suggested that Badillo had made a profit of 10,000 pesos in his agricultural investments, but that he refused to pay any sales taxes. Witnesses confirmed that Badillo had bought and sold products in public markets.

There were other complaints. Badillo gambled and lost money in card games in taverns. He had attended a notorious party at the house of a shoemaker named Josepe Carrión—who, along with several others, had been accused by the provisor in 1568 for boycotting mass.[99] And there was more gossip. Badillo had attended a wedding in Celaya at which he had danced with the bride. He had a habit of sitting too close to the wife of the onetime alcalde Francisco Sarriá, who had dragged his wife home and beat her for dishonoring him. On a different occasion, Badillo had attended a dinner at the Augustinian monastery, where he had joked publicly that the bishop should not be so easily offended by card games. Badillo had said that he had seen a bishop in Spain playing cards, and that it was well known that many bishops had mistresses.

Badillo's cosmopolitan views outraged those who testified against him. He mocked Bishop Medina and stated publicly that the bishop was not his judge, exempt as Badillo was as inquisitional agent. This much was technically true, but Badillo's cavalier attitude toward the typical urbane pleasures of banquets, card games, and salon dances scandalized Pátzcuaro's rustic world. He even bought and sold wine at profit. Citizens were outraged—not so much by the wine but by Badillo's cultural arrogance.

Nothing seemed to outrage those who testified against Badillo more than one particular event. At some point, Badillo had traveled to the sugar-mill town of Zitácuaro in the far southeastern part of the province. Rumors spread that he had gotten drunk and dressed up like a woman in petticoats, making jokes, giggling, and pretending that he was pregnant, and saying, "Fetch the midwife; I am going to have a baby."[100] The partygoers seemed to find this hilarious, but the cathedral canons did not share their sense of humor. It is unclear whether the incident occurred during a Carnival celebration, but other witnesses claimed Badillo's fondness of parties to be well known.

No one seemed to fear the power of the Inquisition or its representative. Instead, there was an organized campaign to demand that inquisitors replace their agent. As scandalous as Badillo's sense of humor may have been, the accusation of profiting financially from his position and extorting funds from the cathedral worried the inquisitors more. They issued a legal summons on 20 July 1577, ordering Badillo to present himself within two days—a short period for this kind of case, suggesting that they were enraged.[101] Badillo, however, took more than two weeks to appear: on 8 August 1577, he presented himself in Mexico City. He was very sorry it had taken so long, he explained, but the roads had been flooded.

Badillo made a brief confession on 9 September in which he stated that he supposed he had been summoned to answer questions about his involvement with Santa Cruz. He asked the inquisitors to grant him house arrest in Mexico City while they conducted their investigation, and they wearily granted the request. The inquisitors had not formally charged Badillo with any crime, but simultaneously, they had demanded that Badillo's principal accuser, Santa Cruz, appear before them, to ratify the sworn statements in evidence, and Santa Cruz appeared on 19 September. Badillo asked to be allowed to return to Michoacán, and the inquisitors complied. But their consent came with a terrible price. On 7 October 1577, Badillo appeared before the inquisitors again in their chambers, and they stripped him of his commission as inquisitional deputy. They ordered Badillo to return immediately to Michoacán to settle the accounts of the cathedral that he had been accused of extorting.

The political campaign against Badillo revealed the limits of inquisitional power and the extent to which local resistance to that power could be effectively deployed. Indeed, local residents not only openly defied the Inquisition's deputy, but succeeded in having him removed from office. The Inquisition's ability to impose its hegemony on Michoacán was limited; or rather, the Inquisition simply could not rein in the province. Attempts at the unilateral imposition of social discipline failed.

THE FALL OF BADILLO

Badillo reported to inquisitors on 4 November 1577 that he had returned to Pátzcuaro. Though the patent is not extant in the case file, he informed the inquisitors that he had returned the commission that they had revoked, along with the various inquisitional testimonies in his possession. He groveled, asking to be reinstated as inquisitional deputy, noting that he was humiliated by the stripping of his title. For the first time in four years, he signed his letter simply as "arcediano de Michoacán" (archdeacon of Michoacán), omitting the second title, "comisario del Santo Oficio" (deputy of the Holy Office), which had embellished his signatures between 1573 and 1577.[102]

If Bishop Medina's word is to be believed, Badillo's life back in Pátzcuaro was more bizarre than one could ever imagine. The bishop wrote to inquisitors on 14 December explaining that Badillo had refused to submit to ritualized correction by the bishop—kneeling and kissing his ring, for example, and begging forgiveness. Stripped of his commission as inquisitional agent, he refused to celebrate mass, or, for that matter, even attend mass. Moreover, the bishop lamented, Badillo refused to work as a lawyer because he had returned to Michoacán "without office." This bit is uncertain because the Inquisition did not strip him of his law license. In any case, the bishop concluded that as a result of Badillo's diminished professional state, "Michoacán had no licensed attorney." Law was, in effect, suspended. But the most bizarre detail of Bishop Medina's letter was personal. He claimed that Badillo spent all his time "going from this party to that party," and had become "a very close friend of the maestrescuela"—none other than Orduña. Finally, on 30 January 1578, Bishop Medina told the inquisitors that Badillo was a toxin that must be purged.[103]

This detail offers a fascinating psychological twist. Was the bishop telling the truth? Did he attempt to taint Badillo with guilt by association, even though he had enough ammunition without the charge? The comment seems too offhand to be contrived; it appears genuine, since his complaint was not that Badillo had be-friended Orduña, but that he had abandoned his clerical duties and refused to bow before the bishop. If Badillo had befriended Orduña, what was going on? Did they make amends and become drinking buddies? Orduña had not testified against Ba-dillo in the 1577 case. Perhaps Badillo and Orduña had bonded over their mutual hatred for the bishop. Or was Badillo a changed man after his experience on the other side of the law? It would hardly be the first time in human history that a man dedicated to an idealized system became disillusioned and turned in the other di-rection, to debauchery and anarchism. Or did he decide to become a *michoacano*, rejecting his Spanish, Mexico City identity? It falls to the conclusion of this book to remark on this, but it may very well be the case that he now saw Michoacán in a different light.

After Badillo returned to Michoacán in the winter of 1577–1578, ecclesiastical justice ground to a standstill. The diocese in effect had no court; the Inquisition had vacated its own power by revoking Badillo's commission. The province had no letrado to examine legal disputes. Badillo returned to his sinecure and collected the archdeacon salary, unperturbed by the tedium of official business. Then, in February 1581, information was gathered concerning an Augustinian friar, Ginés de Ludeña, of minor orders who had celebrated mass in Taximaroa even though he was not an ordained priest. The Inquisition contacted Orduña, as the maes-trescuela, to investigate the case as inquisitional agent, even though they stopped short of a formal appointment as comisario.[104]

Why did the inquisitors select Orduña? He had never been the provisor of the diocese, and, after all, that same inquisition had already convicted him, after the diocesan court had convicted him as well. Maybe the inquisitors had given up on Michoacán and merely opted for the only long-term cathedral dignitary who actu-ally lived in the region. Only five of the ten canons of the cathedral even lived in the diocese, and few of them attended to their tasks. Diego Caballero Bazán, who had advocated for Badillo's removal, had gone to back live in Mexico City because he found life in Valladolid unpleasant.[105] Then, in July 1582, Orduña wrote to the in-quisitors in Mexico City to apply officially to be Valladolid's inquisitional deputy.[106] One can only speculate as to why Orduña thought that he would be appointed by the same institution that had condemned him twice.

In 1583 or 1584, Badillo's career was ruined once and for all. He was still the archdeacon, but presumably his status was much reduced; he had been humili-ated, even to the point of seeing his worst enemy commissioned by the Inquisition he once served.[107] His activities as a clergyman went unnoted in local bureaucratic records, but Bishop Medina held a grudge against him. At some point in 1583, Me-dina ordered Badillo to appear before the provisor, Alonso Ruiz, to answer charges on an unrelated crime for which we do not have the case file. Badillo became angry with the provisor and slapped him in the face.[108] The provisor prosecuted Badillo, in a clear case of conflict of interest, and with astonishing rapidity—within three days—convicted him of assault. The outlandish sentence called for twelve years of galley slavery, a public flogging, and a twelve-year suspension of his office.[109] Badillo appealed the decision to the archdiocese, and the provisor in Mexico lessened the penalty, but sustained a penalty of ten years of exile. Badillo then appealed to Mexico's Audiencia, which vacated the original sentences while sustaining the archdiocesan court's decision.

Badillo left for Spain in the hope of having the entire case dismissed by the papal nuncio.[110] His departure created another power vacuum for the Inquisition: in effect, no one exercised any inquisitional power for several years. And even during the five years when Badillo was the official inquisitional deputy, he was never able to prosecute many cases, given the local hostility toward him and rejection of his power. In 1584, after Badillo had left for Spain, Orduña submitted his genealogy to the inquisitors, asking to be installed as the inquisitional deputy for the capital of Michoacán.[111] The man had some hubris.

A SOCIOLOGY OF INSULT

The Inquisition could convince no one to respect its authority. Few trembled in its presence; royal officials and priests openly mocked it and assaulted its agents. Surely, if it was possible, a law professor like Badillo could put the fear of God and Crown and Inquisition into this unruly bunch of ranchers and encomenderos. But he could not.

Perhaps what was most remarkable about the rise and rapid fall of Badillo's position in Michoacán is the success of a local populace in forcing the Inquisition to revoke its own agent and, in turn, accept defeat. If we assume the Inquisition was mighty, the case of Michoacán must be a cautionary tale. Indeed, on the first formal installation of a central Holy Office in Mexico, the Inquisition was incapable of imposing its will on Michoacán. Residents in Michoacán did not cower before the Inquisition's might. Instead they successfully removed the Inquisition's agent from office through a combination of political sabotage, legal maneuvers, and ordinary stonewalling.

Accordingly, if the expressions of public dishonor were intended to disparage the Inquisition, they worked, at least to the extent that they blocked the court's effective installation. The public assaults, insults, and slanderous statements against the Yepeses, Badillos, and Orduñas of a region like Michoacán took place within a hypermasculine world not only of clergy but of public political culture. In other words, public insult expressed a public "semiotics of power."[112] While male, like female, honor was closely guarded as a public commodity, such visible assaults on the dignity of personal space operated in linguistic anthropological terms within a "grammar of violence."[113] Attacks on the head and face were often made by men against women—particularly wives and mistresses—but public violence was considered plebeian and therefore undignified for members of the upper classes. Other assaults on dignity surfaced in actions such as refusing to ask someone to sit, or forcing a man to stand while another was seated, which implied superiority for the seated man. Accordingly, simple analyses of Iberian sexualized and family honor do not fully explain the subtle insults to dignity—the slapping down of a lawyer's bonnet; the sotto voce insults designed to impugn status without uttering formal fighting words—seen in these sagas. These aggressions were orchestrated according to a cultural script that understood such actions as grievous assaults on dignity that could only be restored through further violence.

There were peculiar ironies of class and culture involved in Michoacán's public fights. Orduña's favored assault on the symbols of the licenciate class could be seen as particularly plebeian methods of settling scores. Indeed, the cultural script of "injury as a social metaphor" understood such crass public actions as appropriate only for members of the lower classes.[114] In early modern Spanish culture, such brazen actions were "metaphors of value systems."[115] Orduña thus upended the acceptable semiotics of power, and in so doing, he showed his rivals that he did not care one fucking bit if they thought he was a plebeian thug. His assault on the Inquisition and its official dignitary was simultaneously an assault on the priggish arrogance that he was determined to mock.[116]

If political and ecclesiastical violence was endemic in the provincial capital, another frontier region, Colima, was so violent that the murder of magistrates was common. Political enemies found themselves having their ears sliced off in reprisal for being on the wrong side of a municipal election. River crocodiles ate unfortunate people crossing rivers in an attempt to make the journey to Mexico City to appeal arbitrary legal decisions. We now travel to Colima to watch the spectacular violence of a region so remote that it had no lawyers.

THE CROWN'S MAN: AN "INCORRIGIBLE DELINQUENT," IN WHICH A BUNCH OF SKETCHY AND MURDEROUS DUDES WROUGHT HAVOC IN COLIMA

Setting: Colima
Years: 1530–1610

The mountain villages had no inns, and the forests were full of monsters, giant bugs, and spooky cacao plantations overseen by private militias. Somewhere, a man's ear lay on the ground. The rivers were full of crocodiles and swift enough during summer thunderstorms to sweep away a house. The rivers, valleys, mountains, and roving gangs in Colima and Motines made travel, well, difficult. But one lucky friar, Juan Bautista Moya, had a magic crocodile that bore him across the raging rivers that lay deep in valleys and gullies, so that he could preach to the poor people unable to ford the torrents. Residents in Colima who braved the long journey to Mexico City to appeal to the royal court faced a treacherous mountainous landscape full of rattlesnakes, swarming insects, several varieties of stinging nettles, poison ivy, "scrotum-swelling" poison sumac, and . . . crocodiles. No one knows how many people the hungry river monsters consumed, but people in Colima agreed that travel was dangerous. Many who went to Mexico City never returned—starved, drowned, done in by fever . . . or eaten by crocodiles.[1]

The expanse of mountains from Colima to Motines was vast. Ensconced in the far western corner of New Spain, Colima was lush but surrounded by topographic as well as cultural barriers. In a 1555 lawsuit, Francisco Preciado declared, "It is notorious that there are no lawyers in this province."[2] The paucity of legal talent commended the place to many. Preciado had made the remark to the alcalde ordinario of Colima, an office he had held himself just a year earlier. Having only recently assumed control of vast cacao plantations and encomiendas once owned by his wife Elvira de Arévalo, Preciado was the target of multiple lawsuits, a court conviction for insulting a priest, and assassination attempts.

In 1554, Preciado survived the first assassination attempt against him. A second such attempt finished the job in 1557.[3] And yet through it all, Francisco Preciado

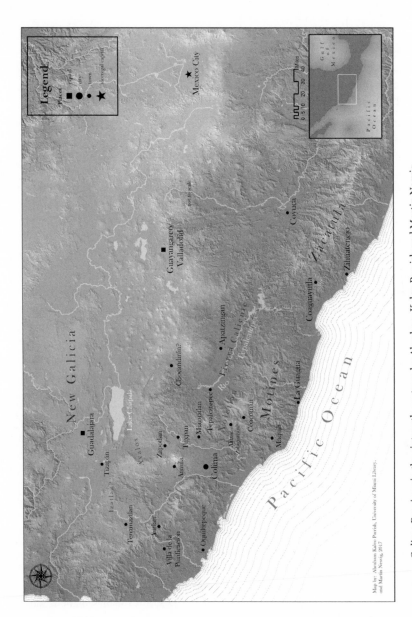

MAP 5.1. Colima Province in the sixteenth century, by Abraham Kaleo Parrish and Martin Nesvig.

insulted and stabbed priests, mocked the royal inspector who fined him for land fraud. He may have been a well-known anticlerical criminal schemer, but he wore his convictions with pride. The feuds and lawsuits and stabbings and land grabs went on and on.

The royal officials who were to apply royal law in Colima were a rough and criminal lot, and the Preciado clan exemplified this tendency. The geographic and juridical isolation of Colima and Motines enabled a regional elite to wield tremendous power and fostered a sense of political impunity.[4] Colima was in fact a refuge from the oversight of royal justice; it was where the very representatives of royal justice hid from the state apparatus they putatively served. That said, resident Spaniards who did not wield such power complained bitterly about the legal and juridical isolation.[5]

Colima was home to a densely settled encomienda and plantation economy based on lucrative cash crops—particularly cacao and coconut—which concentrated wealth in a planter class. There existed an outsized power imbalance between the encomenderos, wealthy plantation owners, and civil authorities, on the one hand, and, on the other, the indigenous pueblos and rancherías (hamlets) and the Spanish, mestizo, and mulato farmers. The situation was ironic in that the bearers of royal justice sought refuge from the authorities above them and distance from a centralized state, and yet did not hesitate to subject those under them to a harsh exercise of authority. But both their escape from royal oversight and their assertion of power constituted a rebuttal to royal control of local politics.[6]

How was a clan like the Preciado family able to obtain, keep, and exploit power as alcaldes despite their thuggish ways? Those who felt themselves to be disenfranchised in the region appealed to royal justice to curb the disproportionate power of alcaldes, residential judges, plantation owners, and Crown-sponsored forced resettlement programs. Their lawsuits reflected the political culture of the region. Spaniards attempting to escape penalties imposed by various tribunals in fact found a region that welcomed convicted criminals.

The economic development of the area as a plantation economy is important to the story of political centralization. In Colima and Motines, indigenous communities appealed to the viceroy, the Audiencia, and the General Indian Court to seek redress of economic grievances, land encroachment, and labor exploitation.[7] Although their cases are instructive on many counts, it is the biased application of the law by the Spanish agents of royal authority—or the agents' failure to address their cases in anything like a timely manner—that allowed the encomenderos, wealthy plantation owners, and civil authorities to develop such a sense of impunity.[8] The indigenous appeals to royal justice explained their grievances in both economic and cultural terms. This was the case, for example, in 1604, when communities in Maquilí claimed that the local judge and agent of forced resettlement had exacted outrageous labor demands, forced them to work on religious holidays and on Sundays, and scandalously opened up an illegal store selling coconut liquor.[9] Even the Spanish residents of the region viewed the economic and political power of the plantation class as ominous. The cacique rule of the region did not just affect indigenous communities; the entire region took part in a collective political misery.

Spanish appeals to royal justice, however, focused on the abuse of legal authority. To the Spanish, the concentration of political and legal power in the local magistrates was unacceptably corrupt, and the colonial class exhibited an egregious abuse of authority. The abuses, for them, constituted judicial, though not necessarily economic, violence. And although they attempted to wrest jurisdictional control away from this class of local officials, their efforts were unsuccessful.

CULTURAL GEOGRAPHY

Colima's climate and population density made it a choice spot for a plantation economy. The region was home to a largely Nahuatl-speaking population, with a mixture of peoples identified as Xilotlanzincas, Coacomanos, and Piñoles. The region as a whole was never subject to the Purépecha Federation, and a Nahua migration from central Mexico likely took place in the fourteenth or fifteenth century. That population then diverged linguistically and culturally from its cousin culture in the Valley of Mexico.[10] We know even less of the region variously described as Motines, Zacatula, and Coacomán.[11] The various original languages of the Zacatula and Motines region, including Cuaucomeca, Huahuan, Motintlan, Maquilan, and Cuitlatecan, were not known outside the region. A kind of Nahuatl identified as "coarse Nahuatl" (*mexicano tosco*) was introduced as a practical form of communication.[12] For example, in Coacomán in northwestern Motines, the original language was Quaucomeca, but by 1580 everyone understood Nahuatl.[13]

The provinces of Colima, Motines, and Tuxpan-Zapotlan were remote and at contact their population densities were remarkably high. For this reason, Cortés assigned the entirety of Colima and Zapotlan to himself.[14] Nuño de Guzmán disputed these encomiendas, and the Mexico Audiencia took judicial possession of them in 1529.[15] By the 1530s, the Crown had seized control of the Cortés encomiendas of Colima and Zapotlan. Others came to Colima in a second wave of land speculation.[16] Martín Monje, for example, a conquistador of Tenochtitlan, received Coyutla in encomienda from Cortés. For his service in New Galicia in the Mixtón War, Monje also received Tenamaztlan.[17] So extensive were Monje's encomiendas that they were called the "pueblos de Martín Monje."[18] The final site of the villa of Colima was probably the original site of the altepetl Tuxpan, whose residents (numbering in the thousands) were forcibly relocated to the broad plains east of the Colima volcano.[19] Like the highland meseta tarasca, Colima, Tuxpan, and Motines sustained a powerful encomienda class, although, given the remoteness of the region, in Colima the encomenderos became major plantation owners with outsized power.

COLIMA'S PLANTATION CLASS

Political violence in viceregal Colima was lavish and sensualist. Plantation wealth in the region derived from two principal products: cacao and coconut liquor. By the 1550s, Colima was home to a Spanish plantation class that had effectively taken over the region, including the area farther east, into the nebulously defined Motines and Coacomán region, in the coastal mountain range of southern Michoacán.[20] Colima was such a desirable region for the encomenderos that these properties were highly litigated. The tribute payments in Colima were among the most lucrative in the entire Michoacán region at least until the plagues of the 1550s and the 1570s.

The plantation economy shaped the political culture of the region. Vast cacao plantations were established by the 1530s. By 1540, there were at least twenty-three plantations in the region, which collectively had close to half a million cacao trees.[21] By 1553, more than thirty plantations were cultivating 726,000 cacao trees.[22] By the seventeenth century, the cacao industry in Colima and Motines was declining, as cultivation was increasingly moving to Soconusco, in southern Chiapas, and to Venezuela. Planters in Colima and Motines began to supplant cacao with coconut palms as their principal cash crop as early as the 1570s, however, following the introduction of coconut palm seeds into Colima (most likely in the 1560s from Philippine sailors). The principal product was a coconut liquor, or wine, which by the seventeenth century had become extremely popular. Unlike cacao, coconut required very little labor, and it proved a cheap investment. By 1600, coconut palms were extensive along the Colima and Michoacán littoral, and by 1612 the region had close to 140,000 coconut palm trees for production of coconut wine.[23] The consumption of this wine was estimated at 10,000 botijas (bottles or flasks each containing between five and eight liters) annually; it was sold primarily in Colima and Michoacán, but also as far away as San Luis Potosí and Parral.

The coconut-liquor industry revealed the extent to which plantation owners could challenge, and even disregard, royal authority. Coconut liquor was considered a vino de tierra (literally, wine of the earth, meaning native to Mexico). All vinos de tierra (including pulque, the fermented drink made from agave cactus) were technically illegal but nevertheless widely available. Spanish coconut plantation owners flouted these regulations and litigated against them.[24] In 1612, for example, the Audiencia of Mexico ordered all coconut palms razed in order to shut

down the coconut-liquor industry. The cabildo of Colima and individual plantation owners opposed viceregal oversight, seeking to preserve their economic interests in coconut-liquor production by resisting the court's attempts to suppress the
industry.[25] Colima's coconut-liquor industry survived by virtue of an exemption
from the general prohibition on vinos de tierra. That Colima was able essentially
to receive absolution for profiting from a technically illegal liquor is the perfect example, in agricultural-economic terms, of the region's political culture.[26] Cultivation of coconut and cacao was not only profitable for plantation owners, but dele-
terious for indigenous communities. Immense swaths of land normally dedicated
to subsistence agriculture were instead cultivated for cash crops. Onerous labor
demands were placed on both encomienda inhabitants and the general population, which was subjected to a kind of peonage. This system, coupled with the high
mortality rates associated with semi-enslavement in copper and gold mines, and
epidemic diseases such as measles and smallpox, led to some of New Spain's most
dramatic demographic declines. In Coacomán, for example, the population in 1535
was approximately 1,920, but by 1580 the town was reduced to 800 inhabitants.[27]
Similar devastation occurred throughout the region. In 1535, Tepalcatepec (strad-
dling the line between Colima and Zacatula) could count approximately 3,840
residents, but by 1555 the population had declined to 2,400, and by 1561, to 1,264.
By 1597, at or near its nadir, Tepalcatepec's population had been reduced to some
520 inhabitants.[28] Unlike the more temperate regions of the meseta tarasca, where
cacao cannot be cultivated, the hotter lowland regions in and around Colima and
Motines proved ecologically ideal for cacao plantations, and the labor abuses associated with cacao cultivation sped the demographic decline of the region.

The outsized wealth produced by cacao and coconut plantations led to a social
and political hierarchy featuring a tiny and wealthy local elite exercising fantastic levels of power. Though many encomenderos were absentee landowners, and
were chided by viceregal authorities for this, their power was nevertheless vast.[29]

LOCAL POWER

Colima was an extreme expression of the concentration of wealth in Spanish landowners seen in the rest of Michoacán. But Colima's political culture was a product
not only of its plantation economy, but also of its jurisdictional isolation. In 1524,
Cortés established Colima as a villa with a resident alcalde mayor (the first was
his cousin, Francisco Cortés). The original jurisdiction of the villa was vast: to the
northwest to Autlan, to the north to Tuxpan and Zapotlan, and to the east to Motines and Coacomán. With Cortés's conquest of Tamazula, Colima, Amula, and
Autlan, and in presuming to assign himself Amula and Tamazula as encomiendas, these regions were considered extensions of the Tarascan Federation and were

thus joined to New Spain.[30] Beginning in the 1530s, these satellite regions were turned into corregimientos, but they remained subject to the alcalde of Colima well into the 1570s.[31] In practical terms, although these remote regions had resident magistrates, they were still subject to the villa of Colima, and, as such, to the alcalde mayor as the ruling judge of first instance. New Spain claimed the entire region, despite the fact that regions as far west as Autlan were even farther west than Guadalajara, which belonged to New Galicia. Some residents, in places like Tuxpan, lived eighty miles from Guadalajara and yet five hundred miles from their overseeing Audiencia in Mexico. In some cases the geography of jurisdiction was absurd: residents in Agualuco, some forty miles due west of Guadalajara, would have had to travel *through* Guadalajara to travel to Mexico City, more than five hundred miles away, to reach the court which oversaw the town.

Francisco Preciado became the prototypical criminal-alcalde of Colima, exploiting the weak oversight from the government of New Spain to great political gain and emboldening his family in the process. The holders of royal power—whether alcaldes, corregidores, or notaries—exploited the concentration of wealth and power at the local level. Municipal officials, such as alcaldes, were a rogue's gallery of scammers, slave-runners, and mafiosos. Francisco Preciado, like so many local political functionaries, was a middling colonial, by his own admission not a lawyer or even a letrado with a rudimentary education. He was a striver as well, having entered into a strategic marriage after proving his bona fides as a second-generation member of Spanish expeditions.

A middling second-generation conquistador, then, Preciado used his influence to obtain substantial economic and political power. Born in Spain, he appeared in New Spain around 1530 and became a member of the Cortés expedition to Teguantepec in 1533. In 1539 he was part of the Ulloa expedition to California. Preciado produced a description of the expedition, later published in Italian in 1556.[32] He was married in Spain to Luisa Gómez, but she evidently remained in Spain.[33] At some point around 1540, Preciado moved to Colima. It was at this point that he began his long, complicated journey from reportedly impoverished and undistinguished middling member of two unsuccessful expeditions to fantastically wealthy plantation owner, alcalde, and virile producer of multiple children.

Preciado's move to Colima was part of a calculated strategy to trade his social prestige for a strategic marriage, despite already having a wife in Spain, although she may have died in the 1530s. In 1540 or 1541, he married Elvira de Arévalo, the widow of the conquistador Diego Garrido. Preciado acquired control of Garrido's encomiendas through his marriage to the grieving widow.[34] Arévalo probably married him for social stability and not for money, as witnesses in later lawsuits agreed that Preciado was broke when he married her.[35] Arévalo was the daughter of the conquistador Alonso de Arévalo, originally a member of the Narváez entrada that shifted allegiance to Cortés to participate in the conquest of Tenochtitlan. Alonso de Arévalo was also part of the early entradas in Zacatula. The Crown had awarded him encomiendas in Xolotlan (in the Motines mountains) and Miaguatlan (just south of Tuxpan).[36] On his death in the late 1540s, his widow, Doña Beatriz López, Elvira de Arévalo's mother, inherited his encomiendas. The family married Elvira to the conquistador Diego Garrido, who was also a former member of the Narváez entrada, in about 1537. The Crown awarded Garrido several encomiendas in the Motines region, including Zapotlanejo and Suchitlan. He died sometime around 1540, leaving the encomiendas to his widow, Elvira, who then married Preciado.[37] By all accounts, Preciado acquired a fortune by marrying her and taking control of these encomiendas. The estates may have brought in as much as 5,000 pesos in tributes annually.[38]

But Preciado's strategic marriage proved dangerous. The law considered Arévalo the technical owner of the estates, though paterfamilial cultural mores dictated that her husband administer the properties. In 1550, Preciado became a citizen (*vecino*) of Colima, the regidor of the villa of Colima, and encomendero of Epatlan. His ability to usurp encomiendas was typical of land acquisition in Colima, which was often bound up in shady deals and frequently featured illegal or questionable possessions. Preciado's mother-in-law, Beatriz López, claimed several encomiendas in the broadly defined Xolotlan region, including Cinacamitlan, Yloli, Chinayo, Omitlan, Xolotlan, Tepenocantitlan, Apapatlan, Miauatlan, Tlalxinastla, Xolotlan de Alcozabi, and Pantla.[39]

Preciado was politically shrewd and baldly cynical. He thought priests were nuisances. In 1550, he publicly insulted the resident curate of Colima, Alonso Sánchez de Miranda. At least two witnesses said he called the curate "a little punk holy man, little punk cleric, little punk vicar."[40] Preciado also told the priest that although he respected the authority of the King and of God, he did not respect the authority of some little priest. Others suggested that Preciado even drew a sword and attempted to stab the priest. Sánchez charged Preciado with sacrilege in his capacity as ecclesiastical judge. Preciado was fined and exiled from Colima for two months, but he returned no worse for the wear.

Arévalo's daughter (by Garrido), Catalina de Arévalo, hotly disputed many of these same encomiendas, planted as they were with vast cacao holdings. Catalina married a man named Pedro de Vivanco in 1552 without Preciado's consent. Vivanco then sued Preciado, apparently in an attempt to retake several of the plantations. The suit turned into a full-fledged showdown over property claims. Preciado's wife had disapproved of Catalina's marriage.[41] At issue was the alleged abduction of Vivanco's bride by her grandmother, Beatriz López, who had evidently tried to stop the couple from consummating the marriage. Vivanco filed suit before the alcalde of Colima claiming that López had in effect kidnapped his new bride just as they were leaving the church. The couple had legally wed in a ceremony before the same curate of Colima, Alonso Sánchez, whom Preciado had insulted. López had allegedly taken Catalina with her to her house by force, and then kept her granddaughter shut in, preventing her from leaving to make her marital bed with her new husband. Vivanco lost the case, but he appealed it to the provisor of the diocese, Juan Zurnero, asking that his bride be given over to the alcalde ordinario, Juan de Aguilar. No such luck. Vivanco then said the alcalde mayor who had heard the case, Luis Ramírez, should have been recused, as he was not a lawyer, and the case should be retried on that account. No dice, said the alcalde. The case stalled, and it is unclear what became of the marriage.[42]

The system both served Preciado and proved his downfall. On the one hand, lawsuits like the one filed by Vivanco highlight the extent to which an alcalde's arbitrary judgment could rupture personal lives and destroy fortunes. A wealthy and powerful woman like Beatriz López could decide that she disapproved of her granddaughter's marital decision and imprison the girl in her own home. The recourse to the alcalde proved useless. Vivanco was within his rights to travel to Mexico City to appeal the decision, but other, more direct methods were generally used.

Preciado's success resulted in part from the free-wheeling political culture of Colima. After his marriage to Arévalo, he assumed control of the vast encomiendas she had inherited from her husband. With this property, he became one of the wealthiest cacao planters of the region. But the wealth that Preciado amassed was clearly achieved as well through extraordinary levels of brutishness. In fact, during his visita, a royal inspector, Lorenzo Lebrón de Quiñones, condemned Preciado for abuse of authority; at least 1,500 indigenous residents had evidently died on his plantations through abuse and overwork.[43]

Colima's citizens even elected Preciado alcalde in 1554. Although many alcaldes in New Spain received their appointments from the viceroy or the Crown, Colima's citizenry appears to have appointed its own magistrates. Even though Preciado had amassed a fortune and held a position as royal magistrate, he was always legally bound to obey the Crown's dictates. But the inspection of the region by Lebrón de Quiñones showed the limitations of the Crown's power to extract penalties against errant encomenderos.

Lebrón de Quiñones had been appointed a judge in the New Galicia Audiencia in 1548 and had a reputation as a diligent critic of encomenderos and mine operators.[44] The Crown commissioned him to undertake a royal inspection of the province of Colima. He targeted landowners connected to the Preciado family, who he charged held no legitimate titles to the land they claimed. For example, when he filed his visita report in 1554, he claimed that Beatriz López could present no legal title to the family properties she claimed were hers. Instead, she held the estates as legal guardian for her son, Pedro de Arévalo, who was the brother of Preciado's wife, Elvira de Arévalo. The visitador was attempting to vacate her claims in order to have the encomiendas escheated to the Crown, as the New Laws of 1542 stipulated that encomiendas were supposed to revert to the Crown after the death of an encomendero, though many exceptions to this rule occurred. But a visita was one thing; actual possession of the lands continued, and López retained the plantations.

The royal inspector held authority only on paper; in practice, he was unable to exact sentences against wealthy planters. When he disputed Preciado's claims to several plantations as illegal, the charges never stuck. For example, in 1554, Lebrón de Quiñones claimed that Preciado had made bogus claims to at least twenty-seven encomiendas in Xolotlan and Motines, including Epatlan, Suchitlan, Alimanci, Vitontlan, Zapotlanejo, and Oquiltepeque.[45] But possession proved more powerful than law, and despite the charges, and the fact that Preciado was unable to present any valid title to the estates, Preciado and his son Juan continued to profit from large cacao plantations in Motines and Zapotlan through the end of the century.

Preciado made financial enemies in the process of asserting his claims. A royal inspector like Lebrón de Quiñones could attempt to vacate a claim to possession, but in practice, it was difficult, and often impossible, to enforce any decision in such matters. A series of lawsuits over the inheritance of Garrido's encomiendas suggests that Preciado simply achieved his wealth by force. In January 1553, when Vivanco filed the suit over his marriage to Catalina and her inheritance of properties from the Garrido estate, one man testified that Preciado had brought no financial resources to the marriage, and had instead enriched himself solely through his wife's encomiendas.[46] Vivanco also attempted to force the alcalde to award him portions of the Garrido estate in 1555, when Elvira de Arévalo died, but he did not succeed.[47]

Preciado had other enemies as well, and sometimes fights broke out. One was Francisco López, a Spaniard born in Seville sometime around 1530.[48] It is unclear whether this López, the López who appears in a lawsuit against Preciado in 1554, was the same man as Francisco López de Avecilla, Colima's notary in the 1560s through the 1580s.[49] In any case, in the 1554 case, López sued Preciado, who was then an alcalde, for an unspecified sum of money.[50] According to the lawsuit, López had spoken to Preciado in front of the town market, demanding payment — for what, exactly, it is not clear, though Preciado did not reject the claim that he owed López money. Reportedly, Preciado had told López that he would pay him later. López found this unsatisfactory and demanded that the payment be made immediately; if Preciado did not pay him then and there, he would file a civil suit against the alcalde. Preciado responded, with a cavalier attitude, that he was free to do as he pleased. López replied that Preciado should expect legal notice, and Preciado offered a classic riposte: "Kiss my ass."[51]

Then the punches flew. Preciado apparently landed several blows on López, crying out, "Defend the Crown!" López eventually drew a dagger and stabbed the alcalde. Preciado survived, though the wound was deep. Bystanders wrestled López into submission even as Preciado screamed, "Son of a whore, faggot, you are going to jail!"[52] And, indeed, off to jail López went. The alcalde declared the sentence, even though he was the aggrieved party. As was often the case, the alcalde in Colima wielded absolute power—in this case, conflating the roles of victim, prosecutor, and judge. López was ordered to pay a fine and exiled from Colima for six years.

Although Preciado refused to die, much to the chagrin of his enemies, and despite the wounds inflicted by López, he remained gravely injured. A year later, in August 1555, the Crown ordered a legal inspection (*residencia*) of Juan de Araña's term as alcalde mayor. Diego de Almodóvar had been involved in some kind of imbroglio that had been described as a quarrel (*desacato*) with Preciado, but Araña had refused to prosecute Almodóvar as required by law.[53] In 1555, Preciado did not exercise the office of magistrate. Instead, he was embroiled in a series of lawsuits over his attempt to take possession of various cacao plantations originally belonging to his step-daughter. The royal inspector Lebrón de Quiñones levied heavy fines and penalties on Preciado during his visita, but Preciado appealed the decision to the Mexico Audiencia in 1555.[54]

The Audiencia affirmed the penalty on Preciado in September 1556. The sentence was delivered in Colima: there would be a fine of 1,191 pesos and 6 tomines— a small fortune.[55] Lebrón de Quiñones returned to Colima in 1556 to collect the money, but to no avail. Preciado took refuge in the local church, fearful that the inspector would have him arrested, and, according to the custom of the times, that was usually sufficient to ensure his safety.

Lebrón de Quiñones came up against the well-organized opposition of the encomendero, plantation, and miner class. He was determined to be a strict enforcer of the New Laws. He had made numerous enemies as audiencia judge in New Galicia for his reforming zeal. Encomenderos like Preciado were determined to undermine the royal inspector's charge. For example, Lebrón de Quiñones condemned a Spanish citizen of Colima for nearly beating to death an indigenous noble of Tuxpan whom Lebrón de Quiñones had vested with power to conduct investigations. The royal inspector sentenced the Spaniard to a two-year exile and a fine of 100 pesos. The Mexico Audiencia vacated the sentence, to Lebrón de Quiñones's chagrin. Eventually, the royal inspector became so unpopular in Colima that encomenderos conspired to have him condemned judicially. They fabricated a series of charges against him and had him jailed. He escaped and went to Mexico City and, ultimately, to Spain, where the Council of the Indies acquitted him of the charges in 1561. But the fate of Lebrón de Quiñones in Colima is instructive in understanding the limits of royal oversight.[56]

If the Audiencia failed to extract the fine from Preciado, his enemies were more successful. In fact, they applied a more final justice—they murdered him. This happened in 1557, when Preciado was again the alcalde of Colima—but his tenure was (to put it mildly) cut short. By then he enjoyed a dizzying network of family and business connections. Sometime in 1551 or 1552, he had granted power-of-attorney to a Spanish man named Garci Garcés de Mancilla to purchase slaves on his behalf.[57] This was the man who murdered him in 1557. The reasons are unknown. Obviously, however, Preciado had made one enemy too many. In August 1557, a man named Bartolomé Sánchez, writing from Colima to Araña in Zalaguacan on a different subject, mentioned the news that Garcés had murdered Preciado and was imprisoned for it.[58]

It seemed like the intrigues would never end, even after his death. Diego de Almodóvar was named legal guardian of Preciado's children in October 1557, to oversee the estate, presumably.[59] This came as Bartolomé Garrido died, throwing the title to the estates into legal limbo. Almodóvar, among others, was named as an executor and had to deal with yet another lawsuit involving the estate, filed by a Spanish man, Juan Fernández Ladrillero.[60] The political and land interest problems came and went in a constant flow, like the ocean's tides.

After Francisco Preciado's murder, the region's tenuous jurisdictional cohesion deteriorated. Spanish residents began to appeal to the Crown to redress the abuse of authority. Yet the Preciado clan continued to assert wide-ranging economic and political power. Francisco Preciado had two wives, indigenous mistresses—or rape victims—and countless children. He had five children by his first wife, Luisa Gómez, in Spain, including Juan de Preciado, who became Colima's regidor in 1561 and 1564 and alcalde mayor in 1577. Juan had inherited a family encomienda by 1568.[61] Lebrón de Quiñones's sentence had left the Preciado family estate in legal limbo. Nevertheless, Juan claimed some of the old Arévalo plantations after his father's death and successfully retained Epatlan throughout the 1560s.[62]

Early in its social and political development, Colima established a reputation for lawlessness and disregard for orthodox decorum. The leading political and economic actors of the region—alcaldes, planters, encomenderos—made few friends or allies among representatives of the Church. Unlike the actions of the Spanish encomenderos of central Michoacán, who offered aid to the missionaries, Colima landholders in fact exhibited a clear contempt for the Church. If anything, its landholders and planters viewed organized Catholicism and royal courts as irritants. This constitutional disregard for religious and royal oversight was the basis of Colima's appeal as a region of refuge from court systems.

LEGAL LIMBO, 1568–1578

Fugitives saw Colima as an excellent place to escape from the inquisitional and diocesan courts. They found a local culture that refused to punish their blasphemies, bigamies, and heresies and that even often embraced them as members of small-town life. Juan Pablos Carrión, a wealthy naval captain from Valladolid, Spain, successfully evaded arrest by the Inquisition for several years in Colima. He came to New Spain in the 1520s and, in one of the earliest attempts at a Pacific crossing to the Philippines, sailed from Zihuatanejo in 1527. The crossing failed, and his whereabouts in the 1530s are uncertain. He traveled to Spain in the 1540s as the treasurer of the archbishop of Seville, in the process marrying a woman named María de Salcedo. He returned to New Spain sometime around 1550 and became a vecino of Colima. He then made a fortune as a naval captain in the armada system and became involved in the provisions trade for the planned Philippine expedition.[63] Though he did not participate in the Legazpi expedition of 1564, he made the port of Villa de Purificación his home.

Around 1566, Carrión married a Spanish woman, Leonor Suárez, in Colima. Upon learning of this detail, in the spring of 1568, the diocesan court opened an investigation against him for bigamy.[64] The case stalled. In October and November 1569, the diocesan inspector traveled to Tuxpan and Zapotlan, where Carrión resided, to depose witnesses in the case. He could find no conclusive evidence, as Carrión insisted that he had never formally married Salcedo in Spain.

Although the inquisitors and their agents, including Cristóbal de Badillo, continued to pursue him, Carrión eluded capture for seven years, through 1575. When he lived in Zapotlan and Tuxpan, the citizenry refused to relinquish him to the inquisitional authorities. The collective refusal to deliver him over was theoretically a crime—they were essentially aiding and abetting a criminal fugitive—but local residents cared little for this legal nicety.[65] It is unclear whether the diocesan Inquisition ever sentenced Carrión. The inquisitional case file of 1572 includes a letter from a Juan de Carrión, purporting to be a relative of his, claiming that Juan Pablos Carrión had at some point been excommunicated by the bishop, but that during Holy Week of 1571 he had confessed before an Augustinian friar to obtain absolution.[66]

On 1 March 1572, Mexico's inquisitional prosecutor Alonso Fernández Bonilla reopened the case, stating that he had evidence indicating that Carrión was a bigamist. Bonilla also suggested that Carrión had sold a considerable amount of property to shell corporations to keep it from being impounded by inquisitional authorities as surety for a bond or fine.[67] Carrión had sold an estate, presumably to be held in name only, to the above-mentioned Juan de Carrión. In December 1573, the Inquisition in Mexico City convicted Carrión in absentia for bigamy.[68] Three months later, on 4 March 1574, the Inquisition reaffirmed this conviction and ordered him to appear in a public auto-de-fé. They exiled him from New Spain for ten years and ordered him to pay an exhorbitant fine of 1,000 ducats.[69] Yet the Inquisition still lacked a prisoner. Carrión was undoubtedly living in Zapotlan. This information wound its way to inquisitors in Mexico City by October, and inquisitors, using the inquisitional comisario, Cristóbal Badillo, as intermediary, ordered the parish priest of Colima to apprehend Carrión.

The priest, Álvaro de Grijalva, deliberately dragged his feet. He unctuously wrote to Badillo saying he was unable to travel to Zapotlan to have Carrión arrested because he had no bailiff to accompany him, and that in any case, the deep canyons and river valleys made the trip much too treacherous. Perhaps, Grijalva offered pusillanimously, the vicar of Tamazula could apprehend Carrión instead? Badillo was not amused and penned an angry reply, informing the unhelpful curate that the Inquisition did not exist for his comfort.[70] Grijalva finally appeared in Zapotlan on 14 November 1574 to gather information about Carrión, hoping to apprehend him.

The inquisitors had no choice but to issue an arrest warrant for Carrión; this they did in February 1575. The inquisitors ordered the comisario of Veracruz to force Carrión to embark for Spain to begin his exile.[71] It is unclear whether he complied, as the inquisitional case file runs cold at this point. Carrión was present in Zapotlan in December 1576, however, when he sold the interests of his Zapuchimilco cacao plantation to a Manuel Salgado for 400 pesos.[72]

Then something remarkable occurred. In an undated letter, Carrión appealed directly to the viceroy, asking him to commute his sentence, and the inquisitors granted the request. On 24 January 1577, they absolved Carrión: he did not have to go into exile; nor, it seems, would he have to pay the fine.[73] Carrión had evaded capture for nearly a decade with the open aid of Spaniards and Nahuas in Zapotlan and Colima. In 1577, he returned to Zapotlan a free man, with a concession in the Philippine provisioning business.[74] His wife, Leonor Suárez, vested with legal power of attorney for her husband, delivered copies of the exculpation to the viceroy in Mexico City in March 1577. The sale of the Zapuchimilco estate remained an open case through 1579. Carrión had escaped inquisitional condemnation. Leonor Suárez, for her part, had affirmed her status as his legitimate wife before the Zapotlan magistrate.[75]

Carrión was just one more Spanish resident flouting the imperial system. Neither the Inquisition, nor local officials, nor the Crown could bring him to heel or force him to behave. Ultimately, he had to answer the charges against him, but neither the accusation against him nor the conviction in a tribunal caused him to suffer serious social harm. It is quite possible that he lived out the rest of his life in Zapotlan on the warm plains beneath the Colima volcano.

Some people viewed Colima as an excellent place to escape legal systems; others saw its lack of legal controls as placing too much power in the local agents of faraway and abstract court systems. The legal situation in Colima led to numerous complaints from Spanish citizens of the region, who would file suit through the city council (*cabildo*) of Guadalajara.[76] The Spanish residents of Zacatula and Colima appealed to the Crown sometime in 1573 to move their region to the jurisdiction of Guadalajara. The Crown obliged, ordering the Guadalajara Audiencia, in a decree of 18 February 1574, to hear all legal appeals from those regions. This decision voided New Spain's jurisdiction over Colima.[77] In March 1576, Guadalajara followed up by asking the Crown to order tributes from Ávalos, Amula, Colima, and Yçatlan to be moved from Mexico to Guadalajara. Guadalajara's cabildo argued that this shift would ease the burden on the indigenous population, as its members would no longer have to travel such a long distance to pay the tribute, and that it would increase tribute payments, since the closer location would allow for a more efficient system.[78] The first explanation was undoubtedly a cynical ploy to increase the wealth of encomenderos and plantation owners; it is unlikely they were concerned about the comfort of the indigenous subjects.

New Spain intervened to nullify the Crown's decision to move the jurisdiction of Colima, Motines, Zacatula, and Zapotlan, and on 5 July 1578, the Crown reversed course and reassigned the pueblos and the villa (Colima) to New Spain.[79] Several citizens of Guadalajara and Colima came forward to litigate the decision — the case dragged on for decades, with the Crown ultimately deciding in favor of New Spain's claims. It is unclear whether a formal suit against New Spain or the Audiencia of Mexico was lodged, and if so, when, but in 1596 the Crown did make note of the fact that it had received many complaints from vecinos of Guadalajara and Colima who were aggrieved by the decision.[80] New Spain retained jurisdiction over Colima by default, because the Crown refused to give legitimacy to the complaints of Colima's residents about remoteness.

CRISTÓBAL PRECIADO, AN "INCORRIGIBLE DELINQUENT" (1572–1581)

Into this jurisdictional free-for-all stepped Cristóbal Preciado, one of the region's most notorious womanizers, drunks, and blasphemers.[81] Francisco Preciado had fathered at least six *criollo* (American-born Spaniard) children with Elvira de Arévalo, and one of them, Cristóbal, had been born in Colima in approximately 1550.[82] Even as a teen Cristóbal had had a flair for offensive language. Witnesses denounced him to the Inquisition for blasphemy in 1572, but no trial ensued.[83] Apparently exculpated, or at least having successfully avoided arrest in the case, Cristóbal moved to Guadalajara in 1572 or 1573 to study, presumably letters or the law. He asked for and received 300 pesos in 1573 from his estate guardian for the costs associated with his education.[84] At some point over the next few years he made a career for himself as a petty letrado, living on the inheritance from his once-wealthy father. In 1579, Cristóbal was at least present in Colima when he asked to be named guardian of the estate of his nieces.[85] Otherwise we know little of his activities, but later inquisitional investigations reveal a man accustomed to the legal impunity he enjoyed who was also fond of young, indigenous girls.

If legal witnesses were accurate, by 1581 Cristóbal and his mestizo half-brother Francisco spent a good deal of their spare time together drinking pulque. Francisco had been born to an unnamed indigenous mistress of the first Francisco Preciado. A mestizo named Martín Hernández denounced the pair before inquisitors in Mexico City. He knew the two in Tizapán (near Lake Chapala) and Chocandirán. Hernández claimed that Francisco had referred to the crucifix around his neck as the devil, and had said that "a man who does not drink alcohol would not enter heaven."[86] The inquisitors in Mexico City never prosecuted the case, but they did investigate it.

The Francisco Preciado investigated by inquisitors in 1581 is a fitting symbol of his father's debauchery. His murdered father had flouted the legal decorum of political office; he had a taste for the good life and, like many other encomenderos, had an indigenous mistress—though by consent or by coercion we cannot know. He had fathered a legitimate son named Francisco around 1549.[87] His will, dated in 1555, mentions a mestizo son to receive 150 pesos. The name Francisco Preciado appears two other times in the archives, and it is not clear whether any of these people are actually the same individual. An indigenous ladino man named Francisco Preciado, a shoemaker by profession, filed a petition in Colima in 1580 noting that he was a vecino. In 1588, the alcalde of Colima prosecuted a forty-something-year-old mestizo named Francisco Preciado for stealing a horse. This mestizo was described as a music and dance teacher.[88] As civil notaries often made snap judgments of ethnic identity, the fact that one was described as indigenous and another as mestizo would not preclude the three Francisco Preciados mentioned in civil documents at this time from being the same man. In Colima and the tierra caliente, terms like mestizo or mulato were slippery, especially given the increasing presence of Africans in the region, the demographic decline of the indigenous population, and the conflation of categories such as mestizo and mulato in common usage.[89]

Cristóbal and his half-brother Francisco were by all accounts good friends. Soon after the dismissal of the 1581 case against Francisco, Cristóbal was living large in Chocandirán. Cristóbal and Francisco had a lot in common; Cristóbal shared his brother's louche ways. Ecclesiastical prosecutors had to investigate Cristóbal's raucous behavior a second time in 1582. By then he had apparently been acting as a notary in Chocandirán for some time but was living in the remote area as a fugitive from justice, having been exiled from the pueblos of Ávalos.[90] This squares with Martín Hernández's statement that he had known the mestizo Francisco in Tizapán and had later come to know Cristóbal in Chocandirán.[91]

It is unclear what brought Cristóbal to Chocandirán. If witness statements are to be believed, it was the sense of impunity he found there and its remoteness. High in the mountains west of Uruapan along an escarpment falling to the valley below in Tingüindín, the region was topographically almost untouchable. Cristóbal had moved to Chocandirán sometime in 1580 or 1581, when he had been installed as a local notary. It was Felipe de Ayala, the beneficed priest of Chocandirán, who compiled the documents against Cristóbal in the 1582 investigation and informed the inquisitors that Cristóbal was the notary—he had been assigned to civil affairs in the town, but had been exiled from Ávalos as a result of bad conduct.[92]

Ayala gathered witness statements about the offensive behavior of this man who had been inflicted on the outpost town as a royal official. Cristóbal had likely fallen from grace in New Galicia and fled across the Audiencia border in search of a halfway decent job. Witnesses from Chocandirán in December 1582 described an irreverent, lascivious young man.[93] Ayala summarized his behavior:

> He goes about sowing disorder and chaos among both the Spaniards and Indians. . . . [H]e is a man of wicked morals and goes about humping the indigenous women from behind, forcing himself on them. He is an incorrigible delinquent who with his bad example goes from house to house semi-naked clothed only in shirtsleeves and white underwear. Because he spends all his time going from house to house, he does not go to mass on Sundays or obligatory feast days. As a result of his example, the Indians have stopped going to mass as well. Because he is the notary for the law, the locals are terrified of him. Moreover, there is no other form of entertainment in this town except to play cards. . . . He also goes about saying scandalous things, such as claiming that even if he commits a mortal sin, he would be absolved only by beating his chest. . . . He has also had carnal access to many women . . . and it is well known that this man Preciado, because of his wicked language, has been exiled from the towns of Ávalos.[94]

The charges against Cristóbal Preciado underscore the general impunity of royal officials in the region. Much like the encomenderos of an earlier generation in Uruapan and Tancítaro, he represented an illustrious tradition of contempt for the social discipline of the Church. But his career and lifestyle could not have been possible in a colonial system with strong enforcement by the Church. Instead, he could live in towns as a representative of the very imperial order that presumably needed to rein him in. The proximity to New Galicia's diocesan border meant that it was easy for someone like him to flee justice and reinstall himself inside the boundaries of Michoacán as a town functionary.

The ecclesiastical judge completed his investigation of Cristóbal Preciado in December 1582. Ayala forwarded the results to the inquisitors in Mexico City, who issued a subpoena for Preciado to appear before them. Then, in February 1583, the alcalde of Colima called him as a witness in a civil proceeding.[95] With Preciado's whereabouts readily apparent, Diego Muñoz, the Franciscan friar, served the inquisitional subpoena.[96] Preciado appeared before the inquisitors on 9 April 1583. Remarkably enough, the inquisitors simply warned him to reform his roguish ways; after keeping him in jail for three nights, they sent him back to Colima.[97]

Once he had been snatched away from his lifestyle in Chocandirán, things did not look good for the young debauchee. Unlike his half-brother Juan, Cristóbal was acculturated to life in rural Michoacán. After the 1572 case, he had disappeared for more than a decade; he had most likely gone to Colima. Sometime before 1583, he had married Doña Isabel de Rojas. It was the same kind of marriage his father had effected, resulting in property and a step up the social ladder. Rojas was the daughter of Juan de Araña and Doña Isabel Ruiz de Monjaraz. Araña was a peninsular who had been corregidor of Amula as early as 1545. He was variously regidor (1550) and alcalde ordinario (1551, 1554, 1559, 1563, and 1564) of Colima and alcalde mayor of Motines (1561 and 1567).[98] Yet his tenure proved complicated as well—he had apparently protected Diego de Almodóvar by shielding him from prosecution in a dispute over insulting Francisco Preciado in 1554 or 1555.[99]

Motines proved critical. Doña Isabel Ruiz de Monjaraz, the daughter of the conquistador Martín Ruiz de Monjaraz, a Cortés partisan, was a scion of conquistador wealth. She had married Manuel Cáceres, another conquistador of Mexico and Cortés partisan who had been given several encomiendas in Colima, including Maquilí and much of Motines. When Cáceres died, sometime before 1550, she married Araña, who stood to gain from the passing of at least part of the encomienda to his new bride.[100]

Thus Cristóbal Preciado married into a wealthy and prestigious family of conquistador-encomenderos, as had his father. Yet criminal problems haunted him. His mother-in-law apparently lived most of her final years in the Motines mountains.[101] In August 1589, she died intestate on her cacao plantation, called Zalaguacan, deep in the mountains of Motines near Alima.[102] The Zalaguacan plantation had already been litigated in the 1550s on several occasions, including by none other than Cristóbal's father, Francisco Preciado.[103]

When Doña Isabel died in 1589, the teniente de alcalde of Motines issued an arrest warrant for Cristóbal. Although the charge is unclear, the magistrate said that Cristóbal had been absent from the Colima-Motines region for six years, and had taken up sanctuary in the Franciscan church in Tuxpan to avoid arrest.[104] Monjaraz's daughter (and Preciado's wife) Doña Isabel de Rojas was presumed to be among the heirs, but Preciado could not be located for a deposition concerning the division of the estate.

Cristóbal Preciado seems to have assumed control of Zalaguacan at some point in the 1590s. He essentially had disappeared in February 1583. Colima's magistrate said as much when, in 1589, he said Preciado had absented himself from the jurisdiction for six years and no one knew where he was. Nor does Preciado appear in any civil contracts in Colima in these years. He merely slipped away. Maybe he was hiding in a remote hamlet. He had been exculpated in the 1582 case, but there may have been something Preciado feared. For all we know he may have been wanted on other criminal charges, or may have owed money to the Monjaraz estate. And indeed, he was to be charged with yet other crimes. But as was the case with his own father, criminal conviction did not prevent him from becoming a royal official.

Cristóbal fell off the archival radar for fifteen years and went into the remote mountains as a cacao plantation owner. But a massive criminal investigation into his behavior in 1598 revealed that he had acquired cacao plantations and houses in Maquilí, Zalaguacan, and Tlazahuayan—places that generally did not exist on maps but were deep in the western end of the Motines mountain range.

In 1598, the alcalde mayor of Colima investigated claims that Cristóbal Preciado was living in the mountains near Alima and, illegally, had claimed authority as the teniente de alcalde.[105] Preciado appears to have lived up to the family name. In these remote cacao plantations, he had traveled with a band of armed men. The alcalde of Colima built a criminal case against him for having falsely claimed he was the local magistrate and for abuse of power. The alcalde traveled to the remote village of Tlazahuayan in November 1598 after the Audiencia dispatched him to investigate the rogue plantation owner. No one knew if he was the local magistrate, since no one had any idea whether he had an actual appointment. But Preciado had arrested a man named Diego Arías and placed him in a dank room in his plantation house. Arías's indigenous servant Esteban Sánchez had the bad luck to be on a remote road between cacao plantations when Preciado and his gang found him. Knowing he was Arías's servant, Preciado had Sánchez bound and flogged to a bloody pulp.[106]

Flogging indigenous residents was not Preciado's only offense to local sensibilities. Various witnesses claimed that he gleefully bragged that his cacao plantations were netting as much as forty *fanegas* of cacao annually, a mind-boggling amount for a single plantation (each fanega would have been about 3 bushels, or about 90 liters—though the quantity varied by locale—or between 100 and 150 pounds of produce). Witnesses believed that the plantation netted a fortune of between 1,000 and 1,800 pesos annually. Preciado probably paid his small militia with the sale of the cacao. Life was good for him. Although we will never know how long he had been in Motines, it was clear that he was comfortably installed, and yet feared. The Audiencia commission to investigate his reign of terror noted that he was a well-known "restless, seditious man and general enemy of all the citizens of that republic."[107] Complaints of abuse of authority and negligence of legal duty characterized his rule. A residencia revealed that he had forced indigenous residents into unpaid service in his home. In one case, he had deliberately refused to investigate a homicide in the region.[108] He may have also had an indigenous mistress, though the claim seemed trivial to the court, which ignored that line of inquiry.[109]

We do not know what ultimately became of Cristóbal Preciado. He simply disappeared from the archival record. He had been a kind of refugee from the rule of law, city life, and royal courts. He had flouted the Inquisition, the city council of Colima, and the Audiencia of Mexico. Maybe someone murdered him. Perhaps he faded into daily life on his remote mountain plantations, wealthy, obscure, and feared. If that was the case, his story was as typical of the region as anyone's.

LAW AND PERSONAL ANIMUS IN A FRONTIER ZONE

Cristóbal Preciado was hardly the last of the criminal alcaldes. In 1577, for example, the alcalde Juan de Iniesta sued Diego Morán for several hundred pesos; Morán claimed he could not pay the debts, and Iniesta ordered Morán's cacao and coconut plantation in Caxtila to be sold at public auction. Juan Fernández de Ocampo, son of the conquistador Juan Fernández el Viejo, and an encomendero of Motines, offered to purchase the plantation for 1,550 pesos, but he was accused of taking possession of the land before making full payment and subsequently jailed. He was to be released upon making the final payment, but it appears that he never did, and the plantation was returned to the Morán family.[110] Fernández de Ocampo was also charged in a series of lawsuits concerning unpaid debts from 1577 to 1579.[111] In a separate suit involving the mortgaging of a cacao plantation in Zapuchimilco (which had belonged to the Carrión family), Fernández de Ocampo was entrusted, in February 1580, with a black slave to be sold as payment for a portion of the mortgage.[112]

Despite his many legal troubles, Fernández de Ocampo had become the alcalde of Motines by August 1581.[113] Yet he was never safe from local enemies. At some point, probably between 1581 and 1585, he appealed some of these cases to the Mexico Audiencia. In 1585, no longer an alcalde, he appeared in person in Mexico City to complain that while he was away from his hacienda near Maquilí, forasteros had stolen his livestock, but that the alcalde had refused to prosecute the case. He also charged the alcalde with having sold his property without just cause.[114] Fernández de Ocampo exercised some degree of economic power, but he found that the manipulation of local power could cut both ways. He had made too many ene-mies, and they, in turn—in the form of the alcalde—prevented actions to be taken on his behalf. Like so many others, he had to choose between making an expensive trip to Mexico City and accepting the alcalde's rule as fiat.

Francisco Preciado, Cristóbal Preciado, and Juan Fernández de Ocampo moved in and out of the legitimate royal court system. Spanish residents of Colima continued to litigate to remove themselves from the oversight of such alcaldes. From November 1597 through February 1598, the Guadalajara Audiencia judge Francisco de Pareja heard testimony from several witnesses about their objections to Colima being placed within the jurisdiction of New Spain. At the core of their reasoning was the fact that any appeals to royal justice in Mexico City were pro-hibitive, and as such royal officials could abuse their authority. At least eight wit-nesses provided depositions in the 1597–1598 appeal, and all of them were Spanish men who claimed citizenship in Guadalajara or Colima.

Their arguments were virtually all the same: Colima was much too far from Mexico City, five hundred miles away, and this distance was prohibitive; the radi-cal changes in the climate and the treacherous terrain, including raging rivers—not to mention the monstrous caimans and the bandits—were dangerous; there were no reliable inns between Colima and Mexico City, whereas between Colima and Guadalajara, one could count on places to stay at regular intervals and places to eat at reasonable prices. Because of the lack of an inn (*venta*) system in the mountainous regions in Motines and Zacatula, one was forced to bring a mule and supplies. Everyone seemed to agree that such a journey would cost about 300 pesos—the equivalent of one year's salary for a parish priest or university profes-sor. Moreover, everyone seemed to know of individuals who had perished on the journey, owing to these very difficulties; indeed, the journey required traversing first the rugged coastal mountain range, which was hot, semiarid, and legendary for its bugs; then the tierra caliente, where the altitude drops to below 1,000 feet above sea level in the Balsas River Basin, and where daytime temperatures hover around 90 to 100 degrees all year; and then back up the mountains of eastern Mi-choacán, a cold region whose mountain passes stand at 8,000 to 9,000 feet above sea level. And then there were the crocodiles.

The result of these difficulties was that any lawsuit valued less than 300 pesos was not worth pursuing in Mexico City, and the local alcaldes and corregidores exploited the situation to their advantage. Witnesses told of alcaldes who extorted ridiculous taxes, arbitrarily confiscated cacao shipments, and committed outra-geous acts of violence. In short, alcaldes and encomenderos could act with im-punity in the region because the available court of appeals was simply too far away for most people to seek recourse there. One planter explained the political violence in startling detail. His name was Francisco Ávila de Çepeda, and he was a citizen of Guadalajara, but he held cacao plantations in Motines and traveled to Colima frequently. He explained that the journey to Mexico City was impractical. But the alcalde of Colima, Miguel Balero, had fraudulently overcharged him the *alcabala*, or royal assessment, and, when he refused to pay it, seized three mules and ten fanegas of cacao. The difficulty of the journey prevented him from appealing his case to the Audiencia. His deposition adds detail to the shifting political geography of the mountainous regions. Ávila noted that he had cacao plantations in Motines, but his final appeal was that the province of La Guaua (a town on the coast) be transferred to New Galicia—yet he also referred to La Guaua as being part of Zacatula.[115] With the sprawling cacao industry in the region, the coastal regions were geographically ill-defined.

The culture of local *caciquismo* only intensified over the years, as might be expected for a region dominated by cash-crop agriculture and characterized by juridical remoteness. Despite the appeal by Guadalajara, the jurisdictional situation did not change, and the Crown left Colima within New Spain. This arrangement allowed local authorities to thwart legal appeals to their authority, to extort both Spanish and indigenous residents, to extract personal revenge, and to stonewall legal remedies. Some of the reported cases were spectacularly gruesome. In the first decade of the seventeenth century, residents accused the alcalde of Colima, Miguel Balero, of stealing royal funds for his private interests. In 1610, the city council elected Juan de Solórzano as alcalde. Balero, who had accused Solórzano of having cut off his ear in a dispute over taxes, appealed to royal justice to block his appointment.[116] The Audiencia of Mexico attempted to intervene from afar, but its actions do not seem to have had much effect in Colima. The severed ear was never found, and business continued as usual in Colima, which is to say, with political and physical violence the norm.

REVERSE REGIONS OF REFUGE

I have only discussed a brief sampling of dozens of such cases in the region. In these and other cases, the Spaniards themselves claimed that the region's jurisdictional isolation created a culture of political corruption. Local appointees of royal authority employed the legal system to their advantage time and again. They were the judges of first instance, and as such they possessed wide-ranging powers to determine the enforcement of royal law. Legal appeal to the Audiencia in Mexico City, let alone to the Council of Indies, was a theoretical abstraction. The alcaldes knew this perfectly well, and their stories highlight how they were able to exploit this jurisdictional frontier to remarkable levels of political self-interest through physical and legal violence.

Biography after biography, family history after family history, cascading over each other as easily as the crocodile-laden rivers of the region, too numerous to count, demonstrate the vast buffet of political violence that typified the first generations of Colima's colonial rule. No king, no viceroy, no royal inspector, no inquisitor could manage to bring the rowdy Spaniards of Colima to heel. The Spaniards snubbed every such attempt even as they happily benefited from the largesse of the very colonial system they purportedly represented but constantly defied.

Many Spaniards appealed as far as Madrid their desire to remove Colima from the jurisdiction of New Spain and the judicial oversight of Mexico City, and yet the villa would remain a kind of jurisprudential and geographical *finis terrae*. That quality shaped and exacerbated the outlaw culture of the region. And just as Spaniards leveled frequent charges against the holders of royal power, so, too, did indigenous residents, though their complaints tended to focus less on the theoretical nature of royal power than on the undue labor and economic burdens that representatives of that authority placed on rural communities.

Everyone seemed to agree that local royal officials in Colima, Motines, and Zacatula were out of control. Spanish and indigenous subjects alike called the local rule of magistrates and delegated judges capricious and noted how they acted with impunity. The king and viceroy might as well have been ghosts. Colima's fraught political culture was symptomatic of its jurisdictional location as a region of refuge from global supervision. Yet the plantation economy and the concentration of power in the local elite were not simply about legal remoteness. A spectacular irony of colonial society drove the political culture of Colima: not only did the Crown fail to impose active oversight in the region, but the local officials set in place to provide that oversight exploited the theoretical power of empire by blocking access to that same system.

Distrust of imperial-colonial political power in Colima and Motines was not ethnically determined, though it did reflect different approaches to royal justice. In fact, both Spaniards and Nahuas expressed dismay at the outsized coercive capabilities of local representatives of royal authority. Local authorities in effect ruled the region as caudillos. In many cases, alcaldes and tenientes were rapists, thieves, or simple criminals. Spaniards tended to view this situation through the lens of legal systems: one could appeal, but appeal would require access to Mexico City. Indigenous communities shared this concern about power imbalance, but they were much more likely to understand it in ethnic terms. If Spaniards saw reprisals and arbitrary actions by magistrates as motivated by personal animus, money, or revenge, Nahuas and Coalcomacans saw abuse of power as an expression of ethnic power imbalances in which Spaniards exploited their position to extract labor and personal service and to effect forcible relocation.

Local officials had minimal legal training. Their understanding of the law was primal, direct, and practical. Their exercise of royal authority owed little to legal theory and everything to the necessity of survival in a dangerous region, a region of refuge from the state that these officials represented. This does not seem to have hampered their ability to retain the exercise of royal authority. Even conviction as a criminal, whether by the Inquisition, by the ecclesiastical court, or by the royal court, seems to have had little long-term negative consequences. Indeed, many criminals wore their convictions as a kind of badge of honor in a freewheeling land of personalist power deeply suspicious of idealized forms of justice. The next chapter turns to the denouement of local power at the height of Don Diego de Orduña's career.

CHAPTER 6

CAUDILLO PRIESTS, IN WHICH THE LOCALS
TRIUMPHED AND TRAMPLED THE CROWN

Setting: Valladolid
Years: 1580–1625

Don Diego de Orduña rode in on horseback followed by a half dozen heavily armed men. He looked like the rancher and everyman that he was. One wonders whether he even dared to wear his priestly garb. No document suggests that he ever did so in public. On an expansive flat plain west of Toluca, a royal judge had herded five hundred head of cattle that he had seized from Orduña's ranch of Tarímbaro. When Orduña arrived to reclaim his property, he shouted insults at the judge. The judge begged him to respect and honor the king. The priest replied, "Oh, sure, the king! You are nothing. You are a squash!"[1] (The Spanish word for squash, *calabaza*, was a traditional symbol of pride and arrogance.)[2] And then Orduña's armed retainers attacked the judge, beating him with clubs and stabbing him repeatedly. Remarkably, the man lived.

The Mexico Audiencia indicted Orduña on charges of land theft in 1598. Indigenous residents of Tarímbaro meanwhile had already filed a lawsuit of their own claiming that Orduña—who by this time was the inquisitional deputy in Valladolid and the cathedral's maestrescuela—had employed dozens of men to forcibly evict the indigenous community from its lands. After he had done so, he turned the expansive plain into a massive ranch with livestock numbering in the thousands. The court ruled against Orduña in the case, sending the royal inspector Antonio Negrete to enforce its order and seize Orduña's livestock. Records of the case and trial fill several volumes; the matter became a cause célèbre, dividing legal and political loyalties.[3]

The Tarímbaro case was among the more spectacular moments of open defiance of royal will and law in Michoacán's religious polity. In an extraordinary act of judicial defiance, the inquisitors in Mexico City vacated the Audiencia's guilty sentence against Orduña, arguing that the royal court had no jurisdiction over the

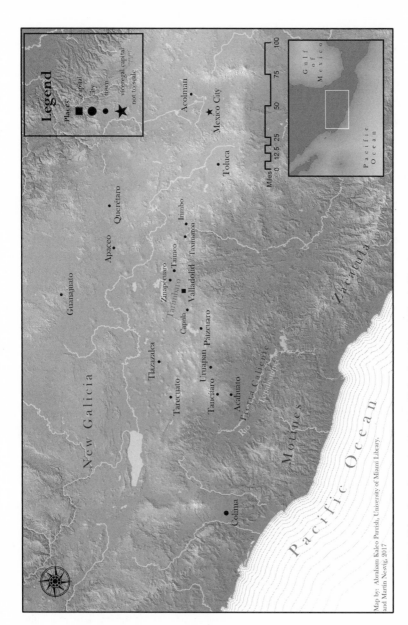

MAP 6.1. Valladolid and environs, by Abraham Kaleo Parrish and Martin Nesvig.

inquisitional deputy. Orduña returned to Valladolid, where, until his death in 1616, he exercised power as a priest and inquisitional deputy, becoming, by all accounts, a very wealthy man.

The breadth of Orduña's violence and his sketchy character paint a spectacular picture of the near total implosion of religious authority in Michoacán. After serving sentences of exile for assault in 1570–1574 and 1575–1576, Orduña managed to embroil himself in scandals serious enough to be brought before the royal or ecclesiastical courts at least three more times in the 1590s: 1593, 1595, and 1598. He was not someone bedeviled by the occasional personally motivated case; instead, he had a three-decade-long history of violence, and the very nature of authority in Michoacán facilitated that violence.

Orduña became one of the most powerful caudillos of Michoacán. He epitomizes everything I have discussed to this point. One might be tempted to say he is this book's antihero. He was a thief, but he was also the cathedral's maestrescuela. As maestrescuela, he was in charge of the basic education of the diocesan parish priests. What did he teach them? How to steal land? How to commit murder? How to slap a lawyer's bonnet off a head?

INQUISITION, INTERRUPTED

When we last heard from Orduña, he was watching with sadistic glee, or perhaps with pathos, when in 1584 his longtime rival (or perhaps friend) Cristóbal de Badillo was leaving New Spain to appeal the unbelievable sentence meted out to him by Bishop Medina. Michoacán remained in what had become its natural political state: a state characterized by entropy and local factionalism. Even those charged with its administration were chronically absent. Of the cathedral chapter's ten canons, only five even resided in Michoacán.[4] In this context, Orduña applied to become the new inquisitional deputy of Michoacán. Inquisitors ignored the request for several years.[5] Maybe they were waiting for someone else to offer himself for the job. No one did—understandably so, given how dangerous it was to act as comisario in Michoacán. In the meantime, Orduña solidified his economic power. He acquired at least one ranch in Apaceo sometime before 1580; by his account, the estate was worth several thousand pesos.[6] In short, Orduña had become rich. His beneficed salary as maestrescuela of the cathedral was probably about four hundred pesos a year, not nearly enough to support the lavish estates filled with livestock that he oversaw.[7] Presumably, his armed guard had been effective in usurping lands from indigenous communities and placing livestock on them as investments.

Orduña, allied with a faction that had long promoted its power over the bishop's, remained the maestrescuela. He and his cronies saw their opening and began to control a cathedral chapter that had long been characterized by rivalry. He and the dean of the chapter, Don Alonso de la Mota, were close. In March 1587, the cathedral chapter fined both of them for leaving the choir loft without permission, in what was likely an orchestrated snubbing of the bishop.[8] When, in 1588, Bishop Medina died, Orduña and his allies effectively took control of the government of the diocese.

Orduña's application to become inquisitional deputy, submitted in 1582 but presumably still under consideration several years later, came at a delicate political moment. The Crown nominated Dominican friar Alonso Guerra as Michoacán's new bishop. Guerra had been the bishop of La Plata in South America, and the Audiencia of Charcas had filed a criminal complaint against him. As a result, in August 1590 Guerra arrived in Michoacán bearing only the royal decree of nomination, without a papal bull approving the appointment, as this had to wait until the lawsuit against him was resolved.[9] The cathedral chapter commissioned Orduña to receive bishop-elect Guerra.[10] We have no documentation about the meeting, but surely the Dominican friar had a rude awakening when he saw what he was getting into.

Guerra sank in the quicksand of the internal politics of the Michoacán cathedral. Quickly after his arrival in Valladolid, sometime in September 1590, he attempted to take control of the Colegio de San Nicolás as a diocesan seminary. The cathedral chapter balked. It refused to relinquish the patronage of the college to the bishop's office even though it was willing to allow the bishop to administer the college personally as long as it remained a possession of the cathedral chapter. The dean de la Mota led the charge. Guerra responded in kind by having three of the canons arrested, including the treasurer, Pedro de Aguayo. The cathedral chapter commissioned Orduña to plead its case in Mexico City.[11] This effort seems to have failed, as Orduña's commission was quickly revoked on 12 February 1591.[12]

The factional dispute continued through 1592. Guerra forced through a variety of appointments. He nominated Marcos de Zayas as rector of the Colegio de San Nicolás, but the cathedral chapter fired him. He appointed a tithe collector for Querétaro, but the chapter refused to acknowledge him. He nominated canon Antonio Ximénez as his vicar general, but the cathedral chapter would not recognize his authority or allow him to be excused from his normal duties as a cathedral dignitary. Moreover, Ximénez charged the majority of the cathedral chapter members with having extraordinary debts to the diocese—8,092 pesos in all.[13] Presumably, cathedral canons and dignitaries were skimming money from tithe collections, not for chapter expenses, but for personal use.

Guerra was still operating without papal confirmation in the summer of 1592. The cathedral chapter again voted to disavow his authority as bishop on 7 July of that year, declaring the diocese unoccupied, and ordered this news to be announced by a public crier.[14] The cathedral's secretary, however, refused to sign the order.[15] The bishop-elect offered a riposte and ordered edicts to be posted on the cathedral door compelling citizens not to obey the dean of the cathedral.[16]

A FRIAR AND A CAUDILLO

Orduña's personality and career stood in remarkable contrast with those of the friar-hermit Diego Muñoz. Born in Cholula around 1550 and almost certainly a criollo, Muñoz joined the Franciscan order in Tzintzuntzan in the 1560s.[17] He spent his entire adult life in Michoacán. In the 1570s and 1580s, he lived in Pátzcuaro and Tzintzuntzan, where he developed an understanding of the local culture—mostly Purépecha, though he was fluent in both Purépecha and Nahuatl. He composed a chronicle of the Michoacán province of the Franciscans around 1585, but it was not published during his lifetime. He became a guardian of the Franciscan houses of Pátzcuaro and Querétaro in the 1590s. The Franciscan order elected Muñoz as Michoacán's provincial (the highest-ranking official of a province) in 1600, making him the first criollo to hold the office in New Spain. He was reelected Michoacán's provincial in 1610. But Muñoz kept going back to his mountain retreat near Tancítaro. On various occasions, he asked his superiors in Mexico City to relieve him of administrative duties.[18] Yet for all his activity and success in administering the Franciscan mission, he preferred a contemplative and solitary life.[19]

Muñoz became an inquisitional notary around 1580 and a deputy around 1590 and spent his time largely in the mountains. He was a voluminous letter writer and composed hundreds of missives, sending them from his mountain retreat to Mexico City. Yet the Inquisition in Mexico City rarely prosecuted the individuals Muñoz investigated, and the friar's remote location meant that his sealed testimonies had a lengthy trip to the capital.

Muñoz lived a peripatetic lifestyle, and his very presence—in a town, in the mountains, in Uruapan—could never be guaranteed. This instability underscored the structural inability of the Inquisition to impose widespread social control on the rural population of Michoacán. There was simply no way the Church could extract obedience when only one roving friar held the office of inquisitional deputy for the entire province outside of the capital city. Rather, semiprivate actors exerted coercive forces that often opposed the royal state's ideological arm, the Church. Microforces within that apparatus battled against each other: in many cases, individuals—such as Orduña—raised their own militias to fend off attempts to impose royal law.

Michoacán's ecclesial polity was a mess. The cathedral chapter refused to recognize the bishop-nominee. The countryside had never had an inquisitional deputy. And meanwhile, priests were stabbing each other, slapping off each other's

bonnets, and beating each other up. Michoacán was thus ripe for the rise of a caudillo priest like Orduña. After decades of political factionalism and violence, the
province's capital had no inquisitional deputy from 1577 to 1592, an extraordinarily
long period of time. Muñoz's first extant case as an inquisitional deputy was in
Tarecuato in 1591.[20] The move of the capital from Pátzcuaro to Valladolid already
had fractured loyalties. The collective memory of Spanish residents was a history
of constant conflict between officers of the Church and Crown with everyday residents and citizens. Neither Church nor Crown could exert the monopoly of force
needed to establish hegemony.

Orduña's audacity paid off and he became Valladolid's inquisitional deputy in
1592.[21] In July of that year, Mexico's inquisitor, Licenciado Francisco Santos García,
was on his way out the metaphorical door of Mexico City to become bishop of
Guadalajara. He approved Orduña's application and appointed him as inquisitional deputy for Valladolid. The background check for such positions (*limpieza
de sangre*) routinely asked witnesses if they knew whether the supplicant (in this
case, Orduña) had been accused or convicted by the Inquisition. All claimed that
he had not.[22] It is possible that no one knew of his two previous convictions, but
in all likelihood, the witnesses simply lied. Surely the former inquisitor, Alfonso
Bonilla, remembered Orduña, since he had convicted him in 1575. Bonilla was now
the archbishop of Mexico; as such, he had an advisory role in the Inquisition he
had served, and, if he had so desired, could have blocked Orduña's nomination.
Santos García probably made the appointment out of desperation—or maybe he
was bribed. It would not have been the first time an inquisitor took a payoff to
ignore evidence.[23] Santos García noted that Michoacán's capital had gone many
years without an inquisitional deputy.[24]

The admission was clear: the Inquisition simply could not find anyone else to
take the job. So, after fifteen years without an inquisitional representative in the
capital of Michoacán, a known criminal took the office. Orduña's cronies cozied up
to the caudillo. In November 1592, for example, the cathedral approved a massive
loan of 1,050 pesos to Orduña from the San Nicolás college treasury.[25] Then, on 15
December, the cathedral chapter refused (again) to recognize Guerra as bishop,
claiming he lacked the necessary papal approval. The cathedral, moreover, did
support Orduña's position as inquisitional deputy, suggesting that he, and not the
bishop, was the reigning ecclesiastical judge in Michoacán.[26]

Whether Orduña obtained his appointment through deceit, institutional disorganization, or bribery, members of the church hierarchy did not welcome him.
Bishop Guerra led the charge. The rivalry between Orduña and his allies on the
cathedral chapter, on the one side, and Guerra and his allies, on the other, ran
deep. The appointment of Orduña as comisario deepened it. Guerra filed a complaint before the Inquisition in Mexico in December 1592 saying that Orduña

should never have been appointed inquisitional deputy.[27] Orduña, he said, was wholly unfit for the job. "He is a vicious man," he wrote, complaining that Orduña was a known gambler, was vain and wore extravagant suits, and spent his time with low and immoral characters. Apparently, this kind of behavior was de rigueur for the inquisitional agent in Michoacán's capital. The charges against Orduña often sounded like those against Badillo fifteen years earlier; the irony was wonderful. Moreover, Guerra continued, Orduña had publicly insulted the bishop by refusing to recognize his authority.[28] Guerra quickly commissioned a cleric, Sebastián de Valderrama (on 17 December), to present the complaint before the inquisitor Santos García. Valderrama appealed to the inquisitor to appoint a deputy morally worthy of the office and not someone like Orduña, whom he considered lascivious and corrupt.[29] Then, in what was surely a deliberate act of provocation, on 2 January 1593 the cathedral chapter nominated both Orduña and the cathedral chapter's treasurer, Aguayo, as the administrative judges of tithes for the diocese (*jueces hacedores*) for the year.[30]

Valderrama's denunciation of Orduña, drafted in early January 1593, read like a scandal sheet.[31] Valderrama explained that the inquisitor had been duped, and that Orduña was well known as having been convicted by the Inquisition for assaulting Badillo. "Because your grace had no notice of the manner of life that don Diego de Orduña has led, you named him deputy. But if your grace had known of his excesses, you never would have nominated him."[32] In addition to recounting this offense, Valderrama expressed doubt that Orduña had completed his sentence from the 1575 trial for assaulting Badillo. Further, he said, Orduña was known to spend his time in taverns, carousing with women and playing cards; in addition, he had a loose tongue and wore silk and damask suits. The scandal, said Valderrama, was too much; Orduña had to go.

Inquisitor Santos García initiated an investigation. Cue the friar-hermit Muñoz: the inquisitor charged Muñoz, on 24 December 1592, with traveling from his current residence in Uruapan to Valladolid to investigate the feud between Orduña and his mortal enemy, Valderrama.[33] He asked Muñoz, in fact, to find out whether Orduña had solicited a man named Juan de Solís to murder Valderrama.[34] This Juan de Solís was possibly the same man who aided and abetted the mestizo imposter Alonso de Montúfar in 1565.[35] Solís was a clear ally of Orduña and acted as witness to the cathedral chapter declaration of 15 December 1592 refusing to recognize Guerra as bishop.[36] There are hints that Solís and Orduña may have been related by family; surely they were linked by clan and political loyalties.

We have only indirect evidence of any familial relationship between the two men. The Solís family included two conquistadors: Francisco and Pedro. Pedro de Solís somehow took control of the encomienda of Acolman, which had originally belonged to Pedro Muñoz (he who would shit on the excommunication). Pedro de Solís died in 1565 and left Acolman to a son named Francisco de Solís Orduña. Another Solís, Juan, had held Comanja in Michoacán between 1523 and 1529. Francisco de Orduña was a conquistador who became the regidor of Puebla.[37] There is no explicit connection between any of these conquistadors and encomenderos to the Juan de Solís and Diego de Orduña of the 1590s. Perhaps this Solís and this Orduña were the sorts of later sons who missed out on the early spoils of the encomienda system enjoyed by other family members, working instead in the rough world of land theft.

In any case, Muñoz traveled to Valladolid to investigate the feud. On 12 January 1593, he began his interrogations.[38] Valderrama had previously testified under oath that Solís was an "impudent vagabond."[39] Alonso de Orta, the corregidor of Tlazazalca, claimed that one day he had been near his house when Valderrama passed by. Solís, Orduña, and two other Spaniards stood nearby. Valderrama was reputed to say to Orta, "May God save you from rogues and liars," indicating Solís. Later that day, on seeing Valderrama, Solís said to Orta, "May God save you from roguish shameless priests."[40] Orta claimed that Orduña later offered to loan Solís a horse for the task of murdering Valderrama.

As one might imagine, there was more to the story than this. Orduña and Aguayo assumed control of the tithe accounts for 1593. But Bishop Guerra had previously given Valderrama the task of collecting the tithes from the lucrative villa of Colima. On 21 January, Orduña and Aguayo assessed the tithes for Colima at 2,530 pesos.[41] In February, Guerra claimed that Orduña and Aguayo had refused to accept a 1,000-peso bond to secure the value of the tithes offered by Gerónimo de Cendejas, the beneficed priest of Guacana. Guerra ascribed their refusal to accept the bond to Orduña's hostility toward Valderrama. In March, the cathedral chapter offered formal opposition to Valderrama as the collector of the tithes for Colima, asserting that the bonds offered were too "fragile."[42]

On 7 February 1593, Orduña entered the fray, asserting himself as the inquisitional deputy for Michoacán's capital city. The case was rich with irony. The bishop and inquisitor had ordered Orduña to be investigated, to determine whether he should be removed from office, and yet, in the midst of the investigation, he was asserting his authority as inquisitional deputy. "The devil never sleeps," Orduña wrote to the inquisitor, explaining that Valderrama had no respect for the Holy Office; that he should be censured because he had disrespected him on 4 February in front of the cathedral church; and that the bishop surely would not issue appropriate punishment.[43] Orduña then summoned two witnesses: the lieutenant magistrate, Francisco Madaleno, and his own ally Aguayo. They claimed that Orduña and Aguayo had been assessing the tithe collections for the diocese when Valderrama had appeared. Orduña accused Valderrama of peculation by deliberate underestimation of the Colima tithe values, presumably pocketing the difference. A shouting match ensued. Valderrama told Orduña, "Shut your mouth—we will see each other again someday."[44] The threat was clear. Aguayo accused Valderrama of offending his honor by refusing to remove his bonnet in his presence. There does not appear to have been any resolution to the case, but on 16 March, the cathedral chapter sent Orduña to Mexico City to argue the case concerning Colima's tithes.[45] Simultaneously, Orduña was commissioned as inspector general of the Santa Fe hospital, further indicating the cathedral chapter's determination to defy Guerra and Valderrama.[46]

It is unclear whether the multiple investigations of 1592 and 1593 led to anything. The tithe dispute offers no clarification except to demonstrate the centrality of money to the conflict. Likewise, the inquisitor appears to have ignored Guerra's and Valderrama's accusations against Orduña's character. Muñoz reported his independent investigation to the inquisitor, who took no action and did not remove Orduña from office. The inquisitional cases involving Orduña, Aguayo, Guerra, and Valderrama were all too obviously about money. Moreover, financial rivalries had existed long before Orduña's nomination as inquisitional deputy. For example, the bishop accused Aguayo, in August 1592, of not having paid the royal assessment (*alcabala*) on investments.[47] When Guerra was unable to obtain convictions against his rivals, Aguayo and Orduña, and when the cathedral chapter openly defied him on questions about the tithes—as was the case with Guerra's selection for tithe collection in Querétaro—Guerra and Valderrama denounced Orduña before the Inquisition as unfit for office. As far as we know, Solís never attempted to murder Valderrama. But, in another ironic turn of events, the cathedral chapter named Valderrama curate of Colima in February 1596.[48]

During Lent of 1594, Orduña pronounced the inquisitional Edict of Faith.[49] It was the first time the edict had been publicly announced in the capital in twenty years. No great inquisitional dragnet resulted; nor did it appear that Orduña even took many testimonies. The principal purpose of the edict was to admonish the citizenry to search their conscience, to confess any doctrinal offenses, and to turn in any neighbors whom they believed to be guilty of heresy. There only appears to have been one witness statement immediately following the feared edict.[50] No depositions or arrests are extant. The city received a free pass. Residents must have loved this kind of Inquisition.

Orduña's appointment as inquisitional deputy became a political fait accompli when Bishop Guerra died in October 1594. But Orduña's actions in the post were almost entirely personal and petty. His first major case, in November 1594, involved a bogus claim that Cristóbal Bravo, the rector of the new Jesuit college in Valladolid, had impeded Orduña's proper exercise of inquisitional prerogatives to take depositions.[51] Bravo turned himself in to inquisitors in Mexico City, who promptly dismissed the case as frivolous. But there is a telling detail: Orduña was living in Puruándiro, on Valladolid's northwestern boundary. He probably had a ranch there. He appears to have been expanding his ranching estates, financing the project at least in part with cathedral chapter money.

Orduña continued to insert himself into partisan squabbles and brawled his way through the capital. By 1595, the cathedral chapter was in a state of virtual daily turmoil. No bishop was in place, and as such, in theory, the chapter ruled the diocese as a corporate body, with the dean, the newly arrived licenciado Melchor Gómez de Soria, as its de facto president. The former dean, Alonso de la Mota, had become bishop of Puebla. The new dean made an almost immediate enemy in Orduña. On 14 May 1595, a group of six indigenous nobles from Zacatula arrived at the Valladolid cathedral church as mass was ending. The cathedral chapter members were assembled in the area where the choir sang, and the indigenous men presented two petitions they had drawn up in which they accused their parish priest of having them flogged. Knowing that the parish priest answered to the diocese, they demanded justice. The canon Joaquín Gutiérrez agreed, received the petitions, and presented them to Orduña, who, as the maestrescuela, was in charge of the education of diocesan priests. Orduña snatched the papers from Gutiérrez's hands and crumpled them up, saying they were not even worth the ink and paper used to produce them.[52]

The conflict escalated. Gutiérrez insisted that Orduña and the cathedral chapter as a whole hear the case. The dean, Gómez de Soria, agreed. Orduña said that it was not a business day. Voices were raised. Orduña called Gutiérrez a rogue. The dean continued to insist that they hear the Zacatulans' case. Orduña refused. And then a fistfight erupted between Orduña and Gutiérrez. Amid the mayhem, Orduña also slapped the dean. Then, in his signature symbolic move, he smacked the dean's lawyer bonnet to the ground. Orduña had once again demonstrated his contempt—not necessarily for the law itself, but for lawyers and the bonnets they wore, which symbolized their licentiate degree. Orduña must have appealed to the inquisitors to defend him, because on 30 May, the inquisitors Don Bartolomé Lobo Guerrero and Don Alonso de Peralta wrote a scathing letter to the dean asking him to reprimand a malefactor—surprisingly, not Orduña but Gutiérrez. The inquisitors asked for an investigation, but noted, in their letter, "We will be most grateful if you make them behave in such a way from now on that there are no further annoyances and quarrels between the maestrescuela and the canon."[53]

No case resulted from the brawl. Maybe Orduña retired to his lucrative ranching trade. There is no evidence that he even bothered to administer inquisitional justice over the next few years. Although he took a desultory witness statement from time to time, he held no actual trials. For all we know, he simply collected his salary from the cathedral. The only witness statement he took, in 1598, was for a matter concerning Irimbo, which was suspiciously close to some of the ranches he eventually claimed to own.[54] He seemed content to leave the exercise of social discipline to Muñoz, who roamed the province's vast rural networks. Orduña's activities as a landholder and a despoiler of indigenous lands near Valladolid nearly proved his final undoing. Technically, after 1592 the capital city, Valladolid, finally had an inquisitional agent; in reality, Orduña enjoyed the position as a supernumerary title, which added a further layer of legal protection, as he counted on both inquisitional and clerical fuero. In addition to Orduña as its comisario, Valladolid had a familiar, Pedro de la Huerta. He was condemned for abuse of power and smuggling in 1594.[55]

THE CAUDILLO TRIUMPHS

Orduña then went about implementing the final steps in his plan as the undisputed caudillo of Michoacán, expanding his ranching empire. In 1598, however, everything seemed to be crashing down when a full-scale jurisdictional war broke out between him and the Audiencia of Mexico. Orduña was accused of massive land fraud, violation of indigenous rights, and illegal land possession in Tarímbaro, a fertile valley just to the north of Valladolid. The case was considered so egregious that the Audiencia even appointed a special prosecutor to investigate, which was unusual to the extent that the Audiencia often simply relied on reports from judges of first instance, such as an alcalde, or referred the case back to the alcalde. But this time, it appears that the indigenous residents of Tarímbaro traveled directly to Mexico City to demand justice.[56]

Land despoilment was hardly new. By the late 1500s, when the indigenous population in Mexico was reaching its nadir, Spanish ranchers, sugar producers, and innkeepers were snatching up more and more lands, claiming, in many cases, that the lands were effectively un-owned. But land disputes had been simmering for decades in Michoacán. Among the most common disputes were those over the damage to indigenous crops when Spaniards introduced livestock, such as pigs, goats, sheep, and cows. In fact, this charge was so common that even a simple listing of them in the sixteenth and seventeenth centuries would run to dozens of pages. Suffice it to say that the Valley of Guayangareo was no stranger to this phenomenon. In Zinapécuaro, the indigenous reported in 1577 that pigs were raising hell, eating everything in their path.[57] In 1588, the indigenous residents sued the Augustinian monastery of Capula for infringement on their land without just title, destruction of crops by the monastery's livestock, and abuse of authority by installing a mill.[58] In 1590, the indigenous residents of Zipiaco filed suit against the owner of an inn (mesón) who, they charged, was extracting unfair demands for supplies and crops.[59] The residents of Taimeo filed suit in 1591 against a Spanish rancher for introducing rapacious livestock that destroyed their crops.[60] And on and on the lawsuits went.

Most of these suits went unanswered by the Audiencia or viceroy, or were simply sent back to the local alcalde with instructions to investigate and assure that indigenous land rights were respected. Such was not the case with Tarímbaro and Orduña. Maybe Orduña had made too many enemies, or the level of his land fraud was so spectacular that it could not be ignored. But Orduña was not the only comisario to be embroiled in controversial land cases or to be accused of outright land theft. The inquisitional deputy of Puebla, the canon Alonso Hernández de Santiago, was prosecuted in a similar matter: he had been accused of stealing four ranches in Cosamaloapa (on the Gulf Coast) from one Francisco Palacio.[61] The case dragged on between 1601 and 1605. Like Orduña, Santiago boasted of a personal militia—in this case of thirty armed men—which he employed to terrorize local landowners like Palacio. According to Palacio, Hernández had usurped four of his large ranches (*sitios de ganado mayor*), asserting authority as a caudillo (the precise word used by Palacio) and despoiling some 2,000 head of livestock. According to Palacio, when he attempted to reason with Hernández, the canon said, "You lie like a Jew dog."[62]

Although Orduña was never specifically called a caudillo, the definition clearly applies. Sebastián Covarrubias, the author of the classic 1611 dictionary, defined a caudillo as a leader of an armed troop. The medieval Spanish law code, the Siete Partidas, defined a caudillo as a military commander, leader, or strongman.[63] Orduña's caudillo status facilitated his schemes to steal indigenous lands. Tarímbaro and Indaparapeo had already been at the center of several previous land disputes (in 1592) when the alcalde filed a complaint against Orduña.[64] Alonso Flores de Ovando, the alcalde, heard a criminal case that the indigenous residents of Tarímbaro and Indaparapeo brought against Orduña, along with García Álvarez Guillén, Juan Martínez de Barrajas, Juan de Vargas, and Tomás Muñoz. They all claimed that Orduña and his partners, with no just title or deed, had brought some 10,000 head of livestock (calves, mules, and cattle) onto the Tarímbaro plains.[65] The alcalde had secured an order from the viceroy, Luis de Velasco the younger (son of the former viceroy of the same name), compelling Orduña and his partners to remove the livestock within thirty days, to pay for the damages to the land, and to reimburse the court for the costs of the investigation.

For five years, Orduña ignored the order. In 1597, Pedro Díaz de Agüero, serving as the Crown's delegated judge for indigenous affairs throughout New Spain (*procurador general de indios*), took up the Tarímbaro case, suggesting that Orduña's brash actions had come to the attention to the viceregal court. Díaz presented a complaint before the Audiencia that claimed that Orduña had relied on his ecclesiastical exemption from civil court prosecution (fuero) to avoid implementation of a civil decree; moreover, because Orduña and his partners were wealthy and powerful, it had been impossible to force them to obey the law. The Audiencia agreed with this assessment and in July 1597 appointed Antonio Negrete as a special delegated judge in the case. He was to travel to Tarímbaro to investigate, empowered with the full authority of royal justice.[66]

By December, Negrete had informed Orduña of his intent to open a criminal investigation against him.[67] Orduña demanded his recusal from the case, and the cathedral chapter supported Orduña. Orduña claimed that as a cathedral maestrescuela and an inquisitional comisario, he was immune to civil proceedings. By February 1598, there was still no resolution in this jurisdictional standoff.[68] After a lengthy investigation, Negrete issued a guilty verdict against Orduña; the sentencing was in March 1598.[69] The judge declared that Orduña had illegally occupied the Valley of Tarímbaro, displacing the indigenous population and introducing at least 4,000 head of livestock without legal title to the land. Negrete thus ruled that one-third of all the livestock was to become royal property. Specifically, the entirety of Orduña's livestock on his illegal ranch was to be rounded up in a rodeo and assessed in quantity and value; one-third of the livestock was to be impounded by Negrete and sold, the proceeds serving as judicial penalty. Moreover, Negrete ordered Orduña to pay an amount equivalent to the salaries of a long list of royal officials for ninety days, which would have amounted to heavy fines. The Audiencia confirmed Negrete's sentence as legal and ordered Negrete to assess the quantity of livestock to be impounded.[70]

The judge proceeded to enforce the sentence, but his actions proved nearly fatal to him. Shortly after pronouncing the sentence, Negrete traveled to the estate of Doña Leonor Ruiz, the widow of Juan Rangel Núñez, and her son Rodrigo Rangel, in Zinzineo, seeking a deed of sale or title to Tarímbaro.[71] Orduña had claimed this property as his own, and this claim was in dispute. On hearing of Negrete's demands, Orduña galloped to the estate, and when he arrived, he found Negrete arresting Rangel for fraud. Orduña attempted to wrest Rangel from the judge, either to defend the young man or to prevent him from being taken into custody.

Orduña openly mocked the royal judge. He warned Negrete that if he went through with his plan to impound his livestock, he could muster a personal militia of twenty men armed with lances and arquebuses (a type of gun similar to a musket). The threat was transparent: Orduña was willing to use physical violence to prevent the sequestration of his property. Negrete reported the incident in his report, noting that Orduña was a menace and that he was terrorizing the indigenous residents. While jailed, Rangel admitted that he had sold a one-eighth portion of the Zinzineo estate to Orduña as a shell corporation in December 1597 with the express purpose of providing legal cover to Orduña. He had needed the money. When Negrete had asked Doña Leonor for a deed of sale, she had refused to produce one, however. Rangel denied having informed Orduña of Negrete's inquiry.[72]

Despite the sentence handed down by Negrete and then affirmed by the Audiencia, Orduña and the cathedral chapter were defiant. Orduña even heard depositions as the acting inquisitional deputy; these took place in Valladolid on 26 March 1598 and in Irimbo in June.[73] The cathedral chapter empowered Orduña to serve as its formal ambassador to receive the new bishop on 27 April, which carried a fee of two hundred pesos.[74]

And then the dam burst. In early or mid-June, Negrete decided that, since he was empowered to remove several hundred head of livestock from Orduña's ranch, he would proceed. He did so with the intention of taking the livestock to Toluca and selling it to pay for the penalties that had been imposed on Orduña and his partners. It proved to be a near-fatal mistake. Orduña summoned a private guard of eight men—a mix of mulatos and mestizos—armed with swords, lances, and guns. They galloped in pursuit of Negrete and found him, along with some 550 head of livestock, in Istlaguaca, just north of Toluca. Negrete presumably traveled with a royal retainer, but Orduña's force clearly outnumbered Negrete's. He had made good on the threat he had made to Negrete in March. Negrete appealed to Orduña's respect for the law. It did not work.

Negrete shouted at them to respect the king when he saw the ominous figures of Orduña and eight heavily armed men arriving on horseback. "Oh sure, you are the king," Orduña replied with sarcasm. "You are a squash!" Negrete must have realized at that point that the matter was not going to be resolved through simple judicial reasoning—if so, he was correct. Orduña's retainers beat him nearly to death, stabbing him in the head and beating him viciously on the ground with pikes and staffs. One marvels that Negrete survived.

With the special prosecutor bloodied and nearly dead, the Audiencia ordered the alcalde of Valladolid to continue the investigation through the summer of 1598. Throughout July and August, he compiled a lengthy case file detailing Orduña's fraud and violence. At this point, apparently, the inquisitional authorities entered the fray. All the while, the Audiencia had claimed that it held jurisdiction in the case, because no one, despite ecclesiastical fueros, could defy an order from the viceroy. Because very old titles from Luis de Velasco the elder protected the rights of the indigenous people of Tarímbaro, it reasoned, Orduña could not claim exemption as an inquisitional official. Orduña was unimpressed, since he had savagely attacked the direct representative of the viceroy in Negrete.

The Inquisition seemed poised to snatch the entire affair from the claims of royal law. Inquisitor Don Alonso de Peralta ordered Orduña to stop interfering with the Audiencia's investigation. But it was the spectacular assault on Negrete in June 1598 in Istlaguaca that must have prompted the inquisitor to intervene. He issued an order for Orduña to be arrested and transferred to Mexico City for trial. Just as Orduña could claim exemption from civil law as an inquisitional representative, so could the Inquisition prosecute its own officials for otherwise civil crimes under its aegis. So Orduña presented himself before the inquisitor. He was granted house arrest, in his own residence in Mexico City, and the trial dragged on for several months.[75]

The inquisitor's ruling is shocking in its reach of power. He voided all claims of the Audiencia and viceroy to the prosecution of Orduña. In fact, he pronounced the sentence null. The decision was a remarkable defense of clerical prerogatives; it drove a thumb in the eye of the Audiencia's defense of the indigenous communities. Orduña had argued before the inquisitor that the case against him was bogus, because, he said, the witnesses to the assault were "vile, low mestizos" and his known enemies. The inquisitional prosecutor, Martos de Bohórquez, rejected Orduña's defense and called on the inquisitor to impose the most severe penalty allowable; even if the witnesses were mestizos and mulatos, he said, this did not mean they did not tell the truth.[76] Inquisitor Peralta demurred.

For months during his house arrest, Orduña complained bitterly, saying he was ill and needed to return to Michoacán to attend to his estate. Ultimately, the inquisitor acquiesced—to a degree. On 23 January 1599, in remarkable defiance of royal defenses of indigenous lands and of viceregal power to investigate assault on its judges, Peralta suspended the charges against Orduña. Orduña was allowed to return to Valladolid, but he was prohibited from leaving Michoacán without express license from the Inquisition. He was also stripped of his office as inquisitional deputy.[77]

Orduña seemed to have been disciplined—one might imagine he would return to Michoacán in ignominy. But that was not what happened. Much to the contrary, he avoided any criminal conviction and presumably was able to keep his illegal ranch on usurped land. His staying power is remarkable for what it says about the assertion of authority by a known criminal, a violent caudillo who thumbed his nose at the royal court and insisted on representing the Catholic Church both as cathedral dignitary and inquisitional agent. As in his previous lawsuits, Orduña simply slipped through the apparatus of control. Or perhaps he and inquisitor Peralta had made a deal. In February 1601, only two years after being judicially removed from office, Orduña was once again taking depositions as inquisitional deputy.[78] In October 1603, he was again receiving witness statements as comisario in Valladolid.[79]

How did Orduña continue to assert authority as comisario after having been stripped of the office by the Inquisition in 1599? He may have applied to be re-instated, but no such request can be found. The Tarímbaro case was appealed to Spain, so a formal exculpation may have come from the Supreme Council of the Inquisition or the Council of the Indies. The more likely explanation is that the inquisitors in Mexico City simply gave up on Michoacán and its rowdy capital. "Let them have Orduña," they may very well have thought. In any case, the very central apparatus of inquisitional control in Michoacán's capital was once again compromised, and it had to accept Orduña as the competent authority. Indeed, he asserted the deputy position for more than a decade, but only in the most sporadic of ways. He probably retired to his ranch.

CAUDILLOS

Orduña remained in Valladolid despite the taint of criminal conviction. While Muñoz crisscrossed the region for two decades, inquisitional investigations in the capital ceased. Orduña did not prosecute anyone during his tenure. The reason for this may be that inquisitors had admonished him, even though they ultimately exonerated him, in the Tarímbaro case. There was a brief dust-up in 1603 when Orduña demanded to see a letter from inquisitors in Spain that a cathedral canon claimed to have in his possession.[80]

There may be another, more sinister explanation, but we cannot know if it is true. Perhaps Orduña used the threat of inquisitional prosecution as a method of political terror. In other words, perhaps he held his power as inquisitional agent over people, in a silent threat to ruin their lives or fortunes. Such a strategy would have been possible, and, indeed, in the 1598 Tarímbaro case against him, prose-cutors noted that Orduña was too powerful and wealthy for ordinary people to extract justice from him. But we cannot know the extent to which Orduña may have used his position to extort payments or land. Given the extensive accusations against him for other forms of personal and political violence, it seems unlikely that he extorted Spaniards openly with threats of inquisitional investigation; still, he may have wielded power in a way that implied an unspoken threat.

It seems evident that the Inquisition effectively ceased to exist in the capital as an ideological instrument. Orduña made what appears to have been his only act of doctrinal investigation in his career in 1609, when he visited the hospital to ask a man named Juan Núñez whether he owned any suspicious copies of the Old Testament. He did not. Orduña still held his post as inquisitional deputy in 1612, though he did not use it.[81]

In short, in the 1610s, four decades after the official founding of the Mexican Inquisition, and eight decades after the establishment of a diocese in Michoacán, no Inquisition had been effected in the province's capital. Instead, Orduña's real passion was ranching. He had owned or stolen estates in Apaceo, Irimbo, Tarímbaro, Coatepec, and probably other places as well.[82] He hated lawyers, and in particular he hated their pretentious bonnets. Orduña died sometime in 1616, almost eighty years old. No will is extant, so we will probably never know whether he died a wealthy man or an impoverished one. Probably the last document he signed was from 24 February 1616, when he took depositions as inquisitional deputy.[83] By then, Orduña's signature was frail, and after this he disappeared from the historical record. In many ways, Orduña's life, career, and death coincided with the trajectory of the Christianization project in Michoacán. He lived through a period of considerable judicial and physical violence, yet he outlasted his rivals. By the time he died, the state of the Christianization apparatus was in near ruins.

Even with the death of Orduña, Michoacán's caudillo priest, the mayhem simply marched on. Other caudillos roamed the countryside, and they, too, often mocked and assaulted inquisitional dignity. In the summer of 1617, the friar-hermit Diego Muñoz dispatched his most recent batch of correspondence to the inquisitors in Mexico City. Things did not work out well. On 18 June 1617, two Purépecha men, Damián Dera and Francisco Chariraqua, carried the official, sealed correspondence to the inquisitor in Mexico City, who then entrusted them with various formal decrees and letters of reply to be delivered to Muñoz. As they worked their slow way west through the mountains, a group of armed men assaulted them, stealing the Inquisition's mail in a valley west of Toluca, along the road back to Michoacán.

The two mailmen brandished the formal letters of safe conduct, which the inquisitor had provided them in order to keep the secret correspondence, under seal, safe. But when they presented the letter and appealed to the assailants' fear of inquisitional power, the man whom the Purépecha identified as the caudillo of the group insulted them. Speaking in Purépecha, the attacker, a mestizo rancher, said, "Come on, that paper isn't worth anything, and whoever wrote it must be like you—come on, you dog, faggot, drunk, cuckold, snitch, asshole."[84] So much for the pedagogy of fear. The group of four men—two mestizos and two mulatos—were later identified as highway bandits known in the region. They worked for a wealthy rancher, Hernando Matías de Ribera. It is unclear whether the Inquisition was ever able to arrest or punish the assailants.

But the Inquisition's system of secrecy often broke down, as it did when Dera and Chariraqua were assaulted and the inquisitional correspondence seized. James Given has shown that such acts of open resistance to inquisitional authorities in medieval France were specific, targeting, for example, the monastery where angry crowds assumed trial records were kept, because the machinery of inquisitional power used the registry and archiving of inquisitional offenses as a tactic of intimidation.[85] Mexico in the sixteenth and seventeenth centuries offers cases of analogous resistance. The Inquisition in Mexico failed to impress upon the residents of places like rural Michoacán the importance of the primacy of inquisitional power. As a result, in a far-flung region with only one deputized representative for the entire rural part of Michoacán, outside of the capital in Valladolid, the Inquisition was obliged to rely on a system of ad hoc couriers, interpreters, and notaries. Indeed, when Dera and Chariraqua returned to Acahuato without the inquisitional correspondence on 7 August 1617, Muñoz deputized his two fellow Franciscan friars to act in the capacity of priests and notaries for the time being, as none yet existed in the town.[86]

The generalized state of religious authority in the capital of Michoacán radiated outward in a kind of reverse effect. Rather than project power to the rural regions, it tended to suck authority into the factional disputes. And so, by 1620, a century after the Spanish Crown had conquered the region and claimed it for Christendom, Michoacán was a kind of stateless province with no Catholic control. Indeed, the only hegemony anyone could muster in the region came from local factotum caudillos. Orduña spent more than four decades mocking the very global empire that made his career possible. He served a Catholic Church that could not impose control over its own clergy. He represented a putatively omnipotent Inquisition that he in turn flouted. He ruined the careers and lives of those who stood in his way.

Orduña was a caudillo, to use the Spanish term, but he was also, to borrow the language of the political scientist Martha Lizbeth Phelps, a "doppelgänger of the state."[87] Orduña pursued private interests and effectively wielded the violence of the state, mimicking the broader aims of the empire that employed him. We may be tempted to reconsider Max Weber's theory that the state is the only human institution that claims a legitimate monopoly on coercive force.[88] Yet other cases shatter this monopoly, much as in the case of Michoacán. Private actors ruling in the name of King Leopold perpetrated mind-boggling violence in the Belgian Congo, for example. Orduña himself succeeded in extracting wealth through illegal ranching, though in terms of resemblance to the mysterious Colonel Kurtz, Joseph Conrad's sadistic madman of the Congo, he may have surpassed Cristóbal de Preciado in his remote mountain plantation.[89] Orduña operated in the capital of Michoacán, openly flouting the very system that had appointed him as its protector.

Orduña's success as a caudillo priest was possible only in a region such as Michoacán, which had for a century been an incubator of local power that mocked global oversight. People laughed at the king and pope and called their judges squashes, putos, and little whiny bitches while stabbing and cracking them and smacking their idiotic, pompous bonnets off their heads. Entropy was the law of the land, and external attempts to control the place sank in the quicksand of contempt for the empire. The empire was a joke, but it was a very seriously unfunny joke for those trying to impose the imaginary rule of law. If you are laughing, you should stop, because this is not funny. Not funny at all.

CONCLUSION

Cristóbal de Badillo died at sea in 1604, and the far-flung inquisitional agents in rural Michoacán who replaced him simply could not, even a century after conquering the province, get people to behave. Michoacán, with its encomienda system a phantom of its former self, remained a rural province with an increasingly pessimistic outlook on the probability of success in its Christianization and Hispanicization projects. Yet, for many, the Edenic ideal remained viable, even if what they sought was an Eden of entropy.

The region was technically a province of New Spain, and, by extension, a royal province of the empire, but the endless derision of metropolitan oversight served as a constant reminder that the place refused to act like a proper arm of royal justice. The rules of imperial governance were inverted. The agents of royal justice exploited the symbolism of empire, if only to flout the very royal oversight that the Crown represented. The century after Spanish arrival in Michoacán was a time of ambivalent conquests and inchoate colonialisms and miniature fiefdoms; of mayhem and judicial violence; and of hilarious insults to the pretentiousness of universalism.

Badillo fled New Spain after his conviction for assault in 1584. Rather than accept the extraordinarily severe sentence of a twelve-year galley servitude, he sought refuge in Spain, where he appealed to both the Council of Indies and the papal nuncio.[1] He spent two decades there, from 1584 to 1604, though he may have also gone to Rome in his attempt to have the sentence vacated. Badillo's efforts appear to have succeeded, though it is difficult to know how he survived financially during those two decades. In these years, he had, by default, fulfilled the sentence of exile from New Spain, though only incidentally, since he appears to have done so out of a desire to vindicate himself and return to his position in the Michoacán cathedral chapter.

Badillo's story was so notorious that it remained part of the memory of the region's religious history. In 1648, the Crown commissioned a survey of the diocese, and a cathedral canon, Francisco Arnaldo de Ysassy, wrote a report in which he related an account of Badillo's imbroglio with the provisor, and the sentence of exile and suspension of his benefice.[2] Badillo had lobbied and received a papal pardon in the case. Sometime in 1594, he had traveled to Cádiz with his papal pardon in hand, ready to embark for New Spain, but for reasons unknown, he had spent another ten years in Spain before finally making his return journey.[3]

This book has portrayed Michoacán as the near opposite of Eden. In terms of political culture, the province was indeed remarkably fractious. But the region held tremendous sway over those who visited the area or lived there. Despite the often brutish quality of local politics, people like Vasco de Quiroga, Pedro de Yepes, Juan Pablos Carrión, Cristóbal Preciado, Cristóbal Badillo, and Diego de Orduña seemed to be incapable of leaving the region, such was its romantic sway over them. For Yepes and Orduña, Michoacán was their natural home, whereas for Quiroga and Badillo, it was their adopted home, and they were willing to fight for what they thought was the proper version of Eden.

Badillo's return to Michoacán after so many years underscored his genuine love of the region. In May 1604, the Crown affirmed his reinstatement as cathedral dignitary of Michoacán. Arguing before the court of the Casa de Contratación in Seville, Badillo produced a copy of a royal decree reinstating him as archdeacon. On 20 May 1604, the Casa de Contratación issued a license allowing him to return to Michoacán.[4] At this point, the case refers to him as a doctor, implying that he had the economic means to pay for a higher university degree, since he had already been a licenciado when he lived in Michoacán in the 1570s. In the Spanish system, a doctorate was educationally superfluous, but it required substantial funds, as the candidate was required to pay for the complex graduation ceremony and for the privilege itself. That Badillo had obtained a doctorate (presumably in law) during his two-decade exile indicates that he was far from impoverished.

Badillo's desire to return to Michoacán seems to have stemmed from an abiding identification with the region. Indeed, his intent to return may have been motivated only partly by economic reasons. Because he had been reinstated to his formal position, he stood to collect a sizable salary in Valladolid—probably around 540 pesos a year.[5] But this does not explain why he did not lobby for a prebend in Spain instead. Badillo's will, drawn up at sea, shows that though he was far from fantastically wealthy, he had not suffered permanent economic damage. He may simply have missed Michoacán and viewed it as his true home. Perhaps Badillo, after a twenty-year hiatus from Michoacán, had become nostalgic, even romantic, about the place. He boarded the ship *Santiago Mayor* in Seville sometime between late May and late June in 1604.

He rented a bedroom in the stern for the trans-Atlantic passage for a fee of 150 ducats. An impoverished man could hardly have afforded such luxury. He traveled with the newly elected chantre of Michoacán's cathedral, Don Mateo Illescas Orejón. It is unclear if they shared a bedroom, or a bed. Badillo brought his personal library of civil and canon law on the journey, which ran to 142 volumes, though we know nothing of the titles.[6] This was not a journey of someone merely looking to resume a professional position. This was a journey of someone returning home.

Badillo fell gravely ill at sea, and the ship's notary, Francisco del Poyo, drew up a last will and testament. On 16 July, Badillo was too feeble to sign his name, and he named Illescas as one of his witnesses. An inventory of assets drawn up on 19 July stated that the ship was at 22 degrees at the Islas de Guadalupe. (This appears to be an error. The islands of Guadaloupe are at 16 degrees latitude. If the position was correct, they may have been situated near today's Caicos Islands.) We do not know the date of Badillo's death, though he had certainly died shortly after finalizing his will, which states that he was too ill to sign it. In October 1604, his library went into receivership, while the document relating his illness was returned to Spain, where it was filed under "goods of the deceased" (*bienes de difuntos*). The will was entered into evidence before the royal fleet notary Martín de Ayala in Veracruz shortly thereafter and later before the Casa de Contratación.[7]

The inventory shows a somewhat sad but optimistic state of affairs. Badillo stated that he had no direct relatives as his inheritors and named as sole beneficiary of his estate a widow named Doña María de Mendoza. He had brought a large collection of old and worn-out clothing with him on the journey. But more telling is that he brought what must have been the majority of his personal possessions: his books, clerical cassocks, two gold rings, two silver cups. He brought his doctor's bonnet. He also had a brass chalice for holy water. He was transporting two mattresses.

One also finds subtle clues as to his cosmopolitanism. Badillo brought a Turkish scimitar and a great deal of Flemish cheese (about twelve pounds). By all accounts, he had traveled widely—from Colima to Pátzcuaro, to Mexico City, and to Campeche, Yucatán, and Veracruz, and presumably to Havana, Seville, Madrid, and possibly Rome. When witnesses denounced him in the 1577 trial, they especially despised what they saw as his excessively loose and urbane cultural sensibilities. Why would this worldly man, with such a high level of education, return to Michoacán? Obviously, it was partly about money and resuming his post as a cathedral dignitary. But we cannot discount two powerful human emotions: vengeance and nostalgia. Perhaps he wanted to prove that he had been right all along. Perhaps there was some score-settling to do. Or maybe, on a simpler level, he missed Michoacán.

Badillo traveled in high style. He must also have brought along an entourage— a servant, an employee, a retainer, a secret lover? The inventory notes the larder he had brought to sustain him and "his people." The quantity of the supplies in the larder suggests, at the least, two people, but probably three or four. The quality of the food indicates that he and "his people" intended not only to eat a good deal, but to eat well, on a journey that would have been expected to take about six weeks. It included five hams. There were still sixteen hens—presumably Badillo had already eaten some of them. There was salt beef, a barrel and two large bottles of wine, a large bottle and a half of oil, a box of garlic and onions, twelve pounds of rice, two *almudes* (close to sixty pounds) of garbanzos, a considerable amount of dry tack, and fresh water for drinking. Unlike the poorer travelers, who would have had to make do with a dreary diet of dry tack and salt beef, Badillo expected to dine in comfort.

But all his plans came to naught. Perhaps the most telling detail of Badillo's deathbed will is his bequest for masses to be said for his soul. When he drew up his final will, he stipulated that all previous versions were nullified. Badillo commissioned two hundred masses to be celebrated for his soul—a perfectly normal practice, but a relatively high number, and a fairly expensive project, since each mass would cost four *reales*, representing an outlay of a hundred pesos. Of these masses, one hundred were to be celebrated in the cathedral church of Michoacán at the altar of indulgences. Clearly, Badillo felt a particular connection with Michoacán. He easily could have stipulated that the masses be celebrated in a church in Mexico City. Of the other one hundred masses, twenty-five were to be celebrated in the monastery of San Francisco in Veracruz, twenty-five in the parish church of Veracruz, twenty-five in Santo Domingo (whether this refers to a church or the city is not clear), and twenty-five in the monastery of San Agustín (he did not stipulate the city). In any case, all of them, like the masses in Michoacán, were to be celebrated at the altars of indulgence in the respective churches.

Badillo had spent twenty years as an exile in his land of birth, Spain, all the while seeking to return to his true, adopted home—Michoacán. The hold the place had on him is remarkable. Even after the place had sent him away, he sought nothing more than to return there. How can one explain this? The place of lakes and streams and white fish and avocadoes and membrillos, of the Purépecha language and soft, warm evenings, of lush pine forest, of roast pig and endless varieties of chiles, of mountain lakes, of black-lacquer pottery, and of crucifixes made from corn paste—maybe Badillo could not bear the thought of never seeing it all again. He would not. But a chaplain would light a candle for his soul and celebrate a hundred masses for the man in the Valladolid cathedral.

Badillo's fate, sad though it may be, demonstrates the lasting influence the region could have on someone's psyche. Despite the political violence and the damage done to his career by Orduña, Badillo simply could not imagine a permanent life in Spain. Yet the region to which he hoped to return was still only partially Christianized. In the decade of his death, the indigenous population reached its lowest point yet. Things had changed. Had Badillo survived the Atlantic journey, he would have been shocked at the state of Michoacán's religious polity. Whole towns had disappeared in vast resettlement programs in the aftermath of wave after wave of epidemic disease. In many rural parts of the province, people had barely heard of the Inquisition, and had only rarely seen a parish priest.

And Michoacán's Catholic empire was falling down—not figuratively, but physically. The Franciscans appealed to the Crown for a massive loan to repair the monastery complex in Valladolid, the one they had begun in the 1540s in defiance of Quiroga. King Philip III ordered an investigation into the decay. According to a report filed in May 1615 by the alcalde Juan Zaldívar Mendoza, at least 30,000 pesos—a fantastic sum—would be required to bring the building up to decent standards. The alcalde described a monastery in near ruins, its walls falling down. Stray dogs roamed the church, and debris littered the compound. Given the population decline of the indigenous residents, alms collections were drastically reduced. The only way to complete the repair was to receive an infusion of royal funding.[8]

Diego Muñoz died in 1624 or 1625. The Inquisition of Michoacán did not exactly die with the friar; rather, it had never really existed.[9] After Orduña's death, cathedral canon Simón Zafra de la Cueva appealed to the inquisitors in Mexico to become the comisario for Valladolid.[10] Inquisitors ignored his 1618 request for years. Apparently, the actions of their previous deputies had made them wary. Or maybe the mail routes were insecure, and someone stole the inquisitors' reply and beat up the mailmen, or shit on an inquisitional order. After Muñoz's demise, inquisitors wearily appointed Zafra as inquisitional deputy.[11]

Zafra reported the state of affairs in Michoacán with apparent horror. In June 1625, he wrote to the inquisitors to explain that the failure to read the Edict of Faith in many parts of the diocese had led to widespread idolatry and superstition, especially in remote regions such as Motines, Zacatula, and Colima.[12] In 1630, a different comisario, Cristóbal Báez, traveled to Taximaroa to discover that local residents—Spaniard, mestizo, mulato, and indigenous—seemed to have no knowledge of a local priest. Many of them were ingesting hallucinogenic mushrooms as a spiritual device.[13] By all appearances, many people in rural Michoacán had never seen a priest or an inquisitional agent. No one from the home office ever visited the area. Most of the residents of rural and remote towns figured there was some vague conceptual inquisition somewhere, but they had never actually seen an inquisitor, let alone a deputy, or even a familiar. Inquisition? What is that?

FINAL THOUGHTS

In the preceding pages, I have endeavored to show that most Spaniards in Michoacán were indeed Catholic, theoretically derived their political authority from the Crown, and abstractly believed in empire. But if we think of empire as something conceived in a broad sense, at the everyday and local level this empire—Crown, Church, Inquisition—needed builders, carpenters, plumbers. Those charged with the construction and maintenance of the empire distrusted the more conservative and orthodox elements of that project.

This series of microhistorical biographies reminds us that imperial power needed individual actors. Those individuals were hard to control. Power was promiscuous in this region precisely because so many different kinds of power overlapped. And many different local agents tried to control the application of a vast global abstraction—the Spanish Empire—when the quotidian reality was a kind of banal free-for-all.

But one would be very hard-pressed to locate a genuinely effective apparatus of persecution or royal hegemony. The persecuting society that many historians see for the later medieval period failed to materialize in Michoacán. The crusading spirit of the reconquest of the Iberian Peninsula has been revived as part of the historiographic tradition.[14] This crusading Catholicism putatively traveled along with the conquistadors of the Americas. Yet the violence of Michoacán was inward-looking. Constant mayhem, rivalry, and localism all blunted the effects of any triumphalist Catholicism. Michoacán looks more like Catalonia than Castile in the sixteenth and seventeenth centuries in that sense: it was a largely unpoliced population with little regard for the demands of conservative religion.[15] To that end, Michoacán also was a region only barely Christianized in the extensive doctrinal sense.

On the secular side of this equation, empire was in effect parceled out to private operators. True, these private operators—bishops, parish priests, magistrates, encomenderos, and indigenous pipiltin—enjoyed the fully vested royal powers associated with their vicarious positions as agents of the Spanish Crown. They enjoyed the outsized local power that came with the semi-privatization of empire and the distance from global regulation. But the semi-privatization of empire backfired whenever the Crown and its ministers decided it was time to control the unruly region.

Michoacán ultimately set the tone for a long period of decentralized and absentee colonialism. Far from the image of effective conquest—political, spiritual, and cultural—the region was a laboratory in all the most prosaic kinds of human desires. Yet Michoacán's hold on the imagination of its residents, then as now, proved hypnotic. Eden it was not, and yet it was a pretty good place to be.

First, yes, Spain had a king, and Mexico was part of its far-flung empire. But residents of Michoacán understood the king only as an abstract concept. On the ground, the empire was a mishmash of individual agents of royal authority. Those agents of royal justice mocked the very law that they served. The same can be said of many of the representatives of a Catholic order. Inquisitional deputies enriched themselves and flouted the rule of law. In effect, Michoacán was a region of refuge. But unlike Maroon slaves or indigenous groups, who might seek refuge from would-be rulers, the Spanish colonials were fleeing the very rule they represented. It was a supremely ironic kind of refuge—as if the Spanish imperial agents were hiding from themselves.

We may be tempted to think about Richard White's magisterial treatment of a "middle ground" in the North American Great Lakes region.[16] He presented a portrait of similar forms of colonial violence but suggests that through all the mayhem both settlers and indigenous peoples worked out a modus vivendi for cultural, social, and political survival. In the estimation of some readers, Michoacán may simply represent the usual state of affairs for frontier regions. To that extent one finds similarities in the case of Chile in the sixteenth century, where Spanish imperial ambition reached the limits of expansion in the Araucanian War and the proverbial line in the sand in Bío-Bío.[17] I argue that while Michoacán may have offered similar levels of violence and evasion of global oversight, it was remarkable because of how the very representatives of order were instead agents of disorder. In that vein, we might even suggest that local royal officials functioned as actors of resistance to imperial expansion. On first glance such a statement appears ridiculous. But consider that these local actors—parish priest, cathedral canon, missionary, inquisitional deputy, magistrate—saw it as their charge to defend local custom and power. That the state which they putatively served sought to rein in that local power only reinforced their belief that they were instead agents of local republics and empires in miniature.

Second, the Catholic Church was incapable of imposing social discipline in Michoacán. Neither friar nor parish priest nor bishop nor inquisitional deputy was able to impose order on the unruly province. In some cases, the absence of social control was a function of political attention being spent on factional battles. But there is something more fundamental operating in this case. The Catholic Church could not impose social control because it could not draw on the corroborating force of cultural expectations and norms. In other words, the formal Church—in the form of its diocesan structure and Inquisition—could not harness the cooperation of the population as a whole. The thesis of a pedagogy of fear supposes that the Church could count on the citizenry to reinforce its message of orthodoxy and behavioral conservatism. Because the Inquisition had such a thinly spread infrastructure, the only way it could impose hegemony was if the population reinforced its message through quotidian cultural policing. But in Michoacán, the residents mocked the Inquisition and refused to participate in its message of behavioral control. The Inquisition in Michoacán was, in short, a spectacular cultural failure.

Third, the Spanish Crown was incapable of maintaining a monopoly on force. Power was personalist in Michoacán: caudillos (often priests) wielded both political authority and armed force. In modern parlance, one would be tempted to think about the region as one without a state. Instead, it was a concatenation of fiefdoms and estates. This decentralized system may be typical of preindustrial states in general, but Michoacán provides a case study in which the very agents of the state mocked the system they served. The imperial endeavor in Michoacán was partially privatized. By the same token, Michoacán's jurisdictional isolation, coupled with its plantation and ranching economy, helped to create a local class of caudillos who wielded power in name of a state, but strictly for their own ends. When their interests conflicted with the royal law, they invariably chose their own interests, rarely paying much penalty for those decisions.

Fourth, I have sought to revise the perception of Michoacán as a peaceable Eden. If anything, my portrait reveals a violent, tumultuous, and rancorous colony. Yes, Quiroga and many Augustinians viewed Michoacán as ripe for grandiose and utopian socio-religious engineering. But their projects met with resistance not only from indigenous residents but also from Spanish colonials. Mayhem, political rivalry, fraud, gambling, stabbings, and assassinations were the order of the day. Michoacán, in the political sense, was anything but peaceful or Edenic. But it would be crass to suggest that it did not exert a tremendous emotional influence on its residents. Badillo, after all, was willing to return after all that had happened.

The Eden thesis makes more sense if we think about the lack of reach of the royal state. I have presented evidence that political violence was common. But much of the violence was a reaction to the perceived imposition of hegemony. Those reactions show that everyday life in much of Michoacán was unregulated by external authorities. In that sense, Michoacán was truly self-sustaining, to the extent that external oversight was unnecessary for its everyday operation, and, when oversight arrived, the local reaction was violent. The hostility to outside influence suggests a region where most residents saw very few official agents of the state or church.

Finally, the long-standing assumption that the early modern Spanish state, in the form of the Crown, formed an effective alliance with the Church to impose hegemony is inaccurate. Once we disentangle the component parts of the state and church in Michoacán, we see that the individual parts ignored the broader imperial model. A key component of the Black Legend assumes that the Crown-Church alliance formed a monolithic force that crushed lives, ruined careers, dismayed the soul, and made everyone tremble in fear before the mighty premodern totalitarian Leviathan. Nothing could be further from the reality of everyday life in Michoacán in the sixteenth century. Instead, it was a farce of the empire, a satire of formal Catholicism, a place where a man could chop off a rival's ear, threaten to shit on a legal writ, or slap and smack down a priest and suffer no long-term legal or political consequences.

One may wonder whether the first century of Michoacán under Spanish rule was simply one more example of the decentralized tendency of the early modern state, Spanish or otherwise. Certainly, Michoacán shared tendencies of the broader systems of delegation of authority in the Spanish Empire. But imperial governance was from day one delegated to corporate interests who acted as a bulwark against any centralized ambitions. This corporatist concentration of power existed in a jurisdictionally remote region only technically brought under oversight—by institutions like the Crown and its viceroy, the Church and its bishop, and the Inquisition and its deputies—after corporate interests had enjoyed free rein into the 1540s, in the case of royal magistrates, and into the 1570s, or, really, the 1590s, in the case of the Inquisition. The result was that the region was constitutionally inured to distrust of external authority.

There was no king, and no empire, in Michoacán. There were, instead, a lot of little empires in miniature, none of them especially respectful of the king, who was a mere abstraction. To an extent, then, Michoacán did resemble Eden, but, in the analogical sense, immediately after the Fall. The people tasked with minding the empire refused to apply the logic of empire; they were, instead, wholly concerned with localism.

I will end with a question. If a region as rich socially and economically and as strategically important as Michoacán had no empire, no king, and no law, what does that say about the overall strength of the Spanish Empire in the sixteenth and seventeenth centuries? Perhaps, in unmaking empire in Michoacán, the various local agents of the Crown, the Church, and the Inquisition simply acted to prevent the imposition of power from afar. Power in Michoacán was promiscuous precisely because claims to competence and authority constantly overlapped. But if extensive ethnohistorical scholarship shows that indigenous communities showed social, cultural, and linguistic continuity under Spanish rule, we need to reevaluate the very nature of that Spanish rule. In the case of Michoacán, it turns out, that rule of law was diffuse. It was spread thin by the competing claims to power at the local level that forever stifled global ambitions.

ABBREVIATIONS

ACCM Archivo del Cabildo de la Catedral de Michoacán (Archive of the Cathedral Chapter of Michoacán), Morelia, Mexico

AGI Archivo General de Indias (General Archive of the Indies), Seville, Spain

AGN Archivo General de la Nación (Mexican General National Archive), Mexico City, Mexico

AHEC Archivo Histórico del Estado de Colima (Historical Archive of the State of Colima), Colima, Mexico

AHMC Archivo Histórico del Municipio de Colima (Municipal Historical Archive of Colima), Colima, Mexico

AHMP Archivo Histórico Municipal de Pátzcuaro (Municipal Archive of Pátzcuaro), Pátzcuaro, Mexico

AHN Archivo Histórico Nacional (National Historical Archive), Madrid, Spain

AVC *Archivo de la Villa de Colima de la Nueva España: Siglo XVI*, ed. and trans. José Miguel Romero de Solís, 2 vols. (Colima, Mexico: Archivo Histórico del Municipio de Colima, 1998–2005)

De la Rea Alonso de la Rea, *Chronica de la Orden de N. seraphico P.S. Francisco, prouincia de S. Pedro. y S. Pablo de Mechoacan en la Nueua España* (Mexico City: Por la viuda de Bernardo Calderón, 1643)

Escobar Matías de Escobar, *Americana Thebaida: Vitas patrum de los religiosos hermitaños de N.P. San Agustín de la provincia de S. Nicolás Tolentino de Mechoacán* (Mexico City: Imprenta Victoria, 1924 [1729])

exp. expediente (file)

Gerhard Peter Gerhard, *A Guide to the Historical Geography of New Spain, 1519–1821*, rev. ed. (Norman: University of Oklahoma Press, 1993)

Himmerich y Valencia Robert Himmerich y Valencia, *The Encomenderos of New Spain, 1521–1555* (Austin: University of Texas Press, 1991)

Inq. Inquisición (section of AGN)

leg. legajo (section of an archival file)

Muñoz Diego Muñoz, *Descripción de la provincia de San Pedro y San Pablo de Michoacán, en las Indias de la Nueva España*, intro. José Ramírez Flores (Guadalajara, Mexico: Instituto Jalisciense de Antropología e Historia, 1965 [c. 1585])

Quiroga v. OSA "El obispo de Mechoacán: Vasco de Quiroga contra el provincial de la órden de San Agustín de Nueva España, fray Agustín de Coruña, sobre el asiento de dicha órden en la iglesia de Tlazazalca. AGI Justicia 163," versión paleográfica de Alberto Carrillo Cázares y Silvia Méndez Hernández, in Alberto Carrillo Cázares, *Vasco de Quiroga: La pasión por el derecho*, 2 vols. (Zamora, Mexico: El Colegio de Michoacán, 2003), 1:219–524, 2:525–721

RM   [Jerónimo de Alcalá], *La relación de Michoacán* (Barcelona: Editorial Linkgua, 2011 [c. 1541])

s/n   *sin número* (without number), for unnumbered file or folio references

UNAM   Universidad Nacional Autónoma de México (National Autonomous University of Mexico)

Vida michoacana   Rodrigo Martínez Baracs and Lydia Espinosa Morales, eds., *La vida michoacana en el siglo XVI: Catálogo de los documentos del siglo XVI del Archivo Histórico de la Ciudad de Pátzcuaro* (Mexico City: Instituto Nacional de Antropología e Historia, 1999)

INTRODUCTION

1. Alonso de la Rea, *Chronica de la Orden de N. seraphico P.S. Francisco, prouincia de S. Pedro. y S. Pablo de Mechoacan en la Nueua España* (Mexico City: Por la viuda de Bernardo Calderón, 1643) ("De la Rea" hereafter), 2. The original: "Las aguas, que riegan este Paraýso terrenal, y fertilizan su copia, son las mas abundantes, que goza el Reyno, tan dulces, y potables como las pide el desseo: y assí no ay Pueblo, Ciudad, o Villa que no tenga su Socorro en Fuentes, o Rios."

2. In Spanish, *meseta tarasca*.

3. See classic studies such as José Miranda, *La función económica del encomendero en los orígenes del régimen colonial de Nueva España (1521-1535)* (Mexico City: Universidad Nacional Autónoma de México [National Autonomous University of Mexico, UNAM hereafter], 1965); Leslie Byrd Simpson, *The Encomienda in New Spain: The Beginning of Spanish Mexico* (Berkeley: University of California Press, 1950); Silvio Zavala, *La encomienda indiana* (Mexico City: Porrúa, 1973).

4. I will cite all these stories in due course.

5. The term derives from Gonzalo Aguirre Beltrán, *Regiones de refugio: El desarrollo de la comunidad y el proceso dominical en mestizo América* (Mexico City: Instituto Nacional Indigenista, 1967). I discuss the analytical model below.

6. Anthony Pagden, *Spanish Imperialism and the Political Imagination: Studies in European and Spanish-American Social and Political Theory, 1513-1830* (New Haven, CT: Yale University Press, 1990), 3.

7. William B. Taylor, "Between Global Process and Local Knowledge: An Inquiry into Early Latin American Social History, 1500-1900," in Olivier Zunz, ed., *Reliving the Past: The Worlds of Social History* (Chapel Hill: University of North Carolina Press, 1985), 145.

8. For a short listing, see J. H. Elliott, *Empires of the Atlantic World: Britain and Spain in America, 1492-1830* (New Haven, CT: Yale University Press, 2007); Jack P. Green and Philip D. Morgan, eds., *Atlantic History: A Critical Appraisal* (Oxford: Oxford University Press, 2008); Henry Kamen, *Empire: How Spain Became a World Power, 1492-1763* (New York: Harper Perennial, 2004).

9. The literature is too extensive to cover here. For overviews, see James Lockhart, *Nahuas and Spaniards: Postconquest Central Mexican History and Philology* (Stanford, CA: Stanford University Press; Los Angeles: UCLA Latin American Center Publications, University of California, Los Angeles, 1991), esp. 159-201, and Matthew Restall, "The History of the New Philology and the New Philology in History," *Latin American Research Review* 38 (2003): 113-134.

10. Here I am indebted to some of the "classics" of microhistory: Natalie Zemon Davis, *The Return of Martin Guerre* (Cambridge, MA: Harvard University Press, 1983); Carlo Ginzburg, *The Cheese and the Worms: The Cosmos of a Sixteenth-Century Miller*, trans. John and Anne Tedeschi (Baltimore, MD: Johns Hopkins University Press, 1992); Luis González y González, *Pueblo en vilo:*

Microhistoria de San José de Gracia (Mexico City: El Colegio de México, 1968); Emanuel Le Roy Ladurie, *Montaillou: The Promised Land of Error*, trans. Barbara Bray (New York: Vintage, 1979), as well as the more recent Craig Harline, *Miracles at the Jesus Oak: Histories of the Supernatural in Reformation Europe* (New Haven, CT: Yale University Press, 2011). For a brilliant reconstruction of an infamous event (the Albigensian Crusade) using a microhistorical approach, see Mark Gregory Pegg, *A Most Holy War: The Albigensian Crusade and the Battle for Christendom* (Oxford: Oxford University Press, 2008). Also see the genre's historiographic elaboration: Edward Muir and Guido Ruggiero, eds., *Microhistory and the Lost Peoples of Europe* (Baltimore, MD: Johns Hopkins University Press, 1991).

11. Mikhail Bakhtin, *Problems of Dostoyevsky's Poetics*, ed. and trans. Caryl Emerson, intro. Wayne C. Booth (Minneapolis: University of Minnesota Press, 1984).

12. Mikhail Bakhtin, *Rabelais and His World*, trans. Hélène Iswolsky (Bloomington: Indiana University Press, 1984). I make no claim about the relative merit of Bakhtin's theories of the carnivalesque, interpreting carnival as a time of cultural liberation, inverting the oppressive order of things. Natalie Zemon Davis offered an influential counterargument, suggesting that carnival reiterated cultural hierarchies by putting them on display, albeit in mockery, in "The Reasons of Misrule: Youth Groups and Charivaris in Sixteenth-Century France," *Past & Present* 50 (1971): 41–75.

13. Archivo General de la Nación (Mexican General National Archive), Mexico City (AGN hereafter), Inquisición ("Inq." hereafter), vol. 228, expediente (file; "exp." hereafter) s/n (without number), fols. 157–159.

14. AGN, Inq., vol. 5, exp. 17, fol. 326: "Santa Catalina era cornuda puta y Santa Magdalena era buxarrona." The English translation is a little tricky. Generally, the masculine form *cornudo* (cuckold) is common; using the feminine of the word, *cornuda*, presents a complicated linguistic question. Did López mean to say that Saint Catherine was an adulteress or that she was the object of a philandering husband? Sebastián de Covarrubias, in *Tesoro de la lengua castellana, o española* (Madrid: Luis Sánchez, 1611), 240–241, offers a tellingly lengthy discussion of the term *cornudo*, and at no point does he mention a concept of a cornuda. No succinct single word in English really captures the meaning, so I have opted for "adulterous whore" for the phrase. Likewise, *buxarrona* is unusual, since the masculine, *bujarrón* (roughly equivalent to a negative use of the word "queer") was more common. Covarrubius, *Tesoro*, 157, identifies "buxarrón, vale tanto como horadado, quasi bucorón." That is to say, a buxarrón was the bottom in anal sex and, as such, in early modern Spanish culture, an object of scorn for having taken the "female" role in sexual penetration. Again, "buxarrona" has no specific English equivalent, so the pejorative word for a lesbian, "dyke," seems like an appropriate translation, given the intensely negative emotion expressed in the modern word. Curiously enough, *buga* and *bugarrón* in modern parlance refer to hyper-macho men who have sex with other men but are socially identified as heterosexual and limit themselves to the active role.

15. AGN, Inq., vol. 281, exp. s/n, fol. 28 [528]: "El cardenal protector estaua amancebado con el guardián de Nápoles, diffinidor de la prouincia romana, y era la putana, y por su respecto le auían hecho guardián y diffinidor." True, *puttana* in Italian technically means "whore," but like *puto/puta* in Spanish, it can take on more generic terms that do not always specifically translate as "whore"/"prostitute" in English. It is not entirely clear whether the speaker meant to say that the entire situation was whorish, but it seems likely that he was implying that the cardinal gave the position to the friar because he was good-looking and that he was the cardinal's lover.

16. AGN, Inq., vol. 18, exp. 1, fol. 4: "En la calle del padre Francisco de la Çerda junta a la puerta este testigo le dixo que abía parado bien y entonces el dicho Alonso Gómez dixo que abía corrido en México en un caballo desbocado y que le abía hecho parar como un serafín y a este testigo le

dixo como paraban los serafines y el dicho Alonso Gómez dixo que era así una manera de dezir y que no le oyó dezir otras palabras malsonantes."

17. AGN, Inq., vol. 17, exp. 4, fol. 109: "De axí muy colorado que tenía color de sangre de Cristo," and fol. 114: "Caldo que venía colorado de chile o especias como sangre del justo."

18. AGN, Inq., vol. 10, exp. 8, fol. 306: "Pedro de Áviles les abía dicho y respondido que fuesen al rrío que por allí pasaba e trajesen cantidad de çauzes y los quemasen y que dellos hiziesen çeniça que el se la pondría."

19. The classic study remains Simpson, *Encomienda in New Spain*.

20. J. Benedict Warren, *The Conquest of Michoacán: The Spanish Domination of the Tarascan Kingdom in Western Mexico, 1521–1530* (Norman: University of Oklahoma Press, 1985).

21. For discussion of the functions and evolution of the Audiencia, see Pilar Arregui Zamorano, *La Audiencia de México según los visitadores, siglos XVI y XVII* (Mexico City: UNAM, 1981); Ismael Sánchez Bella, "Las audiencias y el gobierno de las Indias (siglos XVI–XVII)," *Revista de Estudios Histórico-Jurídicos* 2 (1977): 159–186.

22. France V. Scholes and Eleanor B. Adams, eds., *Proceso contra Tzintzicha Tangaxoan, el caltzontzin formado por Nuño de Guzmán año de 1530* (Mexico City: Porrúa, 1952).

23. Pedro Torres, "La 'bula omnimoda' de Adriano VI (9 Mayo 1522) y su aplicación durante el primer siglo de las misiones de Indias," *Missionalia Hispánica* 3 (1946): 7–52.

24. De la Rea, 29–33; Matías de Escobar, *Americana Thebaida: Vitas patrum de los religiosos hermitaños de N.P. San Agustín de la provincia de S. Nicolás Tolentino de Mechoacán* (Mexico City: Imprenta Victoria, 1924 [1729]) ("Escobar" hereafter), 71–73.

25. Robert Ricard coined the term, which retains considerable explanatory power. See *The Spiritual Conquest of Mexico: An Essay on the Apostolate and the Evangelizing Methods of the Mendicant Orders in New Spain, 1523–1572*, trans. Leslie Byrd Simpson (Berkeley: University of California Press, 1982 [1933]).

26. I discuss his assaults, referenced in contemporaneous correspondence, in Chapter 2 (see AGN, Inq., vol. 43, exp. 7, and vol. 226, exp. s/n, fols. 64–66), and in a lengthy lawsuit between Quiroga, in "El obispo de Mechoacán: Vasco de Quiroga contra el provincial de la órden de San Agustín de Nueva España, fray Agustín de Coruña, sobre el asiento de dicha órden en la iglesia de Tlazazalca. AGI Justicia 163," paleographic version by Alberto Carrillo Cázares and Silvia Méndez Hernández, in Alberto Carrillo Cázares, ed., *Vasco de Quiroga: La pasión por el derecho*, 2 vols. (Zamora, Mexico: El Colegio de Michoacán, 2003), 1:219–524, 2:525–721 ("*Quiroga v. OSA*" hereafter).

27. The literature is vast. The classic model of the Inquisition as an omniscient, malevolent force was elaborated over a century ago. See Henry Charles Lea, *History of the Inquisition in Spain*, 4 vols. (New York: Macmillan, 1906–1907). The Chilean bibliographer and book historian José Toribio Medina offered similarly negative, if slightly less anti-Catholic, conclusions in *Historia del Tribunal del Santo Oficio de la inquisición de Lima (1569–1820)* (Santiago: Imprenta Gutenberg, 1887), and *Historia del tribunal del Santo oficio de la inquisición en México* (Santiago: Imprenta Elzeviriana, 1905). Modern studies, which have tended to see a less effective form of repression, include Richard Greenleaf, *The Mexican Inquisition in the Sixteenth Century* (Albuquerque: University of New Mexico Press, 1969); Henry Kamen, *The Spanish Inquisition: A Historical Revision*, 4th rev. ed. (New Haven, CT: Yale University Press, 2014); William Monter, *Frontiers of Heresy: The Spanish Inquisition from the Basque Lands to Sicily* (Cambridge: Cambridge University Press, 1990); and Stuart B. Schwartz, *All Can Be Saved: Religious Tolerance and Salvation in the Iberian Atlantic World* (New Haven, CT: Yale University Press, 2009). One can also look to the extensive literature of the social history of the Inquisition developed among French, Spanish, and Latin

American historians of the 1970s, 1980s, and 1990s as indicative of a shift away from the Black Legend. For noted examples of this literature, see Solange Alberro, *Inquisición y sociedad en México, 1571–1700* (Mexico City: Fondo de Cultura Económica, 1988); Ángel Alcalá, ed., *Inquisición española y mentalidad inquisitorial* (Barcelona: Ariel, 1984); Jean-Pierre Dedieu, *L'Administration de la foi: L'Inquisition de Tolède (XVIe–XVIIIe siècle)* (Madrid: Casa de Velázquez, 1989); Laura de Mello e Souza, *O diabo e a Terra de Santa Cruz: Feitiçaria e religiosidade popular no Brasil colonial* (São Paulo: Companhia das Letras, 1986); René Millar Carvacho, *Inquisición y sociedad en el virreinato peruano: Estudios sobre el tribunal de la Inquisición de Lima* (Lima: Instituto Riva-Agüero, Pontificia Universidad Católica del Perú; Santiago: Instituto de Historia, Ediciones Universidad Católica de Chile, 1998); Joaquín Pérez Villanueva, ed., *La Inquisición española: Nueva visión, nuevos horizontes* (Madrid: Siglo Veintiuno de España, 1980); Joaquín Pérez Villanueva and Bartolomé Escandell Bonet, eds., *Historia de la Inquisición en España y América*, 3 vols. (Madrid: Biblioteca de Autores Cristianos, Centro de Estudios Inquisitoriales, 1984–[2000]); Ronaldo Vainfas, *Trópico dos pecados: Moral, sexualidade e inquisição no Brasil* (Rio de Janeiro: Editora Campus, 1989). For a more recent reprisal of both the historiographic debates as well as a comprehensive treatment of contemporaneous debates about the Spanish Inquisition, see Stefania Pastore, *Il vangelo e la spada: L'inquisizione di Castiglia e i suoi critici (1460–1598)* (Rome: Edizioni di storia e letteratura, 2003).

28. Irene Silverblatt, *Modern Inquisitions: Peru and the Colonial Origins of the Civilized World* (Durham, NC: Duke University Press, 2004), claims that the Inquisition was a harbinger of twentieth-century totalitarianism. In *Escravidão, homossexualidade e demonologia* (São Paulo: Icone, 1988), and *O sexo proibido: Virgens, gays e escravos nas garras da Inquisição* (Campinus, Brazil: Papirus Editora, 1988), Luiz Mott draws a direct line from the Portuguese Inquisition to modern homophobia and the murder of gay men. Christine Caldwell Ames, in *Righteous Persecution: Inquisition, Dominicans, and Christianity in the Middle Ages* (Philadelphia: University of Pennsylvania Press, 2009), makes a compelling argument that the Inquisition was born of a mentality of persecution within the Dominican order. Similarly, and while not explicitly treating the Inquisition, Franco Mormando's spellbinding study *The Preacher's Demons: Bernardino of Siena and the Social Underworld of Early Renaissance Italy* (Chicago: University of Chicago Press, 1999) shows how sociological factors could undergird a socially repressive cultural message.

29. AGN, Inq., vol. 11, exp. 4, fol. 304: "Mierda para la notificación y para la de escomunión y para quien me lo notificare."

30. His will of the 1570s indicates considerable wealth. See Archivo del Cabildo de la Catedral de Michoacán (Archive of the Cathedral Chapter of Michoacán)(ACCM hereafter), Ramo Colegio de San Nicolás, legajo ("leg." hereafter) 4, exp. 20.

31. See Alejandro Cañeque, *The King's Living Image: The Culture and Politics of Viceregal Power in Colonial Mexico* (New York: Routledge, 2004), and Sonya Lipsett-Rivera, *Gender and the Negotiation of Daily Life in Mexico, 1750–1856* (Lincoln: University of Nebraska Press, 2012).

32. Claudia Paulina Machuca Chávez, "Cabildo, negociación y vino de cocos: El caso de la villa de Colima en el siglo XVII," *Anuario de Estudios Americanos* 66 (2009): 173–192.

33. AGN, Inq., vol. 182, exps. 3, 6.

34. Archivo Histórico Nacional (National Historical Archive), Madrid (AHN hereafter), Consejo de Inquisición, 1728, exp. 8. The term squash (*calabaza*) also implied superciliousness and pretension. See Covarrubias, *Tesoro*, 171.

35. John Lynch, *Argentine Dictator: Juan Manuel de Rosas, 1829–1852* (New York: Oxford University Press, 1981); and Domingo F. Sarmiento, *Facundo: Civilización y barbarie*, ed. Roberto Yahni (Madrid: Cátedra, 1990 [1845]).

36. AGN, Tierras, vol. 3702, exp. 5, and Inq., vol. 316, exp. s/n, fols. 594–599.

37. Archivo General de Indias (General Archives of the Indies), Seville (AGI hereafter), México 28n26.

38. AGN, Inq., vol. 510, exp. 22.

39. Ibid., vol. 316, exp. s/n, fols. 594–599.

40. Ibid., vol. 340, exp. 5, and vol. 346, exp. 11.

41. For a short listing, see J. H. Elliott, *The Count-Duke of Olivares: The Statesman in an Age of Decline* (New Haven, CT: Yale University Press, 1989); Henry Kamen, *Philip of Spain* (New Haven, CT: Yale University Press, 1997); Geoffrey Parker, *The Grand Strategy of Philip II* (New Haven, CT: Yale University Press, 1998). For a classic study of court grandees, see Francisco Tomás y Valiente, *Los validos en la monarquía española del siglo XVII (estudio institucional)* (Madrid: Instituto de Estudios Políticos, 1963).

42. Standard discussions include John Edwards, *The Spain of the Catholic Monarchs, 1474–1520* (Oxford: Wiley-Blackwell, 2001); J. H. Elliott, *Imperial Spain, 1469–1716* (New York: St. Martin's Press, 1964); Benjamín González Alonso, *Sobre el estado y la administración de la Corona de Castilla en el Antiguo Régimen: Las comunidades de Castilla y otros estudios* (Madrid: Siglo Veintiuno de España, 1981); John Lynch, *Spain, 1516–1698: From Nation State to World Empire* (Oxford: Wiley-Blackwell, 1994), and *Spain Under the Hapsburgs* (Oxford: Blackwell, 1964).

43. José Luis Bermejo Cabrero, *Poder político y administración de justicia en la España de los Austrias* (Madrid: Ministerio de Justicia, Secretaría General Técnica, 2000); John B. Owens, *"By My Absolute Royal Authority": Justice and the Castilian Commonwealth at the Beginning of the First Global Age* (Rochester, NY: University of Rochester Press, 2005).

44. Aurelio Espinosa, *The Empire of the Cities: Emperor Charles V, the Comunero Revolt, and the Transformation of the Spanish System* (Leiden: Brill, 2009); Joseph Pérez, *Comuneros* (Madrid: Esfera de los Libros, 2001). On the relationship between law and state in early modern Spain, see Franciso Tomás y Valiente, *Gobierno e instituciones en la España del antiguo régimen* (Madrid: Alianza 1982). An homage to Tomás y Valiente followed up on the debate about the relationship between rule and consent in early modern Spain: Francisco Javier Guillamón Álvarez and José Javier Ruiz Ibáñez, eds., *Lo conflictivo y lo consensual en Castilla: Sociedad y poder político, 1521–1715. Homenaje a Francisco Tomás y Valiente* (Murcia, Spain: Universidad de Murcia, 2001).

45. For a classic of high-level viceregal politics, see Jorge Ignacio Rubio Mañé, *Introducción al estudio de los virreyes de Nueva España, 1535–1746* (Mexico City: Ediciones Selectas, 1955). Perhaps the best study of Viceroy Mendoza's politics is Ethelia Ruiz Medrano, *Gobierno y sociedad en Nueva España: Segunda Audiencia y Antonio de Mendoza* (Zamora, Mexico: El Colegio de Michoacán, Gobierno del Estado de Michoacán, 1991).

46. An excellent study of the political culture of letrados is Stafford Poole, *Juan de Ovando: Governing the Spanish Empire in the Reign of Phillip II* (Norman: University of Oklahoma Press, 2004).

47. On the colonial state in general, see Mario Góngora, *El estado en el derecho indiano: Época de fundación (1492–1570)* (Santiago: Editorial Universitaria, 1951); Clarence H. Haring, *Spanish Empire in America* (New York: Oxford University Press, 1947); José María Ots Capdequí, *El estado español de las Indias* (Mexico City: El Colegio de México, 1941). Also see Lorenzo Santayana Bustillo, prologue by Francisco Tomás y Valiente, *Gobierno político de los pueblos de España, y el corregidor, alcalde y juez en ellos* (Madrid: Instituto de Estudios de Administración Local, 1979).

48. For a good discussion of this cultural flexibility, see António Manuel Hespanha, *La gracia del derecho: Economía de la cultura en la edad moderna* (Madrid: Centro de Estudios Constitucionales, 1993).

49. See Simpson, *Encomienda in New Spain*. A complex and deeply researched study of land and society in colonial Guerrero is Jonathan D. Amith, *The Möbius Strip: A Spatial History of Colonial Society in Guerrero, Mexico* (Stanford, CA: Stanford University Press, 2005).

50. For an overview of the conflict, see Margarita Menegus, Francisco Morales, and Oscar Mazín, *La secularización de las doctrinas de indios en la Nueva España: La pugna entre las dos Iglesias* (Mexico City: UNAM, Instituto de Investigaciones sobre la Universidad y la Educación, 2010).

51. See Pedro de Leturia, *Relaciones entre la Santa Sede e Hispanoamérica*, 3 vols. (Caracas, Venezuela: Sociedad Bolivariana de Venezuela, 1959–1960); Jesús María López Andrés, *Real patronato eclesiástico y estado moderno: La Iglesia de Almería en época de los Reyes Católicos* (Almería, Spain: Instituto de Estudios Almerienses, 1995); John F. Schwaller, *The Church and Clergy in Sixteenth Century Mexico* (Albuquerque: University of New Mexico Press, 1987).

52. For recent discussion of the phenomenon, see Ashley D. Ellington, "The Council of the Indies and Religion in the Spanish New World" (MA thesis, Georgia Southern University, 2014).

53. For excellent overviews of the legal history of the Spanish Inquisition, see José Antonio Escudero, ed., *Perfiles jurídicos de la inquisición española* (Madrid: Instituto de Historia de la Inquisición, 1989). For an excellent microhistory of the earliest years of the Spanish Inquisition in the 1480s, see Gretchen D. Starr-Lebeau, *In the Shadow of the Virgin: Inquisitors, Friars, and Conversos in Guadalupe, Spain* (Princeton, NJ: Princeton University Press, 2002).

54. The standard-bearer English-language studies are Richard Greenleaf, *Mexican Inquisition in the Sixteenth Century*, and *Zumárraga and the Mexican Inquisition, 1536–1543* (Washington, DC: American Academy of Franciscan History, 1961). For more recent studies, see John F. Chuchiak IV, ed. and trans., *The Inquisition in New Spain, 1536–1820: A Documentary History* (Baltimore, MD: Johns Hopkins University Press, 2012); David Tavárez, *The Invisible War: Indigenous Devotions, Discipline, and Dissent in Colonial Mexico* (Stanford, CA: Stanford University Press, 2011). Among Mexican scholars, see Alberro, *Inquisición y sociedad en México*, and Noemí Quezada, Martha Eugenia Rodríguez, and Marcela Suárez, eds., *Inquisición novohispana*, 2 vols. (Mexico City: UNAM, 2000). For discussion of the installment of an inquisitor general in Mexico, see Stafford Poole, *Pedro Moya de Contreras: Catholic Reform and Royal Power in New Spain, 1571–1591* (Berkeley: University of California Press, 1987).

55. Ginzburg, *The Cheese and the Worms*, 61.

56. For a defense of the importance of human biography in understanding inquisitors and, thus, the Inquisition, see Laurent Albaret, ed., *Les Inquisiteurs: Portraits de défenseurs de la foi en Languedoc (XIIIe–XIVe siècles)* (Toulouse, France: Editions Privat, 2001), and Karen Sullivan, *The Inner Lives of Medieval Inquisitors* (Chicago: University of Chicago Press, 2011).

57. The phrase comes from James E. Wadsworth, *Agents of Orthodoxy: Honor, Status, and the Inquisition in Colonial Pernambuco, Brazil* (Boulder: Rowman and Littlefield, 2006). An excellent study of the intersection of local interest and inquisitional agents is Maria Sofia Messana, *Inquisitori, negromanti e streghe nella Sicilia moderna, 1500–1782* (Palermo, Italy: Sellerio, 2007). For other excellent studies of "agents of orthodoxy," see Bruno Feitler, *Nas malhas da consciência: Igreja e inquisição no Brasil* (São Paulo: Alameda, 2007), and Kimberly Lynn, *Court and Confessional: The Politics of Spanish Inquisitors* (Cambridge: Cambridge University Press, 2013).

58. In this vein I am indebted to Paul J. Vanderwood's final book, *Satan's Playground: Mobsters and Movie Stars at America's Greatest Gaming Resort* (Durham, NC: Duke University Press, 2010), which helped me think about how to evoke the mood of a place in a particular moment in history.

59. For a superb study of the ways that local magistrates interpreted law in colonial Latin America, often without access to printed law codes, see Víctor Tau Anzoátegui, *La ley en América hispana: Del descubrimiento a la emancipación* (Buenos Aires: Academia Nacional de la Historia,

1992). Inquisitional interviews of passengers entering Mexico in Veracruz also provide a detailed portrait of the books entering Mexico. The numbers are only representative because inspections are not extant for every year. But in the 1580s, eight such inspections, with 130 witness statements, reveal at least 48 editions of Hours, by far the most popular kind of book of the sixteenth century. These same inspections reveal only one copy each of: civil law, canon law, works of Bartolus, the *Siete Partidas*, the *Recopilación*, Justinian's Institutes, the *Leyes de Toro*, and a work of jurist Covarrubius. For ship inspections, see AGN, Inq., vol. 43, exp. 12; vol. 169, exp. 2; vol. 170, exps. 3, 4; vol. 171, exps. 1, 1a, 1b. These figures are consistent with the secondary literature, which shows that, while books of chivalry (such as *Amadís* and *Primaleón*), adventure tales and epic poetry (*Orlando Furioso*, for instance), devotional works (for example, by Luis de Granada), and, in the seventeenth century, *Don Quijote*, were extremely popular, law books generally only belonged to high-level jurists, inquisitors, and bishops. See Teodoro Hampe Martínez, *Bibliotecas privadas en el mundo colonial: La difusión de libros e ideas en el virreinato del Perú, siglos XVI–XVII* (Frankfurt: Vervuert; Madrid: Iberoamericana, 1996); Irving A. Leonard, *Books of the Brave: Being an Account of Books and of Men in the Spanish Conquest and Settlement of the Sixteenth-Century World* (Ann Arbor: University of Michigan Press, 1949); Pedro Rueda Ramírez, *Negocio e intercambio cultural: El comercio de libros con América en la carrera de Indias (siglo XVII)* (Seville, Spain: Universidad de Sevilla, 2005).

60. Charles Gibson, *The Aztecs Under Spanish Rule: A History of the Indians of the Valley of Mexico, 1519–1810* (Stanford, CA: Stanford University Press, 1964); Irving A. Leonard, *Baroque Times in Old Mexico: Seventeenth-Century Persons, Places and Practices* (Ann Arbor: University of Michigan Press, 1959); Leslie Byrd Simpson, *Many Mexicos* (New York: G. P. Putnam's Sons, 1946).

61. For more recent but by no means exhaustive examples of the literatures on negotiated empires and the ethno-political complexities of empire, see Mark Christensen, *Nahua and Maya Catholicisms: Texts and Religion in Colonial Central Mexico and Yucatan* (Stanford, CA: Stanford University Press, 2013); Susan M. Deeds, *Defiance and Deference in Mexico's Colonial North: Indians Under Spanish Rule in Nueva Vizcaya* (Austin: University of Texas Press, 2003); Raphael Brewster Folsom, *The Yaquis and the Empire: Violence, Spanish Imperial Power, and Native Resilience in Colonial Mexico* (New Haven, CT: Yale University Press, 2014); Laura E. Matthew, *Memories of Conquest: Becoming Mexicano in Colonial Guatemala* (Chapel Hill: University of North Carolina Press, 2014); Gabriela Ramos and Yanna Yannakakis, eds., *Indigenous Intellectuals: Knowledge, Power, and Colonial Culture in Mexico and the Andes* (Durham, NC: Duke University Press, 2014); Ethelia Ruiz Medrano and Susan Kellogg, eds., *Negotiation Within Domination: New Spain's Indian Pueblos Confront the Spanish State* (Boulder: University of Colorado Press, 2010).

62. Inspired by Inga Clendinnen's masterful study of the conflicts of early Christianization in the Yucatán, *Ambivalent Conquests: Maya and Spaniard in Yucatan, 1517–1570* (Cambridge: Cambridge University Press, 1987). For a riff on the term while analyzing conversion processes, see Rick Warner, "'Ambivalent Conversions' in Nayarit: Shifting Views of Idolatry," *Journal of Early Modern History* 6 (2002): 168–184.

63. A model of the approach is Emmanuel Le Roy Ladurie, *Carnival in Romans*, trans. Mark Feeny (New York: G. Braziller, 1979).

64. This approach proved to be crucial in the second half of the sixteenth century. See Philip Wayne Powell, *Soldiers, Indians and Silver: The Northward Advance of New Spain, 1550–1600* (Berkeley: University of California Press, 1952).

65. Peter Gerhard, *A Guide to the Historical Geography of New Spain, 1519–1821*, rev. ed. (Norman: University of Oklahoma Press, 1993) ("Gerhard" hereafter), 349.

66. One can compare the studies of viceroys, such as Rubio Mañé, *Introducción al estudio de los*

virreyes, with studies of ordinary colonials, such as Clare Anderson, *Subaltern Lives: Biographies of Colonialism in the Indian Ocean World, 1790–1920* (Cambridge: Cambridge University Press, 2012).

67. The classic of this model, the New Philology, is James Lockhart, *The Nahuas After the Conquest: A Social and Cultural History of the Indians of Central Mexico, Sixteenth Through Eighteenth Centuries* (Stanford, CA: Stanford University Press, 1992).

68. This is not a book about the fashionable kind of subalterns, as described in works such as Rosalind C. Morris, *Can the Subaltern Speak? Reflections on the History of an Idea* (New York: Columbia University Press, 2010), and Gayatri Chakravorty Spivak, "Subaltern Studies: Deconstructing Historiography," in Ranajit Guha and Gayatri Chakravotry Spivak, eds., with a foreword by Edward Said, *Selected Subaltern Studies* (Oxford: Oxford University Press, 1988), 3–34.

69. See Matthew Restall, "The New Conquest History," *History Compass* 10 (2012): 151–160. Also see Florine G. L. Asselbergs, *Conquered Conquistadors: The Lienzo de Quauhquechollan. A Nahua Vision of the Conquest of Guatemala* (Leiden: CNWS, 2004; Boulder: University Press of Colorado, 2008); *Defending the Conquest: Bernardo de Vargas Machuca's Defense and Discourse of the Western Conquests*, ed. Kris Lane, trans. Timothy F. Johnson (University Park: Pennsylvania State University Press, 2010); Laura E. Matthew and Michel R. Oudijk, eds., *Indian Conquistadors: Indigenous Allies in the Conquest of Mesoamerica* (Norman: University of Oklahoma Press, 2012); Matthew D. Restall, *Seven Myths of the Spanish Conquest* (Oxford: Oxford University Press, 2004); Susan Schroeder, ed., *The Conquest All Over Again: Nahuas and Zapotecs Thinking, Writing, and Painting Spanish Colonialism* (Portland, OR: Sussex Academic Press, 2010); Stuart B. Schwartz, ed., *Victors and Vanquished: Spanish and Nahua Views of the Conquest of Mexico* (New York: Bedford/St. Martin's, 2000); Stephanie Wood, *Transcending Conquest: Nahua Views of Spanish Colonial Mexico* (Norman: University of Oklahoma Press, 2012).

70. For an overview, see Restall, *Seven Myths*.

71. See Camilla Townsend, *Malintzin's Choices: An Indian Woman in the Conquest of Mexico* (Albuquerque: University of New Mexico Press, 2006). Emblematic of this emphasis on fluidity are Juliana Barr, *Peace Came in the Form of a Woman: Indians and Spaniards in the Texas Borderlands* (Chapel Hill: University of North Carolina Press, 2007); William F. Connell, *After Moctezuma: Indigenous Politics and Self-Government in Mexico City, 1524–1730* (Norman: University of Oklahoma Press, 2011); Dana Velasco Murillo, *Urban Indians in a Silver City: Zacatecas, Mexico, 1546–1810* (Stanford, CA: Stanford University Press, 2016); Yanna Yannakakis, *The Art of Being In-between: Native Intermediaries, Indian Identity and Local Rule in Colonial Oaxaca* (Durham, NC: Duke University Press, 2008).

72. Rebecca Earle's study of food and colonial Latin America, *The Conquistador's Body: Food, Race and the Colonial Experience in Spanish America, 1492–1700* (Cambridge: Cambridge University Press, 2012), is an excellent study of "everyday" colonialism.

73. Aguirre Beltrán, *Regiones de refugio*. James Scott applied the model to Southeast Asia in the modern era in his study *The Art of Not Being Governed: An Anarchist History of Upland Southeast Asia* (New Haven, CT: Yale University Press, 2009).

74. An example of this assumption of the Inquisition as oppressor par excellence is Silverblatt, *Modern Inquisitions*.

75. James Krippner, *Rereading the Conquest: Power, Politics, and the History of Early Colonial Michoacán, Mexico, 1521–1565* (University Park: Pennsylvania State University Press, 2001); Bernardino Verástique, *Michoacán and Eden: Vasco de Quiroga and the Evangelization of Western Mexico* (Austin: University of Texas Press, 2000).

76. Julián Juderías coined the term "Black Legend" in his study titled *La leyenda negra y la verdad histórica: Contribución al estudio del concepto de España en Europa, de las causas de este*

concepto y de la tolerancia política y religiosa en los países civilizados (Madrid: Tip. de la Revista de Archivos, Bibliotecas y Museos, 1914); for a comprehensive overview of the history of the idea of generalized Spanish villainry, see Ricardo García Cárcel, *La leyenda negra: Historia y opinión* (Madrid: Alianza, 1998).

CHAPTER 1

1. The story is so well known that it forms a central place in Juan O'Gorman's mural in the Pátzcuaro public library. Begun in 1941, the same year in which Bernal Jiménez's opera *Tata Vasco* premiered in Pátzcuaro, the mural depicts Quiroga, who is contrasted with the sadistic Nuño de Guzmán, as a gentle father figure. For discussion, see Hilary Masters, *Shadows on a Wall: Juan O'Gorman and the Mural in Patzcuaro* (Pittsburgh: University of Pittsburgh Press, 2005).

2. Donald Chipman, *Nuño de Guzmán and the Province of Pánuco in New Spain, 1518–1533* (Glendale, CA: Arthur H. Clark, 1967), offers a less one-sided view of the slaver. "One reader assessed my book as having improved the image of Nuño de Guzmán from that of an ogre to a scoundrel" (personal correspondence with Donald Chipman, 24 July 2017).

3. Leslie Byrd Simpson, *Many Mexicos*, 4th ed. (Berkeley: University of California Press, 1966), 38. David J. Weber, in *Myth and the History of the Hispanic Southwest: Essays* (Albuquerque: University of New Mexico Press, 1988), 12, described Guzmán as a "rapacious thug."

4. The mythology was incorporated into the collective mainstream assumptions of historiography by Edmundo O'Gorman, *Santo Tomás More y "La Utopía de Tomás Moro en la Nueva España"* (Mexico City: Alcancia, 1937). One of Mexico's greatest social historians, Silvio Zavala, lionized Quiroga as a Renaissance visionary in *Ideario de Vasco de Quiroga* (Mexico City: El Colegio de México, 1941). One can also find an expression of this rose-tinted legend in Ross Dealy, *The Politics of an Erasmian Lawyer: Vasco de Quiroga* (Malibu, CA: Undena Publications, 1976); Francisco Miranda Godínez, *Vasco de Quiroga, varón universal* (Mexico City: Editorial Jus, 2007); and Bernardino Verástique, *Michoacán and Eden: Vasco de Quiroga and the Evangelization of Western Mexico* (Austin: University of Texas Press, 2000). For relatively neutral treatments, see José Aparecido Gomes Moreira, "Don Vasco de Quiroga: Pensamiento indígena y jurídico-teológico" (Tesis de Maestría, Escuela Nacional de Antropología e Historia [Mexico], 1989). Further studies include Benjamin Jarnés, *Don Vasco de Quiroga, obispo de utopía* (Mexico City: Ediciones Atlántida, 1942); Carlos Pellicer, *Don Vasco de Quiroga y los hospitales pueblos* (Mexico City: Ediciones Monroy Padilla, 1968); Manuel Ponce, ed., *Don Vasco de Quiroga y arzobispado de Morelia* (Mexico City: Editorial Jus, 1965); Felipe Tena Ramírez, *Vasco de Quiroga y sus pueblos de Santa Fe en los siglos XVIII y XIX* (Mexico City: Editorial Porrúa, 1977).

5. Gerhard, 346.

6. See Ida Altman, *The War for Mexico's West: Indians and Spaniards in New Galicia, 1524–1550* (Albuquerque: University of New Mexico Press, 2010).

7. For excellent analysis of the period's politics, especially relating to land policy, see Ethelia Ruiz Medrano, *Gobierno y sociedad en Nueva España: Segunda Audiencia y Antonio de Mendoza* (Zamora, Mexico: El Colegio de Michoacán, Gobierno del Estado de Michoacán, 1991).

8. Gerhard, 346. The various Spanish words *alcalde*, *corregidor*, and *teniente* pose dilemmas for translations. To some extent they all mean "magistrate," as they were judges of first instance at the local level. Although they exercised judicial authority, however, they also formed part of the local town council, or *cabildo*, if they were assigned to a town (*villa*) that had such an organization. I have used the Spanish terms and the general English equivalent (magistrate) interchangeably throughout the book.

9. Rodrigo Martínez Baracs and Lydia Espinosa Morales, eds., *La vida michoacana en el siglo XVI: Catálogo de los documentos del siglo XVI del Archivo Histórico de la Ciudad de Pátzcuaro* (Mexico City: Instituto Nacional de Antropología e Historia, 1999) (*"Vida michoacana"* hereafter), 234–235.

10. Judicial activity in Michoacán between 1522 and 1542 involved lawsuits over encomiendas and visitas as well as trials against indigenous peoples for idolatry, as in the notorious execution of the caltzontzin in 1530. The earliest extant case of a royal authority undertaking a regular judicial proceeding comes from November 1542, when the corregidor prosecuted two Spanish men for usurping land belonging to the indigenous cacique of Zacapu. See *Vida michoacana*, 29.

11. Reproduced in Jesús García Gutiérrez, ed., *Bulario de la Iglesia mejicana: Documentos relativos a erecciones, desmembraciones, etc., de Diócesis mejicanas* (Mexico City: Editorial "Buena Prensa," 1951), 35–36. For a good discussion of the bull's ecclesiology, see Pedro Torres, "La 'bula omnímoda' de Adriano VI (9 Mayo 1522) y su aplicación durante el primer siglo de las misiones de Indias," *Missionalia Hispánica* 3 (1946): 7–52.

12. Marcia Castro Leal, *Tzintzuntzan: Capital de los tarascos* (Morelia, Mexico: Gobierno del Estado de Michoacán, 1986).

13. There is extensive discussion of the cultural geography of the region. See Ulysis Beltrán, "Tarascan State and Society in Prehispanic Times: An Ethnohistoric Inquiry" (PhD diss., University of Chicago, 1982); Donald D. Brand, "Bosquejo histórico de la geografía y la antropología en la región tarasca," *Anales del Museo de Michoacán* (Morelia, Mexico: [Imp. y Lit. del Gobierno en la Escuela de Artes], 1952), and "An Historical Sketch of Geography and Anthropology in the Tarascan Region: Part I," *New Mexico Anthropologist* 6–7 (1943): 37–108; Shirley Gorenstein and Helen Pollard, *Tarascan Civilization: A Late Prehispanic Cultural System* (Nashville, TN: Vanderbilt University Press, 1983); Alfredo López Austin, *Tarascos y mexicas* (Mexico City: Fondo de Cultura Económica, 1981); Pedro Márquez Joaquín, ed., *¿Tarascos o Purépecha? Voces sobre antiguas y nuevas discusiones en torno al gentilicio michoacano* (Morelia, Mexico: Universidad Michoacana de San Nicolás de Hidalgo, 2007); Lucio Mendieta y Núñez, *Los tarascos: Monografía histórica, etnográfica y económica* (Mexico City: UNAM, 1940); Helen P. Pollard, "Ecological Variations and Economic Exchange in the Tarascan State," *American Ethnologist* 9 (1982): 250–268; Dan Stanislawski, "Tarascan Political Geography," *American Anthropologist* 49 (1947): 46–55.

14. The 1532–1533 report to the Audiencia on the region noted the dominance of Otomí in the region of Matalzingo (on the Michoacán-Mexico border). See Pedro Carrasco, *Los Otomíes: Cultura e historia preshispánicas de los pueblos mesoamericanos de habla otomiana* (Mexico City: UNAM, 1950); Antonio de Herrera y Tordesillas, *Historia general de los hechos de los castellanos en las islas y en tierra-firme de el mar océano*, prologue by J. Natalicio González, 10 vols. (Asunción, Paraguay: Editorial Guaranía, 1944– [c. 1601–1615]), década 4a, lib. 9, cap. V.

15. The Colima group was also called Xilotlanzincas. See discussions of the Tarascan Federation and its attempts at expansion in the west in Gonzalo Aguirre Beltrán, *Problemas de la población indígena de la Cuenca de Tepalcatepec* (Mexico City: Instituto Nacional Indigenista, 1952); Carl O. Sauer, *Colima of New Spain in the Sixteenth Century* (Berkeley: University of California Press, 1948). For discussions of the Tarascan expansion toward the east and the uneasy détente with the Mexica in the Maravatío and Tuzantla regions, see Mary Ann Hedberg, "Conflicts and Continuities: Chapters in the History of Tuzantla, a Town in Colonial Mexico," 2 vols. (PhD diss., University of Minnesota, 1994). Also see Shirley Gorenstein and Helen Pollard's excellent study of Mexica-Purépecha border towns, *Acámbaro: Frontier Settlement on the Tarascan-Aztec Border* (Nashville, TN: Vanderbilt University Press, 1985).

16. The region may have spoken proto-Nahuatl (Xilotlanzinca) prior to the 1520s. See Donald

Brand, *Coastal Study of Southwest Mexico* (Austin: Department of Geography, University of Texas, 1957–1958); Gerhard, 78–80.

17. The region represented the westernmost reach of Nahuatl use in Mesoamerica. The original location of Tuxpan is where the Spanish villa of Colima was established; indigenous residents were forcibly moved to higher regions near Tuxpan. See Sauer, *Colima*.

18. De la Rea, 5.

19. Escobar, 5–15.

20. Ibid., 27–28; De la Rea, 16–17; [Jerónimo de Alcalá], *La relación de Michoacán* (Barcelona: Editorial Linkgua, 2011 [c. 1541]) (RM hereafter), 43, 89–90.

21. Escobar, 30: "Ceremonioso el tarasco, y por consiguiente cuidadoso mucho en el culto y reverencia; y así hoy en la ley nuestra que profesan, es muy reverente y serio; que sus iglesias son las más bien servidas y adornadas de este Occidente, cuya relación reservo para adelante."

22. Pablo de la Purísima Concepción Beaumont, *Crónica de Michoacán* (Mexico City: Talleres Gráficos de la Nación, 1932).

23. J. Benedict Warren, *The Conquest of Michoacán: The Spanish Domination of the Tarascan Kingdom in Western Mexico, 1521–1530* (Norman: University of Oklahoma Press, 1985), 29.

24. RM, 179.

25. See J. Benedict Warren, "Fray Jerónimo de Alcalá: Author of the *Relación de Michoacán?*," *The Americas* 27 (1971): 307–326. Rodrigo Martínez Baracs, in *Convivencia y utopía: El gobierno indio y español de la "ciudad de Mechuacan," 1521–1580* (Mexico City: INAH; Fondo de Cultura Económica, 2005), 297n1, argues that the question mark in Warren's study should be eliminated, given the discovery in Carlos Paredes Martínez, ed., *Lengua y etnohistoria purépecha: Homenaje a Benedict Warren* (Morelia, Mexico: Universidad Michoacana de San Nicolás de Hidalgo, 1997), of incontrovertible evidence that Alcalá was the primary "author" of the chronicle. For good discussions of the relationships between indigenous peoples and Spaniards in the construction of hybrid texts, see three works by Mark Christensen—"The Tales of Two Cultures: Ecclesiastical Texts and Nahua and Maya Catholicisms," *The Americas* 66 (2010): 353–377; *Translated Christianities: Nahuatl and Maya Religious Texts* (University Park: Pennsylvania State University Press, 2014); and "The Use of Nahuatl in Evangelization and the Ministry of Sebastian," *Ethnohistory* 59 (2012): 691–711—and also Gabriela Ramos and Yanna Yannakakis, eds., *Indigenous Intellectuals: Knowledge, Power, and Colonial Culture in Mexico and the Andes* (Durham, NC: Duke University Press, 2014); David Tavárez, "Nahua Intellectuals, Franciscan Scholars and the *Devotio Moderna* in Colonial Mexico," *The Americas* 70 (2013): 203–235.

26. See Rafael Heliodoro Valle, *Cristóbal de Olid, conquistador de México y Honduras* (Tegucigalpa, Honduras: Secretaría de Cultura, Artes y Deporte, 1997).

27. Gil González Dávila, *Teatro eclesiástico de la primitiva iglesia de las Indias occidentales, vidas de svs arzobispos, obispos, y cosas memorables de svs sedes* (Madrid: D. Díaz de la Carrera, 1649), 107.

28. RM, 181. On the term *nahuatlato*, see Ascención Hernández de León-Portilla, "*Nahuatlahto*: Vida e historia de un nahuatlismo," *Estudios de Cultura Nahuatl* 41 (2010): 193–215.

29. RM, 180.

30. The auxiliaries were Nahua or Totonac. See Warren, *Conquest of Michoacán*, 296n7, citing Fernando de Alva Ixtlilxochitl, *Obras históricas*, ed. Alfredo Chavero, 2 vols. (Mexico City: Oficina tip. de la Secretaría de Fomento, 1891–1892), 1:383. Alva Ixtlilxochitl claims that when Cortés partitioned his indigenous allied forces for the conquest of Tenochtitlan, the brother of the first Ixtlilxochtil (Fernando's grandfather), Tetlahuehuezquititzin, provided 50,000 men from Tziuhcohuac to Olid's contingent, and that Olid's Spanish contingent consisted of 33 men on horseback

and 180 foot-soldiers. Alva Ixtlilxochitl describes them as "people . . . from northern provinces subject to the kingdom of Tezcuco." See Amber Brian, Bradley Benton, and Pablo García Loaeza, eds. and trans., *The Native Conquistador: Alva Ixtlilxochitl's Account of the Conquest of New Spain* (University Park: Pennsylvania State University Press, 2015), 37. Also see Gerhard, 228.

31. Ricardo León Alanís, *Los orígenes del clero y la iglesia en Michoacán, 1525–1640* (Morelia, Mexico: Universidad Michoacana de San Nicolás de Hidalgo, Instituto de Investigaciones Histó-ricas, 1997), 153, and Warren, *Conquest of Michoacán*, 82. Both discuss the presence of these men.

32. RM, 182: "Esta gente todos deben ser médicos, con nuestros médicos que miran en el agua lo que ha de ser."

33. RM, 177, 186.

34. RM, 182–186.

35. Martínez Baracs, *Convivencia y utopía*, 123–126; Warren, *Conquest of Michoacán*, 51–52.

36. RM, 185.

37. RM, 193.

38. Juan de Torquemada, *Monarquía Indiana*, 3 vols. (Madrid: Nicolás Rodríguez, 1723), 3:332.

39. Warren, *Conquest of Michoacán*, 84.

40. De la Rea, 29; Diego Muñoz, *Descripción de la provincia de San Pedro y San Pablo de Michoacán, en las Indias de la Nueva España*, intro. José Ramírez Flores (Guadalajara, Mexico: Instituto Jalisciense de Antropología e Historia, 1965 [c. 1585]) ("Muñoz" hereafter), 36.

41. De la Rea, 34–36; Muñoz, 36–37.

42. Though not limited to Michoacán, a good overview of the phenomenon in Mexico is Joaquín García Icazbalceta, "La destrucción de antigüedades," in *Obras*, vol. 2 of 10 (Mexico City: Imprenta V. Agüeros, 1896).

43. De la Rea, 33.

44. See Angélica Jimena Afanador-Pujols, *The Relación de Michoacán (1539–1541) and the Politics of Representation in Colonial Mexico* (Austin: University of Texas Press, 2015), and Cynthia L. Stone, *In Place of Gods and Kings: Authorship and Identity in the Relación de Michoacán* (Norman: University of Oklahoma Press, 2004).

45. RM, 194.

46. De la Rea, 36: "De assentar el fin del Euangelio, y cortó el lazo de la carne y nudos de los casamientos: con que tuuo lugar para assentar los preceptos de nuestra ley, é introducer la verdadera adoración, y reprobar la professión de su falsa secta: derribando, y destruyendo todos los Templos de Tzintzuntzan, à vista de toda la Ciudad. Con que tuuo lugar de coger todos los Ídolos de oro, y plata, y otras piedras preciosas, y hazerlas pedaços: y haziendo dellos vn gran montón, los arrojó en la laguna con el desprecio ygual á su falsedad; con que cayeron en la cuenta de todos los concurrentes, pues veían á sus Dioses sepultados en la laguna. Otros juntó en medio de la plaça, y los quemó, para que las cenizas arrebatadas del viento, les diessen en los ojos, y los sacasse de su ceguedad, y aduirtiessen el engaño passado, y la verdad presente."

47. Muñoz said that among those who assisted in this early mission were the friars Ángel de la Salzeda, Juan Badía, Miguel de Bolonia, Juan de Padilla, and one whom Muñoz identified simply as "Fray Gerónimo," and whom he said was the first Franciscan to learn Purépecha—probably Jerónimo de Alcalá. See Muñoz, 36. Francisco Gonzaga, *De origine Seraphicae Religionis Franciscane* (Rome: Ex typographia Dominici Basae, 1587), and Torquemada, *Monarquía Indiana*, 3:332, repeat Muñoz's list verbatim. Another friar was Diego de Santa María, whom friar Antonio de Ortiz identified in a 1532 deposition as a resident friar and interpreter of Purépecha. See Warren, *Conquest of Michoacán*, 86–87.

48. RM, 194.

49. Peggy K. Liss, *Mexico Under Spain, 1521–1556: Society and the Origins of Nationality* (Chicago: University of Chicago Press, 1975), 52.

50. Juan de Ortega's 1528 visita also identified Ortiz as a resident at the time. See Warren, *Conquest of Michoacán*, 86.

51. The incident is well known. See Joaquín García Icazbalceta, *Don Fray Juan de Zumárraga: Primer Obispo y arzobispo de México*, 2 vols. (Mexico City: Antigua Librería de Andrade y Morales, 1881), 2:66–67.

52. Ibid., 2:63, quoting from Zumárraga's response to the judicial complaint of the Audiencia judge (Delgadillo) in the Consejo de Indias: "No contento Delgadillo con infamar constantemente en esta corte al obispo y religiosos de México. . . . Suplico, constando lo que digo, que le castigue como calumnioso infamador. . . . Sus vicios, sus exorbitancias, los malos tratamientos a los naturales dispertaron mi celo para amonestarle."

53. León Alanís, *Orígenes*, 61–62.

54. Ibid., 85–86.

55. Ibid., 85. The visita report is found in lawsuits spread throughout the AGN's Hospital de Jesús section and in the Justicia section of the Archivo General de Indias (General Archives of the Indies), Seville, Spain (AGI hereafter). J. Benedict Warren transcribed and published the four descriptions in the Spanish edition of his classic work *La conquista de Michoacán, 1521–1530* (Morelia, Mexico: Fímax, 1977), 386–408.

56. Warren, *Conquest of Michoacán*, 73–80, and Warren, *Conquista de Michoacán*, 386–408.

57. Warren, *Conquista de Michoacán*, 386–408.

58. Aguirre Beltrán, *Cuenca de Tepalcatepec*, 76.

59. AGN, Mercedes, vol. 4, exp. s/n, fol. 169v [170v]. The viceroy's figures are difficult to interpret, as they were estimates made in order to determine the macehual labor requirements for the indigenous governor (Huitziméngari) and did not specify gender or age. Aguirre Beltrán, *Cuenca de Tepalcatepec*, 81–82, estimated the entire population of the meseta tarasca at 16,800 in 1565 and 23,488 in 1520.

60. "Suma de visitas," in Francisco del Paso y Troncoso, ed., *Papeles de Nueva España: Segunda serie, Geografía y estadística*, 9 vols. (Madrid: Estab. Tip. "Sucesores de Rivadeneyra," 1905–1919), 1:220–221.

61. AGN, Mercedes, vol. 4, exp. s/n, fol. 170v [171v]; "Suma de visitas," *Papeles de Nueva España*, 1:253.

62. Aguirre Beltrán, *Cuenca de Tepalcatepec*, 53; Warren, *Conquest of Michoacán*, 51.

63. Lawsuits between the Audiencia and Cortés can be found in AGN, Hospital de Jesús, leg. 265, exp. 9; leg. 276, exp. 86; and "Juicio seguido por Hernán Cortés contra los licenciados Matienzo y Delgadillo," *Boletín del Archivo General de la Nación* 9 (1938): 339–407. Parts of the residencia report concerning Cortés from 1528 are in AGI, Justicia, 220–225.

64. Warren, *Conquest of Michoacán*, 260–285.

65. Ibid., 86, 260. Warren notes that the original of the Ortega visita is no longer extant, although copies exist in AGI, Justicia, 130, and in the Archivo Histórico del Instituto Nacional de Antropología e Historia, Col. Gómez de Orozco, ms. 171.

66. De la Rea, 29; Muñoz, 36. In *Monarquía Indiana*, 3:332, Torquemada says there were far too few friars in all of New Spain between 1525 and 1528 for more than two or three of them to accompany Martín de Jesús in Michoacán at any given time.

67. Alberto Carrillo Cázares, *Vasco de Quiroga: La pasión por el derecho. El pleito con la Orden*

de San Agustín (1558–1562), 2 vols. (Zamora, Mexico: El Colegio de Michoacán; Morelia, Mexico: Arquidiócesis de Morelia, Universidad Michoacana de San Nicolás de Hidalgo, Instituto de Investigaciones Históricas, 2003), 1:39. Gerardo Sánchez Díaz, in *La costa de Michoacán: Economía y sociedad en el siglo XVI* (Morelia, Mexico: Universidad Michoacana de San Nicolás de Hidalgo, 2001), 45–46, and León Alanís, in *Orígenes*, 154, estimated that Martínez began as parish priest of Zacatula in 1525.

68. There is no direct evidence, but Francisco Martínez is referenced in an inquisitional trial as parish priest of Zacatula. See AGN, Inq., vol. 2, exp. 2. In *Conquest of Michoacán*, 82, Warren claims that Martínez was parish priest of Zacatula "as early as November 3, 1525, and as late as 1529." León Alanís, in *Orígenes*, 154, claims there were parish priests in Colima and Zacatula as early as 1525 and that they were Michoacán's first secular parish priests.

69. Carrillo Cázares, *La pasión por el derecho*, 1:39.

70. Warren, *Conquest of Michoacán*, 281.

71. "Suma de visitas," *Papeles de Nueva España*, 1:220, lists Tuxpan as having 986 married men (the number of wives is not listed), 626 widows and widowers, and 1,093 children over the age of eight. One can assume there were hundreds of uncounted children below the age of eight. These numbers indicate a population of somewhere around 4,000, suggesting an adult mortality rate as high as 15 percent, though we cannot know how many of those 626 widowed adults had spouses who died of non-epidemic-related causes.

72. Warren, *Conquest of Michoacán*, 279.

73. "Suma de visitas," *Papeles de Nueva España*, 1:254.

74. AGN, Mercedes, vol. 4, exp. s/n, fol. 169v [170v].

75. The provenance of the *cédulas*, the rightfulness of the grant, and the legality of the First Audiencia, operating as an arm of the queen with secret instructions to despoil Cortés of encomiendas, are all a subject of controversy and complexity, covered by Robert Himmerich y Valencia, *The Encomenderos of New Spain, 1521–1555* (Austin: University of Texas Press, 1991) ("Himmerich y Valencia" hereafter), 177; Martínez Baracs, *Convivencia y utopía*, 143–146; Warren, *Conquest of Michoacán*, 165–171.

76. Warren, *Conquest of Michoacán*, 171.

77. For good overviews, see John K. Chance, "The *Caciques* of Tecali: Class and Ethnic Identity in Late Colonial Mexico," *Hispanic American Historical Review* 76 (1996): 475–502; Stephen M. Perkins, "*Macehuales* and the Corporate Solution: Colonial Secessions in Nahua Central Mexico," *Mexican Studies/Estudios Mexicanos* 21 (2005): 277–306. For specific analysis of Michoacán's indigenous elites, see Delfina López Sarrelangue, *La nobleza indígena de Pátzcuaro en la época virreinal* (Mexico City: UNAM, Instituto de Investigaciones Históricas, 1965); María Teresa Martínez Peñalosa, "Noble purépecha, intérprete en el Juzgado de Indios," in *Uandani, Mensaje Cultural Michoacano* (Morelia, Mexico: Imp. Elite, 1982); Carlos Salvador Paredes Martínez, "La nobleza tarasca: Poder político y conflictos en el Michoacán colonial," *Anuario de Estudios Americanos* 65 (2008): 101–117.

78. Guzmán claimed that he traveled with four hundred Spanish horsemen and foot-soldiers, though he conveniently ignored the indigenous allied force. See Ida Altman, "Conquest, Coercion, and Collaboration: Indian Allies and the Campaigns in Nueva Galicia," in Laura E. Matthew and Michel R. Oudijk, eds., *Indian Conquistadors: Indigenous Allies in the Conquest of Mesoamerica* (Norman: University of Oklahoma Press, 2012), 7; Warren, *Conquest of Michoacán*, 213–214, 319n8.

79. RM, 201.

80. RM, 203–204.

81. France V. Scholes and Eleanor B. Adams, eds., *Proceso contra Tzintzicha Tangaxoan, el caltzonztin formado por Nuño de Guzmán año de 1530* (Mexico City: Porrúa, 1952).

82. Ibid.; RM, 201–203. The trial against the caltzontzin is notorious enough, though the claim that it was judicially unusual is false. Numerous other Spanish courts in the sixteenth century engaged in judicial torture, pronounced the death penalty, or settled imperial expansion with legal tactics. See Francisco Tomás y Valiente, *La tortura judicial en España* (Madrid: Crítica, 2000).

83. This is how it is remembered in the RM, 202: "Muestra los pellejos de los cristianos que tienes; si no los haces traer aquí, aquí te tenemos que matar."

84. *Proceso contra el caltzontzin*, 65. The trial transcript simply states that Guzmán, as judge, ordered Don Pedro to bring the skins before him under pain of death: "Hizo parecer ante sí al dicho Pedro Prança, al cual le preguntó y apercibió que la diga la verdad que adónde tiene los dichos pellejos de cristianos . . . y que él [don Pedro] enviará luego por ellos y vendrá de aquí mañana. . . . Y luego su señoría le mandó que traiga en el dicho término los dichos pellejos de cristianos ante su señoría so pena de muerte."

85. *Proceso contra el caltzontzin*, 66. The sentence is vague, as it simply states that the caltzontzin was guilty of the charges against him—obfuscation of tribute resources and precious metals, idolatry, murder, and sodomy. By the standards of the day, the hastiness of the guilty sentence stands out for its brevity, as ordinarily a royal judge was required to elaborate guilt on each charge. The charge of sodomy was not proven in the case; most witnesses claimed they knew nothing of it.

86. *Proceso contra el caltzontzin*; RM, 203.

87. *Proceso contra el caltzontzin*, 35. The extent to which the Purépecha engaged in sex between men is beyond the scope of this analysis. For a discussion of the caltzontzin's trial as it concerns homosexuality, see Zeb Tortorici, *Sins Against Nature: Sex, Colonialism, and Archives in New Spain (1530–1821)* (Durham: Duke University Press, 2018), chap. 2. Sex between men among the Purépecha was rumored to be common. As late as 1605, extensive networks of Purépecha men who had sex with men (in and around Tzintzuntzan) were widespread. See Zeb Tortorici, "'Heran todos putos': Sodomitical Subcultures and Disordered Desire in Early Colonial Mexico," *Ethnohistory* 54 (2007): 35–67. In 1576, a man named Juan del Vado was imprisoned in the Pátzcuaro jail on charges of sodomy. We do not know his ethnicity, though the name suggests he was Spanish. See *Vida michoacana*, 119.

88. Evidence for homosexuality in pre-Hispanic Mesoamerica is complicated by the lack of a category like the Spanish label of "sodomy." See Pete Sigal, *The Flower and the Scorpion: Sexuality and Ritual in Early Nahua Culture* (Durham, NC: Duke University Press, 2012). For discussions of sex between men in Spain, see Rafael Carrasco, *Inquisición y represión sexual en Valencia: Historia de los sodomitas, 1565–1785* (Barcelona: Laertes, 1985); Francisco Núñez Roldán, *El pecado nefando del Obispo de Salamina: Un hombre sin concierto en la corte de Felipe II* (Seville, Spain: Universidad de Sevilla, 2002); Francisco Tomás y Valiente, "El crimen y el pecado contra natura," in *Sexo barroco y otras transgresiones premodernas* (Madrid: Alianza, 1990). For a discussion of homosexuality in colonial Mexico post-contact, see Serge Gruzinski, "Los cenizos del deseo," in Sergio Ortega, ed., *De la santidad a la perversión: O de por qué no se cumplía la ley de Diós en la sociedad novohispana* (Mexico City: Grijalbo, 1986); Tortorici, *Sins Against Nature*.

89. "Muñoz" appears in the documentation. See AGN, Inq., vol. 11, exp. 4, and AGN, Mercedes, vol. 2, exp. 567, fol. 230.

90. Gerhard, 160, 175, 312, 344; Himmerich y Valencia, 203–204.

91. Gerhard, 175–176, claims that this grant occurred between 1534 and 1537; Himmerich y Valencia, 204, says that the encomienda was granted "around 1536." AGN, Mercedes, vol. 2, exp.

567, fol. 230, notes that in 1543 he continued to hold Xiquipilco in encomienda. Guzmán stopped in an encomienda held by Muñoz in late December 1529 only three days after he left Mexico City. Xiquipilco may have already been assigned to Muñoz at this stage, since his other possessions had been despoiled by then and were, in any case, either in the wrong direction (Acolman, to the northeast of Mexico) or too far (Capula) to have been reached by Guzmán's large force in only three days.

92. *Proceso contra el caltzontzin*, 32–33.

93. Warren, *Conquest of Michoacán*, 215.

94. *Proceso contra el caltzontzin*, 26–36.

95. RM, 203.

96. Ibid., 202.

97. Ibid., 204.

98. Himmerich y Valencia, 192–193.

99. This is the only case where I offer freestyle adaptation of someone's thoughts without quoting directly from archival or chronicle sources. The adaptation owes methodological inspiration from studies on the history of emotions, including Pilar Gonzalbo Aizpuru, Anne Staples, and Valentina Torres Septién, eds., *Una historia de los usos del miedo* (Mexico City: El Colegio de México, 2009); Pilar Gonzalbo Aizpuru and Verónica Zárate Toscano, eds., *Gozos y sufrimientos en la historia de México* (Mexico City: El Colegio de México, 2007); Javier Villa-Flores and Sonya Lipsett-Rivera, eds., *Emotions and Daily Life in Colonial Mexico* (Albuquerque: University of New Mexico Press, 2014).

100. For the inquisitional trial against Rangel in 1527 that was initiated by the friar Domingo de Betanzos, see AGN, Inq., vol. 1, exp. 10bis. Rangel was a frequent blasphemer. He was also accused of hating friars to the point of encouraging his indigenous subjects to shoot arrows at them when they arrived on Rangel's encomienda. For a discussion of the circumstances of the case, see Richard Greenleaf, *The Mexican Inquisition in the Sixteenth Century* (Albuquerque: University of New Mexico Press, 1969), 11–26, which shows that Betanzos prosecuted pro-Cortés conquistadors for blasphemy in what was surely a politically motivated Inquisition in 1527. My numeration of files in volume 1 differs from Greenleaf's.

101. Gerhard, 114; Himmerich y Valencia, 220.

102. AGN, Inq., vol. 1, exp. 10bis.

103. Motolinía made claims to inquisitional authority based on the broad privileges given the Franciscans in the Omnimoda. Mexico in the 1520s experienced a jurisdictional vacuum, because the Spanish Inquisition did not clearly delegate inquisitional authority to anyone, and there was no bishop until Zumárraga was appointed in December 1527. Canon law recognized the right of bishops to prosecute heresy in Lucius III's 1184 bull *Ad abolendam*, which was incorporated into the *Decretales Gregorii IX* in the 1230s. There are no extant inquisitional trials for Mexico prior to May 1527, but there are indications in AGN, Inq., vol. 1, exps. 1 and 2, that there was an inquisitional trial against Marcos de Acolhuacan in 1522. Martín de Valencia engaged in "Inquisition-like functions in 1524 in Tlaxcala, and in 1525 in Mexico City," according to Greenleaf, in *Mexican Inquisition*, 10. Civil authorities—for example, the alcalde Leonel de Cervantes—prosecuted blasphemy cases in 1524 and 1525, though the trials are not extant. For an overview of questions of competence and authority, see Miguel Ángel González de San Segundo, "Tensiones y conflictos de la Inquisición en Indias: La pre-Inquisición o Inquisición primitiva (1493–1569)," in José Antonio Escudero, ed., *Perfiles jurídicos de la Inquisición española* (Madrid: Instituto de Historia de la Inquisición, 1989), and José Toribio Medina, *La primitiva inquisición americana (1493-1569)* (Santiago: Imprenta Elziviriana, 1914).

104. Most of the conquistadors convicted of blasphemy in 1527 by Betanzos were fined much less. Juan Bello was fined 12 pesos (AGN, Inq., vol. 1, exp. 9). Gil González de Benavides was fined 3 pesos (AGN, Inq., vol. 1, exp. 10). The alcalde Cervantes held a criminal trial against Diego de Morales for blasphemy in 1525 or 1526; Morales was sentenced to pay a fine of 4,000 maravedíes, theoretically equivalent to about 15 pesos (AGN, Inq., vol. 1, exp. 8, fols. 29–30). The case file is not extant; only fragments of it remain in the inquisitional case file for blasphemy against Morales in 1528 (AGN, Inq., vol. 1, exp. 8). There is some confusion in general about the case, given what Greenleaf called the "nearly impossible" paleography of the existing file. Cervantes and his wife Doña Leonor testified in the 1528 trial; Cervantes stated that he remembered the sentence. For discussion of the various cases and sentences of conquistadors that Betanzos prosecuted in 1527, see Greenleaf, *Mexican Inquisition*, 11–26.

105. Rangel was a close partisan and friend of Cortés who testified on Rangel's behalf in the inquisitional trial. See AGN, Inq., vol. 1, exp. 10bis.

106. Cortés testified in the case that Rangel suffered from *bubas* (likely syphilis).

107. AGI, México, 242B, n. 44.

108. Gerhard, 345; Himmerich y Valencia, 159.

109. Gerhard, 268, 387; Himmerich y Valencia, 133–134.

110. Aguirre Beltrán, *Cuenca de Tepalcatepec*, 77–78.

111. Gerhard, 268.

112. A classic is Julian Pitt-Rivers, *The Fate of Shechem, or, the Politics of Sex: Essays in the Anthropology of the Mediterranean* (Cambridge: Cambridge University Press, 1977). For an evaluation of honor and shame in colonial Latin America, see Lyman Johnson and Sonya Lipsett-Rivera, eds., *The Faces of Honor: Sex, Shame, and Violence in Colonial Latin America* (Albuquerque: University of New Mexico Press, 1998).

113. Gerhard, 292.

114. Ruiz Medrano, *Gobierno y sociedad*, 352.

115. Himmerich y Valencia, 118.

116. Ibid., 124–125.

117. Ruiz Medrano, *Gobierno y sociedad*, 379.

118. Ibid., 356, 370–371.

119. For an excellent discussion of masculinity and friar-missionaries, see Asunción Lavrin, "Masculine and Feminine: The Construction of Gender Roles in the Regular Orders in Early Modern Mexico," *Explorations in Renaissance Culture* 34 (2008): 3–26.

120. Diego de Basalenque, *Historia de la Provincia de San Nicolás de Tolentino de Michoacán, del Orden de N.P.S. Agustín*, intro José Bravo Ugarte (Mexico City: Editorial Jus, 1963).

121. De la Rea, 51–52; Muñoz, 41.

122. Neither De la Rea, 41–42, nor Muñoz, 43–45, gives a date for the founding of Uruapan. Aguirre Beltrán, in *Cuenca de Tepalcatepec*, 80, lists Friar Juan as *guardián* (overseer of a monastery) of Uruapan in 1536.

123. See discussions in De la Rea, 16–18, and RM, 43, 89–90.

124. De la Rea, 16: "Tzacapu, Metrópoli de Mechuacán, y Mátriz de su grandeza, como Roma en todo el mundo."

125. De la Rea, 14: "Viueza del ingenio del Tarasco . . . su ygualdad . . . y assí en su política, y religión Antigua, fue tan circunspecto, que no deuió nada al establecer sus leyes a Saturno, Lysianias, y Radamantho, ni al Legislador Licurgo: porque assí en la rectitud, como en la obseruancia, se preció de tan seuero, que reprehendía a los demás, con el cumplimiento, de sus leyes, con que su gouierno, Repúblicas, y Templos fueron los mas celebres, que repite oy este Occidente."

126. De la Rea, 15: "Porque en ellos tan nativa la circunspección, que entre todos los de esta tierra se conoce un tarasco; así en la viveza de las palabras, como en la sutileza y disposición de sus negocios. Son eminentes en todos los oficios, de tal manera que sus curiosidades han corrido a todo el mundo, con aplauso general; particularmente en la escultura son tan consumados, que confiesa la fama de ser la mejor de estas partes."

127. Muñoz, 43.

128. Muñoz, 42, says he was from the province of San Miguel, based in Plasencia, a dependent of the broader province of San Gabriel. Also see Sebastián García, "San Francisco de Asís y la Órden Franciscana en Extremadura," in *El culto a los santos cofradías, devoción, fiestas y arte* (San Lorenzo El Escorial [Madrid]: Ediciones Escurialenses; Real Centro Universitario Escorial-María Cristina, 2008), 768.

129. Torquemada describes Garrovillas as a Purépecha language expert in *Monarquía Indiana*, 3:334–335, and for "having removed the abominable sacrifices of the province of Çacatula . . . destroying in one day 1000 idols." The date is unclear. De la Rea, 55–57, cites and repeats Torquemada's story, which copies Muñoz's original recounting.

130. Muñoz, 42–43: "Pasó a estas partes, especial en los motines de Zacatula, donde usaban horrendos y abominables sacrificios, costa del mar del Sur, tierra en extremo calurosa y de increíble aspereza, a la cual iba el apostólico varón a pie, discurriendo de pueblo en pueblo y de sierra en sierra. Mostró Nuestro Señor la largueza de su divina mano para con él en el mucho fruto que hizo, porque de todo punto destruyó la idolatría, poniéndose muchas veces a peligro de perder la vida, y plantó la santa fe católica en la cual permanecen hoy día, libertados de la diabólica sujección. Aconteció quemar más de mil ídolos juntos, y hacer que los mismos que los adoraban, los ayudasen a quemar."

131. José Eduardo Zárate Hernández, ed., *La tierra caliente de Michoacán* (Zamora, Mexico: El Colegio de Michoacán, 2001), 27, and Sánchez Díaz, *La costa de Michoacán*, 42.

132. Agustín de Vetancurt, *Menologio Franciscano de los varones mas señalados: Que con sus vidas exemplares, perfeccion religiosa, ciencia, predicacion evangelica, en su vida, y muerte ilustraron la Provincia de el Santo Evangelio de Mexico* (Mexico City: Doña María de Benavides, Viuda de Juan de Ribera, 1697), 75.

133. León Alanís, *Orígenes*, 92.

134. Martínez Baracs, *Convivencia y utopía*.

135. For example, see Juan Martínez Araujo, *Manual de los santos sacramentos en el idioma de Michuacan* (Mexico City: Doña María de Benavides, Viuda de Juan de Ribera, 1690); Ángel Serra, *Manual de administrar los santos sacramentos à los Españoles, y naturales de esta provincia de Michuacan* (Mexico City: Doña María de Benavides, Viuda de Juan de Ribera, 1697).

136. Aguirre Beltrán, *Cuenca de Tepalcatepec*, 80.

137. See Elinor G. K. Melville, *A Plague of Sheep: Environmental Consequences of the Conquest of Mexico* (Cambridge: Cambridge University Press, 1994), for the original interpretation; for a reevaluation, see Georgina H. Enfield and Sara L. O'Hara, "Degradation, Drought, and Dissent: An Environmental History of Colonial Michoacán, West Central Mexico," *Annals of the Association of American Geographers* 89 (1999): 402–419. For an excellent broad overview, see Alfred Crosby, *The Columbian Exchange: Biological and Cultural Consequences of 1492*, foreword by Otto van Mering (Westport, CT: Greenwood, 1973).

138. De la Rea, 38: "Cuando llevado de su espíritu trepaba los montes y se arrojaba a sus abismos buscando almas que convertir, donde los bárbaros, como fieras con cuartana, le mostraban las garras para despedazarle. Pero la virtud de sus palabras era tan activa, que las reducía y trocaba en cordilleros mansos; y al retirarse a su convento le salían a buscar balando por aquellas sierras

y siguiendo sus huellas, como de tierna madre, para volver a nacer entre sus tiernos brazos. No quedó cumbre, gruta o monte en toda esta provincia, que no discurrió a pie, descalzo y desnudo; ayunando casi todo el año, sin perder un punto las horas del oficio divino, aunque fuese entre tigres y leones, cuya descortesía tal vez corregía con las disciplinas ordinarias."

139. Aguirre Beltrán, *Cuenca de Tepalcatepec*, 80.

140. Quoted in ibid., 80: "Los naturales de la dicha provincia de Michoacán andaban desnudos, sus vergüenzas de fuera . . . huían de los religiosos . . . e se iban a los montes e no obstante esto se huían por sus costumbres de idolatrías, e a emborracharse, y hacer otras cosas muy en servicio del demonio e no de Dios Nuestro Señor."

141. Ibid., 80; De la Rea, 41–43.

142. De la Rea, 39: "Porque privar a uno de su gusto, nadie lo sabe sino el que se ve forzado. Y así veremos los imposibles que este siervo de Dios tendría para arrancar a estos indios de su natural asiento y de las delicias que gozaban con la latitud del barbarismo, sin ceñir su libertad a ley que impedía la facultad del apetito, y que forzosamente habían de sujetarse a una cabeza los que jamás superion tenerla. Cosa es ésta la más repugnante al natural del chichimeco que se ve en el mundo, porque su vida, ser y natural es andar vagueando por los montes, cazando fieras y vistiendo su ropaje."

143. Ibid., 41.

144. Ibid., 41, described Uruapan as particularly fecund. While the period 1598–1605 was the zenith of the congregación project in New Spain, there were earlier, experimental efforts: in 1557 in San Bartolomé Calpulhac (AGN, Tierras, vol. 2303, exp. 7); in 1579 in Huatlatlahuca (AGN, Tierras, vol. 2702, exp. 17); and in 1579 in Jilotepec (AGN, Tierras, vol. 2764, exp. 5). Also see Peter Gerhard, "Congregaciones de indios en la Nueva España antes de 1570," *Historia mexicana* 26 (1977): 347–395. For a classic case study from the peak period of the congregación project, see Hilda J. Aguirre Beltrán, *La congregación de Tlacotepec, 1604-1606: Pueblo de indios de Tepeaca, Puebla* (Mexico City: SEP Cultura, 1984). Also see Howard F. Cline, "Civil Congregations of the Indians of New Spain, 1598-1606," *Hispanic American Historical Review* 26 (1949): 349–369.

145. Escobar, 59–61, 72: "Era pesca de hombres y Michoacán en el nombre, quiere dezir Prouincia de pezes, y discurrieron y asertaron la gran pesca, que se les preuenía pues era tanta la multitud de pezes, que ya se les rompían las redes, a los Venerables Padres Franciscanos."

146. See Luis G[ómez] Canedo, *Educación de los marginados durante la época colonial: Escuelas y colegios para indios y mestizos en la Nueva España* (Mexico City: Porrúa, 1982).

147. For biographical overviews, see Mauricio Beuchot et al., *Fray Alonso de la Veracruz: Antología y facetas de su obra* (Morelia, Mexico: Gobierno del Estado de Michoacán; Universidad Michoacana de San Nicolás de Hidalgo, 1992); Arthur Ennis, *Fray Alonso de la Vera Cruz, O.S.A. (1507-1584): A Study of His Life and His Contributions to the Religious and Intellectual Affairs of Early Mexico* (Louvain, Belgium: E. Warny, 1957).

148. See, for example, Beaumont, *Crónica de Michoacán*. While clearly valuable as a source, Beaumont's telling, for my interpretation, is better considered a sort of secondary source, and one which says more about the eighteenth-century mentality than about sixteenth-century religious politics.

149. To this end, Lavrin's essay "Masculine and Feminine" is instructive.

150. Escobar, 62–64: "A cada paso encontraban Circes y Medeas, y muchas veces visibles demonios que en forma de dragones defendían las manzanas de oro de las almas."

151. Escobar, 87: "langostas racionales."

152. Escobar, 114: "Salieron los pueblos enteros con danzas y vailes a su Antigua usanza, po-

blando de ramas, flores, el campo de sus triunfos, cuyos alegres jubilos manifestaban ya evidentes la muerte de la idolatría."

153. Gerhard, 348, says that a curate was established in 1536 in the encomienda of San Nicolás Guango, but I have seen no mention of such curates elsewhere.

154. The term was notably used by James C. Scott in *Domination and the Arts of Resistance: Hidden Transcripts* (New Haven, CT: Yale University Press, 1990).

155. For a compelling application of Scott's term, which shows that "gendered power is relayed via everyday transactions and relationships" in higher education, thus adversely affecting women, see Louise Morley, "Hidden Transcripts: The Micropolitics of Gender in Commonwealth Universities," *Women's Studies International Forum* 29 (2006): 543–551.

156. For a broad study of the phenomenon, see Scott K. Taylor, *Honor and Violence in Golden Age Spain* (New Haven, CT: Yale University Press, 2008). Most of the scholarly literature on honor, violence, and shame revolves inexorably around questions of class-status and of gender, family, and sexuality. But there appears to be relatively little on the question of violence between men as expressions of competition for its own sake, bereft of these contexts of social class or family-gender. For an *abbreviated* listing of scholarship on Mediterranean sexual honor culture, see J. G. Peristiany and Julian Pitt-Rivers, eds., *Honor and Grace in Anthropology* (Cambridge: Cambridge University Press, 1992); *El placer de pecar y el afán de normar*, Seminario de Historia de las Mentalidades (Mexico City: Joaquín Mortiz; Dirección de Estudios del Instituto Nacional de Antropología e Historia, 1988).

CHAPTER 2

1. The baby-snatching incident is recorded in AGN, Inq., vol. 226, exp. s/n, fol. 65r. The generally nefarious activities of Gordillo are detailed in *Quiroga v. OSA*. The Tlazazalca case is also discussed in Ricardo León Alanís, *Los orígenes del clero y la iglesia en Michoacán, 1525–1640* (Morelia, Mexico: Universidad Michoacana de San Nicolás de Hidalgo, Instituto de Investigaciones Históricas, 1997), 220–224, and referenced by Gilberti in AGN, Inq., vol. 43, exp. 7.

2. For a good overview of the royal oversight of crimes against the indigenous peoples of Mexico, see Woodrow Borah, *Justice by Insurance: The General Indian Court of Colonial Mexico and the Legal Aides of the Half-Real* (Berkeley: University of California Press, 1983).

3. Eight decades have passed since the publication of Robert Ricard's classic study *The Spiritual Conquest of Mexico: An Essay on the Apostolate and the Evangelizing Methods of the Mendicant Orders in New Spain, 1523–1572*, trans. Leslie Byrd Simpson (Berkeley: University of California Press, 1982 [1933]), which has provided a framework, whether consciously or unconsciously, for historians of mendicant missionaries in Mexico ever since. The study offered an elegantly simple thesis—friar-missionaries were a species of spiritual conquistador working to achieve a global Spanish Catholic empire in the Americas. Fittingly enough, Nobel-prize winning novelist J. M. G. LeClezio, a fan of Michoacán's Eden, adopted the framework for his doctoral thesis, published in Spanish as *La conquista divina de Michoacán* (Mexico City: Fondo de Cultura Económica, 1985). For a reconsideration of the phenomenon using different terminology, see James Muldoon, ed., *The Spiritual Conversion of the Americas* (Gainesville: University Press of Florida, 2004). Also, for debating the relative ongoing value of the concept, see Sarah Cline, "The Spiritual Conquest Reexamined: Baptism and Christian Marriage in Early Sixteenth-Century Mexico," in John F. Schwaller, ed., *The Church in Colonial Latin America* (Wilmington, DE: Scholarly Resources, 2000). For an excellent study of the role of mendicant orders in urban civic development,

see Karen Melvin, *Building Colonial Cities of God: Mendicant Orders and Urban Culture in New Spain, 1570–1800* (Stanford, CA: Stanford University Press, 2012). A complex reconsideration of "internal missions" and the missionary's cultural world is David Rex-Galindo, *To Sin No More: Franciscans and Conversion in the Hispanic World, 1683–1830* (Stanford, CA: Stanford University Press, 2017). Related studies of the political and cultural consequences of conversion projects (focusing on the semiotics and theatrics of conversion) include Othón Arróniz, *Teatro de evangelización en Nueva España* (Mexico City: UNAM, 1979), and Jaime Lara, *City, Temple, Stage: Eschatological Architecture and Liturgical Theatrics in New Spain* (Notre Dame, IN: University of Notre Dame Press, 2004).

4. Ricard, *Spiritual Conquest*, 15.

5. See, for example, Luis Nicolau D'Olwer, *Fray Bernardino de Sahagún (1499–1590)*, trans. Mauricio J. Mixco, foreword by Miguel León-Portilla (Salt Lake City: University of Utah Press, 1987); Miguel León-Portilla, *Bernardino de Sahagún: Pionero de la antropología* (Mexico City: UNAM, 1999); John F. Schwaller, ed., *Sahagún at 500: Essays on the Quincentenary of the Birth of Fr. Bernardino de Sahagún* (Berkeley, CA: Academy of American Franciscan History, 2003).

6. Scholars of this approach have taken traditional missionary sources such as chronicles and combined a reading of criminal cases, ethnographic description, census reports, population figures, travel accounts, and land disputes to provide a multilayered portrait of indigenous societies living in contact with or under the presumed political rule of Spanish missionaries. The term "new mission history" was expressly adopted in Erick Langer and Robert H. Jackson, eds., *The New Latin American Mission History* (Lincoln: University of Nebraska Press, 1995), and David A. Boruchoff, "*Tanto puede el ejemplo de los mayores*: The Self-Conscious Practice of Missionary History in New Spain," *Colonial Latin American Review* 17 (2008): 161–183. A short listing of works in the genre includes: Susan M. Deeds, *Defiance and Deference in Mexico's Colonial North: Indians Under Spanish Rule in Nueva Vizcaya* (Austin: University of Texas Press, 2003); Robert C. Galgano, *Feast of Souls: Indians and Spaniards in the Seventeenth-Century Missions of Florida and New Mexico* (Albuquerque: University of New Mexico Press, 2005); Barbara Ganson, *The Guaraní Under Spanish Rule in the Río de la Plata* (Stanford, CA: Stanford University Press, 2003); Lisbeth Haas, *Saints and Citizens: Indigenous Histories of Colonial Missions and Mexican California* (Berkeley: University of California Press, 2013); Stephen W. Hackel, *Children of Coyote, Missionaries of Saint Francis: Indian-Spanish Relations in Colonial California, 1769–1850* (Chapel Hill: University of North Carolina Press, 2005); Julia S. Sarreal, *The Guaraní and Their Missions: A Socioeconomic History* (Stanford, CA: Stanford University Press, 2014); Maria F. Wade, *Missions, Missionaries, and Native Americans: Long-Term Processes and Daily Practices* (Gainesville: University Press of Florida, 2008); Rachel M. Wheeler, *To Live Upon Hope: Mohicans and Missionaries in the Eighteenth-Century Northeast* (Ithaca, NY: Cornell University Press, 2008).

7. William B. Taylor, *Magistrates of the Sacred: Priests and Parishioners in Eighteenth-Century Mexico* (Stanford, CA: Stanford University Press, 1996), 12.

8. For an excellent study challenging assumptions about the uniformity of the Spanish Catholic message and mediation of that message for an indigenous audience, see Osvaldo F. Pardo, *Honor and Personhood in Early Mexico* (Ann Arbor: University of Michigan Press, 2015).

9. Louis Châtellier, *The Europe of the Devout: The Catholic Reformation and the Formation of a New Society*, trans. Jean Birrell (Cambridge: Cambridge University Press, 1989); Jean Delumeau, *Catholicism Between Luther and Voltaire: A New View of the Counter-Reformation*, intro. John Bossy (London: Burns and Oates; Philadelphia: Westminster Press, 1977); Lino Gómez Canedo, *Evangelización y conquista: Experiencia franciscana en Hispanoamérica* (Mexico City:

Porrúa, 1977); Nicholas Griffiths and Fernando Cervantes, eds., *Spiritual Encounters: Interactions Between Christianity and Native Religions in Colonial America* (Birmingham, UK: University of Birmingham Press, 1999).

10. Charles E. Dibble, "The Nahuatlization of Christianity," in Munro S. Edmonson, ed., *Sixteenth Century Mexico: The Works of Sahagún* (Albuquerque: University of New Mexico Press, 1974), and Osvaldo F. Pardo, *The Origins of Mexican Catholicism: Nahua Rituals and Christian Sacraments in Sixteenth-Century Mexico* (Ann Arbor: University of Michigan Press, 2004).

11. Jennifer D. Selwyn, *A Paradise Inhabited by Devils: The Jesuits' Civilizing Mission in Early Modern Naples* (Aldershot, UK: Ashgate, 2006; Rome: Institutum Historicum Societatis Iesu, 2006).

12. An exception to this general trend is the work of John F. Schwaller in *The Church and Clergy in Sixteenth Century Mexico* (Albuquerque: University of New Mexico Press, 1987), and *Origins of Church Wealth: Ecclesiastical Revenues and Church Finances, 1523–1600* (Albuquerque: University of New Mexico Press, 1985).

13. The depiction of Quiroga as a beloved champion of the downtrodden Purépecha is at least as old as the eighteenth-century biography of him by Juan Joseph Moreno, *Fragmentos de la vida y virtudes del v. illmo. y rmo. Sr. Dr. Don Vasco de Quiroga* (Mexico City: En el imprento del real, y más antiguo colegio de S. Ildefonso, 1766). Quiroga was also famously lionized in Miguel Bernal Jiménez's 1941 opera, *Tata Vasco*, as a beloved friend of the indigenous, which was a powerful part of the *indigenista* ideology of the 1940s. Recent studies have generally agreed with this evaluation. See James Krippner, *Rereading the Conquest: Power, Politics, and the History of Early Colonial Michoacán, Mexico, 1521–1565* (University Park: Pennsylvania State University Press, 2001), and Bernardino Verástique, *Michoacán and Eden: Vasco de Quiroga and the Evangelization of Western Mexico* (Austin: University of Texas Press, 2000).

14. The classic depiction of Quiroga as a follower of More's utopian dreams is provided in Edmundo O'Gorman, *Santo Tomás More y "La Utopía de Tomás Moro en la Nueva España"* (Mexico City: Alcancia, 1937). In this vein, also see Ross Dealy, *The Politics of an Erasmian Lawyer: Vasco de Quiroga* (Malibu, CA: Undena Publications, 1976); Francisco Miranda Godínez, *Vasco de Quiroga, varón universal* (Mexico City: Editorial Jus, 2007); Nicolás León, *El Ylmo Señor Don Vasco de Quiroga, Primer Obispo de Michoacán: Grandeza de su Persona y de su Obra* (Morelia, Mexico: Universidad Michoacana de San Nicolás de Hidalgo, 1984 [1904]). A relatively balanced, if still slightly rosy, depiction of Quiroga is J. Benedict Warren, *Vasco de Quiroga y sus pueblos-hospitales de Santa Fe* (Morelia, Mexico: Universidad Michoacana de San Nicolás de Hidalgo, 1997).

15. "Información en derecho," in Rafael Aguayo Spencer, ed., *Don Vasco de Quiroga; documentos: Biografía de Juan José Moreno, Ordenanzas de los hospitals, Testamento, Información en derecho, Juicio de residencia, Litigio por la isla de Tultepec*, introducción y notas críticas por Rafael Aguayo Spencer (Mexico City: Editorial Polis, 1939).

16. Ricardo León Alanís, *El Colegio de San Nicolás de Valladolid: Una residencia de estudiantes, 1580–1712* (Morelia, Mexico: Universidad Michoacana de San Nicolás de Hidalgo, Instituto de Investigaciones Históricas, 2001); Miranda Godínez, *Don Vasco de Quiroga*.

17. For vast amounts of material concerning the moves between Tzintzuntzan, Pátzcuaro, and Valladolid, see AGN, Tierras, vols. 713, 714, 715, 716.

18. Warren, *Vasco de Quiroga y sus pueblos-hospitales*.

19. Carlos Herrejón Peredo, *Los orígenes de Morelia: Guayangareo-Valladolid*, 2nd ed., foreword by Juan Carlos Ruiz Guadalajara (Mexico City: Frente de Afirmación Hispanista; Zamora, Mexico: El Colegio de Michoacán, 2000), 67.

20. See AGN, Mercedes, vol. 1, exp. 213, fols. 83v–84r, and exp. 417, fol. 195v; vol. 2, exp. 2, fol. 1.

21. In numerous viceregal decrees. See, for example, AGN, Mercedes, vol. 1, exp. 274, fol. 129r; exp. 415, fol. 195.

22. For comprehensive treatment of the expedition, see Richard Flint and Shirley Cushing Flint, eds. and trans., *Documents of the Coronado Expedition, 1539–1542: "They Were Not Familiar with His Majesty, Nor Did They Wish to Be His Subjects"* (Albuquerque: University of New Mexico Press, 2012). For a discussion of the political-military context in New Galicia, see two works by Ida Altman: "Conquest, Coercion, and Collaboration: Indian Allies and the Campaigns in Nueva Galicia," in Laura E. Matthew and Michel R. Oudijk, eds., *Indian Conquistadors: Indigenous Allies in the Conquest of Mesoamerica* (Norman: University of Oklahoma Press, 2012), and *The War for Mexico's West: Indians and Spaniards in New Galicia, 1524–1550* (Albuquerque: University of New Mexico Press, 2010).

23. AGN, Mercedes, vol. 1, exp. 207, fol. 99; exp. 415, fols. 194v–195r.

24. Spencer, ed., *Don Vasco de Quiroga*, 79–80.

25. AGN, Mercedes, vol. 2, exp. 210, fol. 83; exp. 211, fol. 83v.

26. Ibid., exp. 212, fol. 83v.

27. Herrejón Peredo, *Orígenes de Morelia*, 82–84.

28. There is a bewilderingly extensive literature on Antonio de Montesinos, the Dominican friar who delivered an infamous sermon in Santo Domingo in 1511 lambasting the encomenderos, and on Las Casas and missionary critiques of the encomienda system. Overviews include Lewis Hanke, *The Spanish Struggle for Justice in the Conquest of America* (Philadelphia: University of Pennsylvania Press, 1949); Anthony Pagden, *The Fall of Natural Man: The American Indian and the Origins of Comparative Ethnology* (Cambridge: Cambridge University Press, 1986); D[eme-trio] Ramos, *La ética en la conquista de América: Francisco de Vitoria y la Escuela de Salamanca* (Madrid: Consejo Superior de Investigaciones Científicas, 1984).

For a comprehensive analysis of land acquisition by friar monasteries, see Ryan Crewe, "Building a Visible Church: The Mexican Mission Enterprise in the Early Spanish Atlantic, 1521–1600" (PhD diss., Yale University, 2009). Ricard's *Spiritual Conquest* also gives broad brush treatment of the topic. For an excellent discussion of the process of constructing Augustinian convents in New Spain (in a physical as well as a cultural and sociopolitical sense), see Antonio Rubial García, *El convento agustino y la sociedad novohispana, 1533–1630* (Mexico City: UNAM, 1989).

29. Especially by Rodrigo Martínez Baracs, *Convivencia y utopía: El gobierno indio y español de la "ciudad de Mechuacan," 1521–1580* (Mexico City: INAH; Fondo de Cultura Económica, 2005), 143–146; J. Benedict Warren, *The Conquest of Michoacán: The Spanish Domination of the Tarascan Kingdom in Western Mexico, 1521–1530* (Norman: University of Oklahoma Press, 1985).

30. AGN, Mercedes, vol. 1, exp. 415, fols. 194v–195r.

31. Ibid., exp. 274, fol. 129r.

32. Ibid., exp. 207, fol. 99r.

33. Herrejón Peredo, *Orígenes de Morelia*, 82, 131.

34. Escobar, 73: "Casi todas las tierras para el convento . . . [y] para el aseo de la Iglesia nos dejó opulentas minas de Curucupaseo."

35. Raúl Arreola Cortés, *Tacámbaro, Carácuaro-Nocupétaro, Turicato* (Morelia, Mexico: Gobierno del Estado de Michoacán, 1979), 92.

36. Escobar, 112. Also see Gloria Angélica Álvarez Rodríguez, *La capilla de Cristóbal de Oñate: Santa María Magdalena en Tacámbaro* (Mexico City: Morevallo, 2006).

37. Arreola Cortés, *Tacámbaro*, 88–91; Escobar, 112–113.

38. AGN, Mercedes, vol. 3, exp. 123, fol. 56.

39. For comprehensive overview, see Herrejón Peredo, *Orígenes de Morelia*, 51–116.

40. Herrejón Peredo, *Orígenes de Morelia*, 131, cites a census and account book for the newly founded monastery from 1555 to 1559 found in Archivo de Casa de Morelos (Morelia), leg. 1, Negocios Diversos, Inf. Matrimonial, 1555–1599. The Augustinians were not unique in their role as proto-bankers, though they were unusual to the extent that monasteries as credit agencies tended to be run by nunneries and not by friaries. For a classic study of the system (albeit for the eighteenth century), see Gisela von Wobeser, *El crédito eclesiástico en la Nueva España, siglo XVIII* (Mexico City: UNAM, 1994).

41. Himmerich y Valencia, 165–166. For reconsiderations of the presumed conspiracy of 1566, see Shirley Cushing Flint, "Treason or Travesty: The Martín Cortés Conspiracy Reexamined," *Sixteenth Century Journal* 39 (2008): 23–44, and Ethelia Ruiz Medrano, "Fighting Destiny: Nahua Nobles and Friars in the Sixteenth-Century Revolt of the Encomenderos Against the King," in Ethelia Ruiz Medrano and Susan Kellogg, eds., *Negotiation Within Domination: New Spain's Indian Pueblos Confront the Spanish State* (Boulder: University of Colorado Press, 2010).

42. The 1568 Chamacuero dispute alludes to the lawsuit. See AGN, Tierras, vol. 24, exp. 5.

43. Antonio de Herrera y Tordesillas, *Historia general de los hechos de los castellanos en las islas y en tierra-firme de el mar océano*, prologue by J. Natalicio González, 10 vols. (Asunción, Paraguay: Editorial Guarania, 1944– [c. 1601–1615]), década VI, lib. 7, cap. 9; Peter Boyd-Bowman, *Índice geobiográfico de cuarenta mil pobladores españoles de América en el siglo XVI*, 2 vols. (Bogotá, Colombia: Instituto Caro y Cuervo, 1964), 2:59.

44. AGN, Tierras, vol. 24, exp. 5. Various witness statements referring to the 1543 and 1544 settlement of Chamacuero as having taken place "more than twenty years ago" and "twenty-four years ago" date the original depositions filed by Doña Leonor's children, Doña Isabel de Figueroa and Luis de Moscoso, in 1568. The further reference to the two children as being legal minors, the daughter under twenty-five and the son under fourteen, also suggest that Doña Leonor de Alvarado bore the daughter around the same time as, or shortly after, the death of her first husband, González de Ávila (Benavides), in 1544.

45. William B. Taylor, "Between Global Process and Local Knowledge: An Inquiry into Early Latin American Social History, 1500–1900," in Olivier Zunz, ed., *Reliving the Past: The Worlds of Social History* (Chapel Hill: University of North Carolina Press, 1985), 150.

46. Gerhard, 172–173; Ethelia Ruiz Medrano, *Gobierno y sociedad en Nueva España: Segunda Audiencia y Antonio de Mendoza* (Zamora, Mexico: El Colegio de Michoacán, Gobierno del Estado de Michoacán, 1991), 168.

47. León Alanís, *Orígenes*, 310.

48. Ruiz Medrano, *Gobierno y sociedad*, 169.

49. AGN, Mercedes, vol. 1, exp. 229, fol. 106v.

50. For an excellent discussion of the ways in which the pipiltin sought to maximize their appeal to the Spanish Crown as loyal subjects, genuine Catholic converts, and immemorial aristocrats of Mesoamerica, see Peter B. Villella, *Indigenous Elites and Creole Identity in Colonial Mexico, 1500–1800* (New York: Cambridge University Press, 2016), esp. 29–72. For other discussions of indigenous elite political strategies, see María Castañeda de la Paz, "Apropiación de elementos y símbolos de legitimidad entre la nobleza indígena: El caso del cacicazgo tlatelolca," *Anuario de Estudios Americanos* 65 (2008): 21–47; Eréndira Nansen Díaz, "Los intérpretes jurados como auxiliares de la administración de justicia colonial en Michoacán," in Carlos Paredes Martínez and Marta Terán, eds., *Autoridad y gobierno indígena en Michoacán*, 2 vols. (Zamora, Mexico: El Colegio de Michoacán, INAH, CIESAS; Morelia, Mexico: Universidad Michoacana de San Nicolás de Hidalgo, 2003), 1:173–182.

51. For a case study of indigenous elite governance, albeit in a different region, see Robert S. Haskett, *Indigenous Rulers: An Ethnohistory of Town Government in Colonial Cuernavaca* (Albuquerque: University of New Mexico Press, 1991).

52. AGN, Mercedes, vol. 1, exp. 33, fol. 18.

53. Ibid., exp. 383, fol. 177r.

54. León Alanís, *Orígenes*, 89.

55. Herrejón Peredo, *Orígenes de Morelia*.

56. AGN, Mercedes, vol. 1, exp. 52, fols. 24v–25r.

57. Antonio Arriaga, *Organización social de los tarascos: Reglas y ordenanzas para el gobierno de los hospitales de Santa Fe de México y Michoacán* (Morelia, Mexico: Departamento de Extensión Universitaria, 1938).

58. For overviews of these projects, neither of which came anywhere near to physical fruition during Quiroga's lifetime, see León Alanís, *El Colegio de San Nicolás*, and Guillermina Ramírez Montes, *La catedral de Vasco de Quiroga* (Zamora, Mexico: El Colegio de Michoacán, 1986).

59. Óscar Mazín Gómez, *El cabildo catedral de Valladolid de Michoacán* (Zamora, Mexico: El Colegio de Michoacán, 1996), 83–84.

60. León Alanís, *Orígenes*, 309, 316, 320.

61. The ACCM, book 1, for the cathedral chapter records does not list tithes prior to 1561, so the actual amounts collected between 1538 and 1561 are anyone's guess, though presumably it was less than the 7,700-peso annual average of the 1560s calculated in León Alanís, *Orígenes*, 283–285.

62. Spencer, ed., *Don Vasco de Quiroga*, 83.

63. Mazín Gómez, *Cabildo catedral*, 84.

64. Zurnero appears as early as March 1549, in a letter to Quiroga in which he references his role as provisor in the previous year. See Alberto Carrillo Cázares, *Vasco de Quiroga: La pasión por el derecho. El pleito con la Orden de San Agustín (1558–1562)*, 2 vols. (Zamora, Mexico: El Colegio de Michoacán; Morelia, Mexico: Arquidiócesis de Morelia, Universidad Michoacana de San Nicolás de Hidalgo, Instituto de Investigaciones Históricas, 2003), 1:38, and León, *El Ylmo Señor Don Vasco de Quiroga*, 316a. Zurnero asserted his position as provisor after Quiroga's return to Mexico in 1554, adopting also the titles of maestrescuela and vicario general from 1556 to 1559. See AGN, Inq., vol. 15, exps. 1, 7; vol. 23, exp. 8bis.

65. Wigberto Jiménez Moreno, *La colonización y evangelización de Guanajuato en el siglo XVI* (Mexico City: Editorial Cultura, 1944); Isauro Rionda Arreguín, "Acámbaro indígena, colonizador y evangelizador," in *Ciudades guanajuatenses a la orilla del milenio* (Guanajuato, Mexico: Universidad de Guanajuato, Centro de Investigaciones Humanísticas, 1996), 61–78.

66. AGN, Tierras, vol. 24, exp. 5.

67. Carrillo Cázares, *Pasión por el derecho*, 1:37–38.

68. AGN, Mercedes, vol. 3, exp. 494, fol. 180v.

69. Ibid., exp. 496, fol. 181.

70. AGI, Patronato, leg. 60n2, ramo 3. See Villella, *Indigenous Elites and Creole Identity*, for discussion of the pipiltin strategy in the mid-sixteenth century of appealing to royal sensibility to prove their inclusion as loyal vassals of the Crown.

71. AGI, Justicia, 157n1.

72. AGN, Mercedes, vol. 3, exp. s/n, 181v [204v]–182r [205r].

73. AGN, Tierras, vol. 2956, exp. 62. The trial record is not extant, and we only have the sentence, in favor of the macehuales.

74. Ibid., vol. 2075, exp. 10.

75. AGN, Mercedes, vol. 4, exp. s/n, fol. 265 [267].

76. The feud and paper war are chronicled in *Quiroga v. OSA*.

77. Carrillo Cázares, *Pasión por el derecho*, 1:36.

78. Ibid.

79. Mazín Gómez, *Cabildo catedral*, 84–85.

80. León Alanís, *Orígenes*, 130.

81. For an overview of Veracruz's political imbroglios, see Paula López Cruz, "Los escándalos de Fray Alonso de la Veracruz," in Mauricio Beuchot et al., *Fray Alonso de la Veracruz: Antología y facetas de su obra* (Morelia, Mexico: Universidad Michoacana de San Nicolás de Hidalgo, Gobierno del Estado de Michoacán, 1992).

82. José Antonio Almandoz Garmendía, ed., *Fray Alonso de Veracruz O.S.A. y la encomienda indiana en la historia eclesiástica novohispana (1522–1556): Edición crítica del texto* De dominio infidelium et iusto bello, foreword by Ernest J. Burrus (Madrid: J. Porrúa Turanzas, 1971–1977).

83. AGN, Mercedes, vol. 4, exp. s/n, fol. 175.

84. Ibid.

85. Ibid., exp. s/n, fol. 289.

86. Ibid., exp. s/n, fol. 279.

87. Himmerich y Valencia, 234.

88. José María Kobayashi, *La educación como conquista (empresa franciscana en México)* (Mexico City: El Colegio de México, 1974).

89. For overviews of the council and Montúfar's politics, see Magnus Lundberg, *Unificación y conflicto: La gestión episcopal de Alonso de Montúfar, OP, arzobispo de México, 1554–1572*, trans. Alberto Carrillo Cázares (Zamora, Mexico: El Colegio de Michoacán, 2009); Ethelia Ruiz Medrano, "Los negocios de un arzobispo: El caso de Fray Alonso de Montúfar," *Estudios de Historia Novohispana* 12 (1992): 63–83. For the council's proceedings, see Francisco Antonio de Lorenzana, ed., *Concilios provinciales primero, y segundo, celebrados en la muy noble, y muy leal ciudad de México, presidiendo el Illmo. y Rmo. Señor D. Fr. Alonso de Montúfar, en los años de 1555, y 1565* (Mexico City: Imprenta de el Superior Gobierno, de Joseph Antonio de Hogal, 1769).

90. *Apologia pro religiosis trium ordinum mendicantium, habitantibus in nova Hispania*, a presumed original copy (which I was not able to consult for this study), is located in the Real Biblioteca del Monasterio de San Lorenzo del Escorial. See Arthur Ennis, *Fray Alonso de la Vera Cruz, O.S.A. (1507–1584): A Study of His Life and His Contributions to the Religious and Intellectual Affairs of Early Mexico* (Louvain, Belgium: E. Warny, 1957).

91. Georges Baudot, *La pugna franciscana por México* (Mexico City: Alianza Editorial Mexicana; Consejo Nacional para la Cultura y las Artes, 1990), 122: "Porque tanto es el poder, favor y mando de los religiosos en estas partes que puede y vale más un fraile lego que un arçobispo de México."

92. Ibid.; "Carta de Montúfar," 20 June 1558, in Francisco del Paso y Troncoso, ed., *Epistolario de Nueva España*, 16 vols. (Mexico City: Antigua Librería Robredo, de J. Porrúa e hijos, 1939–1942), 8:186.

93. There is some discrepancy in the precise dates offered by De la Rea, 58. For the 1556 time in Tzintzuntzan, see J. Benedict Warren, "Introducción," in Maturino Gilberti, *Arte de la lengua de Michuacan* (Morelia, Mexico: Fímax, 1987 [1558]), 17.

94. Juan Baptista de Lagunas, *Arte y dicionario: con otras obras, en lengua Michuacana* (Mexico City: Pedro Balli, 1574). See De la Rea, 57–59.

95. AGI, México, 212n24.

96. De la Rea, 58.

97. On Gilberti's work as a writer and Purépecha scholar, see Warren, "Introducción" in Gil-

berti, *Arte*, and José Bravo Ugarte, "Preface," in Maturino Gilberti, *Diccionario de la lengua ta-rasca o de Michoacán* (Guadalajara, Mexico: n.p., 1967). Also see Román Zuláica Garate, *Los fran-ciscanos y la imprenta en México en el siglo XVI* (Mexico City: Ed. Pedro Robredo, 1939), 125–168.

98. Muñoz, 47.

99. De la Rea, 58, repeats Muñoz's tale of gout, but expands on the legend of Gilberti's popu-larity as a preacher, including the detail about the litter in which he was carried. The quotation above: "Cuando los indios eran tantos, como si fueran hijos de Abraham, que solo la arena de la tierra y estrellas del cielo, pudieron ser símbolo de su multitud."

100. As claimed in an inquisitional case against a man for blasphemy. See AGN, Inq., vol. 128, exp. 8.

101. For an excellent overview of Gilberti's criticism, see Rodrigo Martínez Baracs, *Caminos cruzados: Fray Maturino Gilberti en Perivan* (Zamora, Mexico: El Colegio de Michoacán, INAH, 2005). For a biographical discussion of Gilberti, see Bravo Ugarte, "Preface," in Gilberti, *Diccio-nario*; and Warren, "Introducción," in Gilberti, *Arte*.

102. Gilberti's critiques of Quiroga are in AGN, Inq., vol. 43, exp. 6; vol. 72, exp. 35.

103. AGN, Inq., vol. 43, exp. 6, fols. 202–203.

104. Gilberti's manuscript translation of liturgical scripture into Purépecha was never pub-lished, probably for fear of inquisitional censure. Nevertheless, at least one manuscript copy (clearly in Gilberti's hand) remains extant. See "Thema para que oyga la boz del señor," in the John Carter Brown Library, Codex Ind 6. I thank Ken Ward for refreshing my memory.

105. Around 1618, the Franciscan friar Ambrosio Carrillo, a longtime resident of Michoacán and confidant of the inquisitional deputy Diego Muñoz, drew up an inventory of his personal library, found in AGN, Jesuitas, III-26, exp. 13. Among his books, he reported the *Diálogo* of Gil-berti, noting that it was titled "Diálogo de la lengua de Mechoacán con los Evangelios y Epístolas de todo el año y doctrina christiana en la misma lengua por Fray Maturino Gilberti."

106. The 1554 and 1559 indexes that elaborated the ban on vernacular Scripture are reproduced in J. M. de Bujanda, *Index espagnols, 1551–1559*, in *Index de livres interdits* (Sherbrooke, Quebec: Centre d'études de la Renaissance, Editions de l'Université de Sherbrooke; Geneva: Droz, c. 1984–c. 1996). For discussions, see Lorenzo Amigo Espada, "Las Biblias en romance y Biblias en ladino: Evolución de un sistema de traducción," *La ciudad de Dios* 203 (1990): 111–142; Sergio Fernández López, *Lectura y prohibición de la Biblia en lengua vulgar: Defensores y detractores*, prologue by Luis Gómez Canseco (León, Spain: Universidad de León, 2003); J. I. Tellechea Idígoras, "La cen-sura inquisitorial de Biblias de 1554," *Anthologica Annua* 10 (1962): 89–142. The ban on vernacular Scripture produced a rancorous debate in Mexico, especially in the 1570s, which swept up Gil-berti's works and discovered several manuscripts of Nahuatl translations of Ecclesiastes and other books. For discussion of the controversy, see Martin Nesvig, "The Political Epistemology of Ver-nacular Scripture in Sixteenth-Century Mexico," *The Americas* 70 (2013): 165–201.

107. J. Benedict Warren, "Introducción," in Maturino Gilberti, *Vocabulario en Lengua de Me-chuacan* [Edición facsimilar de la de 1559], ed. and intro. by J. Benedict Warren (Morelia, Mexico: Fímax, 1991), 17.

108. AGN, Inq., vol. 43, exp. 6.

109. Ibid., exp. 7.

110. The account of the fire and the case surrounding it are told in the witness statements in *Quiroga v. OSA*.

111. Carrillo Cázares, *Pasión por el derecho*, 1:31.

112. Ibid., 1:30; Ricard, *Spiritual Conquest*, 75.

113. *Quiroga v. OSA*, 1:158–160.

114. The discussion that follows is based on a reading of the trial transcripts in *Quiroga v. OSA*.

115. Promulgated by Innocent IV in 1245; incorporated into the Sextus, lib. V, tit. V, cap. IV: *Auctoritate*.

116. See James Lockhart, *The Nahuas After the Conquest: A Social and Cultural History of the Indians of Central Mexico, Sixteenth Through Eighteenth Centuries* (Stanford, CA: Stanford University Press, 1992), 210–215, 636.

117. See, for example, Carlos M. N. Eire, *War Against the Idols: The Reformation of Worship from Erasmus to Calvin* (Cambridge: Cambridge University Press, 1986).

118. AGN, Inq., vol. 226, exp. s/n, fol. 65.

119. León Alanís, *Orígenes*, 223–224.

120. AGN, Inq., vol. 43, exp. 6.

121. Warren, "Introducción," in Gilberti, *Vocabulario*.

122. Overviews of this thinking and Franciscan millenarianism include Georges Baudot, *Utopia and History: The First Chroniclers of Mexican Civilization (1520–1569)*, trans. Bernard R. Ortiz de Montellano and Thelma Ortiz de Montellano (Niwot, CO: University Press of Colorado, 1995); John Leddy Phelan, *The Millennial Kingdom of the Franciscans in the New World* (Berkeley: University of California Press, 1956); Josep Ignasi Saranyana and Ana de Zeballa, *Joaquín de Fiore y América* (Pamplona, Spain: Ediciones Eunate, 1992). Gilberti's activity as translator and writer was prolific. Among the various works known to have been penned by him can be included more than a dozen works in Purépecha. Around 1552 or 1553, he may have been commissioned by his order to compose a small *doctrina* in Purépecha, which has been lost. In 1558, Juan Pablos published his *Arte de la lengua tarasca*, and in 1559 his *Devocionario*, the *Tesorero espiritual*, the *Vocabulario en lengua de Michoacán*, and the *Diálogo de Doctrina Cristiana*—all in Purépecha. Also in 1559 was published a now lost "Cartilla para los niños en lengua tarasca," which Ricardo León Alanís supposes formed part of a later publication of 1575, *Tesorero espiritual de pobres en lengua de Michoacán*, printed by Antonio de Espinoza. Additional works by Gilberti in Purépecha include *Sermones*; *Pláticas sobre los Evangelios del año*; *Confessionario*; and a saints' calendar with the name *Fiesta del año*.

123. AGN, Inq., vol. 43, exp. 6.

124. In the 1564 bull *In Principis Apostolorum Sede*.

125. AGN, Inq., vol. 43, exp. 20.

126. Ibid., exp. 6, fols. 202–203.

127. Ibid., fol. 202.

128. Ibid., fol. 203: "Mancebos idiotas nacidos acá y criados entre los pechos de las indias."

129. Ibid., fols. 202–203.

130. Ibid., vol. 72, exp. 35, fol. 291.

131. AGN, Mercedes, vols. 5/6, exp. s/n, fol. 230v [481v].

132. Copies of the 1557 Audiencia rulings and the Periban subjects' reply are in Archivo Histórico Municipal de Pátzcuaro (Municipal Historical Archive of Pátzcuaro) (AHMP hereafter), caja 2, exp. 35, and related in *Vida michoacana*, 75.

133. Gerhard, 387; Himmerich y Valencia, 133–134.

134. *Vida michoacana*, 75.

135. Ibid., 75–76.

136. Ibid., 31.

137. Muñoz, 32–33, lists Tancítaro, Tarecuato, and Uruapan as monasteries of indigenous towns. He also lists "Piruán" in this category, which likely refers to Periban.

138. *Vida michoacana*, 212–214.

139. His testimony is in AHMP, caja 2, exp. 35, and reproduced in *Vida michoacana*, 213–214. For an overview of Gilberti's activities in Periban, see Martínez Baracs, *Caminos cruzados*.

140. AGN, Inq., vol. 226, exp. s/n, fol. 65.

141. Steven C. Caton, "Anthropological Theories of Tribe and State Formation in the Middle East: Ideology and the Semiotics of Power," in Philip S. Khoury and Joseph Kostiner, eds., *Tribes and State Formation in the Middle East* (Berkeley: University of California Press, 1990), 80. For elaboration of his analysis of the "anthropology of the event," see Steven C. Caton, *Yemen Chronicle: An Anthropology of War and Mediation* (New York: Hill and Wang, 2005).

CHAPTER 3

1. AGN, Inq., vol. 11, exp. 4, fol. 304.

2. In "the more things change the more they stay the same" category, James B. Given's study of southern France in the thirteenth and fourteenth centuries shows that the tithe was also particularly hated in that region and often a starting point for inquisitional prosecution. See *Inquisition and Medieval Society: Power, Discipline, and Resistance in Languedoc* (Ithaca, NY: Cornell University Press, 1997).

3. No indigenous peoples were targeted, even though they were subject to inquisitional oversight until 1569, at which point indigenous peoples were transferred to the jurisdiction of the *Provisorato de Indios*. There are echoes here of Javier Villa-Flores's excellent study *Dangerous Speech: A Social History of Blasphemy in Colonial Mexico* (Tucson: University of Arizona Press, 2006), especially in his chapter on gambling.

4. Enumerated in *Ad abolendam* in the *Decretales Gregorii IX*.

5. I analyzed the phenomenon and offered more detailed analysis of the broader caseload than provided here in the article "Heterodoxia popular e Inquisición diocesana en Michoacán, siglo XVI," *Tzintzun* 39 (2004): 9–38.

6. AGN, Inq., vol. 4, exps. 1, 6; vol. 7, exp. 12; vol. 8, exp. 2; vol. 9, exps. 1, 2; vol. 17, exps. 18, 19; vol. 18, exp. 1; vol. 20, exp. 4; vol. 38, exp. 10; vol. 41, exp. 4; vol. 44, exp. 4; vol. 71, exp. 6; vol. 91, exp. 4; vol. 113, exp. 1; vol. 114, exp. 3; vol. 128, exp. 1.

7. AGN, Inq., vol. 10, exp. 8; vol. 20, exp. 2; vol. 21, exp. 3; vol. 39, exps. 2, 3; vol. 45, exp. 3; vol. 46, exp. 4; vol. 72, exps. 8, 12 (*dos procesos*); vol. 109, exps. 3, 6; vol. 110, exps. 2, 5, 7; vol. 111, exp. 12; vol. 114, exp. 1; vol. 181, exp. 2.

8. AGN, Inq., vol. 1A, exp. 34; vol. 2, exp. 14; vol. 3, exps. 4, 5, 6, 7, 13, 16, 17; vol. 15, exps. 2, 3, 4, 5, 6, 9, 10, 10bis, 11, 13, 16; vol. 16, exps. 8, 9, 14; vol. 17, exps. 5, 7, 11; vol. 18, exps. 5, 9, 15; vol. 22, exp. 16; vol. 24, exps. 1, 3, 5, 6; vol. 25, exp. 8; vol. 32, exps. 2, 16; vol. 36, exp. 9bis; vol. 37, exps. 8, 9, 10; vol. 42, exps. 14, 15, 16; vol. 43, exps. 1, 3, 5, 8; vol. 71, exps. 4, 5; vol. 90, exp. 2; vol. 98, exp. 3; vol. 181, exp. 1; vol. 601, exp. 12.

9. For comprehensive assessment of inquisitional punishment before 1700, see Jaime Contreras and Gustav Henningsen, "Forty-Four Thousand Cases of the Spanish Inquisition (1540–1700): Analysis of a Historical Data Bank," trans. Anne Bonn, in Gustav Henningsen and John Tedeschi, eds., in assoc. with Charles Amiel, *The Inquisition in Early Modern Europe: Studies on Sources and Methods* (DeKalb: Northern Illinois University Press, 1986).

10. See John F. Chuchiak IV, "La inquisición Indiana y la extirpación de idolatrías: El castigo y la represión en el Provisorato de Indios en Yucatán, 1570–1690," in Ana de Zaballa Beascoechea, ed., *Nuevas perspectivas sobre el castigo de la heterodoxia indígena en la Nueva España, siglos XVI–XVIII* (Bilbao, Spain: Servicio Editorial de la Universidad del País Vasco, Euskal Herriko Unibertsitateko Argitalpen Zerbitzua, 2005).

11. Richard Greenleaf, *Zumárraga and the Mexican Inquisition, 1536–1543* (Washington, DC: American Academy of Franciscan History, 1961).

12. AGN, Indiferente Virreinal, Inq. caja 826, exp. 1. The case echoes the man-god tradition in Mesoamerica outlined by Serge Gruzinski, *Man-Gods in the Mexican Highlands: Indian Power and Colonial Society, 1550–1800*, trans. Eileen Corrigan (Stanford, CA: Stanford University Press, 1989).

13. For the 1539 case against Don Carlos de Texcoco, see AGN, Inq., vol. 2, exp. 10. For the 1537 case against Andrés Mixcoatl, see AGN, Inq., vol. 38, exp. 7.

14. He was not a conquistador of Mexico but was involved in Panama in the 1510s. He received Istapa in encomienda in 1528. In 1530, he purchased an estate in Guayangareo from the famed conquistador Bernardo de Albornoz. See Carlos Herrejón Peredo, *Los orígenes de Morelia: Guayangareo-Valladolid*, 2nd ed., foreword by Juan Carlos Ruiz Guadalajara (Mexico City: Frente de Afirmación Hispanista; Zamora, Mexico: El Colegio de Michoacán, 2000), 30, 35–36; Himmerich y Valencia, 163–164.

15. On the original trial, see AGN, Inq., vol. 2, exp. 2. For a transcription and critical edition of the trial, see Álvaro Ochoa, ed., with an introduction by J. Benedict Warren and Richard E. Greenleaf, *Gonzalo Gómez primer poblador español de Guayangareo (Morelia): Proceso inquisitorial* (Morelia, Mexico: Fímax, 1991).

16. J. Benedict Warren, *The Conquest of Michoacán: The Spanish Domination of the Tarascan Kingdom in Western Mexico, 1521–1530* (Norman: University of Oklahoma Press, 1985), 171.

17. AGN, Inq., vol. 2, exp. 2, and *Gonzalo Gómez*.

18. AGN, Inq., vol. 22, exp. 12.

19. Ibid., vol. 14, exp. 37bis.

20. Ibid.

21. Ibid.

22. Only seven cases of ecclesiastical-inquisitional justice in Michoacán are extant for the years 1537 through 1559. See AGN, Inq., vol. 14, exp. 37bis; vol. 15, exps. 1, 7; vol. 22, exp. 12; vol. 23, exp. 8bis; *Archivo de la Villa de Colima de la Nueva España: Siglo XVI*, ed. and trans. José Miguel Romero de Solís, 2 vols. (Colima, Mexico: Archivo Histórico del Municipio de Colima, 1998–2005) (AVC hereafter), 1:23–25; José Miguel Romero de Solís, *Cirujano, hechicero y sangrador: Medicina y violencia en Colima (siglo XVI)* (Colima, Mexico: Archivo Histórico del Municipio de Colima, 1993).

23. AGN, Inq., vol. 15, exps. 1, 7; vol. 23, exp. 8bis.

24. Ibid., vol. 23, exp. 8bis.

25. Ibid., vol. 15, exp. 1.

26. Ibid., vol. 4, exps. 1, 6; vol. 17, exps. 18, 19; vol. 18, exp. 1; vol. 38, exp. 10; vol. 71, exp. 6; vol. 114, exp. 3; vol. 128, exp. 1.

27. Ibid., vol. 4, exp. 1.

28. Innocent III solidified this traditional view in the bull *Cum ex iniuncto*: "Laymen may not preach, nor may they make secret assemblies, nor censure priests" (translation mine), incorporated into the law in *Decretales*, lib. 5, tit. 7, c. 12: "Laici non praedicent, nec occulta conventicula faciant, nec sacerdotes reprehendant."

29. AGN, Inq., vol. 71, exps. 4, 7.

30. Ibid., exp. 6, fol. 365.

31. Gerhard, 172.

32. AGN, Inq., vol. 71, exp. 6, fol. 265.

33. François Chevalier, *Land and Society in Colonial Mexico: The Great Hacienda*, trans. Alvin Eustis, ed. Leslie Byrd Simpson (Berkeley: University of California Press, 1970), 77.

34. Gerhard, 173.

35. AGN, Inq., vol. 71, exp. 6, fol. 366.

36. Gerhard, 172.

37. John D. Early, *The Maya and Catholicism: An Encounter of Worldviews* (Gainesville: University Press of Florida, 2006).

38. AGN, Inq., vol. 71, exp. 6.

39. *Ordenanças del Ilustriss[im]o y reverendissimo señor D. Fr. Marcos Ramirez de Prado, del consejo de Su Magestad, obispo de Mechoacan; para los curas, beneficiados, y vicarios de toda su dioecesi* (Mexico City: n.p., 1657).

40. AGN, Inq., vol. 71, exp. 6, fol. 401: "Desnudo de la cintura arriba, una soga a la garganta a todas las manos le den alderedа de la santa iglesia desta ciudad con una coroça en la cabeça; le den doçientos açotes públicamente y con pregón que manifeste su delicto y después de açotado se esté a la puerta de la yglesia hasta que se acaben los ofiçios divinos." The *coroza* (peaked crown) was a mark of shame of inquisitional conviction.

41. AGN, Inq., vol. 71, exp. 6, fol. 401.

42. Ibid., vol. 7, exp. 12.

43. Ibid., fol. 225: "Y que no eran yndios para se lo mandar."

44. It is difficult to render the phrase in English. Ortega said "mozos de hornachos," which, literally, means "boys of/from mountain mines." But there are clear racial undertones, since most of the mine workers were press-ganged indigenous peoples or African slaves.

45. AGN, Inq., vol. 7, exp. 12, fol. 225: "Que nadie le abía de hazer fuerça a oyrse sermón que el yría quando quisiese a oyrle y quando no, no."

46. Ibid., vol. 7, exp. 12.

47. Ibid., vol. 9, exp. 2.

48. The case file and testimonies do not give any more information on Gaspar and Juan, simply describing them as "un negro Gaspar" and "un esclavo negro Juan." Gaspar was presumably a free black man, given the tendency in sixteenth-century nomenclature to specify slave status.

49. AGN, Inq., vol. 9, exp. 2, fol. 67: "vellaco traidor."

50. Ibid.: "Tiró un bote con la dicha partesana e me [al fiscal] dió una herida en el rostro en el carrillo isquierdo de la qual me cortó cuero y carne del dicho rostro y me salió mucha sangre y en este ynter todos los demás vinieron sobre mí y a palos e con las dichas partesanas me echaron del cauallo abaxo en el suelo."

51. Ibid., fol. 64.

52. Ibid., fol. 67: "Tiró un bote con la parthesana." The weapon was a kind of lance that is also known as a "partisan polearm."

53. Ibid.: "Mata a ese uellaco traidor ladrón robador puto desuella cara robador en los caminos y así se fueron dándose fabor unos a otros diziendo contra Vuestra Merced [the provisor] que era un ladrón robador y que les auía robado sus haziendas y que era un ereje luterano y que así se lo prouaría." It is nearly impossible to translate the word *puto*. Even in today's Spanish it lacks a sufficient rendering in English, although the most common translation is "faggot." But it is also often used with no explicit reference to sexual orientation and can mean terms that in English might be rendered as "bastard," "punk," or "bitch." It can also be an all-purpose insult implying infidelity, especially if used by a woman to insult her boyfriend or husband. The term *punk* dates to at least the 1940s and refers to, among other things, (a) a male who is on the bottom in male-male anal sex, that is, a "passive male homosexual"; (b) a male who is "turned out" as a functional female in prison sexual relationships; and (c) a "worthless fellow . . . [or] petty criminal." See *Shorter Oxford English Dictionary*, 5th ed. (Oxford: Oxford University Press, 2002), s.v.

"punk"; and Wayne S. Wooden and Jay Parker, *Men Behind Bars: Sexual Exploitation in Prison* (New York: Da Capo, 1984).

54. The case file refers to their cases, but their prosecutions are not extant. Only the sentence and trial against Muñoz are included in the current file. For the sentence against Muñoz, see AGN, Inq., vol. 9, exp. 2, fol. 120.

55. It is difficult to provide an equivalence, but a *maravedí* was a medieval coin, no longer in circulation in the sixteenth century, worth ⅓₄ of a real, which was itself valued at ⅛ of a peso. In short, "two maravedíes" was a phrase intended to indicate a sum of little value, i.e., pennies.

56. AGN, Inq., vol. 9, exp. 1.

57. Muñoz held Acolman and Capula in encomienda until 1528, and Xiquipilco from at least 1537, though possibly as early as 1529. Gerhard, 160, 175–176, 312, 344; Himmerich y Valencia, 203–204; Warren, *Conquest of Michoacán*, 215. He held Xiquipilco in encomienda as late as 1543. See AGN, Mercedes, vol. 2, exp. 567, fol. 230.

58. See Chapter 1.

59. AGN, Mercedes, vol. 2, exp. 567, fol. 230.

60. Ibid., vol. 5, exp. s/n, fol. 215.

61. We have no records regarding the excommunication portion of the litigation, which was probably contested in communication or at the diocesan court.

62. AGN, Inq., vol. 11, exp. 4, fol. 304: "Mierda para la notificación y para la de escomunión y para quien me lo notificare."

63. Ibid., vol. 11, exp. 4.

64. The rancher who offered shit balls (*cagajones*) for the saints was Pedro de Trejo, prosecuted twice for heresy and blasphemy, in 1569 and 1574. See Ibid., vol. 8, exp. 2; vol. 113, exp. 1.

65. The connections between filth and sociocultural taboo were famously explored by Mary Douglas in *Purity and Danger: An Analysis of Concepts of Pollution and Taboo* (New York: Routledge, 2002).

66. Valerie Allen, *On Farting: Language and Laughter in the Middle Ages* (New York: Palgrave Macmillan, 2010), 3, in her hilarious history of the philosophy of bodily detritus and "butthole scholarship." Martin Luther's untranslated "table talks" are notoriously scatological. See *Tischreden* (Berlin: Evangelische Verlagsanstalt, c. 1948).

67. Early modern Spaniards were supposed to be the sharp end of the Counter-Reformation stick, yet studies of popular religion suggest distrust of centralized Catholicism. See, for example, Jodi Bilinkoff, *The Avila of Saint Teresa: Religious Reform in a Sixteenth-Century City* (Ithaca, NY: Cornell University Press, 1989); Sara T. Nalle, *God in La Mancha: Religious Reform and the People of Cuenca, 1500–1650* (Baltimore: Johns Hopkins University Press, 2008).

68. Luther had little core popularity in sixteenth-century Spain beyond the opinion of many that he was an okay guy and had some good ideas about the stupidity of tithing and indulgences. See John Longhurst, *Luther's Ghost in Spain (1517–1546)* (Lawrence, KS: Coronado, 1969). For an intellectual history of Luther's supposed theological presence (despite the general absence of his printed works) in New Spain, see Alicia Mayer, *Lutero en el Paraíso: La Nueva España en el espejo del reformador alemán* (Mexico City: Fondo de Cultura Económica; UNAM, Instituto de Investigaciones Históricas, 2008).

69. Quoted in John Witte Jr., "'The Law Written on the Heart': Natural Law and Equity in Early Lutheran Thought," in Wim Decock, Jordan J. Ballor, Michael Germann, and Laurent Waelkins, eds., *Law and Religion: The Legal Teachings of the Protestant and Catholic Reformations* (Göttingen, Germany: Vandenhoeck and Ruprecht, 2014), 231.

70. For analysis of his scatological language from a theological perspective, see Heiko A. Ober-

man, *Luther: Man Between God and the Devil*, trans. Eileen Walliser-Schwarzbart (New Haven, CT: Yale University Press, 1989), 106–110. Though not explicitly focused on language, Erik Erikson's notorious psychohistorical analysis of Luther explained his personality in terms of Freudian developmental stages (including—of course—the anal stage). See Erikson, *Young Man Luther: A Study in Psychoanalysis and History* (New York: Norton, 1958). For anti-Catholic propaganda, see Miriam Usher Chrisman, "From Polemic to Propaganda: The Development of Mass Persuasion in the Late Sixteenth Century," *Archiv für Reformationsgeschichte-Archive for Reformation History* 73 (1982): 175–196; Robert Scribner, *For the Sake of Simple Folk: Popular Propaganda for the German Reformation* (Cambridge: Cambridge University Press, 1981).

71. AGN, Inq., vol. 20, exp. 2: "Votaba a Dios que no abía de sembrar por no pagar diezmo."

72. Ibid.

73. The case file described her variously as *morisca* (a vaguely defined term meaning someone mostly Spanish and partly African, or a Moor), *morena* (a generic term for a dark-skinned woman), and *mulata* (of African and Spanish background).

74. AGN, Inq., vol. 38, exp. 10, fol. 237.

75. Ibid., vol. 39, exp. 2.

76. Susan Socolow, *The Women of Colonial Latin America* (Cambridge: Cambridge University Press, 2000), 53–54; Peter Boyd-Bowman, *Patterns of Spanish Emigration to the New World (1493–1580)*, Special Studies No. 34 (Buffalo, NY: SUNY Buffalo, Council on International Studies, 1973).

77. Richard Boyer, *Lives of the Bigamists: Marriage, Family, and Community in Colonial Mexico* (Albuquerque: University of New Mexico Press, 1995).

78. AGN, Inq., vol. 104, exp. 3.

79. Ibid., vol. 66, exp. 8. He received a license from the Casa de Contratación to travel to New Spain on 15 April 1535. See AGI, Contratación, 5536, vol. l, exp. 3, fol. 213(5).

80. Óscar Mazín Gómez, *El cabildo catedral de Valladolid de Michoacán* (Zamora, Mexico: El Colegio de Michoacán, 1996), 90.

81. AGN, Inq., vol. 66, exp. 8, fols. 155–170. A copy of this genealogy appears as part of his nephew Rodrigo's 1575 application to be an inquisitional official, included in the same archival file.

82. Mazín Gómez, *Cabildo catedral*, 83, 86; Ricardo León Alanís, *Los orígenes del clero y la iglesia en Michoacán, 1525–1640* (Morelia, Mexico: Universidad Michoacana de San Nicolás de Hidalgo, Instituto de Investigaciones Históricas, 1997), 160, 314. In 1560, Pedro Díaz requested a canonship to replace Yepes, who was promoted from canon to treasurer.

83. AGN, Inq., vol. 10, exp. 8; vol. 20, exp. 2; vol. 21, exp. 3; vol. 39, exps. 2, 3; vol. 45, exp. 3; vol. 46, exp. 4; vol. 72, exps. 8, 12 (*dos procesos*); vol. 109, exps. 3, 6; vol. 110, exps. 2, 5, 7; vol. 111, exps. 2, 12; vol. 114, exp. 1; vol. 116, exp. 2; vol. 181, exp. 2.

84. On 3 September 1579, he was alive; on 30 July 1580 a notary document listed him as deceased. See *Vida michoacana*, 128, 134. By contrast, Zumárraga prosecuted 110 cases in six years (1536–1541), delegating several others to auxiliary judges: see AGN, Inq., vols. 1, 2, 14, 22, 23, 30, 34, 36–38, 40, 42, 125, 212. For discussion of his tenure and activity, see Richard Greenleaf, *Zumárraga and the Mexican Inquisition, 1536–1543* (Washington, D.C.: Academy of American Franciscan History, 1961).

85. AGN, Inq., vol. 110, exp. 2.

86. Ibid., exp. 5.

87. León Alanís, *Orígenes*, 160, 309, 314, 316.

88. Ibid., 309, 314, 316.

89. Ibid., 283–285, 320.

90. As attested in a case in December 1562 against Hernando Ortiz, who swore in public in front of Yepes's stores. See AGN, Inq., vol. 17, exp. 19, fol. 481.

91. León Alanís, *Orígenes*, 283–285.

92. *Vida michoacana*, 92.

93. León Alanís, *Orígenes*, 236.

94. ACCM, Ramo Colegio de San Nicolás, leg. 4, exp. 20.

95. Stafford Poole, *Pedro Moya de Contreras: Catholic Reform and Royal Power in New Spain, 1571–1591* (Berkeley: University of California Press, 1987), 30–33.

96. AGN, Indiferente Virreinal, Inq. caja 5304, exp. 61, fols. 5v–6r.

97. For an analysis of his life as a poet and of his poetry, see Luis Carlos Arredondo Treviño, "Obra completa de Pedro de Trejo" (Tesis de maestría, Universidad Autónoma de Nuevo León, 1995); Edmundo O'Gorman, ed., "Poesías sagradas y profanas de Pedro de Trejo (1569)," *Boletín del Archivo General de la Nación* 15, no. 2 (1944): 209–312; Francisco Pérez Salazar, "Las obras y desventuras de Pedro de Trejo en la Nueva España del siglo XVI," *Revista de literatura mexicana* 1 (1940): 117–132.

98. AGN, Inq., vol. 72, exp. 37, fol. 295.

99. Ibid., vol. 116, exp. 9, fol. 308.

100. Ibid., vol. 46, exp. 4, fol. 21.

101. Elegantly expressed by Bartolomé Bennassar, "Modelos de la mentalidad inquisitorial: Métodos de su 'pedagogía de miedo,'" in Ángel Alcalá, ed., *Inquisición española y mentalidad inquisitorial* (Barcelona: Ariel, 1984); reprised by Javier Villa-Flores, "Wandering Swindlers: Imposture, Style, and the Inquisition's Pedagogy of Fear in Colonial Mexico," *Colonial Latin American Review* 17 (2008): 251–272. James Given's classic study of power and Inquisition in southern France, *Inquisition and Medieval Society*, suggests that the Inquisition employed technologies of fear, but that there was considerable resistance to its political hegemony. The ability of the Inquisition to harness a pedagogy of fear was limited; local citizens even stole the symbolic powers of punishment of the Inquisition only to mock them. See, for example, Luis Corteguera, *Death by Effigy: A Case from the Mexican Inquisition* (Philadelphia: University of Pennsylvania Press, 2014).

102. Expressed notably in R. I. Moore, *The Formation of a Persecuting Society: Power and Deviance in Western Europe, 950–1250* (Oxford: Blackwell, 1987). David Nirenberg's study *Communities of Violence: Persecution of Minorities in the Middle Ages* (Princeton, NJ: Princeton University Press, 1998) follows in a similar line, though he argues that violence was rational, an expression of a new language of repression. For a nuanced discussion of martyrdom and a superb study of medieval southern France, see Louisa A. Burnham, *So Great a Light, So Great a Smoke: The Beguin Heretics of Languedoc* (Ithaca, NY: Cornell University Press, 2008).

103. See Henry Kamen, *The Phoenix and the Flame: Catalonia and the Counter Reformation* (New Haven, CT: Yale University Press, 1993), and *The Spanish Inquisition: A Historical Revision*, 4th rev. ed. (New Haven, CT: Yale University Press, 2014), and Josefina Edith Ruiz y Torres, "A puerta cerrada: Lectura e inquisición en el siglo XVI novohispano" (Tesis de licenciatura, Escuela Nacional de Antropología e Historia [México], 1998).

104. Notably in Irene Silverblatt, *Modern Inquisitions: Peru and the Colonial Origins of the Civilized World* (Durham, NC: Duke University Press, 2004).

105. Loath as I am to invoke the most over-invoked theorist of the late twentieth century, it seems apt here to use the most terrible F-word of our language: Foucault. In his study of sexuality, he asked why, if Victorians were so repressive, everyone was so obsessed with talking about sex all the time. His "repressive thesis" is most clearly elaborated in Michel Foucault, *The History of Sexu-*

ality, vol. 1, trans. Robert Hurley (New York: Pantheon Books, 1978). If prisons were so successful at surveilling everything and everyone, why would there be a need to inscribe the panopticon into legible treatises? Echoes of this concern about surveillance and the obsessive need to record the results are found in Michel Foucault, *Discipline and Punish: The Birth of the Prison*, trans. Alan Sheridan (New York: Pantheon Books, 1977). For a study that argues in explicitly Foucauldian terms that confession and Inquisition in medieval France produced a "discipline and punish" power dynamic, see John H. Arnold, *Inquisition and Power: Cathars and the Confessing Subject in Medieval Languedoc* (Philadelphia: University of Pennsylvania Press, 2001).

CHAPTER 4

1. Several letters complaining about Badillo's conduct in 1577 repeated that the Inquisition should be of grand authority but that Badillo was not. See the discussion below. The letters are found in AGN, Inq., vol. 83, exp. 1.

2. Ibid., vol. 80, exp. 9, fol. 227.

3. Ibid., vol. 78, exp. 10, fol. 236.

4. Ibid., vol. 66, exp. 8.

5. Ibid., vol. 80, exp. 9.

6. Ibid., vol. 83, exp. 1.

7. See Ángel Alcalá, "Herejía y jerarquía: La polémica sobre el Tribunal de Inquisición como desacato y usurpación de la jurisdicción episcopal," José Antonio Escudero, "Inquisidor General y Consejo de la Suprema: Dudas sobre competencias en nombramientos," and Antonio González de San Segundo, "Tensiones y conflictos de la Inquisición en Indias: La pre-Inquisición o Inquisición primitiva (1493–1569)," in José Antonio Escudero, ed., *Perfiles jurídicos de la inquisición española* (Madrid: Instituto de Historia de la Inquisición, 1989); Ma. del Carmen Espinosa, "Conflictos políticos y jurisdiccionales en la inquisición Episcopal a mediados del siglo XVI," in Noemí Quezada, Martha Eugenia Rodríguez, and Marcela Suárez, eds., *Inquisición novohispana*, 2 vols. (Mexico City: UNAM, 2000).

8. Inquisitors general periodically issued summaries of inquisitional law and procedural instructions in lieu of extensive inquisitional manuals, such as Nicolau Eymeric's *Directorium Inquisitorum* (Rome: In aedibus pop. rom., 1578), which were often in short supply outside of the private libraries of high-ranking jurists and clerics, universities, and major friaries. See "Las instrucciones de la Inquisición española: De Torquemada a Valdés (1484–1561)," in Escudero, ed., *Perfiles jurídicos de la Inquisición española*. For an overview of questions of competence, see Jaime Contreras, "La infraestructura social de la inquisición: Comisarios y familiares," in Ángel Alcalá, ed., *Inquisición española y mentalidad inquisitorial* (Barcelona: Editorial Ariel, 1984).

9. Carlos Herrejón Peredo, *Los orígenes de Morelia: Guayangareo-Valladolid*, 2nd ed., foreword by Juan Carlos Ruiz Guadalajara (Mexico City: Frente de Afirmación Hispanista; Zamora, Mexico: El Colegio de Michoacán, 2000); Rodrigo Martínez Baracs, *Convivencia y utopía: El gobierno indio y español de la "ciudad de Mechuacan," 1521–1580* (Mexico City: INAH; Fondo de Cultura Económica, 2005).

10. In his confession before inquisitors in August 1577 (AGN, Inq., vol. 83, exp. 1, fol. 89), Badillo said he was forty years old, which would put his birth around 1537, but his *méritos y servicios* of 1566 (see note 12 below) suggests he was born in 1540. John F. Schwaller, *The Church and Clergy in Sixteenth Century Mexico* (Albuquerque: University of New Mexico Press, 1987), 35, pegs his birth at 1539.

11. One witness testimony for Diego de Orduña's defense in 1575 refers to Badillo as "Don"

(AGN, Inq., vol. 80, exp. 9), but otherwise this does not appear in regular documentation. Juan de Benavides, the notary for the investigation against Badillo in 1577 by Bishop Medina, also generically refers to Badillo as Don (AGN, Inq., vol. 83, exp. 1). But correspondence from inquisitors generally did not use this title for Badillo.

12. The outline of this trajectory is summarized in his *méritos y servicios* deposition before the Mexico Audiencia in January 1566 (which included copies from a 1560 deposition drawn up in Seville) (AGI, México 281). Many thanks to Tatiana Seijas for dragging a photocopy of this case file across an ocean for me from Seville. Other portions of the 1566 *méritos y servicios* exist in AGI, México 209n2. Witness statements in his *méritos y servicios* petitions all say, in January 1566, that Badillo had lived in Mexico City for two or two and a half years.

13. AGI, México 209n2.

14. Ibid.; AGI, México 281.

15. AGI, México 211n5.

16. AGI, México 209n2. He oversaw one case in the Yucatán, in AGN, Inq., vol. 7, exp. 13, which refers to him as licenciado.

17. Michoacán cathedral canon Juan de Velasco repeated the rumor. See AGN, Inq., vol. 80, exp. 9, fols. 212, 217.

18. AGI, México 211n5. See Schwaller, *Church and Clergy*, 36.

19. AGI, México 211n5. The licenciado exam in law required that the applicant quote verbatim and comment on an undisclosed chapter of the law.

20. Schwaller, *Church and Clergy*, 35–37.

21. Alberto María Carreño, *La Real y Pontificia Universidad de México 1536–1865* (Mexico City: UNAM, 1961); Cristóbal Bernardo de la Plaza y Jaén, *Crónica de la real y pontificia universidad de México*, ed. Nicolás Rangel (Mexico City: Talleres Gráficos del Museo Nacional de Arqueología, Historia y Etnografía, 1931).

22. AGN, Inq., vol. 63, exp. 3; vol. 86, exp. 44.

23. Schwaller, *Church and Clergy*, 37.

24. AGN, Inq., vol. 63, exp. 3.

25. For studies of the relative liberality of Spanish and Spanish-American urban life in the sixteenth and seventeenth centuries, see José N. Alcalá-Zamora, ed., *La vida cotidiana en la España de Velázquez* (Madrid: Ediciones Tema de Hoy, 1999); Irving A. Leonard, *Baroque Times in Old Mexico: Seventeenth-Century Persons, Places, and Practices* (Ann Arbor: University of Michigan Press, 1959); Francisco Núñez Roldán, *La vida cotidiana en la Sevilla del Siglo de Oro* (Madrid: Sílex, 2004), and *Ocio y vida quotidiana en el mundo hispánico en la Edad Moderna* (Seville, Spain: Universidad de Sevilla, 2007).

26. AGN, Inq., vol. 80, exp. 9, fol. 227.

27. Ibid., vol. 99, exp. 5, and AGN, Indiferente Virreinal, Inq. caja 5304, exp. 61, fol. 53.

28. AGN, Inq., vol. 80, exp. 9, fol. 233.

29. *Vida michoacana*, 238.

30. AGI, México 209n2.

31. *Vida michoacana*, 109.

32. Ibid., 112.

33. AGN, Inq., vol. 80, exp. 9, fol. 233: "Dixo al arçediano sois un desvergonçado rapaz que pareció tan mal de un hombre Viejo. . . . y respondióle el arçediano con toda modestia assí tratáis a los officiales comissarios del santo offiçio."

34. AGN, Inq., vol. 80, exp. 9, fol. 231.

35. Ibid., fols. 235–239.

36. Ibid., fol. 227.

37. Ibid., vol. 78, exp. 10, fol. 236.

38. Ibid.

39. The original signed commission for the position is not extant. The cover sheet of his application, AGN, Inq., vol. 66, exp. 8, fol. 136, states that he was nominated for the position of comisario, but it also notes: "Información de la limpieza del linage de Rodrigo de Yepes, nombrado del comisario deste Santo Oficio en Mechoacán." Rodrigo de Yepes did serve as the inquisitional notary on one notorious case—the prosecution of cathedral canon Orduña for his assault on the comisario Badillo in witness statements in August 1575. See AGN, Inq., vol. 80, exp. 9.

40. A man who signed a 22 July 1577 letter from the convened cathedral chapter in Michoacán signed as "el canónigo Go[nzalo] Yepes." See AGN, Inq., vol. 83, exp. 1, fol. 20. Also see Ricardo León Alanís, Los orígenes del clero y la iglesia en Michoacán, 1525–1640 (Morelia, Mexico: Universidad Michoacana de San Nicolás de Hidalgo, Instituto de Investigaciones Históricas, 1997), 322.

41. A linguistic curiosity is that the term employed was zacate, a Nahuatlism.

42. AGN, Inq., vol. 80, exp. 16.

43. Ibid., exp. 9.

44. For the cultural script concerning seating arrangements, such as the relative status of a certain kind of chair or cushion, with particular relevance to physical church settings, see Sonya Lipsett-Rivera, Gender and Negotiation of Everyday Life in Mexico, 1750–1856 (Lincoln: University of Nebraska Press, 2012), 2–3, 19, 252.

45. AGN, Inq., vol. 80, exp. 9.

46. Ibid., vol. 72, exp. 12; vol. 80, exp. 9.

47. Ibid., vol. 190, exp. 7, lists his genealogy. When in 1575 he appeared before inquisitors in Mexico City, he claimed to be forty years old. See AGN, Inq., vol. 80, exp. 9, fol. 165.

48. Decades later, in 1582, when he applied to be an inquisitional agent, he submitted this genealogy to the Mexican Inquisition, which recorded the petition as submitted by "Don Diego de Orduña, maestrescuela de Michoacán." See AGN, Inq., vol. 190, exp. 7. I thank Linda Arnold for providing a digital copy of this document, which I had read in the AGN several years ago, but of which I had no copy for cross-reference when I revised this manuscript.

49. León Alanís, Orígenes, 242.

50. AGN, Inq., vol. 44, exp. 5.

51. León Alanís, Orígenes, 283–285, 306–312. Parish priests in the 1560s and 1570s received salaries of about 150 pesos, cathedral canons around 180 pesos.

52. AGN, Inq., vol. 39, exp. 2; vol. 72, exp. 12.

53. Schwaller, Church and Clergy, 81.

54. AGN, Inq., vol. 80, exp. 9.

55. Ibid., fol. 245: "El dicho Andrés García dixo que apelaua de todo porque tenía por sospechoso a su señoría diziendo que al Obispo y al dicho vicario y al dicho Francisco de Hermosilla [']nos tenía a todos por sospechosos e vió que yo [Hermosilla] le dixe no tenéis razón que el obispo mi señor haze siempre justiciar sin pasión y así hazemos lo que nos manda['] que entonces el padre vicario le dixo es bellacamente ablado eso que vos no abéis de poner lengua en el Obispo."

56. AGN, Inq., vol. 80, exp. 9, fol. 245. Continuing from above: "Se fue hazia a Andrés García que auía respondido al dicho vicario . . . el dicho vicario dixo al dicho alcalde mayor que como era notorio clérigo y vicario en estas minas que no le prendiese."

57. Ibid., fols. 243–245.

58. Ibid., fol. 258v.

59. The original trial against Orduña in 1570 does not appear to be extant, but a copy of the

investigation was drawn up when Orduña was charged in 1575 for assaulting Badillo. In the copy drawn up, it appears that Orduña was given a rather severe sentence. See AGN, Inq., vol. 80, exp. 9.

60. AGN, Inq., vol. 80, exp. 9.

61. Ibid.

62. Numerous witnesses in the 1577 investigation into Badillo's behavior attested to his ostentatious dress. See AGN, Inq., vol. 83, exp. 1.

63. AGN, Inq., vol. 80, exp. 9, fol. 1. The alcalde, in a covering letter to inquisitors, referred to Orduña as *canónigo* (canon).

64. AGN, Inq., vol. 80, exp. 9, fol. 149v.

65. Ibid., fol. 167: "Una falsa artifiçiosa y estudiada confesión de su culpa en que añadiendo delicto a delicto se [h]a perjurado."

66. AGN, Inq., vol. 80, exp. 9.

67. Ibid., vol. 104, exp. 12.

68. Martínez Baracs, *Convivencia y utopía*, 367.

69. León Alanís, *Orígenes*, 136–137.

70. AGN, Inq., vol. 80, exp. 16.

71. Ibid., fol. 331.

72. Ibid., vol. 80, exp. 16.

73. Ibid., fol. 350: "Así juntos se acordó ser el conocimiento y castigo deste de la justicia real y así lo auemos declarado pesándonos mucho de que el mal término inquietud y liuiandad del Rodrigo de Yepes nos aya atado las manos de nuestro poder y jurisdicción." We also have the case file of his genealogy and application to be an inquisitional official. The cover sheet, in AGN, Inq., vol. 66, exp. 8, notes that the Inquisition had revoked his title for a criminal case in the Inquisition's secret court for his resisting an alcalde's authority: "Información de la limpieza del linage de Rodrigo de Yepes, nombrado del comisario deste Santo Oficio en Mechoacán. Tiene título. Quitósele. Quitósele el títtulo por cierto delito que cometió en Mechoacán resistiendo a un alcalde hordinario de que ay proçeso en el secreto entre el dicho proçeso de offiçiales y familiares."

74. For excellent analyses of cases of imposture, manipulation of the pedagogy of fear and punishment, and inquisitional responses in colonial Mexico, see Luis R. Corteguera, *Death by Effigy: A Case from the Mexican Inquisition* (Philadelphia: University of Pennsylvania Press, 2014), and Javier Villa-Flores, "Wandering Swindlers: Imposture, Style, and the Inquisition's Pedagogy of Fear in Colonial Mexico," *Colonial Latin American Review* 17 (2008): 251–272. For a fascinating analysis of religious "underworlds" that considers related topics, while not explicitly ascribing to the Bennassar thesis, see Matthew D. O'Hara, "The Orthodox Underworld of Colonial Mexico," *Colonial Latin American Review* 17 (2008): 233–250.

75. The file for the civil case against Rodrigo de Yepes is not extant, but Badillo referenced it in his correspondence with the inquisitors of 30 November. See AGN, Inq., vol. 80, exp. 16, fol. 351.

76. *Corsarios franceses e ingleses en la Inquisición de la Nueva España, siglo XVI* (Mexico City: Archivo General de la Nación; Imprenta Universitaria, 1945).

77. AGN, Inq., vol. 80, exp. 25.

78. Ibid., exp. 9, fol. 164.

79. Ibid., fol. 277.

80. Ibid., vol. 227, exp. s/n, fols. 219–220.

81. Ibid., vol. 80, exp. 9, fol. 280r.

82. Ibid., vol. 223, exp. 18, fol. 50 [47].

83. Ibid., vol. 80, exp. 9, fol. 281.

84. Ibid., fol. 282; AGN, Indiferente Virreinal, Inq. caja 5304, exp. 61, fol. 32.

85. A *ladina* (Spanish-speaking) indigenous woman, Gerónima de Contreras, called in an unrelated investigation, said that she lived on Orduña's estate in Apaceo in July 1580. See AGN, vol. 229, exp. s/n, fol. 151.

86. AGN, Inq., vol. 80, exp. 9, fols. 284r, 286–288.

87. Ibid., fols. 286–288.

88. Ibid., fol. 284r.

89. Ibid., fol. 288v.

90. Ibid., fol. 285.

91. A letter dated 27 May 1577 from the Michoacán cathedral chapter to the inquisitors is signed by, among others, "el maestrescuela de Mechoacán," in Orduña's distinct hand. See AGN, Inq., vol. 83, exp. 1, fol. 23r. Likewise, witnesses called against Badillo in July 1577 referred to Orduña as the maestrescuela, though Orduña was not summoned in the case. See AGN, Inq., vol. 83, exp. 1, fols. 59v, 61v.

92. Ibid., fols. 8–9. Words like "loose" (from *libre*) and "giggle" (*da voces*) are contextual translations based on the tone of the letter, which, in today's language, we would characterize as vaguely homophobic and racist: "Entiendo que si uviese personas que abisasen a Vuestra Señoría . . . aviso que el comisario Vadillo no tiene el término que debe en el usar de su ofiçio porque no guarda en el secreto que era justo antes trata los negocios muy al descubierto, haciendo alharacas y ruidos amenazando los hombres y disfamándolos. Es hombre que no tiene las calidades que se requieren para semejante ofiçio. Muéstrase liviano y de poca autoridad siendo çacerdote arcediano comisario del santo ofiçio. Váse a las bodas y desposorios dondequiera que los ay. Come y bebe demasiado de donde le causan algunas libiandades. Amigo de mujeres al descubierto. Es libre anda de noche con armas házese temer. Presume de rico. Trata y contrata al descubierto. Es bullicioso demasiado. Mal gusto y toma vasido [?] y opinions. Bayla con la novia públicamente con hoga y beca y bonete. Haze burlas de manos. Tócase como mujer y viste de sayas. Y hazela parida diziendo que quiere parir que le llamen la partera y da bozes diziendo que ya está parida y otras cosas semejantes que son de hombres bajos y plebeyes y no de su calidad. Asimismo se dize públicamente que es de casta sospechosa morisco y riñiéndose con el selo an dicho en la cara. Y dize que es de esa casta que es de los caballeros turcos de Turquía."

93. AGN, Inq., vol. 83, exp. 1.

94. Ibid., vol. 80, exp. 9.

95. Ibid., vol. 83, exp. 1.

96. Ibid., fol. 29. The letter from Bishop Medina of 19 July 1577 to inquisitors is the only time I have seen reference to the family connection between Infante and Farfán, though others may have noted this. On Infante, see Gerhard, 344–345; Himmerich y Valencia, 177.

97. AGN, Inq., vol. 83, exp. 1, fol. 33: "El arçediano como lo supo vino a mí mui desbaratado con la color mudada echando fuego por los ojos pidiéndome que le diese los proçesos. Yo lo rrespondí con todo comedimiento que no se le podían dar porque era no hacer el deuer con forma a justiçia que no era justo entregar el proçeso a las partes que viniese un letrado . . . respondió con mucho enojo que cosas de más calidad se fiauan del y no faltó sino meterme los dedos en los ojos sin rrespetarme como a hombre que tenía la vara de su magestad."

98. AGN, Inq., vol. 83, exp. 1, fol. 20.

99. Ibid., vol. 7, exp. 12. I discuss the case in Chapter 3.

100. Ibid., vol. 83, exp. 1, fols. 8–9: "Tócase como mujer y viste de sayas. Y haze la parida diziendo que quiere parir que le llamen la partera y da bozes diziendo que ya está parida."

101. Ibid., fol. 31.

102. Ibid., fols. 111–113.

103. Ibid., fols. 115–116: "Él no a ido a la iglesia sino aquel y aquel fiesta y no a hecho nada sino buscar papeles. . . . ni diçe missa ni aún la oye que sola una cantada pareçe a dicho despues que desa çiudad vino sin officio . . . y como no ay aquí letrado acude a el pleiteçillos y aboga se [ha] hecho gran amigo del maestrescuela."

104. AGN, Inq., vol. 174, exp. 1, fols. 6–13.

105. León Alanís, *Orígenes*, 237.

106. AGN, Inq., vol. 190, exp. 7.

107. León Alanís, *Orígenes*, 237–238, says 1584; Schwaller, *Church and Clergy*, 37, says 1583.

108. AGN, Inq., vol. 83, exp. 1.

109. The events were notorious enough that in 1648 a cathedral canon, Francisco Arnaldo de Ysassy, discussed the case in a report on the history of the diocese commissioned by the Crown. The report is found in the Ayer Collection in the Newberry Library in Chicago. For its transcription, see Arnaldo de Ysassy, "Demarcación y descripción de el obispado de Mechuacán y fundación de su Iglesia Catedral," in *Bibliotheca Americana* 1 (1982): 60–178.

110. Schwaller, *Church and Clergy*, 37–39.

111. AGN, Inq., vol. 190, exp. 7.

112. See Alejandro Cañeque, *The King's Living Image: The Culture and Politics of Viceregal Power in Colonial Mexico* (New York: Routledge, 2004), and Steven C. Caton, "Anthropological Theories of Tribe and State Formation in the Middle East: Ideology and the Semiotics of Power," in Philip S. Khoury and Joseph Kostiner, eds., *Tribes and State Formation in the Middle East* (Berkeley: University of California Press, 1990).

113. Lipsett-Rivera, *Gender and the Negotiation of Everyday Life*, 172. "Grammar of violence" has also been used in the modern context to analyze heterosexual rape as violence that operates according to a cultural script. See Sharon Marcus, "Fighting Bodies, Fighting Words: A Theory and Politics of Rape Prevention," in Constance L. Mui and Julien S. Murphy, eds., *Gender Struggles: Practical Approaches to Contemporary Feminism* (Lanham, MD: Rowman and Littlefield, 2002), 166–185.

114. María Alejandra Fernández, "Familias en conflicto: Entre el honor y la deshonra," *Boletín del Instituto de Historia Argentina y Americana* 3a serie, nú. 20 (1999), 14: "La injuria ha sido interpretada como una metáfora social."

115. Marta Madero, *Manos violentas, palabras vedadas: La injuria en Castilla y León (siglos XIII–XV)* (Madrid: Taurus, 1992), 21, cited also in Fernández, "Familias en conflicto."

116. For further discussion of class-based assumptions about the nature of public honor, dignity, and acceptable levels of violence in early modern Spanish culture, see Julio Caro Baroja, "Religión, visiones del mundo, clases sociales, y honor durante los siglos XVI y XVII en España," in Julian Pitt-Rivers and John Peristiany, eds., *Honor y gracia* (Madrid: Alianza, 1993); Lyman L. Johnson and Sonya Lipsett-Rivera, eds., *The Faces of Honor: Sex, Shame, and Violence in Colonial Latin America* (Albuquerque: University of New Mexico Press, 1998).

CHAPTER 5

1. José Corona Núñez, *Carácuaro de Morelos* (Morelia, Mexico: Universidad Michoacana de San Nicolás de Hidalgo, 1991), 30, recounts a tale that colonial peoples told about the friar Bautista riding a river caiman. Escobar, 116–117, tells of the missionaries' terror of the region, enumerating various poisonous plants, including *venberecua*, *chupiri* (a tree, probably *Euphorbia calyculata*, which emits a burning sap—the word comes from the Purépecha word for "to burn"), and a plant

identified as *Rhus infarta testes* (probably a type of poison oak or poison sumac; different species of *Rhus*, usually a poison oak or sumac, exist in Mexico, but one type of poison ivy is sometimes colloquially called *hinchahuevos*). It is a little unclear to what species Escobar was referring. Escobar said he would not name it in Spanish in order not to offend innocent ears: "Hay otro árbol cuyo nombre omito (*Rhus infarta testes*) por no manchar castos oídos, es tan cálida su sombra, y tan maligno su contacto, que es suficiente éste para llenar de horrorosas vejigas al que llega a coger una rama o tocar una hoja" (p. 117). Witnesses in a 1597 case before the Crown who asked for Colima's jurisdiction to be moved to Guadalajara told of citizens who had attempted the long journey and perished on the way because of the changes in climate, the altitude, the raging rivers, or starvation. The same witnesses explained that there were no inns or places to eat in the remote mountain areas: AGI, Guadalajara 48n24. One cacao plantation, Zalaguacan, somewhere southeast of the city of Colima in the mountainous area near Alima in Montines, lay in ruins when its owner, Doña Isabel Ruiz de Monjaraz, died intestate in 1590. Archivo Histórico del Municipio de Colima (Municipal Historical Archive of Colima), Colima, Mexico (AHMC hereafter), caja A-12, exp. 7.

2. The marital dispute first appeared in 1552 in AHMC, caja A-2, exp. 5. For transcriptions of this and the statement of Preciado about lawyers, see AVC, 1:43, 57. Preciado's statement: "Digo que ya es notorio como en esta Provincia no hay letrado."

3. José Miguel Romero de Solís, *Andariegos y pobladores: Nueva España y Nueva Galicia (siglo XVI)* (Colima, Mexico: Universidad de Colima, 2001), 436.

4. For an excellent overview of the political history of colonial Colima, see Claudia Paulina Machuca Chávez, *El cabildo de la villa de Colima en los albores del siglo XVII* (Colima, Mexico: Universidad de Colima, 2009).

5. Various sustained indigenous appeals against the predations of Spanish plantation owners are found in AGN, Congregaciones, vol. 1; AGN, Indios, vol. 2, exps. 229, 230, 231, 274; AGN, Mercedes, vol. 4, fols. 265v, 267r-v, 269v, 270r-v; AGN, Tierras, vol. 37, exp. 1; vol. 2811, exps. 11, 12; vol. 2926, exp. 7.

6. James C. Scott, *The Art of Not Being Governed: An Anarchist History of Upland Southeast Asia* (New Haven, CT: Yale University Press, 2009), *pace* Gonzalo Aguirre Beltrán, *Regiones de refugio: El desarrollo de la comunidad y el proceso dominical en mestizo América* (Mexico City: Instituto Nacional Indigenista, 1967).

7. The literature on indigenous vassals seeking legal regress through appeal is extensive. See Woodrow Borah, *Justice by Insurance: The General Indian Court of Colonial Mexico and the Legal Aides of the Half-Real* (Berkeley: University of California Press, 1983); Tamar Herzog, "Colonial Law and 'Native Customs': Indigenous Land Rights in Colonial Spanish America," *The Americas* 69 (2013): 303–321; Brian Owensby, *Empire of Law and Indian Justice in Colonial Mexico* (Stanford, CA: Stanford University Press, 2008).

8. Indigenous communities appealed to abuse of authority in a wide range of cases. They asked the viceroy to prohibit their forced labor as *tamemes*—or bearers, who carried a variety of goods on their backs—and in road construction from the 1550s to the 1580s. See AGN, Indios, vol. 2, exps. 229, 230, 231, and AGN, Mercedes, vol. 4, fols. 265v, 267r-v, 269v, 270r-v. Other disputes concerned unfair labor practices and poor pay. See AGN, Indios, vol. 2, exp. 274. Still other communities resisted forced resettlement in the first decade of the seventeenth century. See AGN, Congregaciones, vol. 1, fols. 14–16, and AGN, Tierras, vol. 2926, exp. 7.

9. AGN, Tierras, vol. 2811, exp. 5.

10. We have no reliable information for the pre-1520s, but as early as the 1540s various geographic summaries and sociolinguistic details emerge. See Donald Brand, *Coalcoman and Mo-*

tines de Oro: An Ex-Distrito of Michoacán, Mexico (The Hague: Published for the Institute of Latin American Studies at the University of Texas, Austin, by Martinus Nijhoff, 1960), and *Coastal Study of Southwest Mexico* (Austin: Department of Geography, University of Texas, 1957–1958); "Juicio seguido por Hernán Cortés contra los licenciados Matienzo y Delgadillo," *Boletín del Archivo General de la Nación* 9 (1938): 339–407; Carl O. Sauer, *Colima of New Spain in the Sixteenth Century* (Berkeley: University of California Press, 1948); "Vecinos y pueblos en Colima en 1532," *Boletín del Archivo General de la Nación* 10 (1939): 5–23.

11. Brand, *Coalcoman and Motines*.

12. Ramón López Lara, *El obispado de Michoacán en el siglo XVII—informe inédito de beneficios, pueblos y lenguas* (Morelia, Mexico: Fímax, 1973), 128–130. Also see Gerhard, 192–193.

13. "Relación de Quacomán" of 1580, quoted in Sauer, *Colima*, 71.

14. Gonzalo Aguirre Beltrán, *Problemas de la población indígena de la Cuenca de Tepalcatepec* (Mexico City: Instituto Nacional Indigenista, 1952), 76; Sauer, *Colima*, 24–25.

15. The feud is well known. For some discussion of the dispute over Colima, see "Juicio seguido por Hernán Cortés contra los licenciados Matienzo y Delgadillo," *Boletín del Archivo General de la Nación* 8 (1937): 556–572; "Nuño de Guzmán contra Cortés sobre los descubrimientos y conquistas de Jalisco y Tepic [1531]," *Boletín del Archivo General de la Nación* 8 (1937): 365–400.

16. Gerhard, 78–79, 192–193, 338–339.

17. AVC, 1:63.

18. Sauer, *Colima*, 38–39.

19. Sauer, *Colima*.

20. For a discussion of the poorly understood remote region, see Brand, *Coastal Study of Southwest Mexico* and *Coalcoman and Motines*; Gerardo Sánchez Díaz, *La costa de Michoacán: Economía y sociedad en el siglo XVI* (Morelia, Mexico: Universidad Michoacana de San Nicolás de Hidalgo, 2001).

21. Sánchez Díaz, *La costa de Michoacán*, 90.

22. Ernesto Terríquez Sámano, ed., *Relación sumaria de la visita que hizo en Nuevo España el licenciado Lebrón de Quiñones á doscientos pueblos* (Colima, Mexico: Gobierno del Estado de Colima, Secretaría de Cultura, 2006 [c. 1553]); Sánchez Díaz, *La costa de Michoacán*, 93–94.

23. Coconut palms were autochthonous to the western Pacific, probably introduced to Mexico by Philippine sailors in the Pacific galleon trade. The trees needed close to ten years to reach maturity and produce fruit. See Henry Bruman, "Early Coconut Culture in Western Mexico," *Hispanic American Historical Review* 25 (1945): 212–223; Claudia Paulina Machuca Chávez, "Cabildo, negociación y vino de cocos: El caso de la villa de Colima en el siglo XVII," *Anuario de Estudios Americanos* 66 (2009): 173–192.

24. See Claudia Paulina Machuca Chávez, "Vino de cocos," chap. 6 in "El cabildo de Colima en el siglo XVII" (PhD diss., CIESAS Occidente, 2010).

25. Machuca Chávez, "Cabildo, negociación y vino de cocos," and "Vino de cocos."

26. For example, the presumed value of one tree, either cacao or coconut, was assessed at one peso: at the height of the cacao industry in the region in the mid-sixteenth century, the value of the cacao plantation trees was close to 750,000 pesos; by the 1610s, the coconut palm plantation trees were worth less than 150,000 pesos.

27. Aguirre Beltrán, *Cuenca de Tepalcatepec*, 68.

28. Ibid., 64.

29. The viceroy ordered several Colima and Motines encomenderos to return to their properties in 1550. Lebrón de Quiñones lamented the practice of absenteeism by encomenderos in his 1554 visita. See AVC, 1:29, and Sámano, ed., *Relación sumaria*.

30. Sauer, *Colima*, 9–26.

31. Gerhard, 79–80.

32. For a Spanish edition, see Julio César Montané Martí, *Francisco de Ulloa: Explorador de ilusiones, con la traducción del italiano de la Relación de Francisco Preciado por Ramón Miranda Camou* (Hermosillo, Mexico: Universidad de Sonora, 1995).

33. Romero de Solís, *Andariegos*, 436–437.

34. Gerhard, 80, 192; Himmerich y Valencia, 218; Romero de Solís, *Andariegos*, 436.

35. AVC, 1:43–49, 57–58, 64.

36. Gerhard, 193, 339; Himmerich y Valencia, 121.

37. Gerhard, 80, 192; Himmerich y Valencia, 162; Romero de Solís, *Andariegos*, 436.

38. AVC, 1:49.

39. Sámano, ed., *Relación sumaria*, 89.

40. The insults are difficult to render in English: "Beatillo, cleriguillo, vicariuelo," are simple diminutives, but in the context of Preciado's general irreverence they take on negative connotations. AVC, 1:23–25.

41. Preciado and Arévalo sued the couple over her dowry and control of the Motines encomienda, appealing in 1552 to the visitador of New Spain, Lebrón de Quiñones, because there were no licensed lawyers in Colima. See AVC, 1:43–44.

42. AVC, 1:43–44.

43. Romero de Solís, *Andariegos*, 436.

44. J. H. Parry, *The Audiencia of New Galicia in the Sixteenth Century: A Study in Spanish Colonial Government* (Cambridge: Cambridge University Press, 1948), 41, 67–68, 72.

45. Sámano, ed., *Relación sumaria*, 75.

46. AVC, 1:45–49.

47. Ibid., 1:57–58.

48. López stated for the record in 1575 that he was "more than 40 years old" (AHMC, caja A-7, exp. 19); in 1580, he stated that he was "more than 50 years old" (Romero de Solís, *Andariegos*, 281).

49. Archivo Histórico del Estado de Colima (Historical Archive of the State of Colima), Colima, Mexico (AHEC hereafter), Fondo Virreinal, caja 2, caja 3; AHMC, caja A-7, exp. 20; Romero de Solís, *Andariegos*, 280–282; AGN, Inq., vol. 116, exp. 2. López de Avecilla was the notary of the villa of Colima for many years, asserting the office in Colima possibly as early as 1560, again in 1573, and then from 1575 through 1590.

50. AHMC, caja A-2, exp. 10; AVC, 1:52–55.

51. AVC, 1:52–55. Expressed variously in the case as "que lo besase en el culo" and "bésame el culo."

52. AVC, 1:52–55, elaborated by witnesses as either "puto traidor" or "hi[jo] de puta, puto, no os queréis ir a la cárcel."

53. AVC, 1:65.

54. Felipe Sevilla del Río, *Prosas literarias e históricas* (Colima, Mexico: Universidad de Colima, 2005), 151–152.

55. Ibid., 152.

56. Parry, *Audiencia of New Galicia*, 71–76.

57. AVC, 1:34.

58. Ibid., 1:71.

59. Ibid., 1:17.

60. Ibid., 1:65.

61. Romero de Solís, *Andariegos*, 435–436, 438–439.

62. Gerhard, 193.

63. AVC, 1:31; Felipe Sevilla del Río, *Breve estudio sobre la conquista y fundación de Coliman*, 2nd ed. (Mexico City: Talleres Galas de México, Colección Peña Colorada, 1977; Colima, Mexico: Gobierno del Estado de Colima, 1986).

64. AGN, Inq., vol. 93, exp. 2.

65. Ibid.

66. Ibid., fol. 225.

67. Ibid., fol. 135.

68. Ibid., fol. 253.

69. Ibid., fols. 255–256.

70. Ibid., fol. 273. The letter is worth quoting in part as a model of bureaucratic sarcasm: "Mui magnifico y mui reverendo señor. Por que para los negocios del Santo Oficio se excoje las personas que conviene y el negocio que a V.Md. envié no se puede ya dar a otro respondo a lo que en esto V.Md. me avisa como va ordenado pues quando esta llegue avrán cesado los inconvenientes que se me signfican e ubiera inportado la brevedad como avise sea V.Md. [. . .] que sin dilaçión se effetue."

71. AGN, Inq., vol. 79, exps. 19, 21.

72. AHMC, caja A-18, exp. 1.

73. AGN, Inq., vol. 93, exp. 2.

74. AHMC, Reyes 662.

75. AHMC, caja A-18, exp. 1.

76. For overviews of jurisdictional issues between Colima and New Spain, and between New Galicia and New Spain, see Claudia Paulina Machuca Chávez, "Colima entre las Audiencias de México y la Nueva Galicia. Historia de un conflicto jurisdiccional," in Juan Carlos Reyes G., ed., *IV Foro Colima y su Región: Arqueología, antropología e historia* (Colima, Mexico: Gobierno del Estado de Colima, Secretaría de Cultura, 2008); Parry, *Audiencia of New Galicia*.

77. AGI, Guadalajara 230, l, 2, fols. 5–6.

78. Ibid., Guadalajara 31n18.

79. Ibid., Guadalajara 48n24.

80. Ibid., Guadalajara 48n24. The appeals continued at least through 1602. See AGI, Guadalajara 30n25, fol. 183.

81. This Cristóbal was presumably the son of Francisco Preciado and Elvira de Arévalo. See AGN, Inq., vol. 112, exp. 2; vol. 114, exp. 1.

82. Romero de Solís, *Andariegos*, 435.

83. AGN, Inq., vol. 112, exp. 2; vol. 114, exp. s/n, fol. 398.

84. Romero de Solís, *Andariegos*, 435.

85. AVC, 2:156–158.

86. AGN, Inq., vol. 143, exp. 5, fol. 24.

87. Romero de Solís, *Andariegos*, 436.

88. Ibid., 437–438.

89. Although it analyzes a much later period, the following is instructive: Andrew B. Warren, "Negotiating Two Worlds: The Free-Black Experience in Guerrero's Tierra Caliente," in Ben Vinson III and Matthew Restall, eds., *Black Mexico: Race and Society from Colonial to Modern Times* (Albuquerque: University of New Mexico Press, 2009). For a more general discussion, see Robert C. Schwaller, *Géneros de Gente in Early Colonial Mexico: Defining Racial Difference* (Norman: University of Oklahoma Press, 2016).

90. AGN, Inq., vol. 120, exp. 4.

91. Ibid., vol. 143, exp. 5, fol. 24.

92. Ibid., vol. 120, exp. 4, fol. s/n. The hand is difficult to read, but it states that Cristóbal Preciado "sirbe de [. . .] [escribano?] nombrado a la justicia desde dicho pueblo . . . y por su mala lengua y mal bibir a sido desterrado de la provincia de Ábalos."

93. Ibid., vol. 120, exp. 4.

94. Ibid., fol. s/n: "Anda rebolbiendo y sizañando a los vezinos españoles unos con otros y con los naturales rebolbiéndolos con los saçerdotes y que es un ombre de mal bibir con anda tras las mugeres de los naturales requiriéndolas y a otras a cometiéndolas por fuerça y que es un ombre facinoroso yncorregible que de su bibir da mal exemplo a los naturales andando de casa en casa desnudo en camisa con unos calçones blancos y que por andarse de casa en casa dexa de oyr misa los domingos e fiestas de guarder y por dejar de ir el suso dicho a misa muchos de los naturales la dejan de oyr por que darse a guardar su casa teniéndose del dicho Preçiado y como sirbe de [. . .] [escribano?] nombrado a la justicia desde dicho pueblo tiene a los naturales muy temorizados diziéndoles que les a de buscar las vadas [vidas?] y los dichos naturales como es gente miserable le temen y que en este dicho pueblo no tiene entretenimiento ninguno sino es jugar naypes con quantos pasatiempo este dicho pueblo jugando mal con engaños [. . .] ansimismo dize y habla palabras malsonantes escandalosas como es dezir y a dicho públicamente que aunque se cometa un pecado mortal no se acusen dello que con solo dezir señor [. . .] que dándose golpes en los pechos está en [. . .] cia y que así mismo a dicho que de tener acceso carnal con mugeres que no lo tiene en [. . .] da y que era un poco daire de lo qual se escandalizan las personas que se lo an oydo dezir y que el dicho Preçiado por su mala lengua y mal bibir a sido desterrado de la provincia de Ábalos por que traya los dichos pueblos rebueltos a yndios con religiosos y españoles [el uno?] con otro y que así mismo lo an echado otras partes y que por sus malas costumbres y ser testimoniero no cabe en parte [. . .] y entremetiéndose y sustentando por fras [. . .] sas delicadas que no entiende e para la [. . .] tal y sosiego de los naturales y españoles y que de aquí en adelante no aya a las re [. . .] tas que a bridio y al presente como es notorio por el mal y males que dello puede [. . .] dir a redamder [?] en el dicho pueblo y sup [. . .] do y para que su señoría reberendísima ponga [. . .] llo el remedio convinyente y necesario y por el buen engemplo [exemplo] de los naturales."

95. AVC, 2:278.

96. AGN, Inq., vol. 120, exp. 4.

97. Ibid.

98. Romero de Solís, *Andariegos*, 64–65.

99. AVC, 1:57–58.

100. Gerhard, 193; Himmerich y Valencia, 133, 231.

101. AHMC, caja A-12, exp. 7.

102. Ibid.

103. AHMC, caja A-1, exp. 10; caja A-3, exp. 2.

104. Ibid., caja A-12, exp. 7.

105. AGN, Tierras, vol. 2811, exps. 11, 12.

106. Ibid., vol. 2811, exp. 11. It is not entirely certain that his surname was Sánchez, though an educated deduction from the abbreviation in the case file suggests it.

107. Ibid., vol. 2811, exp. 11, fol. 207 [54]: "Hombre sediçiosso en aquella inquieto y enemigo general de todos los vezinos della y azendado en el dicho valle."

108. Ibid., vol. 2811, exp. 12.

109. Ibid., exp. 11.

110. AHMC, caja A-8, exp. 16.

111. Ibid., exp. 10; caja A-9, exps. 1, 6, 14.

112. Ibid., caja A-18, exp. 1.

113. AGN, Inq., vol. 116, exp. 2; AVC, 2:247–251.

114. AGN, Tierras, vol. 2968, exp. 148.

115. AGI, Guadalajara 48n24, fol. 2.

116. AGN, Tierras, vol. 2941, exps. 53, 111.

CHAPTER 6

1. "Vos sois una calabaza" was the phrase. AGN, Inq., vol. 218, exp. 17.

2. See Sebastián de Covarrubias, *Tesoro de la lengua castellana, o española* (Madrid: Luis Sánchez, 1611), 171.

3. As the original case seems to be missing and we must rely on copies drawn up by the notaries of the Inquisition and the Audiencia, we can only infer the trajectory of the case. There are multiple copies of the case and they mostly repeat each other, which also suggests that the case was being reviewed at the highest levels of royal and inquisitional justice. In fact, there are copies drawn up by the royal notary for the Audiencia (AGN, Inq., vol. 218, exp. 17), a copy drawn up by the Inquisition (AGN, Inq., vol. 217, exp. 13), and a copy of a criminal trial delivered to the Suprema in Madrid (AHN, Consejo de Inquisición, 1728, exp. 8).

4. Ricardo León Alanís, *Los orígenes del clero y la iglesia en Michoacán, 1525–1640* (Morelia, Mexico: Universidad Michoacana de San Nicolás de Hidalgo, Instituto de Investigaciones Históricas, 1997), 236–238.

5. AGN, Inq., vol. 190, exp. 7.

6. A ladina indigenous woman, Gerónima de Contreras, called in an unrelated investigation, said that she lived on Orduña's estate in Apaceo in July 1580. See AGN, vol. 229, exp. s/n, fol. 151.

7. León Alanís, *Orígenes*, 283–285.

8. ACCM, Libro 1/s/n/1.

9. León Alanís, *Orígenes*, 239–240.

10. ACCM, Libro 1/89/1.

11. León Alanís, *Orígenes*, 241–243.

12. ACCM, Libro 1/98/1.

13. Óscar Mazín Gómez, *El cabildo catedral de Valladolid de Michoacán* (Zamora, Mexico: El Colegio de Michoacán, 1996), 116.

14. Ibid., 116. The administrative term for this was *sede vacante*.

15. León Alanís, *Orígenes*, 243–244.

16. Mazín Gómez, *Cabildo catedral*, 116.

17. De la Rea, 95–98, details his biography. For rules prohibiting non-Spaniards from taking orders in the Mexican Church and Franciscan order, which were occasionally overlooked, see Francisco Morales, *Ethnic and Social Background of the Franciscan Friars in Seventeenth Century Mexico* (Washington, DC: Academy of American Franciscan History, 1973), and Magnus Lundberg, "El clero indígena en Hispanoamérica: De la legislación a la implementación y práctica eclesiástica," *Estudios de historia novohispana* 38 (2008): 39–62.

18. See Morales, *Ethnic and Social Background*, 69n69, and AGN, Inq., vol. 292, exp. s/n, fols. 30–32.

19. De la Rea, 95–98, discusses his life as a hermit and recluse.

20. AGN, Inq., vol. 239, exp. s/n, fol. 77.

21. Ibid., vol. 190, exp. 7.

22. Ibid.

23. For a massive scandal surrounding inquisitors and prosecutors of the Mexican Inquisition of the 1640s and 1650s convicted of bribery and suborning perjury, see Richard Greenleaf, "The Great Visitas of the Mexican Holy Office, 1645–1669," *The Americas* 44 (1988): 399–420. For the notorious corruption of the Mexico Audiencia of the 1580s, see Stafford Poole, *Pedro Moya de Contreras: Catholic Reform and Royal Power in New Spain, 1571–1591* (Berkeley: University of California Press, 1987), 94–100.

24. AGN, Inq., vol. 190, exp. 7.

25. ACCM, Libro 1/117/1.

26. AGN, Inq., vol. 234, exp. s/n, fol. 33v.

27. Ibid., fols. 31–32.

28. Ibid.: "Absolutamente es tenido por hombre muy vicioso."

29. Ibid., vol. 182, exp. 3, fols. 67–68.

30. ACCM, Libro 1/118/1.

31. AGN, Inq., vol. 182, exp. 3.

32. Ibid., fol. 66: "No teniendo Vuestra Señoría notiçia del modo de vivir que a tenido y tiene don Diego de Orduña maestrescuela le nombró por su comisario . . . que si Vuestra Señoría tubiera notiçia de sus exçesos no le nombrara por tal comisario."

33. Ibid., vol. 214, exp. 10, fols. 173–176.

34. Ibid., fol. 176.

35. Ibid., vol. 71, exp. 6.

36. Ibid., vol. 234, exp. s/n, fol. 33v.

37. Gerhard, 312, 344–345; Himmerich y Valencia, 208, 244–245.

38. AGN, Inq., vol. 214, exp. 10, fol. 177.

39. Ibid., fol. 170: "hombre vagabundo, soltero y atrevido."

40. Ibid., vol. 214, exp. 10: "Dios libre a Vuestra Merced de vellacos, fulleros" and "que Dios libre a Vuestra Merced de clérigos desvergonzosos."

41. Ibid., vol. 234, exp. s/n, fols. 41–42.

42. Quoted in Mazín Gómez, *Cabildo catedral*, 117, from the cathedral chapter's *actas capitulares* of 16 March 1593.

43. AGN, Inq., vol. 214, exp. 10, fol. 121: "El diablo nunca duerme."

44. Ibid., vol. 182, exp. 6, fol. 122: "A grandes voces calla maestrescuela que vos y yo nos veremos algún día."

45. ACCM, Libro 1/119/2.

46. Ibid., 1/119/3.

47. Mazín Gómez, *Cabildo catedral*, 99, original in AGI, México 374.

48. ACCM, Libro 1/159/1.

49. AGN, Inq., vol. 239, exp. s/n, fol. 500.

50. Ibid.

51. Ibid., vol. 216, exp. 3.

52. Ibid., exp. 8.

53. Ibid., fol. 59: "Le damos poder y commisión en forma y estimaremos en mucho que allá los compussiesse de manera que no passassen Adelante las mohínas y pessadumbre que entre los dichos maestrescuela y canónigo ay."

54. For example, Orduña took one deposition in June 1598 in Irimbo against a Spanish man, Sebastián de Tafoya, who reportedly had ordered his indigenous servant to remove the sciatic nerve from a leg of lamb in order to make it kosher (AGN, Inq., vol. 252, exp. s/n, fols. 25–26). Orduña had heard a similar denunciation in Valladolid in March 1594 (AGN, Inq., vol. 239, exp.

s/n, fol. 500). In March 1595, Orduña farmed out testimonies to Félix Peñafiel as the curate in Colima (AGN, Inq., vol. 240, exp. 17bis).

55. AGN, Inq., vol. 182, exp. 12.

56. See Ibid., vol. 217, exp. 13, and vol. 218, exp. 17; AHN, Consejo de Inquisición, 1728, exp. 8.

57. AGN, Tierras, vol. 2811, exp. 4.

58. Ibid., vol. 2075, exp. 10.

59. Ibid., vol. 2682, exp. 18.

60. Ibid., vol. 2729, exp. 14.

61. So extensive was the fraud that the investigation into the case fills three entire volumes of material (AGN, Inq., vols. 258–260).

62. AGN, Tierras, vol. 3702, exp. 5, and Inq., vols. 258, 259, 260. The phrase he used was "mientes como perro judío."

63. Covarrubias, *Tesoro*, 212: "El guiador de la hueste, quasi capdillo, â capite, de donde tambien se dixo capitan, que sinifica lo mesmo, vel caudillo, quasi cauens alium, porque ha de cuidar de toda su gente. De las calidades del que ha de ser cabdillo habla la ley 4. tit. 23. par. 2 y dizen alli la glossa de Montaluo, verbo Cabdillos." See also Siete Partidas, Partida 2a, tit. 23.

64. For disputes from 1571 to 1590, see AGN, Tierras, vol. 2695, exp. 2; vol. 2721, exps. 35–38, 79; vol. 2737, exps. 5–6, 10–11, 94; vol. 2976, exp. 117.

65. AGN, Inq., vol. 218, exp. 17, fol. 37.

66. Ibid., fols. 38–39.

67. Ibid., vol. 217, exp. 13; vol. 218, exp. 7; AHN, Consejo de Inquisición, 1728, exp. 8.

68. AGN, Inq., vol. 218, exp. 17, fols. 157–158.

69. Ibid., fol. 161.

70. Ibid., fols. 157v–161r.

71. Ibid., vol. 217, exp. 13.

72. Ibid.

73. Ibid., vol. 246, exp. s/n, fols. 15–53; vol. 252, exp. s/n, fols. 25–26.

74. ACCM, Libro 1/206/1.

75. AGN, Inq., vol. 217, exp. 3.

76. Ibid., fol. 274.

77. Ibid., fol. 276.

78. Ibid., vol. 312, exp. s/n, fol. 352.

79. Ibid., vol. 270, exp. s/n, fols. 70–79.

80. Ibid.

81. Ibid., vol. 455, pt. 1, exp. 3bis, fols. 171–181.

82. The only formal deed for land that I have seen for Diego de Orduña was for a pasture (*potrero*) in Coatepec (which could have been anywhere, given the fact that it is a common placename). See AGN, Mercedes, vol. 22, exp. s/n, fol. 213.

83. AGN, Inq., vol. 312, exp. s/n, fols. 353–355.

84. Ibid., vol. 316, exp. s/n, fols. 594–599. I have approximated some of the terms, which have no precise English equivalent. We do not know whether the two Purépecha men reported insults in Spanish or in Purépecha, as the two mailmen spoke no Spanish and reported the assault through a bilingual interpreter in Acahuato. The notary, Friar Pedro Zavala, recorded the words given to him by the interpreter Friar Juan de Espinosa as "Esse papel no vale nada y el que lo scrivió deve de ser como tu, anda perro, puto, borracho, cornudo, cabrón, chivato."

85. James B. Given, *Inquisition and Medieval Society: Power, Discipline, and Resistance in Languedoc* (Ithaca, NY: Cornell University Press, 1997).

86. AGN, Inq., vol. 316, exp. s/n, fol. 597.

87. Martha Lizbeth Phelps, "Doppelgangers of the State: Private Security and Transferable Legitimacy," *Politics and Policy* 42 (2014): 824–849.

88. Max Weber, "Politics as a Vocation," in Tony Waters and Dagmar Waters, trans. and eds., *Rationalism and Modern Society* (New York: Palgrave Books, 2015).

89. For the hideous violence of the Congo, see Adam Hochschild, *King Leopold's Ghost: A Story of Greed, Terror, and Heroism in Colonial Africa* (New York: Houghton Mifflin, 1998; Boston: Mariner Books, 1999). Hochschild makes a compelling argument that Joseph Conrad's famous creation, Colonel Kurtz (from *The Heart of Darkness*), was not fictional but a real man who was emboldened by the orgy of violence in that place and time.

CONCLUSION

1. I have not been able to locate documents in Spanish archives confirming the exact nature of his legal appeals.

2. Arnaldo de Ysassy, "Demarcación y descripción de el obispado de Mechuacán y fundación de su Iglesia Catedral," in *Bibliotheca Americana* 1 (1982): 60–178.

3. John F. Schwaller, *The Church and Clergy in Sixteenth Century Mexico* (Albuquerque: University of New Mexico Press, 1987), 37–39.

4. AGI, Casa de Contratación 528n4, and AGI, Catálogos de pasajeros a Indias 1, 8, exp. 2639.

5. Ricardo León Alanís, *Los orígenes del clero y la iglesia en Michoacán, 1525–1640* (Morelia, Mexico: Universidad Michoacana de San Nicolás de Hidalgo, Instituto de Investigaciones Históricas, 1997), 283–285, summarizes the tithe collections for the diocese from 1600 to 1608. They averaged 17,732 pesos annually for the period, which, based on the shareholding rules for cathedral dignitaries, would result in 1605 in an annual salary for the canons at 414 pesos, the dean at 591; the various other dignitaries presumably collected salaries of about 540 pesos.

6. AGI, Casa de Contratación 268B, n. 1, r. 21.

7. His will and testament are recorded in AGI, Casa de Contratación 268B, n. 1, r. 21. I have relied on this document for the discussion here. There are two notarial hands at work. Francisco del Poyo drew up the will on board the ship. But Martín de Ayala, a royal notary and notary of the fleet, entered it into evidence before the court in the port of Veracruz. One of the linguistic curiosities of the deposition is the willful use of the letter "l" in place of "r" in the word "alsediano" by Ayala. This is a curious linguistic moment, presumably of Andalusian origin, which highlights the later Puerto Rican pronunciation of words like "Puerto Rico" as "Puelto L/Rico."

8. AGI, México 28n26.

9. Muñoz wrote to the inquisitor from Acahuato on 22 August 1624. This letter was only received by the inquisitor on 2 September 1626. See AGN, Inq., vol. 303, exp. s/n, fols. 34–35. The August 1624 letter is the last signed letter from Muñoz of which I am aware. Inquisitors continued to write to Muñoz throughout 1625 and 1626, although, by September 1626, they had ceased to communicate with him. The many unanswered letters from inquisitors in 1625, coupled with a two-year delay in the delivery of the August 1624 letter, suggest that Muñoz died in the interim. See AGN, Inq., vol. 510, exps. 87, 89, 90, 92, 99.

10. AGN, Inq., vol. 317, exp. 16.

11. Ibid., vol. 346, exp. 2.

12. Ibid., vol. 510, exp. 22, fol. 65.

13. Ibid., vol. 340, exps. 4, 5.

14. Joseph F. O'Callaghan, *Reconquest and Crusade in Medieval Spain* (Philadelphia: University of Pennsylvania Press, 2013).

15. Elaborated especially in Henry Kamen, *The Phoenix and the Flame: Catalonia and the Counter Reformation* (New Haven, CT: Yale University Press, 1993).

16. Richard White, *The Middle Ground: Indians, Empires, and the Republics in the Great Lakes Region, 1650–1815* (Cambridge: Cambridge University Press, 1991).

17. Álvaro Jara, *Guerra y sociedad en Chile: La transformación de la guerra de Arauco y la esclavitud de los indios* (Santiago: Editorial Universitaria, 1971).

Note: Italic page numbers refer to illustrations.

68–70, 76, 79, 210nn104–106, 211n122; on Vasco de Quiroga, 69–70, 75–77; in Tzintzuntzan, 68, 209n93; in Uruapan, 78
Given, James B., 170–171, 212n2, 217n101
Gómez, Alonso, 5
Gómez, Gonzalo, 31, 84
Gómez, Luisa, 136, 141
Gómez de Ávila, Pero, 80
Gómez de Soria, Melchor, 163
González, Beatriz, 84–85
González, Martín, 97
González de Benavides, Gil, 57, 200n104, 207n44
Greenleaf, Richard, 199n100, 199n103, 200n104
Grijalva, Álvaro de, 143
Guadalajara, 62–63, 136, 144–145, 150–151, 159
Guanajuato, 20, 62, 63, 70, 112–113
Guango, 70
Guaniqueo, 56
Guatemala, 88
Guayangareo: Augustinian monastery of, 57, 207n40; as capital of Michoacán, 54, 55, 57, 60, 66, 67, 79, 105, 117–119; cathedral church construction in, 117; Franciscan monastery of, 56, 67; and indigenous land disputes, 164; and inquisitional prosecution, 84, 99; repartimientos for construction of city, 57, 60. *See also* Valladolid (today Morelia)
Guerra, Alonso, 157–160, 161, 162
Guerrero, Bartolomé Lobo, 163
Guillén, García Álvarez, 165
Gutiérrez, Joaquín, 78, 163
Guzmán, Manuel, 40
Guzmán, Nuño de: and Hernán Cortés's encomiendas, 133; execution of Tzintzincha Tangaxoan, 6, 15, 18, 32, 35, 37, 40, 46, 193n10; goals of conquest of Michoacán, 13, 18, 27, 40; indigenous allies of, 32, 47, 197n78; Pedro Muñoz's collaboration with, 34, 93, 199n91; in Juan O'Gorman's mural, 15, 192n1; and Cristóbal de Oñate, 66; as president of Audiencia, 6, 15, 28; reputation of, 15, 192nn1–3; role in Spanish conquest, 18, 46–47; terror inflicted on Michoacán, 16, 18, 35, 40; and trial of

Tzintzincha Tangaxoan, 32–35, 198n82, 198n84

hallucinogenic mushrooms, 1, 9, 177
heresy, 82, 83, 86, 92–93, 105, 162
Hermosilla, Francisco de, 113–114
Hernández, Martín, 145, 146
Hierro, Juan del, 117–118, 123
Himmerich y Valencia, Robert, 197n75, 198n91
Hispanicization project, 4, 173
Hochschild, Adam, 232n89
Honduras, 22
hospital-pueblos, 60
Huahuan language, 133
Huejotzinca group, 32
Huiramángaro, 87, 88
Huitziméngari, Antonio, 24, 32, 44, 59, 60, 63–64, 67, 196n59
Huitziméngari, Tariácueri, 59
Huitziméngari clan, 50, 63, 64
human sacrifice: and Purépecha group, 20–21, 32, 34, 41; and trial of Tzintzincha Tangaxoan, 33
Hurtado de Mendoza, Luis, 65–66

Iberian Peninsula, reconquest of, 10, 178
Illescas Orejón, Mateo, 175
imperial agents: and power dynamics, 3, 13, 47, 178. *See also* local imperial agents; local imperial rule
imperial theory, quotidian enforcement of, 4, 9, 11, 181
Indaparapeo, 165
indigenista ideology, 205n13
indigenous churches, 90
indigenous communities: of Colima, 132, 152; and land claims, 64; and land encroachment, 132, 156, 224n8; and Alonso de Montúfar, 89; and plantation owners, 132, 135; pueblos, 85, 87, 132; and Vasco de Quiroga, 13, 15
indigenous education, 56, 59, 67
indigenous elites: and alliances with friar-missionaries, 50–51, 59–60; and Augustinians, 7, 44, 48, 50, 59, 63–64, 67; education of, 67; and Franciscans, 7, 50; inquisitional prosecution of, 84; lawsuits